# THE DESERT ROAD TO TURKESTAN

## Books by Owen Lattimore

*America and Asia*
*High Tartary*
*The Inner Asian Frontiers of China*
*Manchuria: Cradle of Conflict*
*Mongol Journeys*
*The Mongols of Manchuria*
*Nationalism and Revolution in Mongolia*
*Nomads and Commissars*
*Ordeal by Slander*
*Pivot of Asia*
*Situation in Asia*
*Solution in Asia*
*Studies in Frontier History*

with Eleanor Lattimore:
*Silk, Spices, and Empire*

with Fujiko Isono:
*The Diluv Khutagt*
*China Memoirs*

"The life and vivid record of a modern pioneer in a far-off frontier . . . of the new century."  —*New York Herald Tribune*

"Mr. Lattimore . . . was the first to follow 'the Winding Way' throughout with a conscious interest in its history. . . . He . . . tasted the full flavour of this immemorial method of travel, which he describes with gusto."  —*New Statesman*

"The poetic, subjective note struck in many passages throughout this book lends it an unusual charm . . . of rare value and interest."  —*Geographical Review*

"The author speaks Chinese and had absorbed enough of the Chinese spirit to make him, like his companions, adaptable in the strangest of circumstances."  —*London Times Literary Supplement*

# THE DESERT ROAD
# TO TURKESTAN

BY
OWEN LATTIMORE

WITH PREVIOUSLY UNPUBLISHED PHOTOGRAPHS AND
A NEW INTRODUCTION BY DAVID LATTIMORE

KODANSHA INTERNATIONAL
New York • Tokyo • London

Kodansha America, Inc.
114 Fifth Avenue, New York, New York 10011, U.S.A.

Kodansha International Ltd.
17-14 Otowa 1-chome, Bunkyo-ku, Tokyo 112, Japan

Published in 1995 by Kodansha America, Inc.

First published in 1929 by Little, Brown and Company.

This is a Kodansha Globe book.

Library of Congress Cataloging-in-Publication Data

Lattimore, Owen, 1900–
    The desert road to Turkestan / by Owen Lattimore.
        p.    cm. — (Kodansha globe)
    "With previously unpublished photographs and a new introduction
    by David Lattimore."
    Includes index.
    ISBN 1-56836-070-3
        1. Mongolia—Description and travel. 2. Asia, Central—
    Description and travel.    I. Series.
    DS793.M7L3   1995
    915.8'40486—dc20                                        95-31036

Printed in the United States of America

95  96  97  98  99  Q/FF  10  9  8  7  6  5  4  3  2  1

To
H. G. W. WOODHEAD, C.B.E.
TO WHOM I OWE MY CARAVAN DAYS

# CONTENTS

# CONTENTS

# INTRODUCTION

In the nineteenth century the United States was not a colonial power in the sense that Britain and France were, yet just as in those countries, there were families that spread across the planet in search of careers and fortune. My father, Owen Lattimore, came from one such family. Of the five Lattimore brothers and sisters in my grandfather's generation who survived to maturity, only one lived out her life in America.

My grandfather's father, Alexander Williamson Lattimore, was the son of an Indiana frontier preacher. He had married a cousin of Mary Todd Lincoln, and was involved in the beginnings of the Sanitary Commission, which created the railway hospital service in the Civil War. As my father told the story, Alexander lost his religion in mid-life after reading Darwin. His older children, born in the 1860s, were raised as Christians; his younger children, born in the 1870s, as agnostics.

Mary, the eldest, learned from Alexander Graham Bell how to teach the deaf; she became a Presbyterian missionary, and opened the first "deaf-and-dumb" school in China, at Suzhou, where she spent her life. Her brother John, the eldest son, was infatuated with everything military, but Alexander, who had lost faith in war along with his faith in God, refused to use his political connections to get the young man into West Point. The frustrated John worked as a clerk on a railway post-office car; he stole money from the mails and squandered it. Following the custom of the time, John, as the son of a "good family," was allowed to join the army instead of going to jail, on the condition that his family make restitution for the theft. John got his military career—as a noncommissioned officer in the Philippines—but the family, which lived in Washington, D.C., was now impoverished and unable to provide a college education for the precocious younger sons, David Sr. (my father's father) and Alexander Jr.

David and Alec belonged to a milieu of young men, some of them attachés of embassies, who exchanged lessons in languages and other subjects; the Greek and Latin learned at home had been well learned, and on the strength of this informal education David became a public high school teacher. Both brothers—the shy, reserved David and the flamboyant, upredictable Alec—were poets, and translators of poetry; both destroyed all their verses.

David married a fellow schoolteacher, Margaret Barnes, whose father had "run away with a Spanish dancer" and become U.S. consul in a banana republic. Owen, their second child and first son, was born in Washington, D.C. on July 29, 1900. Later he claimed to be the first Lattimore in five hundred years to have been born in the same place as his father.

Owen was born during the Boxer Rebellion, as the Legation Quarter of Beijing lay under siege. After the defeat of the antiforeign Boxers, the imperial government of China began to found modern state universities that would prepare students for advanced training abroad. The new secular institutions competed with Christian missionary colleges, and the missionaries resented them, but blood was presumably thicker than baptismal water, and Mary, the missionary teacher, helped her agnostic younger brother David get a professorship of modern languages (English, French, and German) in a new Chinese secular university. (Later she would do the same for Alec, although he had turned from an agnostic into something even more bizarre to good Protestant stock like the Lattimores—a Roman Catholic.)

David and Margaret, with their children Katharine and Owen, arrived at Shanghai in 1901. Over the next twenty years David took part successively in the founding of three Chinese universities, at Shanghai, Baoding, and Beiyang University at Tianjin (then called Tientsin).[1] My father's earliest childhood memory was of Shanghai, at four: shown the first automobile in the city, he ran out and kicked its tire. But mostly he remembered Baoding, by which time there were three more children. All were taught at home, chiefly French and Latin. As they moved from nursery to schoolroom they were discouraged from speaking Chinese. My grandparents wanted them to have a chance at life in America, and didn't want them "going native."

The little girls, Isabel and Eleanor, drew pictures and wrote stories. Later in life they were artists. Eleanor (as Eleanor Frances Lattimore) wrote and illustrated children's books, some of which, such as *Little Pear*, remained in print for decades.[2] Richmond became a poet who translated Homer and Pindar from Greek, as well as many tragedies and the New Testament. Unlike Owen he stayed home long enough to learn Greek as well as Latin from his father and uncle. He was a Rhodes scholar and the first American, I believe, to graduate from Oxford with a Double First in Greats (*Literae humaniores*). Like his father he was shy and humorous. He taught all his life at Bryn Mawr, declining offers of professorships from large and grand universities.

As non-Chinese and nonmissionaries the Lattimores were doubly isolated. In a manuscript memoir Eleanor Frances wrote, "It was lucky there were five of us, because there were times when we had no playmates except each other."[3] My grandparents forbade the use of vogue words such as "cute," so the children substituted "snoof." In fact, they developed something of a private language. Stuffy and self-righteous people were "mish," and the worst were "pi-mish," *pious* missionaries.

In 1912 Margaret took the five children to Lausanne, Switzerland, for two years of regular schooling. Owen went to an ordinary lycée, not a boarding school for rich foreigners. The family was in England when World War I began. The others returned to China, but it was thought that there was no school in China suitable for Owen, and the crossing to America was perilous because of U-boats. While in England they had met uncle Alec, who felt at home there; for a while he had been co-owner of a student boarding house in Oxford. Now he found Owen a place at St. Bee's, probably the smallest, most remote, and cheapest of ancient and honorable public schools.

Owen flourished at St. Bee's in his beloved Lake District. His earlier training left him stumped by mathematics, but the school let him drop that subject and teach himself German instead. Later he wrote self-deprecatingly about his school performance, but a number of prize books survive with certificates of award inscribed to him for merit in examinations and "form work." In fact he was the best scholar of his years, but captained the second Rugby team, not the first, and so failed to become student head of the school. At provincial St. Bee's an interest lingered in the medievalism and guild socialism of William Morris. Owen wrote with a quill, read Chesterton and Belloc, and took instruction, briefly, from a Catholic priest, ministrant to Irish laborers in the neighborhood. The priest's dimness and prurience cooled Owen's enthusiasm, but he was too proud to admit this in letters to his irreligious father in China. (Later Owen liked and admired Catholic missionaries in Mongolia and Turkestan.)

Owen spent two summers tramping and tenting in the north of England, working as a farm laborer. If the war had lasted another year he would have been a subaltern in the British trenches. He passed examinations to enter Oxford but did not obtain the full scholarship he would have needed. Work study was unheard of, and his father was paid in an illiquid Chinese currency. Full scholarships were exceedingly uncommon in those days; excellent and persistent students without wealth, such as J. R. R. Tolkien, might work at menial jobs and take examinations twice (or many times) before winning the support they needed. But Owen was more a man of action and omnivorous curiosity than a scholar with a calling to book learning for its own sake. He used to quote with amusement his mother's remark that "Richmond is a real scholar; Owen just learns languages because he can't bear not to know what other people are saying."

At nineteen, with the war over, he sailed back to China. For seven years he worked in a British (originally Austro-Danish) import-export firm, Arnhold and Co., chiefly at Tianjin (Tientsin), with a year off in which he reported for the *Peking and Tientsin Times*. Owen's parents returned to the United States in 1921 with his younger sisters and brother. Owen inherited the oversight of his uncle Alec who, after a few years at Wuchang University in Wuhan, had joined his brother in teaching modern languages at Beiyang.

Uncle Alec was apparently a large part of the entertainment available in Tianjin, and he was a beloved figure in the foreign community. According to a memoir of him left by Marcel Wolfers, Tianjin chief of Arnhold's, "he was certainly the queerest fish that ever landed in the harbour of Tianjin."[4] His oversight included the frequent need to extract him, drunk, in the wee hours from one of the specialized bordellos he fancied. He once paid a tipsy early morning call on the Wolfers and was met by Mrs. Wolfers, a daughter of the American Chargé d'Affaires at Beijing. Arnhold's at this time was in the process of being acquired by the great Sassoon family of Anglo-Iranian-Jewish merchants. "Hush, Alec darling," said Mrs. Wolfers, "Marcel is just now talking with Mr. Sassoon." "Sassoon!" Alec replied in a *very* loud voice. "Is that a musical instrument, or just a big wind?"

A favorite pastime of Owen's was racing on the Hai-ho, followed by steak tartare and black velvets at the Tianjin Rowing Club. As stroke on the Company four he won the Hong Challenge Cup in 1923. In addition to the more conventional activities of Rugby and pony racing he took up falconry and rabbit coursing with his Gansu greyhounds, Lanta and Lilith. His boarding-school aestheticism lingered. As can be seen from illustrations in *The Desert Road to Turkestan*, he wore a monocle. On the Gobi desert, due to high winds he carried a box of two hundred spare monocles. In his introduction to the 1975 reissue of *High Tartary*, looking back with discomfort at what he saw as the "cockiness" of his book (first published forty-five years earlier), Owen said, "I was a young man who was in fact not too sure of himself, who had not long been married, and who was trying to impress his wife."[5] Were the quill, the falcons, and the monocle all an attempt to impress Uncle Alec?

Alec suffered a stroke at Tianjin in 1927. A friendly couple at Beiyang, returning to America on leave, took him in tow, but he died on his way home, in the Mediterranean, and was buried in Genoa.

Young Owen reacted to the philistinism of the treaty ports—the ports, such as Tianjin, in which foreign enclaves enjoyed privileges exacted from China by the so-called Unequal Treaties—not only with quill-pen dandyism but with a seemingly opposite down-to-earthness. Foreign merchants in the treaty ports rarely learned Chinese, using only a few Pidgin phrases to direct their servants; but Owen mastered Chinese of the slangiest as well as the formal kind, and acquired, too, a command of the written characters sufficient for reading newspapers and business correspondence. (A few years later he could also read historical texts in the classical language.) In dealings with Chinese businessmen and officials he was thus freed from reliance on interpreters who, as Chinese themselves, would be understandably torn in their loyalties between Chinese opposite numbers and a "barbarian" employer.

In his work for Arnhold and Co. Owen volunteered repeatedly for "hardship" details up-country—for example, dealing with a warlord who, in hopes of "squeeze," was holding up a canal-barge shipment of peanuts. Western merchants on such assignments had typically traveled with a cook and a compradore (a native Chinese factotum) as well as a camp bed and camp kitchen; rooms at an inn would be stripped and fumigated for the sahib to camp in, and as Owen wrote, "the impossible was accomplished; the foreigner made his little business trip as if he were not in China at all, but in a private vacuum."[6]

Owen's method was different. Reaching his destination alone, often by mule cart, he would put up in the compound of the local firm that dealt with Arnhold's, spreading his bed roll on the heated brick sleeping platform that he shared with managers, clerks, and apprentices who roomed and ate in company quarters. There, over Mah-Jongg and tea, quizzing no one but just listening, he would pick up the local gossip he needed to brief himself for successful negotiations the following day. (In his later career Owen despised social scientists who traveled into the bush with questionnaires; his prescription for finding out what was worth knowing was to sit by the campfire and listen.) These troubleshooting tours up-country were a valuable apprenticeship for Owen's later low-budget, largely native-style travels in Inner Asia. One of the tours also led directly to those later travels.

Arnhold's had a "godown" or warehouse for wool and cotton at Hohhot (Kuei-hua) where camel caravans, bringing these commodities from Turkestan, descended from the Mongolian plateau to the railway line that ran eastward to Beijing. In February 1925, Owen rode a freight train to Hohhot to expedite a wool shipment delayed because feuding warlords had been commandeering the rolling stock. There in Hohhot he experienced a kind of epiphany. Camel caravans that had crossed Inner Asia from Turkestan—well over a thousand miles of almost unknown steppes and deserts—filed and knelt to be unloaded between the trains in the dusty, snowy railroad yard. For a historical moment, the old order of the caravan had physically meshed with the new order of the railroad. Owen sensed that this moment could not last long:

> There lay the loads, between the lines of camels and the lines of railway wagons: a distance of two paces, perhaps four paces, bridging a gap of two thousand years, between the age when caravans had padded back and forth into the obscure distances dividing the Han Empire from the Roman Empire, and the age of steam, destroying the past and opening the future. [7]

From this experience Owen resolved that he would "follow the caravans to the end of the line, and see what there is to be seen" while it was still there to be seen. [8] The rest—how he quit his job, married, and headed back to the frontier, determined to reach

Turkestan and beyond—is narrated in *The Desert Road to Turkestan*, *High Tartary*, and *Turkestan Reunion*.

The journey described in these, his (and his wife's) earliest books, was a honeymoon trip from Beijing (then called Peking) across Inner Asia and down to India via the five great passes of the Ka-rakoram, all of them more than 16,000 feet above sea level. Because of the conditions at the time, which included civil wars and rev-olutions, and the available means of transport, my parents didn't travel together on the journey's first leg, rather odd for a honeymoon trip. Instead, my mother made a harrowing solo detour through Siberia, and the whole adventure took a year and a half.[9] (As Owen and Eleanor left Beijing, on March 18, 1926, it was to the sound of gunfire—police in Tiananmen Square were firing into a crowd, killing more than forty student demonstrators and bystanders. *Plus ça change . . .*)

What happened after the trip can be briefly told. The Lattimores, meaning to make their travels known, sailed from India to Italy and settled for a year (1927–28) in Rome, understood to be the cheapest European capital. Nearly out of money, they took rooms on the top floor of what is now the Keats-Shelley House at the foot of the Spanish Steps. They lived on "spaghetti and butter," as Eleanor later said. Owen wrote *The Desert Road to Turkestan*. They went to England via Paris, where Eleanor suffered acute appendicitis and Owen a serious infection from abscessed teeth. It is unpleasant to think of what might have happened if these ailments had struck a year earlier in Turkestan.[10]

In England, completely without funds, my parents made contact with Douglas Carruthers, the naturalist author of *Unknown Mon-golia*, who is mentioned several times in *The Desert Road*. Immensely interested in what they had accomplished without any official train-ing or backing, Carruthers arranged for Owen to address the Royal Geographical Society (who eventually awarded him a gold medal) and the Royal Central Asian Society. These occasions required evening dress, which Owen and Eleanor did not have and could not afford. Luckily, they still had some coins and paper money from Chinese Turkestan that had proved inexchangeable in India. Chinese Turkestan (Xinjiang) in the 1920s, under its crafty governor Yang Zengxin (never mentioned by name in the Lattimores' travel books; he was murdered in 1928), was so strictly isolated from the world that the numismatics department of the British Museum had no examples of the province's four currencies; their purchases funded my parents' evening clothes.

The rest was plain sailing. A British publisher was found for the first edition of *The Desert Road to Turkestan* (1928). In America, the Social Sciences Research Council, imaginatively judging the book to be equivalent to a Ph.D., awarded my father a year of "postdoctoral" study in anthropology at Harvard University. More grants followed for further travel and study in China and Inner Asia, one from the Harvard-Yenching Institute and two successive ones from the Guggenheim Foundation. It was during this time that I was born, in Beijing, in 1931. Owen learned Mongol, a language that is unrelated to Chinese, and in subsequent years traveled Mongol-style with a single Mongol companion, Arash, covering much of Inner Mongolia, where in 1926 he once had journeyed with Chinese caravans. These further adventures he narrated in *Mongol Journeys*, his own favorite among his many books.[11]

Owen Lattimore wasn't "college bred," as people used to say; beyond high-school level he was mostly self-taught. He first made his mark on the world not with scholastic achievement but with his daredevil journey and the two books he wrote about that experience, *The Desert Road to Turkestan* and its sequel, *High Tartary*. His travel books are full of observations on geography, history, and custom. Theories and grand perspectives fascinated him. But he was always testing theories against observation, as he had learned from reading T. H. Huxley in his teens. He was always, at bottom, an empiricist, which is why Marxism never interested him. All the more ironic that, in the red-baiting furor of the 1950s, Senator Joseph McCarthy would try to smear Owen by calling him "the top Soviet espionage agent in the U.S." In the great witch-hunt my father defended himself with spirit, and also with tongue-lashings of the senators and their perjured witnesses such as the Capitol Hill committee rooms may have never heard before or since. U.S. senators are rarely accused to their faces in public of "base and contemptible lies," as my father accused McCarthy. Ultimately Owen vindicated himself, but at much cost in peace of mind, and especially in time: five and a half of his prime years.[12]

In his introduction to the 1975 reissue of The Desert Road to Turkestan, my father wrote somewhat disparagingly about this, his first volume. He winced at what he saw as condescension toward "the natives," deplored its bookishness, corrected some mistakes, and concluded that The Desert Road "must be read tolerantly as the work of a young beginner."[13] Perhaps he judged his younger self too harshly. I should like to make a few points in the book's (and the journey's) favor.

My mother's part of the journey made her the first woman to have documented a trip overland from Beijing to India via the Karakoram. In particular, her traversal as a lone woman of the Steppe of the Great Horde in Kazakhstan in mid-winter by horse-drawn sled, at temperatures below those of the North Pole, and in the most unsettled of political and social circumstances, not knowing whether her husband was dead or alive, was remarkable in the highest degree.

But my father's journey by caravan from Hohhot to Turkestan was remarkable too. Chinese and Mongol caravans had traveled this Desert or Winding Road for several years, and had carried a few White Russian refugees, but the route itself was undocumented, although a very few explorers had crossed it at right angles. The first, eastern stretch of the route was an ancient caravan path from Hohhot, the "Blue City," in medieval Tenduc, to Khara-khoto, the ruined "Black City," in medieval Tanggut, on the Edsin Gol. Further west the Winding Road, which crossed the Black Gobi, the most desolate part of Mongolia (including stretches of four and of three waterless stages) was a route of extreme hardship for the caravans, especially in winter, adopted by them only as a desperate recourse because of the closure of the Great Mongolian Road by the Communist-ruled Mongolian Republic, through whose territory it passed.

Members of the Swedish expedition of Sven Hedin traveled approximately Owen's route in the following year, but it is not one that could have been reconnoitered much earlier or much later. Current maps show a motor route, doubtless established for military reasons, along the western and more desolate half of the Desert Road, but not along the eastern half.

My parents didn't have the usual credentials of explorers at that time, in natural history, paleontology, archaeology, or cartography. They probably would not have qualified for membership in a normal expedition with institutional backing. The money they had to travel with was one fifth of what would have been budgeted for a single junior member of well-equipped motorized expeditions such as those of their contemporary, Roy Chapman Andrews of the American Museum of Natural History, celebrated discoverer of the Mongolian dinosaur eggs. What they had going for them was the judgment and organizational skills of my mother and their family servant Moses, my father's exceptional command of Chinese, and his knowledge of history and of the ways of traditional merchants.[14] Much more than members of a scientific expedition would have been, by their poverty they were thrown together with the people of the country; my father's linguistic and cultural acumen, backed by Moses, enabled them to make use of the opportunity. Their journey with camels, ponies, and yaks—the cheap, "native" way of traveling in the 1920s—could not be duplicated today, except perhaps as an expensive stunt for upscale safari customers.

The owner and driver of my father's nine camels, unnamed in *The Desert Road* but referred to simply as the Villainous Camel Puller, was a last-minute substitute fobbed off on him by the original contractor, and had been a "runner" or informant to bandits. Because this man did not know the Desert Road, he and my father were obliged to tag along with regular merchant caravans, led by men who did.

This made the Villainous Camel Puller a blessing in disguise.

While Owen only later received professional training in ethnography, he gained a familiarity with the ways of the merchant caravans that enabled him to include in *The Desert Road to Turkestan* what amounts to a first-rate ethnography of caravan organization, economics, laws, customs, and beliefs. This knowledge, and the friendships that he formed with caravan masters and owners, enabled him in turn to deal with the Villainous Camel Puller.

How this was done supplies much of the drama running throughout *The Desert Road*. The evidently dangerous Camel Puller, fearful of plots against himself and his prerogatives, threatening vengeance upon the imaginary plotters, drastically self-sufficient (for example, in refusing medicine for his tormenting eye ailment), and especially vicious to the weak (the stray youth and old man Owen had picked up along the way), matches with extraordinary exactitude a psychiatrist's profile of a paranoid personality. My father was particularly proud that he had dealt successfully with this man, not by pulling rank as a foreigner, but wholly in accordance with the customary law and practices of the caravans, and backed by the sympathy and help of the caravan merchants. One result was that they saved the life of the stray youth who in *The Desert Road* is called the Chen-fan Wa-wa. Owen's revenge was perhaps too remorseless. The Villainous Camel Puller suffered no bodily harm but lost his pay and his "face," or repute. Joseph McCarthy might have done well to take warning from *The Desert Road to Turkestan*.

While their separate crossings of the Mongolian and Kazakh steppes were the most strenuous and hazardous part of my parents' trip, Owen's entry into Turkestan (*The Desert Road*, chapter XIX) was something of a diplomatic feat. The xenophobic old governor Yang Zengxin, a mandarin graduate of Confucian state examinations in the imperial days before 1911, had ruled Xinjiang since the revolution as if it were his personal inheritance from the Manchu Dynasty, controlling the people (at that time still consisting in the main of non-Han minorities) by the traditional methods of setting them against each other and co-opting their leaders. He forbade the printing of minority-language newspapers and kept the keys to the telegraph station, which he personally unlocked and locked again each day. Yang administered Xinjiang through a clique of fellow provincials from Yunnan; other Chinese, to say nothing of foreigners, were kept out as much as possible, although Xinjiang, as if it were a sovereign power, conducted its own consular relations with British India and the Soviet Union.[15] As he tells in *The Desert Road*, Owen was arrested on entering Xinjiang and detained ten days until he could arrange for a highly placed business acquaintance in Urumchi to stand as his personal guarantor. Many years later he learned that the governor's agents had followed and watched him during his entire nine months in the province.[16]

The route of *The Desert Road* now lies chiefly in the Inner Mongolian Autonomous Region of the Chinese People's Republic. Most of the Desert Road passed through country either uninhabited or with a sparse all-Mongolian population.[17] Owen traveled with Chinese-speaking caravans, owned and mostly manned by Han Chinese. At the time he spoke Chinese but not yet Mongol. He knew, however, that the techniques, social structure, laws, and ritual observances of the caravans had been taken over *en bloc* from the Mongols, deriving from the practices not only of Mongol trading caravans but of the seasonal migrations of all Mongol nomads.

This first exploratory journey of Owen's not only piqued his interest in the Mongols but woke his sympathy for them. While the caravans kept to open country for the grazing that they needed, he knew that as little as ten miles to the south were Mongol lands that Chinese speculators or profiteering officials, underlings of the "Christian General" Feng Yuxiang, were buying at six dollars an acre for resale to famished Chinese peasants from Henan or Hebei—lands, one might add, of uncertain rainfall; Chinese peasants could quickly exhaust their fertility. Nevertheless, ninety percent of the population of Inner Mongolia is now Han Chinese. "I call the whole thing a tragedy," my father wrote, "because it does not give either Chinese or Mongol a fair chance."[18]

Separated early from his family by the First World War, shallowly rooted in his native country, which he hadn't visited between the ages of one and twenty-eight or settled in before the age of thirty-seven, worn down by the congressional follies of the 1950s, devastated by my mother's death, which left him a widower for nineteen years, my father displayed an odd mixture of dependency and feisty individualism. After the years of American demagoguery in the 1950s, and still more after my mother died in 1970, Owen turned his affections to the Mongol people, especially the Outer Mongolians of the Mongolian Republic, the most accessible Mongol territory. In 1969 he became the first foreign member of the Mongolian Academy of Sciences and received an ovation from that body for his unrehearsed address to them in Mongol, ending with five lines that he had composed in traditional alliterative verse.[19] He was rather like a Mongol in his hardihood, his distrust of the comfortable and the settled, and his pride (coupled with friendliness for those who showed respect).

For a stretch of Owen's later years he traveled in Mongolia almost annually. He and I covered 2,500 miles of Mongolia by jeep together in 1964. The Mongols called him La Bagsh, Master Lattimore, a rare honor. Both he and I were personal disciples in the Mongol fashion, although not disciples in faith, of a high Mongol lama, the Diluv Khutagt (Dilowa Khutukhtu).[20] Owen had many Mongol friends and protégés, from Arash in the 1930s to Urgunge Onon, his colleague at Leeds University in the 1960s, and younger scholars in the Mongolian Republic, such as Dalai.

I think it was John K. Fairbank of Harvard who said, with some justice, that to understand Owen's thought one had to see that at bottom he was a Mongol nationalist. In his youth, when many contemporaries were radicalized in college or the labor movement, he was far away and untouched. It was the Spanish Civil War, he said, that politicized him. For a time he deluded himself about the character of Stalin's purges and on a 1944 mission he fell for the Potemkinized labor camps shown him in Siberia. He gave the Soviet Union the benefit of the doubt because he saw it, correctly, as the protector of Outer Mongolia from Chinese population pressure and territorial ambitions.

If for this unusual reason he tilted toward the Soviet Union, his Mongol experiences also caused him to tilt away from Marxism and other deterministic theories of the nineteenth and early twentieth centuries. My father's own deepest interest lay in the development of societies over the long term, measured in millennia. But theories that set down rigid schemes of successive societal stages cannot account for different, but contemporaneous, *kinds* of society, any of which may have experienced periods of devolution as well as evolution. Owen already knew this before he made his relatively late contact with Marxism. He was thus inoculated against Marxism before he came to it. Having never been a Marxist, however, he never felt the sense of betrayal ex-Marxists often feel about their former belief. He remained capable of friendly discourse with Marxists and sometimes borrowed from them ideas that seemed useful.

When Owen wrote *The Desert Road* he already knew that Inner Asian societies had undergone devolution as well as evolution, and like others at the time he accepted the explanation for this put forward by a Yale professor, Ellsworth Huntington, in *The Pulse of Asia* (1907) and later works. According to Huntington, climatic variations over the centuries, especially in rainfall, explained these societal ups and downs. In the 1930s Arnold Toynbee adopted Huntington's theory and made a massive attempt to document it in the third volume of *A Study of History*. Owen, who unlike Toynbee was not exclusively an armchair scholar, had already made field observations that caused him to abandon Huntington's theory.

My father summed up his own ideas in *The Inner Asian Frontiers of China* (1940). One central idea of this large, complex book is that the agricultural society of China and the nomadic societies of the steppe, rather than being survivals of successive evolutionary stages, were different specializations developed simultaneously out of a single earlier, less specialized type of society, one that had practiced a mixture of hunting, herding, and primitive agriculture; moreover, the later, specialized societies required a symbiotic relationship with each other to survive, and continued to influence each other (thus nomad empires rose in response to unification of the Chinese empire).

Research in the history and archaeology of China and Inner Asia has progressed a good bit over the fifty-five years since its first publication, yet the ideas in *The Inner Asian Frontiers of China* have survived remarkably well. They have, for example, been applied to agricultural-nomadic frontiers in Africa.[21] Reviewing negatively a book by another author who had attempted a new work of synthesis to supplant *Inner Asian Frontiers*, a writer in the *Journal of Asian Studies* concluded in 1991 that "for students and non-specialists (even specialists), the works of Owen Lattimore . . . have not yet been superseded."[22]

While Mongols in the 1960s called my father La Bagsh, Mongols in the 1930s called him by a different name: Ganchar Siltei, meaning "solitary glass," or monocle. Owen sometimes explained that he wore a monocle while riding on the steppe because the flash of sunlight reflected from the single glass identified him to Mongols from a distance. About a year after his death my daughter Maria, who had traveled in China and Mongolia with her grandfather in 1981, wrote a poem called "Ganchar Siltei":

> They launched a telescope in space today
> To see as far throughout the heavens' past
> As man has ever told on prayer beads.
> I know that in this new-old firmament
> There shines somewhere a far-off unnamed star,
> That glimmers like the solitary glass
> Worn as a signature by our old man
> In his young days with ancient caravans.

David Lattimore
March 1995

Notes to this introduction can be found on pp. 373–374.

# INTRODUCTION TO THE 1975 EDITION

BETWEEN the end of the First World War in 1918 and the Great Wall Street Crash in 1929, the years in which this journey was made and this book was written, the world was crawling with adventurous youngsters trying to find their way into countries that had been cut off from them during the war years. They headed for Asia more than for Africa and Latin America because Asia, in the language of a later generation of youth, was "where the action was at." Japan had risen to a new level of power. China and India were stirring with revolutionary nationalism.

A large proportion of these young wanderers were Americans, if only because America had been enriched by the war, while European countries had been impoverished. In America, more than any other country, publishers had the money to pay for books by new, unknown authors and a public that would buy anything by a traveller who, having set foot almost anywhere in Asia, would describe himself as "following in the footsteps of Marco Polo." Under these conditions the traveller, ignorant of the history, customs and language of the people among whom he (or frequently she) was travelling, substituted "adventure" for the gathering of information, and turned incompetence in the art of travel into "endurance of hardship."

It was partly out of reaction against the temper of the times that for a couple of years before starting out on my journey I read everything about Mongolia and Sinkiang that I could lay my hands on, and carried all the way with me such classics as Yule's "The Book of Ser Marco Polo," Douglas Carruthers' "Unknown Mongolia;" Sir Aurel Stein's "Ruins of Desert Cathay," and a good many others. I also worked hard to make my spoken Chinese less like the genteel style of my first teacher—an opium-smoking Manchu petty bureaucrat of the old regime, who had come down in the world—and more like the language of workers, peasants, and especially merchants who dealt with the caravan trade. I had not yet met the caravan men themselves.

This course of training had its merits. It enabled me to learn more while traveling than if I had not tried to prepare myself. It also helped to account for some of the defects of the book, however. "The Desert Road to Turkestan" is too bookish a book. It reflects a young man's effort, sometimes too strained an effort, to show how much he knows, how thoroughly he has mastered his problems, how deeply he has penetrated the lives of people whose nature the reader could never understand without his help.

As for "penetrating the lives of people," there is also a kind of condescension that makes me wince today, 45 years later when I read some of the pages—a once-fashionable condescension of "the white man among the natives." I particularly regret some of the patronising remarks about my loyal companion, "Moses", because they belong to the bad old tradition of praising the "faithful native servant" as an indirect way of building up one's superiority. There are also passages that show that in spite of my love of venturing into the deep interior, I had by no means thrown off the social snobbery and appalling political insensitivity of the Treaty Port foreigner on the coast of China in the 1920's.

Another weakness of the book, but a weakness for which I could not be blamed, is that at that time I knew no Mongol, and so missed a great deal that might have been learned. Nor could I acquire truly Mongol information through the Chinese caravan men, because caravan men are like sailors, who travel to distant places but never learn the local languages, except a few words to use when in search of drink or women. Only rarely was I able to learn the meaning of a Mongol word as used by Chinese, for the Mongol and Chinese languages are phonetically so different that a Mongol word which has passed into the Chinese vocabulary, or a Chinese word borrowed by the Mongols, are always mispronounced.

Thus *hu-la-mao'rh* (p. 68), a "mixed" caravan—mixed, that is, in ownership of camels and goods, but travelling by agreement to a common destination, I took at the time to be a word from the patois of Shansi or Suiyan. I rendered it as "jerrycummumumble," because it looked as if it belonged to the same family of expressions as *hsi-la-hu-tu* which is more or less "by guess and by God," and *ma-ma-hu-hu* "any old way." It is in fact simply the Mongol word *kholimag* "mixed." I believe that caravans of this kind are more likely of Mongol than of Chinese origin; or perhaps one should say frontier origin. The principle of organization is like that of the Russian *artel'*—a union of individuals for a limited purpose, to be carried out in a limited time.

When the syllables *hu-la-mao-erh* are written down in Chinese characters, they form a word that has no meaning of it's own. The characters are used simply for their phonetic value. There is another class of these jargon words, however in which the syllables, in addition to their phonetic value, form a word that appears to have a meaning, though the meaning is misleading. An example (not found in this book, but in "High Tartary," the next book that I wrote), is *yang-kao-tze*. As written in Chinese, this means "lamb," but the real meaning is *"prostitute."* It is a garbling of the Mongol word for "prostitute," *yangan* (older spelling, *yanggan*). Following the trail a little farther, I believe that this word may in fact be a Mongol borrowing from one of the Central Asian Turkish languages.

Another word for "prostitute" used by the caravan men is *K'ou-k'ou-tze* (the *-tze* here gives the sense of a diminutive). It is from the Mongol "Khuukhen," "girl," "Unmarried woman," and by extension "girlfriend," "woman living with a man but not married to him." Among Mongols below the status of the aristocracy and the wealthy commoners, it often meant, in pre-revolutionary times, simply "wife."

There are, of course, reverse examples. In 1860–61 there was a mongol Prince Senggerinchen, who fought for his feudal overlord, the Manchu Emperor, against the French and British who marched from Tientsin to Peking and burned the famous Old Summer Palace outside of Peking. Senggerinchen, like a great many other personal names, came into Mongolia with the Lama-Buddist religion (just as many "Christian" names are in fact Hebrew). The second half of the name, *rinchen* is the Tibetan for "treasure." (As I do not know Tibetan, I have not gone into the possibility that it may be a Tibetan borrowing from an Indian language.) The first half, *sengge* is unmistakably from a North Indian, Indo-European language. It means "lion," and is the same as Singh, a standard component of Sikh personal names. The Chinese rendering of Senggerinchen is Seng-k'o-lin-ts'in. From this the British troops against whom the valiant prince was fighting contrived the happy variant, Sam Collinson.

Some of these transformed words are of special interest. Ma-tsung Shan (see Chapter XV, "The House of the False Lama") is explained on p. 245 as "horse-hoofprint hills." This was how the name was explained to me by the caravan men. It was only many years later that I divined the true derivation and meaning of this name. It is from the Mongol Metsin (old spelling, Bechin) Uhl, "Ape Mountains." For the significance of this name, turn to pages 185 and 186 and the references there to "Hairy Wild Men" and various kinds of bears. To these can be added Mongolian tales from Altai Mountains about a not-quite-man, not-quite-bear creature which the Mongols call *almas*. In other words what we have here is an extension, the colonial geography, so to speak, of the folklore world of the fabulous Abominable Snowman of Tibet.

In Chapter XV also I told the story of the False Lama. I called him that because his name was pronounced and explained by the caravan men as *Chia* "false." Reading the story again after nearly half a century, I am astonished and pleased at the way in which it demonstrates how much of the historical truth can be preserved in a form of oral history that is very close to folklore. The *chia* in this name is in fact the Mongol (or rather Tibetan) *ja* an abbreviation, in a manner quite usual in Mongolia, of the name Dambijantsan.

Ja Lama or Dambijantsan was a Kalmyk (Kalmuk; properly Khal-imag) from the Volga region. Had I known Russian at the time I would have known that the great Russian scholar and traveller Pozdneev heard about him during his travels of 1893 (E.M. Pozdneev, *Mongoliya i Mongoli*, Vol I, St. Petersburg, 1893; translated as "Mongolia and the Mongols," with the author's name transcribed as Pozdneyev, Bloomington, Indiana, 1971). There is a great deal about him by the trader-scholar A.V. Burdukov, who knew him personally (*V Staroi i Novoi Mongolii*, "In the Old and New Mongolia", with massive and valuable notes and commentary by I. Ya Zlatkin, Moscow, 1969). According to Burdukov there was probably more than one man who called himself Dambijantsan, and one of these was said to have come from the eastern part of what was then Outer Mongolia, and to have studied at the great monastic centre of Delonnor (Doloon nuur) in the Eastern Part of Inner Mongolia. There was a strong Chinese influence at Dolonnor, and many lamas there spoke Chinese.

Evidently the caravan versions that he was really a Russian, or a Russianised Buryat, echo the fact that he was a Kalmyk, that is, not an "ordinary" Mongol of Mongolia, and the version that he was (p. 35) "A Chinese from Manchuria who had served in Mongolia as a herder of ponies for the princely firm of Ta Sheng K'uei" echoes Burdukov's "Alternative" version that he was from the East of Mongolia but had spent many years in the west and could speak like a westerner. A sensational account of him, with striking photographs, is to be found in Hermann Consten, *Weideplätze der Mongolen* Berlin, 1919–20, based on travels in Mongolia at about the time of Dambijantsan's Khobo (Khovd) exploits.

To these accounts may be added the stories told me by Arash, my travelling companion of Inner Mongolian days in the 1930's "Mongol Journeys," New York and London, 1941). Arash was himself a Jakchin from the Altai, and he had a brother (whom I never met) who had been a follower of Dambijantsan. Another source in my possession is in the *Autobiography* of the late Dilowa Hutukhtu (Dilov or Delov Khutagt). My wife had not completed her editing of this material at the time of her death. My partner in research, Fujiko Isono, will complete the work, and I will edit it, but the work is difficult. The Dilowa dictated his account, in snatches, over a rather long period of time; I made a running translation or paraphrase, and my son wrote down this English version. Owing to the method, there are both overlaps and repetitions which have to be matched against each other, and gaps which will have to be filled by writing notes or commentaries.

These references do not exhaust the sources, but one must mention at least V.A. Obruchev (1863–1956), *V Debryakh Tsentral'noi Azii,* "In the Wastes of Central Asia," Moscow 1956. An English version (unfortunately an abbreviated translation), was published as *Kukushkin, A Geographer's Tales,* London, 1961. Obruchev was one of the great geologist-explorers. No other traveller matches him in knowledge and accurate description of the details of different modes of Mongolian and Central Asian travel. It is sad that many of these details are omitted in the English condensation. In his old age he wrote several fictional tales of adventure for young people, of which this is one. It has two young heroes, a Russian whose mother was an Altai Turk, and a Mongol. It is clear that his Russian is modelled on Burdukov (who has been mentioned above, and must have been one of his sources of information). The story includes an account of an adventurer who sets himself up in a desert oasis, protects and exploits the caravan trade, and deals in a shady way with different Chinese provincial potentates. This lively tale, presented as fiction, confirms in general the account given by the caravan men of the "False Lama" and his stronghold in the Matsung Shan.

So much for the past; but much new work is going on. My partner in research, Fujiko Isono, will shortly publish an account of the revolutionary Mongol partisans of 1921, which includes a full translation of the personal narrative of Nanzad, who led the commando that liquidated Dambijantsan. The eminent contemporary Mongol historian, Academician Sh. Natsagdorj (whose biography of Sukbaatar, the great Mongol revolutionary warrior-statesman, my colleague Urgunge Onon and I translated in "Nationalism and Revolution in Mongolia," Leiden, 1955) is writing a monograph on Dambijantsan. He has the advantage of access to unpublished state archives. He will also, probably, write the scenario of a cinemathriller based on his historical research.

My knowledge of Chinese in those days was not as good as I sometimes thought it was. On p. 147 I refer to the Eldest Son of the House of Chou. On p. 148 I say that he was known "by his child name of Liu-tze." But in this application, Liu-tze would mean Sixth Son, which is nonsense for an eldest son. Note, however, that he was an opium smoker. It was only later that I came to understand the nickname. Liu-tze can also mean "the character (sign) for six." In sign language, if the middle fingers of the hand are curled in, as if one were clenching the fist, while the thumb and little finger are left protruding, that is the sign for six. If, in making the sign for "six," the thumb and little finger are extended sideways as far as possible, it becomes the sign for "opium pipe," "opium smoker."

Another example is that I say on p. 163 that the great snow peak of Bogdo Ola (modern Mongol spelling, Bogd Uul), "Holy Mountain," was called "Bread Mountain—Mo-mo shan, or Man t'ou shan" because it was a sign that the caravans were approaching the lands "where men eat their fill of the noble white-flour bread." Two explanations are here mixed up. I was certainly told that Man-t'ou Shan means "Bread Mountain"; but *mo-mo* is a round, soft, steamed roll, and a slang word for a woman's breasts, or tits. Thus a "mo-mo Mountain" is the exact equivalent of the Grand Tetons in the Rocky Mountains.

My understanding of politics was also weak. An example is that I did not do justice to that interesting figure, General Feng Yu-hsiang (whom I came to know personally many years later). All through the war-lord period of the 1920's he was cut off by his rivals from access to the seaports, through which arms could be bought from abroad. In the hinterland, where he had to conserve his ammunition, he could not use force as arbitrarily as his rivals, and had to rely more on public support. He, therefore, taxed more even-handedly than other warlords, restrained his troops from wanton plundering, and favoured small merchants who elsewhere were being driven out of business by bigger firms and especially by "compradore" trade linked with privileged foreign firms. He was in fact what later the communists (who began where he left off) would call a bourgeois democrat, and Americans, perhaps, a populist.

Finally, my knowledge of history as it is imbedded in folklore was weakly developed. I should have tried to learn much more about the links between the caravan trade and trade in general with the period at the end of the seventeenth century and the beginning of the eighteenth century when the Manchu Emperor K'ang Hsi extended his conquests over Mongolia and into Sinkiang. When the caravan men said (p. 157) that "the relations between Chinese and Mongols [were] fixed for all time by K'ang Hsi," they were close to history. Recent research by Mongol scholars has showed how the supply-caravans, manned by Chinese, which followed the advancing armies, engaged also in private trade. The necessity to keep the military supplies moving made it politic to tolerate and even protect these private activities—partly, of course, because war-ravaged Mongolia was in desperate need of goods of all kinds. The origins of the modes of Chinese trade and usury, and the privileges which protected them until the Mongolian Revolution of 1921 (and in Inner Mongolia until the triumph of the Chinese Communists in 1949) are to be found here.

There is historical confirmation also for the account given on pp. 71–72 of the messenger or courier dogs of the famous Chinese firm of Ta Sheng K'uei. In recent years, in the Altai and the West of the Mongolian People's Republic, I have found that these dogs are well-remembered. Moreover a Mongol friend of mine, Ch. Dalai, himself a man of the Altai, has found in the Chinese sources for the history of the Yuan or Mongol dynasty in China, 1260 (or 1280) to 1368, that far to the east, in Manchuria (now the Northeastern provinces of China) there was a state-maintained service of courier dogs.

All in all, it can be seen from the additions and corrections in these few pages that the "field work" results of this journey had some value; but the book must be read tolerantly as the work of a young beginner.

Owen Lattimore
Department of Chinese Studies
University of Leeds
1972

# PREFACE

I HAVE called this book *The Desert Road to Turkestan* because the road I followed in the journey described is the most desert of all the caravan routes which traverse Mongolia, or lead through Mongolia to Chinese Turkestan. Its distinctive name among the caravan men is the Jao Lu, the Winding Road; but in contrast with the others, which lie either in the *ts'ao ti*, the grasslands, or along the edge of the *ming ti*, the "open" or cultivated land, it stands out as the road of the desert. My four months on the desert road to Turkestan were the first part of a journey overland from Peking to India. The Mongolian journey I made alone in 1926, but early in the following year my wife joined me at Chuguchak, on the Siberian border, and together we traveled on through Chinese Central Asia and over the Karakoram route to Leh, Kashmir, and India.

In the first chapters I have sketched in enough of the history and present conditions of the caravan trade in Mongolia to furnish the necessary background for the narrative. On the other hand, I have tried not to overweight the story with too much technical discussion of ancient trade routes and their bearing on the caravan routes now in use, nor have I touched more than cursorily on the economic and political changes which are now going on in the far-away and little-known lands that lie between China and Russia.

As the spelling of names in the regions covered by this account is a difficulty not yet authoritatively resolved, I have felt myself justified in choosing my own standards. In the spelling of Turki names I have followed the recommendations of the Committee on Names of the Royal Geographical Society. For Chinese names, however, I have departed from what is now the usual rule of accepting the official spelling of the Chinese Post Office.

The Post Office system has the advantage of a specious ready-made uniformity; but, though convenient, it is not based on a coherent single method of transliteration. I have therefore taken the Wade system of transliteration, but used my own judgment in the syllabic division of names. A few examples may show the object at which I have aimed: —

Lan Chou (Lan being the name of the city, properly speaking, while Chou is an index of its rank under the old Imperial system)

Kuei-hua (the two hyphenated words forming in combination the name of the city, the index of its rank being commonly dropped in colloquial usage)

Ku Ch'eng-tze (Ku, "Ancient," and Ch'eng-tze, "The City," falling naturally into a two-unit name)

My attempt at rationalizing, to the small degree that is possible, the names of Chinese places, especially in the far interior, is intended chiefly for the benefit of two deserving but little-considered classes of men: the traveler with a knowledge of the vernacular, who, as well I know, may frequently be helped by a hint at the meaning of names; and that still less considered man, the one who likes a clue to help him in hunting place names through the dictionary. Naturally, I have left alone the few names which have a really well-established English version; to dragoon Tientsin back to its native T'ien-ching would be as futile as to insist on Wien for Vienna. As for the names on which I have laid my hands, I have supplemented them in the Index with other spellings — with Lan Chou I have written Lanchow, with Kuei-hua, Kueihuating and Kueihuacheng, with Ku Ch'eng-tze, Kuchengtze and Guchen. For Chinese words other than place names I have also used the Wade system, but once or twice without altering words from a dialect form to the more literary form of Peking "Mandarin" or *kuan-hua*.

There remain the Mongol names and words, which for the most part I have had to spell phonetically, hoping that I heard them right. For these I cannot pretend to accuracy or authority. I may mention that I have kept the spelling *khara*, black, for the Mongol word, as in Khara-khoto, Black City; but for the more old-fashioned Kharashahr, which also means Black City, I have

# PREFACE

XXXV

substituted Qara Shahr, to conform to the system of the Royal Geographical Society, because the Qara here is not Mongol but Turki. It is to be hoped that the recent publication of an official map of Mongolia, in Mongol, may lead to an authoritative method of transliteration.

One word, in its two forms, requires special mention. I have conformed to what is now the best usage in writing Bar Köl for the lake and the mountain range, and Barköl for the town, omitting altogether the official Chinese name for the town, which is Chen-hsi, and the colloquial name, which is Pa-li-k'un, a mere corruption of Barköl.

My "authorities," my references to previous travelers, I have given explicitly in footnotes, instead of lumping them in a bibliography at the end of the volume. I have done so in order to clear myself of the tendency toward two prideful extremes which I have noticed in all but the few really good modern books of travel. One is the pose of having read absolutely everything, including the thoroughly useless and irrelevant, on one's subject. The other is the tendency, regrettably marked among my own countrymen, to omit all references, thus giving the vicious implication that one has been traveling in totally unexplored and unmapped countries. I have therefore indicated, at each point where I have been indebted to a book, the measure to which I have been indebted. I have also tried to make as clear as possible, for the benefit of those interested in the geography of Mongolia, the areas which to the best of my knowledge have hitherto been unexplored. I should add that, owing to the lack of an English translation of the works of Kozloff, I have been restricted to the summary of his explorations (in the areas which I also touched) in *La Géographie*.

A journey in the hinterland of China is not to be lightly undertaken at the present time, and even my own journey, traveling alone and in modest style as I was, could hardly have been successful but for the assistance and goodwill of a large number of people. For some of them the appearance of this book will be an indication that their help was not wasted, and an acknowledgment of my gratitude; but I must mention particularly my indebtedness to Mr. H. G. W. Woodhead, editor of the *Peking and Tientsin Times*, for his initial encouragement and support; to Mr. Pan Tsilu for his friendship and good offices in Turkestan, and to Messrs. Arnhold & Co., Ltd., of Tientsin, my former employers, for letters of recommendation to their Chinese trade agents in the interior. I have also to thank the Società Geografica at Rome, the Société de Géographie in Paris, and the Royal Geographical Society for their kindness in putting books and maps at my disposal after my return.

# THE DESERT ROAD TO TURKESTAN

1. OWEN LATTIMORE WITH BOOTS OF ANTELOPE (GAZELLE) HIDE
(BLACK GOBI)

# I

## THE ROADS TO INNER ASIA

No one knows the beginning of the caravan traffic from China into Mongolia and what is now Chinese Central Asia; but since its beginning men have taken out the manufactures and silk of China and brought back the pelts of wild animals and gold dust and jade. The origins of this trade are obscured by the wars and conquests which crowded along the same primal and inevitable routes. Whenever the barbaric tribes of Central Asia were strong enough, they swarmed about the western and northern borders of China, occupying broad lands and establishing kingdoms and dynasties. Whenever the Chinese in their turn were in the ascendant, they pushed their own conquests far to the west, taking their trade with them; not only establishing touch with Northern India across the Karakoram and Pamirs, but even opening, through Western Turkestan, a route whose farther end they could not guess. Along this route the traders of intermediate kingdoms, receiving the precious, almost fabulous silks of the Chinese, carried them on to the Mediterranean to delight the peoples of Greece and Rome.

The avenue between China and the West of which we know the most is the classical road which still survives, and is commonly known as the Imperial Highway. It leads in our time from the Peking–Hankow Railway (which links the capital and the Yang-tze valley) past Hsi-ngan, the greatest of the ancient capitals of China, and on across the provinces of Shen-hsi and Kan-su as far as Ngan-hsi, near the Jade Gate of classical times, the Chinese taking-off point for the West in all the great ages. From Ngan-hsi the road has taken different entries into Central Asia, according to the conditions of different times and the extent of the power exercised by China over the outer nations. This was the road followed, in one or other of its variants, by the Chinese armies which set up their standards as far away as the Pamirs and Samarqand; by Chinese pilgrims going to Northern India in search of Buddhist scriptures, and by the Western adventurers, like the Polos and Benedict Goes.

Other roads, less known, have existed for as long, linking Peking and Northern China with Mongolia and the cardinal Central Asian routes between Europe and Cathay. They were first followed out by barbarian raiders, and developed by the traders of the lesser principalities and powers, outlying khanates and frontier kingdoms. Under such rulers as Jenghis Khan and his successors, and later under the dynasty established in China by the Manchus, they were confirmed in constant use by the troops and envoys of the great Emperors, on their way out and back between the solid central civilization of China and the far outposts of the Empire, and thronged, under a stable peace, with the camps and caravans of traders.

These are the Mongolian roads, all of them firstly and lastly caravan roads, for though express mounted messengers passed along them in haste, the usual kind of travel was by camel caravan. The Imperial Highway was a cart road, a corridor for the trade and armies of a settled people, but the caravan roads have always belonged to the nomads and the Chinese who learned from the nomads; carts, even when pulled by camels, have not commonly used them.

These are the chief of the Mongolian ways: from Kalgan to Urga and on northward to Kiakhta, on the Siberian border; from Urga to Uliassutai and Kobdo, in the west of Mongolia; from Kuei-hua to Urga; from Kuei-hua to Uliassutai and Kobdo; from Kuei-hua to Ku Ch'eng-tze and so to Urumchi or Hami and the arterial roads of Zungaria and Chinese Turkestan; from Kuei-hua through Pao-t'ou to the valley of the Yellow River and so to Kan-su — a road that could be followed by carts, and offered a connection with the western extension of the Imperial Highway; and from Kuei-hua through Inner Mongolia to either Hami or Ku Ch'eng-tze.

By this last, the vaguest and least known of all the caravan roads, I traveled in 1926 along the length of Mongolia until I came to Chinese Turkestan, on my way to further wanderings on further roads. The way that I followed is in the main an ancient road to which the caravans have turned again only in latter years, because they have been barred from other roads by the troubles that increasingly possess Central and Eastern Asia. It is also one of the very few among the ancient roads that are not likely to change with the shifting world, because of the deserts in which it is hid, the lack of water that fends off campaigning armies, and the huge sands that debar the approach of carts and motor cars. The new world in its time will travel by its new railways and motor roads; but the Winding Road, as it is called, will not be shaped to their use. It will pass out of its own immemorial use into honorable oblivion, guarded by the wilderness.

The beginnings of my own journey did not lie in scientific study, nor was I sent on a "mission" or "expedition" of any kind. I came to it more in the way of an old man dreaming a dream or a young man seeing a vision; but it did proceed, in some sort, from political and economic things — from a sense of the complex unity of history, a stream of grand volume descending from discoverable sources. It all began in a longing to travel the caravan ways in the old manner of caravans, because I had had a glimpse of what they meant — a survival from the past, but more than that: one of the sources or headwaters of our life as it is.

The reason that we know so little of Central Asia between the Middle Ages and the time when rival empires began to enter those countries again is that after the opening of communication by sea between East and West, the stream of missionaries, pilgrims, envoys, and adventurers crossing the dreaded mountains and central deserts fell away. Marco Polo himself on his return from China came as far as India by sea, and after his time the establishment of sea traffic began to effect, very curiously, the isolation of China. So long as the great rulers and conquerors of China had had even the most remote touch with the West by land, the balancing of the advantages and dangers of intercourse with other peoples had kept their imagination lively. With the passing of the ages of migration and tribal wars, and the conquests of the nomads, men of alien races were no longer estimated as potential invaders or allies. The few boatloads of merchant adventurers who came by sea the Chinese and their rulers were disposed to regard as pirates or ruffians of some sort, not dispatched by nations of serious power, and too much awed by the magnificence of the Chinese State to attempt any onslaught. The foreigners themselves bent all their efforts to the effecting of a lodgment in a few seaports; not threatening any war, but using diplomacy or flattery until compelled by contumelious treatment to resort to arms. The petty inroads on their coasts which resulted were still regarded by the Chinese as acts of piracy rather than of war, and though a rich trade was developed by a comparatively small number of men, China and Europe remained essentially farther apart than in the quasi-fabulous period of the overland routes. One of the clues to the psychology of history is that men who come in ships to trade affect the life and customs of a country far less than men who come on camels, or with mule trains, or even donkeys.

During this long period when only the seaways were regarded, the old roads of the caravans were forgotten, except by a few Chinese traders, who kept on tramping the old long stages with the old merchandise, while the count of years ran into generations. It took the Russian " forward policy " of sixty years ago to revive interest in the countries, themselves still mediæval, that still held Europe and Asia apart; and the resuscitation of this policy, in the eastward trend of the foreign policy of Soviet Russia, has once more refreshed the interest of the world in Central Asia.

An economic interest is bound up in this political interest. The caravan trade, which had by the end of the Middle Ages begun to suffer from the competition of trade by sea, came in the end to benefit by it, and to enjoy an unpredictable revival of prosperity for which the foreign traders at the ports of China were directly responsible. The trade was probably at its lowest ebb in the last decades before 1900. Then, with China recovering from the T'ai P'ing and Mohammedan rebellions, and foreign merchants acting with greater security and prosperity after the Boxer war, foreign trade began to take its full effect. It was no longer limited to the more precious cargoes, like tea and silk, but prospered by the demand for raw materials. The markets for wool and hides, goatskins and furs, grew so rapidly that they could not be supplied by the parts of Manchuria and Mongolia nearest to the Chinese border. The demand was felt farther and farther away in the hinterland, and caravan owners grew rich in bringing down produce from the most distant pastures of Outer Mongolia, Chinese Turkestan, and the Tibetan border plateaux. Competition increased when the pressure of the Russian "forward policy" began to bear on Chinese Central Asia and the East, until the caravans were as busy, with Peking impotent and China in political decay, as they had ever been when Peking commanded half the world.

The buying and selling of wool is a mystery or craft. The caravans come to the railway, the railway comes to Tientsin and the river, and the river goes to the sea. There are Chinese brokers, who run between the railway yards and the foreign firms, who will shake and pat a handful of wool and tell you within a few ounces how much dirt there will be in a hundred pounds of it. There are even Americans, Englishmen, and Japanese who will pat it and shake it again, and pull out tufts of it and even smell it, and tell you whether it was sheared on the high pastures of the Koko Nor and marketed at Hsi-ning, or whether it is only "imitation Hsi-ning," picked from the better fleeces of the lower Kan-su levels.

This is not my business, and I know little of it. The men who do know are not fond of going far from their desks, and to motor to the golf club is a Sabbath day's journey for them. Had I been apprenticed to them, I should hardly have come to set foot on the caravan roads. It happened in my fate that I was sent "upcountry" once to try to get hold of some wool, because I could speak Chinese. My companion on this journey was a young Chinese, Pan Tsilu,[1] who had been connected with

---

[1] The ordinary romanization of the Chinese characters would be P'an Chi-lou; but Chinese who write their names in English use as much latitude in the spelling as we do in the spelling of our own names.

my firm, but was preparing to return to his home in Urumchi. His father, who died a few months later, was the P'an Ta-jen of Sir Aurel Stein's books, the scholarly administrator by whose friendly interest his explorations were so well furthered. A scholar and a gentleman of the old tradition, and an able official who had had many high posts, he was beloved throughout the province of Hsin-chiang, where he was known as "P'an the Good." His son, a man of about thirty, had already made his mark. He had traveled between Chinese Central Asia and Peking by the Imperial Highway from Hami to Ngan-hsi and Lan Chou and so through the provinces of Kan-su and Shen-hsi; by the Mongolian Great Road, and a third time through Siberia. As a child in the far interior he had learned French and English from missionaries, and also Russian, and his English he had improved by study in Peking. After his return to Hsin-chiang he was preferred at once to high official position, and his friendship was the deciding factor in the success of my own travels.

I had known that beyond Nan K'ou, the "Southern Gate" from Mongolia to Peking, stood Kalgan; that from Kalgan to Feng-chen, Kuei-hua, and Pao-t'ou ran the Northwestern Province, created out of frontier districts of the provinces of Chih-li and Shan-hsi and those fringes of Mongolia that have been largely occupied by Chinese settlers and brought into unity by one of the newest Chinese railways. I knew that it was a bad season, because it was February, when the weather is coldest and the Chinese, during their New Year holidays, not at all lively about doing business. There was a foreboding of political troubles, and the trains were running badly because of troop movements. Quantities of wool had accumulated at railhead, coming from all the caravan routes that converge toward Kuei-hua. Most of it had been bought by foreign firms, like my own, who were bothered because they could not get it down to the sea to ship it to America in the time demanded by their contracts. My commission was to try to get cars for the wool belonging to my firm.

I expected to find Kuei-hua crude and rude and cold. It was

all of that. What I had never expected was that I should find a world that was a new world to me, but a very old world indeed by its own reckoning, ruled by its own tradition and peopled by men out of earlier centuries. We got down very stiff and cold from a train that was hours late, and were fittingly met by one of those two-wheeled carts, covered with a curved hood, which we call " Peking" carts; but a cart lined with squirrel and leopard skins and silk, and drawn by a mule in brass-plated harness — one of those big Shan-hsi mules that in old days used to be the pride of Peking mandarins.

From that hour I was among men whose very dialect was so strange to me that for the first few days I was quite at a loss. They took me to see caravan owners and agents for railway transport, in whose offices, fitted with carved woodwork, sleek clerks brought tea for uncouth men in the matted sheepskins and crusted dirt of winter travel with the caravans, who were received with deference. Then they took me to the station yard, where the wool had been piling up for months, and was being added to every day as the caravans came in. The outer quarters of the city were thronged with scores and hundreds of camels, which only finished the last march from Chinese Turkestan when they knelt by the shunting lines, squealing back at the engines roaring a few yards away. There the caravan men, steaming with sweat in the frosty air, some of them even stripped to the waist, worked up and down the files, pulling out the clinching pegs, letting the heavy bales of Turfan cotton and Qara Shahr wool bump to the ground, and tugging at frozen knots to free the cordage in which the bales had been slung ever since they had been assembled at Ku Ch'eng-tze, the greatest of all the caravan cities.

Then my Chinese friend went back, and I went on alone by train the ninety miles or so to Pao-t'ou, which means the Head of Packages, the place where loads are delivered. Here the railway runs against the northern bend of the Yellow River, where it returns toward China after rounding the Ordos desert. The progress of the railway is barred by the difficulty of bridging the river, running half a mile wide between low soft banks that crumble and shift with the floods of every year, and the further difficulty of laying a track through the sands beyond.

Down the Yellow River, all the way from Lan Chou, come rafts and boats with the wool and hides of Kan-su and the Koko Nor; and out from Pao-t'ou, the current of the river being too swift for any volume of traffic upstream, go caravan roads to the Ordos and the principality of Alashan in Inner Mongolia, and cart and camel roads to Ning-hsia and Lan Chou in Kan-su. I stayed for a few days in Pao-t'ou, a little husk of a town in a great hollow shell of mud ramparts, where two busy streets made a traders' quarter in a wilderness of frozen cesspools where children whooped, curs wrangled over garbage, and black vagrant pigs went moodily about their occasions. I was lodged in a caravanserai around whose court were the quarters of a score of traders, bankers, and brokers. Here again I was thrown among men whose talk was forever of the prices of wool and camels, of caravan rates and cart hire, of journeys counted in many tens of days from Pao-t'ou into the remote hinterland of Asia, and of the bandits besetting this road or the soldiers obstructing that. Or else their gossip would run on storms and the loss of caravans, or lucky ventures that had made men rich at one blow, and all the chances and alarms of a way of trading and living utterly different from the alien civilization which I had seen creeping up along the railway, but of which they seemed so little aware.

In the last few months bandits had been raiding right up to the walls of Pao-t'ou. The gates were therefore always closed at dusk, cutting off the station, which lay outside the town. Matters had begun to improve a little, however, and a few men who, as they said themselves, were too poor to be of any account stayed out at the station overnight. For fear that the gates might open late, or police formalities there delay me, I slept the last night in the railway yards. I shared the mud-built quarters of a cargo foreman, and the pork and cabbage of his gang. From them, by the light of a twist of cotton in a saucer of oil, I heard more of the talk of the frontier, which was very strong talk, working powerfully. We turned in early, but I stepped out of the reeking frowst of the low-ceiled room for a few long breaths of cold clean air before the Mongol dogs were unchained to range the yards all night. The stars shone big and bold as I looked up from the gloom below towering stacks of wool and cotton in bales. There came on me a feeling that I had known before in other places of interior China — a desire to break with the office life of the fringing coastal ports; to go somewhere a long way off, to countries where men do things as they were done uncounted years ago, because their fathers did things in that way.

I wanted to feel the strange and actual life of that past which we usually accept without thought as the dead background of our present. This time there was more than the desire. I had seen men and heard speech that gave me an earnest of that other world, discovering both a vision and a promise.

That was early in 1925. A few days after returning to Tientsin I gave notice of resignation to my employers. Then, feeling a little dashed by the result of my impulse, I cast about for a way of getting what I wanted. I had very little money, but an old friend, the editor of a British newspaper in Tientsin, gave me all the support he could, and I was able to go on with my plans, though counting on only about a fifth of the money that the average "expedition" allots to one man. There were still many months of delay, which I spent in Peking, still in the employ of my old firm. During this time I read all that I could find of the wide reach of Asia between Peking and India. I ordered a rifle from the Savage Company in America — a slow business, requiring many permits from the Chinese authorities. Then it took months to get a new passport and have it approved by the Chinese Foreign Office, and additionally endorsed by the War Office to cover my arms and munitions.

Nor did the American Legation show any sort of zeal in pushing my requests; they merely raised their eyebrows and submitted them. As I had not the backing of any of those learned societies or museums which make such good advertising use of American travelers, I suppose they must have been anxious to give not the faintest impression of official approval. Thus they would give the Chinese authorities the least possible advantage in the melancholy diplomatic game of "I told you so," were I to come to a spectacularly bad end and the filing clerks be faced with the exhausting task of entering up the name of "Lattimore, Owen, scuppered." American officials abroad are not behind those of any other nation in appreciating the difference between helping a well-advertised celebrity on his booming way and assisting an unwanted adventurer, without a headline to bless himself with, to get into silly scrapes.

During this time my friend Pan set off for his home in Chinese Turkestan by the Russian entry through Siberia. He told me that he would make sure of my welcome if I ever succeeded in attaining the province through Mongolia, but warned me again that the journey was hedged about with more difficulties than had ever been known before. Everybody who knew interior China or Mongolia had the same warning; but those who knew best agreed that it could be done if one went at it quietly and with tact and patience. The main facts against me were that foreigners were definitely debarred from Outer Mongolia, and that the temper of all the Mongols was uncertain. The whole of interior China was still seething with antiforeign feeling, as a result of the business of May 30 in Shanghai. Hsinchiang itself, however, was the single province from which no outbreaks had been reported. As for the foreign governments, ill informed and badly served, they were abashed by the fury of partisan feeling, and, being at a loss to understand the forces at work, accepted with nervous futility the increasingly frequent attacks on foreigners in the interior.

It was March 1926 before I could get away. My rifle, or at least the ammunition for it, had arrived only a few days before. The rifle itself had been stolen in transit, but by great good luck I managed to buy a secondhand rifle of the same make and calibre. I left Peking by the night train. On that very afternoon a crowd of demonstrators had been fired on by the Chinese police, who killed a number of students, some of whom were girls, and a few bystanders. The shooting had taken place within a few hundred yards of the house where we were staying. There was a tense, ominous feeling throughout the city. The gates were closed early and we had difficulty in getting to the station, outside the walls.

In the general and fluttering terror of the servants the only calm voice was that of my man Moses. "This must be looked at in the right way," he said. "It is a good omen. The progress of people marked out by their destiny for a conspicuous fortune is always attended by remarkable public events and all kinds of calamities." Moses, whom I had just brought up from Tientsin, where he had been "lent" to a friend during the last few months, was enjoying Peking. He had begun by recognizing an old acquaintance in our host's cook, who had once worked for a Manchu prince, a refugee in Tientsin after the Revolution. The cook, though a man of lowly country origin, had acquired a fine Peking way of speaking, and tried to come the high and mighty over Moses, whom he despised because he had never become rich on "squeeze" and was bent on following a mad master into scandalous parts of the world. Moses took his revenge by pretending to have been an accomplice of the cook's former rogueries in cheating his Manchu master, and sat up till all hours inventing shocking stories, for the other servants, of the high old, bad old times.

I inherited Moses from my father. He had been, in his boyhood, a Boxer. Then he went to South Africa as an indentured laborer, and there he learned to speak good English; his English was no longer fluent, because he had served for so many years with Chinese-speaking foreigners, but he could understand readily enough. On his return to China he was servant for many years to a foreigner; then, after short experiences as a railway restaurant "boy" and a hotel bar boy, he became my father's "number one boy," in charge of the household, and after my father left China he came to me. He stayed with me several years, both as cook and boy, but I hardly thought him fit to travel through Mongolia, though he was capable, genuine, and honest. He had been married for years, and had a young son to educate; moreover, he had put on a certain well-liking fatness, not unbecoming to a man of forty and an old family servant. I supposed without asking that he would not care for the camp and the caravan, of which he had no experience at all, so when I was making my plans I told him that I would make him as good a present as I could afford, and had already arranged for him a better billet than he had had with me. He was very much hurt. In fact, he refused to be left behind. "Everybody knows," he said, "that I served your father and mother for years and that they said, 'Moses is a good man.' It would be a disgrace to me if you considered that I was not fit to go with you wherever you go. If your father came back to China and said to me, 'Moses, where is my son?' what should I have to say?"

I explained to him the certain physical hardships and the dangers that everybody predicted. "That does not matter," he said. "If I am not afraid, what need you fear for me? Danger is mostly a thing of talk. If all men listened to talk, no men would go to the Hsi-k'ou wai,"—that is, to the parts beyond the western gates of the Great Wall,—"but everybody knows that those parts are full of Tientsin men who have become rich. Besides, if it is a bad time for foreigners in the interior, the more need that I go with you, for I can handle the Chinese and look after you. This is truly a time when you must have a safe man behind your back."

A little against my first judgment, I took him. Before he left Tientsin, his friends invited him to a series of those dinners with which the Chinese preface solemn talk, and begged him to be better advised, but he never showed a sign of wanting to withdraw. He never even asked for extra pay, though in that year few Chinese in foreign service could have been bribed to go. No traveler could have been better served. He was never sick, and he never asked us to shorten a march or make his work lighter. Once, while my wife was with me on the Mongolian borders, we had a horrid experience with an opium-sodden carter. We had to walk a full thirty miles, in a hot sun. Moses, who had not yet hardened, was so tired that in the last two or three miles he could not stagger more than a hundred yards without lying down to rest. When we reached a village, we sent out men to fetch him, but he finished on his own feet and his first question was whether his "missy" were all right. The next morning he said, "This needs practice. I shall learn it yet." He was lame for several days, but when he got his "practice" he could march with the best.

He proved his worth the night we left Peking. There was the kind of confusion at the station that goes with the eve of a Chinese civil war. The third-class carriages were full of first-class passengers, and the first-class of people with third-class tickets and soldiers with no tickets at all. I had a few small, heavy boxes of provisions which I was told I could not possibly take with me. I was going to try smooth words and bribery when Moses nudged me in the back and I withdrew. He told me to get a place in the train and he would see that the boxes came along.

He did. He had recognized in one of the clerks at the station office a relative of a man for whom he had once found a job. He did not remember the man's name, but managed to address him without betraying that. He persuaded the fellow that he was the dearest friend of his whole family clan, and in the end got all the boxes on the train without paying a bribe. Then he found himself a place in a second-class compartment, where he traveled in comfort on a third-class ticket. He granted himself the favor of free food from the train staff.

While he was working his own oracles, I went off rather hopelessly to the train. Most of the carriages were dark, because no one was paid to keep the lamps going. In the darkness I bumped against a train boy, and when he found I could speak Chinese he pulled me at once into a carriage. Then he pushed me into a two-berth compartment and locked the door. The outside of the door was covered with "reserved," "strictly reserved," "reserved by order," and "officially reserved" notices. The train attendant had made them himself. He had probably been in more than one civil war. He knew that there comes a tide in the affairs of China which, taken at the flood, needs no railway tickets. What counts is "face" and personal negotiation. He had sequestered that compartment in good time, as a private investment, knowing that the train would be run more by the soldiers on it than by the railway staff.

Seeing that a civil war was imminent, and that its effects might reach for an undeterminable distance into the interior, it was important for me to get away as soon as possible.  According to our plans, I was to make the journey through Mongolia, the most difficult and certainly the most hazardous part of the whole venture, alone.  When I had reached Urumchi I could send back a message by the wireless station there (one of the two established in the province for the Chinese Government), my wife would come by the rail-and-motor route through Siberia to join me, and we should make our Turkestan travels together.

My wife had come as far as Kuei-hua to see me off.  The return journey to Peking for her already looked very difficult.  The train service was likely to be suspended for several days at a time, on account of troop movements.  Yet we fretted for days in Kuei-hua over unreasonable delays.  My camels had been hired in advance, under good guarantee.  Their owner asked at first for a few days' grace, and, having then no reason to distrust him, I agreed.  He continued, however, with further evasions, and our position became much more difficult, but at last we made him come to terms and the day was fixed.  I should start in the morning and my wife would take the train to Peking on the same afternoon.

The start had to be made in secret.  The police had strict orders to prevent my going, nominally because the bandit country through which I should have to pass was more unsafe than ever.  The real reason was more probably that the "Christian Army" which held the province was receiving munitions of war from Soviet Russia, by motor transport through Mongolia.  Its commander, Feng Yü-hsiang, still rested a great deal of his public attitude on his Christian pretensions, and well knew the value of the advertising he received from the foreign missions.  It would therefore be inconvenient for him to have too much explicit news of his commitments to his Russian backers reaching the foreign press on the coast.

We arranged, therefore, that Moses was to take the camels by the great pass that leads for a long day's march through the hills to the open country.  When I had given them a start, I should stroll out of town, past the police and the military pickets, to a quiet spot by the Mohammedan cemetery, and there vanish into a hooded cart. In this way I should go discreetly through the pass, where if necessary I should represent to the pickets that I was going on local trading business, and had already been passed without question by the town pickets. In the open country I should join my little caravan, and a few forced marches would put me for a while beyond the reach of passport inspectors.

The camels came at dawn to the little house where we were staying. In a gray light and a thin drizzle of rain they were swiftly loaded. One by one they lurched to their feet and sidled out of the gate, led by a grinning pigtailed fellow whom the camel owner had deputed to be my caravan man. Moses, who during his stay in Kuei-hua had learned seven words of Mongol (all wrong) with which he was prepared to face anything, picked up a blue enameled teapot and set off after them. There was an expression in the set of his shoulders that seemed to say, " Well, well, well! So this is a caravan!" To me, left standing in the bareness of the mud-walled compound, caravan travel seemed not so simple. I had a sudden feeling as if I had lost my stomach; that it was going to be horrible saying good-bye to my wife, and that the police, sensible fellows, had really given me a lot of sound advice.

In a little while I set out, with a conscience that, in spite of all the resolution I tried to pretend, felt guilty; but, though I jumped like a detected spy every time a policeman turned to stare at the foreigner abroad so early, I left the town without being questioned at all, and passed the tasseled standard at the quarters of the cavalry picket. As I reached the cemetery and crawled into the cart I reflected, without much comfort, that after all a great many long journeys begin at the cemetery.

There are two Mohammedan burial grounds in Kuei-hua. In one are laid the good Moslems, in the other the backsliders whose repute has been soiled with wine and tobacco and evil dealing. I set out from the resting place of the virtuous, but it was no good omen for all that. We had not gone two miles when the carter stopped, put his head into my little kennel, and said, with the peculiar grin of a man who sees someone else's trouble coming, that my camels were on their way back.

Moses was riding the tallest of them.  He was seated on a load of bedding and informed me, out of a stiff neck, — for, being new to camel riding, he did not feel easy about looking over the edge, — that he had been stopped at the mouth of the pass.  A telephone order had just reached the post there that all camels were to be seized for military use.

Evidently the trouble was going to be serious.  Early as it was, a couple of hundred camels were in sight, being brought back from the hills under escort.  Back in the cart, turning again toward the city, I was worried and depressed.  If the New China was at a pass where it had to risk damaging the caravan trade on which a great part of the prosperity of the province depended, it would probably take a suave delight in chivvying a foreigner.

And it was so.  Moses went with the camels to the *ya-men*, where I could not very well follow them, seeing the unofficial manner of my start.  There he talked with all the command of wile and bluff that fits him to be the Prophet of All Tramps, making out that the camels were only going on a short trading venture, and so on; but to no purpose. .  The camels, not being the property of a foreigner, but hired from a Chinese, must go to the war.  They went the next morning.

The same day we were told that the railway line to Peking was definitely cut.  Even the fitful service that had been maintained till then was no longer possible.  The Christian Army had been holding not only the whole length of the railway, but Peking itself.  Now they had abandoned Peking and taken up a position in the pass of Nan K'ou, through which the railway runs, and fighting had started.  The money I had paid for camel hire had gone, the camels had gone; I could not make a start for Mongolia, nor could my wife and I get back to Peking.

## II

## THE EDGE OF THE BORDER

WE were then at the end of March 1926. Thus, about thirteen months after the first inspiration of my journey, I was arrived again in Kuei-hua, but this time with my wife. What we had at first hoped was a temporary check, when my camels were taken and the railway cut, proved a kind of internment which lasted more than five months. Though we were able to travel a little in the Mongol border country to the north, we spent most of the time in the city, one of the capitals of the caravan trade, which came to be for us a human and accustomed place, and our home.

Kuei-hua stands in a wide valley or enclosure, having on the north the range of the Ta Ch'ing Shan [1] which here forms the southern ramp of the Mongolian plateau, and on the south the outer ranges of Shan-hsi Province. Open and well-watered, this enclosure must always have been a natural grain-growing and supply area for the nomads of the plateau. Of the beginnings of its history, before chronicles were regularly compiled, we can know little until an adequate archæological survey has been made of the natural frontiers here marking the cleavage between nomad tribes and settled peasantry. One thing at least must be taken as a premise; there were many shifting and struggling powers in Mongolia before Jenghis Khan rose up to lift raiding and harrying into the art of war and conquest. The Mongols of our own day are the proof, showing traces of more than one blood and ancestry.

By the thirteenth century we have something more definite. In the accounts of Marco Polo and the letters of John of Monte Corvino, Archbishop of Cambulac or Peking, there is mention

---

[1] For some reason called the Yn-shan or In-shan by early travelers.

of a Nestorian kingdom of Tenduc, a vassal State of the Mongol
Empire then established in China.[1]  This kingdom and its ruling
house they associated with the legend of Prester John.  No
Chinese chronicle records a Nestorian ruling house in this territory, and at present there are no surviving Nestorian evidences;
but it may well come about, when the sites of the ancient cities
near Kuei-hua have been explored, that we shall have more
archæological knowledge of the Nestorians of the Far East than
we yet possess.  That there are several "dead cities" in this
region, which from its geographical position is fitted to be the
mother of early civilizations, is well enough known; but no work
has yet been done to fix the sites historically.  I myself saw, to
the north, the remains of a wall which I think runs with the supposed boundaries of Tenduc, but I will mention that in its own
place.

The conventional history of Kuei-hua begins with the foundation of the present city under the Emperor Wan Li, in about
A.D. 1573, on the site of an old military post.  When the Manchus
in their turn inherited the Empire, Kuei-hua appears to have
been not so much a Chinese military outpost as a Mongol trading
centre, known to the Mongols themselves, who continue in our
time to use the name, as Kuku-khoto, the Blue City.  It was a
temple city, one of those places where the Mongols gathered in
great numbers at seasonal pilgrimages.  Chinese traders have always found their way to such celebrations, however distant, establishing fairs which probably in old days of tribal wars were
protected by a kind of "truce of God."  The greatest fairs were
bound to be at places which, like Urga and Kuei-hua, lay on
natural avenues of trade, so that these fairs expanded inevitably
into settled trading communities.

Kuei-hua, at that time, besides being a great holy place visited
by distant tribes, was the tribal centre of the Tumet Mongols.
In the troubled time that preceded the Manchu conquests, the
Tumets, being threatened by a Mongol conqueror who was
attempting to restore the old unity and power of the Mongol

[1] Yule's *The Book of Ser Marco Polo*, revised by Cordier. London: John
Murray.

Empire, appealed to the distant Tsar of Russia for protection. Getting little good by this, they turned to the approaching Manchus, and were among the first of the Mongols to offer fealty to the Ta Ch'ing Empire. For this they got but a poor reward; the Manchus, aware of the value of the Kuei-hua position, wanted no strong tribe in possession of it. Once in power themselves, they made the old Tumet negotiations with Russia an excuse to deprive them of their hereditary chief, break up their tribal organization, and draft them into "banners" on the Manchu military system, making them directly liable to military service and discipline. In the result, they completely lost whatever independent power had once been theirs. That this was the deliberate Manchu policy is attested by the local Chinese tradition, which says that the Tumets were "hounded until they vanished" by the Manchus. They now survive in small numbers in the valleys and along the foot of the Ta Ch'ing Shan, while their richest lands have long since passed into the hold of Chinese settlers. They still retain, however, their tribal title to much of the land on which the city of Kuei-hua is built, from which their chieftains continue to draw a revenue.

The coming of the Manchus is remembered in a legend of K'ang Hsi, the second Emperor and first consolidator of the new Manchu dominions. K'ang Hsi was a great ruler who knew how to temper the harsh facts of a tryannical rule by the personal appeal of a striking character. When he came to Kuei-hua on one of his Imperial tours, he requested an interview of the head of the religious community, which was the core of the rich trading city. This was one of those Living Buddhas whom the Mongols popularly hold to be a mighty God on earth. At the meeting of the temporal and spiritual powers the Emperor went so far as to bow his head. Instead of making on his own part a diplomatic and graceful recognition, the Living Buddha stared as impassively before him as if he had been confronted by no more than an abject Mongol princeling. Angered by this, for the Manchus had adopted in full the Chinese conception of the divinity of the Emperor, some of K'ang Hsi's bodyguard made as if to force the Living Buddha to prostrate himself. The attendant lamas, horrified in their turn by such a violation of the sacred person, rushed to his defense. In the uproar K'ang Hsi is said to have snatched a robe from a lama, wrapped himself in it, and escaped. The chief of his bodyguard, named Pai, losing sight of the Emperor, believed him to have come to harm; therefore, stabbing the Living Buddha, he fell on his own sword, to atone for the disgrace of having come short of his duty.

In gratitude to his faithful captain the Emperor caused him to be deified, and an image of him was placed in a temple beyond the walls, where it still stands. It is said that the successors of the Living Buddha, held by the Mongols to be his reincarnation, have never dared return to Kuei-hua, but live afar in Mongolia. Were one to return, a baleful emanation from the image of Pai, now himself an immortal, would surely cause him to die.

There may be a confusion in the last part of this legend. A Living Buddha is still associated with Kuei-hua. He is of the rank of Khutukhtu,[1] and the second of the holy personages of Mongolia, of whom there used to be a third in Peking, as a kind of hostage. Indeed, I suppose he is the first now, since the Incarnation at Urga has completed its cycle and is not to be born again. This Living Buddha has a temple in Kuei-hua, but lives usually at another temple, beyond the hills on the plateau. It may be that he inherits from another Incarnation than that concerned in the legend; but it may be that he is the same, and that his temple so far from the city explains the belief of the uninstructed Chinese that he dare not return.

Three centuries ago the Manchus planted beside Kuei-hua the New City of Sui-yuan, garrisoning it with their own people, in the way they had, to watch and tax the caravan trade of the Chinese and the barter trade of the Mongols. From that time, under a firm and settled rule which controlled both China and the tribes, Kuei-hua prospered. Kalgan still held the most part of the trade with Urga, and through Urga with Siberia, and Kalgan sent out in untold camel loads the "overland tea" by which the Russians set such store. Kuei-hua, however, drew to

---

[1] There are several degrees of "divine incarnation," the Khutukhtus of Urga and Kuei-hua having the great Tibetan divinities of Lhasa and Tashilunpo above them and minor Mongolian manifestations below them.

itself all the trade that came down the Yellow River, and led in the vast trade with Western Mongolia and the outlying province of Hsin-chiang; for trade came and went more cheaply with the camel caravans than along the congested roads through China proper, and travel for merchants and officials was faster if not as comfortable. The proudest firms of Kuei-hua date their foundations from the early Manchu reigns — firms whose partners used to lord it among the Mongols, in the old days, as if they held the whole land in fee, and whose account books were the keys to the "state secrets" of more than one princely family. The spring of the city's prosperity lay in its command of the Yellow River route as well as the several caravan routes; of magnificent pastures for camels, and rich farming lands to supply cheap provisions for the men of the caravan trade.

The railway, coming in latter years to Kuei-hua and then going ninety miles west to Pao-t'ou on the banks of the Yellow River, fed its prosperity. Until that time, though there had been enough trade to make a city rich, yet it was in the main a local and inland trade. With a railway to empty its markets as fast as the caravans filled them, Kuei-hua felt in full force the demands of foreign countries beyond the seas. In return for the exports, foreign goods were sent up from the coast, and the men of Kuei-hua carried them on, even until they overpassed the sources of the rivers that fall towards the Pacific.

The final turn of the wheel came when all China began to disintegrate under the influences of civilizations not only assertive and assured, but different in character from its own isolated and static polity. A new generation began to use the new instruments of power to further personal ambitions, and China entered on the cycle of civil wars. The Northwest Province was occupied by Feng Yü-hsiang, with his mercenary army of highly disciplined "Christian soldiers." The "Christian General" was not bound to the interests of his new province in any way. He had risen to a dubious kind of power by political betrayals and treachery in war. To get rid of him, a junta of other military leaders had manœuvred him into this province, which they thought so remote that his influence would be eliminated. With the vivid understanding of practice and performance that had characterized his whole career, however, he made of his place of exile a political stronghold. His championship of Christianity had already muzzled a number of his critics, puzzled the rest, and given him, in the missionary societies, an excellent publicity bureau. As a more positive move he allied himself with the student classes, the prophets of the regeneration of China by theoretic exposition, a cause which needed a champion and a figurehead, and gave him the nucleus of a political party — for which mere Christianity, in China, would never do. Finally, unable to supply himself with arms from the seacoast, he turned the tables on his political rivals, who thought they had debarred him from stealing any more thunder, by coming to terms with the Russian Soviets. In this way his alliance with the Vocal Revolution was confirmed, and he was supplied with munitions overland, through Mongolia. Thus fortified, he sallied from his place of security behind the mountains, seized Peking, and for a while opened communication to the sea through Tientsin. These brilliant successes galvanized the loose opposition against him into a determined coalition; armies were marshaled, and he was compelled to evacuate Peking. The coalition advanced against the line he had taken up in the hills threatening Peking, determined to have done with him. Thus began the civil war which held us bound so long.

The war lasted from spring till autumn. When we came to Kuei-hua, the long stretches of bare brown earth showed that the winter was over, but neither in the fields nor on the trees were there yet to be seen the green tokens that show that spring has surely come. The air was damp from the thawing snows in the hills, and cold damp winds searched restlessly through the valleys and the uplands and ranged across the empty plain.

The spring came; in the daytime my wife and I walked about the streets and outskirts of Kuei-hua and Sui-yuan like prisoners at large, and in the night we heard the geese flying northward. The first trembling green of poplar and willow along the roads matured to the heavy foliage of the short, intense summer, alternately burdened with dust and shaken with pelting rain.

As wheat and oats grew up to cover the naked brown fields, the drab forlorn horizons of winter changed magically to shimmering distances of blue and purple, and the hills stood up to the forbidden north like ramparts of the gods, looking out over the sickly discontented cities of men —

> Nor sound of human sorrow mounts to mar
> Their sacred everlasting calm.

In early August the little market gardens that fringe the mile of road between Old City and New bloomed with the noble splendor of opium poppies, and it seemed that we might live forever bone-idle among the languorous white and luxuriant pink and purple colors, and the sweet heavy scents that permeated with Oriental indifference the sour stink of Oriental backyards.

There was a small foreign community in Kuei-hua, and everybody was very kind to us. To begin with, there was the Swedish Mission, where we stayed for a while, and where I left my wife when at last I made my start. Then there was the Catholic Mission, with its hospital and two Belgian doctors, laymen, with their families. The people who helped us most were two Swedish youngsters, the Söderbom brothers. Born "Beyond the Wall," they had grown up in the border country and had a unique knowledge of local ways and of the very different kind of Chinese one finds in the northwest. They, together with a young Scotchman, were in the employ of a British firm dealing in Mongol sheep. Thousands of their sheep had been seized by the "Christian Army," on the ground that the firm had "violated the treaties," and their affairs were in such a bad way that another Scotchman was sent up, and later an Irishman. Last of all a Dane, Haslund-Christensen, came up from Kalgan, which was on our side of the fighting line. He had spent about five years wandering in Mongolia, spoke the language perfectly, and knew the life of the people in the *yurt* and on the march and even in the temple. In the end it was he who helped my wife to get back to Peking.

We were, however, most of the time by ourselves. We managed to get away from the city to camp in the gorges of the hills and later beyond the hills, on the plateau — a life made exciting by bandit alarms. The two cities we learned to know by custom, until we were familiar with all manner of small inconspicuous beauties that the traveler never sees; but the marks of a changing order were everywhere. No cheery Manchu horsemen rode out from the garrison city with hawk on wrist and greyhound at heel to follow the sport of Imperial days now swept into the unregretting oblivion of the East. Even their bows, beautiful things of old and skillful workmanship, of bamboo and Buffalo horn, bound with bark and strung with silk, were sold ignominiously in shabby booths for a dollar or so, to Chinese who wanted them to shoot the three ceremonial arrows of the marriage rite, or Mongols who would make them into trophies and present them to gods in the chill shadows of dusty temples. All that remained of the Manchu dominion within the yellow-gray walls of the New City was the rich intonation of their speech — that canorous *kuan-hua* of Peking which puts a spell on those who know it and has an odd dignity in contrast with the flat whine of peasant and merchant, all of baser stock, in the villages and the Old City.

In the Old City the walls had been demolished, except at the North Gate, to make way for light, air, and the Advance of Progress. When we were first there, however, we saw a bustle and throng in street and market that had nothing to do with Modern Improvements or Christian Armies or the New China. Buyer and seller went by the old fashions that they understood. It was then that the spring caravans were going out. Owners of caravans were making their final settlements with brokers, and traders their last preparations for the road, while the men who lead the strings of camels on the long marches into the west were buying trinkets and odds and ends in order to do a little business for themselves when they came to the bazars of Ku Ch'eng-tze. They were in the right tradition. Except that the things they bought were gay cotton prints for the Turki, plush Tientsin shoes for Chinese men and women, startling pink hats with gauds and false pearls for Chinese girls and babies, and cigarettes for all comers, their trafficking was the unchanging practice of unnumbered and unchronicled generations.

So long as Kuei-hua stands where the caravans and freight

2. CITY GATE, SUI-YUAN
"Three centuries ago the Manchus planted beside Kuei-hua the New City
of Sui-yuan." (p. 22)

3. A MOSQUE IN KUEI-HUA
" . . . mosques of the Chinese Mohammedans, which have been accommodated almost exactly to Chinese temple architecture." (p. 268)

4. BALLAD SINGER, TEMPLE FAIR, KUEI-HUA

5. OWEN LATTIMORE, KUEI-HUA, 1926

trains exchange their cargoes, the old life will retain its vigor. In our time, though every outward freight the caravans carry goes to work changes in Mongolia and Chinese Turkestan, they carry them in the old timeless way, as if no white men had ever come to Asia. Yet their doom is on them. When, in a time deferred but inevitable, — for time in China goes by the half-century, — those who have learned from the foreigner shall have carried the railway through to Ning-hsia and Lan Chou, the business of the caravans will decline into an affair of peddlers among the sand dunes of Alashan and the pastures of the Great Grasslands. It was a strange thing to walk in those markets, feeling the pulses of the life led through inenarrable yesterdays by the farthest-going caravans, and knowing the shadow of to-morrow would distort all their type and character. When the camel man has done up his little bundle, he shambles away out of the city as if he were expecting to stroll home within half an hour; but he plods on until he finds the camp where the caravan waits behind the hills with its camels at pasture, until its complement of loads be filled; when camp is broken, he plods away again until he fetches up in Central Asia; for the men of his calling, by leaving their houses and pitching tents, depart with no more ado from the civilization of telegraphs and newspapers, bayonets and martial law, into a secret and distant land of which they only know the doors.

This was the Kuei-hua we knew for a short time only. When the camels were led off to serve the armies, and the railway closed, it withered all the dealings of the caravans. We had no news from "inside" — that is, from inside the Great Wall, from a Peking which seemed as remote as Khanbaligh,— for the telegraph was cut off and the mails did not come through except in scraps, by roundabout ways, months overdue. The markets were empty but for a few country folk, and not a camel came near the city. Only the merchants cowered in fresh panics every time a fresh loan was forced out of them. Only the wounded kept coming in from the southeast. Only the new soldiers, peasant youngsters conscripted from the countryside, learned to count the conscript marching step — the tempo of Kuei-hua in those days — *one, two, three, four! One! Two! Three!*—and to sing the conscript hymns.

I tried my best to get fresh transport.  In hiring camels for the Mongolian journeys, difficulties have often to be met after the contract has been made.  Because they must be settled somehow, a broker is absolutely necessary.  Very often there is no written contract, but always there is a broker.  His chief responsibility is this same adjustment of disputes which may come up after he has written or spoken the contract between the parties.  As an arbitrator having business relations with both sides which he is anxious not to impair, he will do his best to make them agree reasonably.  The principals themselves would rather come to an arrangement through him than go to law.  The judge in court would be more likely to weigh the purses of complainant and defendant than the equity of their pleas.  A Chinese law court is a nightmare theatre in which the men of law are the actors and the men who go to law are the audience.  The way of the comedy is that the audience are the entertainers, and the actors, though they pronounce the words the audience have paid to hear, are the entertained.  Moreover, at the end of the performance the audience, whether pleased or not, pay as they go out, in addition to having paid to get in.

I had made a written contract, signed by the broker as guarantor and middleman.  For this he had received from the camel owner a commission of twenty tael cents on each camel hired.  So far as I have ever heard, both brokers and owners, though full of guile when in negotiation, are as strictly fair as they can be when once the bargain has been struck.  The essence of the bargain, for the caravan owner, is that he shall bring the cargo safely to its destination, in spite of any loss to himself.  He may frequently exceed the time limit agreed on for the journey, without being pressed for an indemnity; but safe delivery is the highest of the unwritten laws of the trade.

This was not my own luck.  The caravan owner had been paid by me in advance, according to the usual custom.  With the money he had bought several new camels, which he had hired to me.  This is also a very usual practice.  When his camels were taken, however, he pleaded *force majeure*. I had dealt with him in the first place because he was not a Kuei-hua man, but came from Barköl, far away in the west, so that, being homeward bound, I had thought he would be the keener to make good time on the road. Now, with his camels taken, he had no other property which he could sell or mortgage to return me my money. He owned about seventy other camels, but these had been sent off some weeks before the trouble. He said that all the money he had received for the loads in his main caravan he had invested either in camels or in goods. Nor — and this I could well believe — was it possible for him to raise the money on credit when he had no security at hand, in such uneasy times.

Thus it fell to the broker to square my account, with either cash or camels. He in turn said that he could not get other camels, as the requisition order, which had taken several thousand, had so scared caravan owners that whatever camels were left had been driven to safe hiding at a great distance and would not be brought within reach of the city. The majority of the spring caravans had left, so that there were few fit camels that had not been commandeered. Incoming caravans halted behind the hills and sent in their freight by cart; but their camels, having traveled through the winter, would be in no condition to start again at once. As for money, he said flatly that he had not any.

I did hear later that a few small parties of Chinese travelers had been more honorably dealt by. Owners and brokers together had found a fit camel here and a fit camel there, collected them behind the hills, sent out the passengers by cart, and so got them away, even at a financial loss to themselves. My broker would do no such thing. He knew that I could hardly take public action, because an appeal to the authorities would only make them save themselves trouble by renewing the ban on my going at all. There seemed nothing to do but to wait. All the owners whose camels had been taken got news now and again. The camels had gone down to Kalgan with supplies. Then, instead of being released, they were held idle behind the lines, and ate themselves into fatness on the standing crops. The broker, like everyone else, hoped vainly for their return.

At the beginning of August I heard that caravans were gathering at Pai-ling Miao, on the edge of the grasslands, and there taking up cargo brought out to them by carts, and starting for the west. Most of this freight had been booked in the early spring, but had not been dispatched either because the camels had been commandeered or because they were not fit and had to be put out to grass during the season when they shed their hair. No new contracts were being made. All the freight that had started in January and February had come up by rail the year before. For many months not a single goods train had entered Kuei-hua, but all the time caravans were coming in from the west. When their camels had been pastured through the summer and the owners were looking for outward freights, prices came tumbling down. Owners were willing to take freight at almost any price, for they were beginning to be anxious about the war, which seemed to be turning more quickly against the Christian Army, and they thought it best to get their camels out of the way of a possible retreat. When I came to Kuei-hua, the regular price for freight was forty-four taels (more than five pounds) a load, and sometimes more; by the time I left, eighteen taels was a good price.

If I myself did not get away soon, all our plans would be ruined. The Christian Army would come by in retreat, sweeping every kind of transport with them, and the hills and the "back country" would be filled with stragglers and deserters quite as dangerous as bandits. Renewed pressure on the broker at last brought an unsatisfactory kind of result. I was to advance the camel owner another hundred dollars, the broker (he said) would advance him some more, and he would buy fresh camels and get me away. A new contract was drawn up, giving me a lien on the camels to secure the return of my money.

As before, I was to go out by cart. All my dunnage was to be loaded on four ancient camels, unattractive to the military, which were mysteriously brought forward. They would take me out more than a hundred miles, to the place where the camels that were to take me on the further journey would be in waiting. It was touch and go. The Christian Army was already breaking;

small bands of deserters left the city every day with arms in their hands. In another day or two, troops would be coming back by trainloads from the front, and the tide of defeat would smother us.

This time, after still more agonizing delays and attempted last-minute evasions, I started late on a sultry afternoon, the twentieth of August, 1926. The police, nervous themselves and afraid day and night of mutiny in the conscript barracks, had quite forgotten me. My wife walked out a little way with me, and somehow, when we had said good-bye and I had turned to look back at her standing on a bank under an elm by the sunken earth road, I had less courage than ever. We were to meet again months later — not till next year, had we known it — somewhere in the middle of Asia. In the meantime I was leaving her in an interior city, far away from consuls and gunboats, which in a few days would be full of defeated soldiery and would almost certainly be looted. She would be in less danger, staying in the Mission, than in the bandit country through which I had yet to pass, grown more lawless than ever through months of immunity from military interference; but still, it all began to seem a little bit mad.

A while later, on the edge of night, rain began to fall. I climbed disconsolately into the cart; but, though we had got off in scrambling fashion, things went better this time from the very start. It is only four or five miles from Kuei-hua to the mouth of the pass through the northern hills. We had to get by a local tax station, where questions might have been asked; but either the men did not like to venture out after dark in those nervous days, or they kept indoors from the Chinese dislike of rain. We went on a little way into the hills, and stopped for the night.

All along this lower valley of the pass there are inns with spacious yards in which whole caravans can lie as if in camp. When the times are good, the caravans come all the way in to Kuei-hua; but although the city walls have been demolished there is still a pleasant police rule that "the gates are closed at night." Therefore the caravans halt in the valley on the last night of their journey and enter the city the next morning at sunrise.

We stopped at one of the smallest inns; a cart inn, not a caravan inn. My cart was backed under a huge old crab-apple tree, and around it the camels knelt, seen dimly in the scattered moonlight that came tumbling through the leaves. The clouds had cleared away, the night was cool and fresh and smelled of damp earth (so different from the smell of mud) and of trees and the mountainside that pitched right down to the eaves of the low inn. The house itself was of clean new mud bricks; inside the new woodwork was picked out here and there with crude splashes of red paint, and against the walls were ranged big solid-looking red chests, the pride of every peasant family in these hills.

As for the people, they were subdued and anxious. The straggling village had been looted for food and money on the previous two days, and a third time in the afternoon, a few hours before I came, by small parties of deserters, who had then gone into the hills and might still not be far away. They had no money left but a few paper dollars which they feared, very correctly, would soon be quite worthless.

People came and went restlessly, and now and then a child would dodge out from the inner room, to stare for a moment at the foreigner. Two women were making food — little flat pieces of oatmeal dough rolled into cylinders and steamed in a sieve over boiling water. It is the unrelieved diet of these people all the year through. An old hag crouched in a corner smoking a long pipe, spitting publicly and muttering privately. The women of mountain villages always move more freely among their men than the women of the cities, even joining in the common talk.

I too felt restless, and went to stand in the door, looking into the courtyard. One felt all the time as though something dreadful were about to happen, but the unusualness was only in men's minds — though the villagers, poor souls, had had something real to scare them. In contrast with this nervous feeling the routine of their simple life seemed to bump against one with an almost palpable dullness, and the strain made me fretful. Standing in the doorway, I seemed to feel rather than see or hear the camels

munching their cud, the cart mules stamping, the little black pig-
lets grunting and squealing, and the silent-footed dogs dodging
from moonlight to shadow.   There were voices and reflections
of light from a neighboring courtyard, but nothing stirred along
the road.   Overhead the crab-apple tree rustled faintly now and
then.

    After a while I felt better.   I went back, ate a little Chinese
bread, and smoked and drank tea until the closer air of the room,
the smell of people and dung fuel and Chinese tobacco and new
wood and the matting and felts on the *k'ang* (the sleeping platform), made me a little drowsy.   Then I unrolled my sleeping
bag and lay down on top of it fully dressed.   As I was dozing,
neither awake nor asleep, — that state so delightful when one is
calm, and so like a threat of nightmare when one's nerves are
strung up, — I caught the drift of a whispered conversation.
The whisper of a Chinese peasant is produced in the throat and
sounds like a saw with some of the teeth missing.   I was being
set down as a Soviet officer in the service of the Christian Army,
making an early get-away to Urga.   It annoyed me, but it was
not worth denial, since denial would only strengthen conviction.
But how silly!   Did n't I have enough worries, what with leaving
my wife in a silly place like Kuei-hua and starting off for a silly
place like Mongolia, with a lot of silly camels, without being taken
for a spy or a soldier of fortune or something fantastic of a kind
that is found more often in the newspapers than on a journey?

    Still, that conversation was pregnant, for Moses also heard it,
and it gave Moses a Great Idea.

# III

## TO THE TEMPLE OF LARKS

HAVING safely entered the pass, we were on the high road between Kuei-hua and the grasslands, which runs north through the range of the Ta Ch'ing Shan. The opening of the valley toward Kuei-hua is Pa K'ou, or Mouth of the Pass. The road goes upward without any great incline for thirteen or fourteen miles; then there is a steep ascent, a drop on the other side into a valley turning westward, and a turn into another valley, leading more nearly to the north, by which there is a steady climb to K'o Chen, beyond the mountains. The whole distance from Kuei-hua is on the long side of thirty miles, and the crest in the middle is called the Wu Kung Pa. The word *pa* in Tientsin means to totter, to walk with difficulty, or like a woman with bound feet. In the dialect of the northwest it is used of walking uphill or through heavy sand, and as a substantive it means a mountain pass.

The Wu Kung Pa is the easiest way from Kuei-hua to the "back country," as the whole Mongolian plateau is locally called, but was formerly a very difficult passage for carts. A year or two ago, after several carts had been caught on the pass in heavy snow and a man frozen to death, a new road with an easier gradient was blasted out. This new road was probably intended to serve eventually for motor transport; it is negotiable by motor cars, and in time there will doubtless be a service to supplement the railway in fetching goods to market.

There are many other passes from the plain to the high open country, but they are through narrower valleys, too difficult to allow much traffic by cart or even camel transport. This puts a stop to smuggling on a large scale, but small valuable cargoes like opium can easily be taken into Kuei-hua free of duty by men on ponies, or with a few camels. Men who work with the caravans very commonly invest their money in the west in cheap opium, especially if they are coming back in the winter, because in hot weather opium is too easily detected by the smell. On the way back to Kuei-hua, one man will often be left behind, a few marches from the city, to bring on the lame and tired-out camels by easy stages. Battered packsaddles are left on some of the animals, and in the straw-stuffed pads of these a lot of opium can easily be concealed. The man with the camels brings them down by one of the unfrequented passes, and when he reaches the plain turns aside, to enter Kuei-hua as though he had not come from the great caravan road but from some village not far away, thus making an entrance fee of suspicion.

We had still the pass to climb and one of the main barriers to face in our "escape" from Kuei-hua. On the far side of the Wu Kung Pa is a station maintained by the Kuei-hua authorities to keep a check on the cart and camel traffic, and collect a small additional tax on each load. All travelers and caravans going even on local journeys must have permits on which the number of men and animals, the nature of the loads, and the destination are stated. We were almost on top of the station when the men found that the broker, whose duty it was to provide all the necessary documents, had played us a dirty trick. He had said to Moses that all the papers were in the hands of the man with the camels, while he had told that man that he had given them to us. The truth was that he had not dared ask the police for any papers, for fear of exciting comment.

It was here that Moses acted on the Great Idea suggested to him by the men whispering in the inn the night before. I had gone to sleep in the cart, and he carried out the whole manœuvre himself, with great promptness and decision. Furnished with no papers, and faced with an inspection post where unusual travelers in such panicky times were almost sure to be closely questioned, he saw no alternative to *l'audace, et toujours de l'audace.* He spoke to the camel man, a fellow, like all his kind, with the instincts of a smuggler, and one who could take a hint without having it shouted at him. He took the camels farther ahead, until he had a lead of several hundred yards. When stopped for inspection, he said, like a man with a grievance, that he had been commandeered. He had no papers to show on what service he had been impressed. He and his camels had been hauled in a great hurry to such and such a *ya-men*, where he had taken up his loads. There was a man coming behind who probably knew what it was all about, but the man had a short way with him and did not like to answer questions. Without waiting for permission he moved on, and the men at the station, a little baffled, let him go.

The cart had loitered to let the camels get clear. When it drove up, the men questioned Moses with the politeness of caution. If any tax collector in interior China is polite, it is not only safe to be rude to him, but the best policy. Usually they are a bullying crew. Theirs is a nasty trade, and the kind of men who have a talent for it have a keen eye for the widow's mite and are great discerners of the orphan. If they turn polite, it means that they are uncertain of their ground and afraid to press matters. Moses therefore said in a stout way that he had no authority to speak. If they had any *kung-shih* — authority or official business — they had better ask the gentleman (*wei*, a respectful term) inside. He was asleep. Moses was not one to wake him for small matters. They must take the responsibility on themselves. At this one of the men diffidently peeked in at the side of the curtain over the front of my kennel. He saw a pair of foreign boots and the perspective of a pair of foreign legs. He let the curtain drop. Foreigners might be up to all kinds of funny business, and he knew that the Christian Army made a point of dealing strictly with all foreigners; but if this foreigner had his funny business done for him by a *ya-men*, which is the office of an official, there was probably no humor in it for meddlers. He knew that there were some extra queer foreigners in good standing with the Christian Army. While he was yet in a swither, Moses gave the carter a nudge which was as good as "Drive on, James." James drove.

All this I heard later, when I had got out of the cart to walk awhile. Moses smirked with innocent pride as he told me, while the camel man grinned sardonically, wagging his head. "See what can be done with hard words!" he said. There is nothing a camel man likes better than to score off one of the officials who pop out at awkward corners of the road, where there is no dodging, to ask him questions that must be answered with money.

It was then high noon, and in the early afternoon we fell in with several cumbrous oxcarts, heaving slowly up that stubborn pass, where the road is small shingle and soft sand in the dry bed of a stream. There seemed to be several families of country people on the move, traveling with that odd indifference to political upheaval and military disaster to be seen every once in a while in China. Though everyone along the road was nervous and scared, they straggled on in profound calm. Who would take their oxcarts from them for running away nimbly? Who would even kill an ox of theirs for food, when an ox cannot be taken on the saddle and there are sheep to be had?

They were probably coming from the Kuei-hua plain, to take up bigger fields of cheaper land on the plateau. Everything that could be tied with string or lashed with rope was on the outside of the carts. Everything else banged and jolted inside. The women rode, because the women of Shan-hsi, who must stand on their feet and be about all day, working, cling stubbornly to the old custom of binding their feet very small. They can hobble about the house and farm, but they cannot set out to walk for a day. The men walked. The children pulled each other along by the hair, or sat down in the dust to howl. They were tired and savage. As for the babies, the only way to keep them from being bumped to death was to attach them to the mothers' breasts, where they clung like leeches, rolling complacent eyes at the hot hillsides.

Before long the carts halted. The oxen rested in the shafts, or lay down in their traces. The men, rigging up a few mats and felts for shade, lay down in the road to smoke opium. The women waited and the children quarreled or slept. We too soon stopped, at a clean little new inn, — the only clean inn is a new one, — while the camels were turned loose to graze off the few tufts of harsh grass on the sweltering hillsides. We were trying to cut a day off the journey to Pai-ling Miao, which meant that we did not march a day and rest a night, but marched and rested and started again without taking account of day or night. The inn was kept, had I only known it, by the brother of a bandit I was to meet far away on the other edge of Mongolia; and halting at it to drink tea and smoke opium were two men I was to know well along the road. We did not start until that hour when in high mountain country there is still an afternoon light in the sky, but in the valley it is almost evening and little breezes begin to stir as the hillsides cool. As we went on through sunset and dusk and moonlight the hills became more rounded, the valley began to open out toward the rolling country of the plateau, and when we halted we were within a mile of K'o Chen.

This inn was not new. I realized that when I lay down on the *k'ang* to sleep. The bugs were old hands. Bugs are supposed to be wary of light, but though we kept a wick smoking and smelling all night in a little earthenware bowl filled with oil, they flensed us like stranded whales.

In the morning we started before sunrise. This was one of the most disturbed parts of the country, where deserting soldiers had ravaged in numbers, robbing and killing. We left the smoke of K'o Chen's mud chimneys mounting thinly in the pale light, well to one side. The town was by origin a trading post, as is shown in the Mongol name of it, Kuku-irghen or Blue Cloth, which name is still as current in use as the Chinese. Since the lands about it have been taken from the Mongols and opened to Chinese farmers, it has grown to be a *hsien* or district city, the seat of a magistrate, with the official name of Wu Ch'üan Hsien. This entitles it to a city wall and opens the problem on which all new *hsien* cities must debate. The Chinese like the feeling of being inside a wall, and they like the dignity of gates; but a wall, though a handy thing as between burgher and bandit, is of little use in a war. Also it costs a great deal of money. In K'o Chen they knew what to do. They built a main gate, looking to the south for grandeur and the sake of old custom and because that is whence the higher officials come, and the wall they took as read.

K'o Chen (the least correct name of the place and naturally the most used of all; *K'o* is the first character of the long Chinese transliteration of Kuku-irghen, and a *chen* is a town of inferior rank to a district city), guarding the upper entrance of the pass, is connected with Kuei-hua by a single telephone wire. None of us wanted to have anything to do with a telephone just then. For one thing, boots may do very well now and again as a pass ticket through a mountain valley; but if asked questions over a telephone who would like to try to answer by presenting his boots to the mouthpiece? K'o Chen we were eager to pass. It was the last place, until we should reach Turkestan, with a regular kind of administration, where formalities would have to be treated formally, should we be caught, and where our affairs could be easily referred to higher authorities. Beyond, though there would be people to be met who would claim official standing, what they said and what we said and what they did and what we did would depend on simple things like force and numbers. Sometimes they won and sometimes we did, as will be seen.

Luckily, all the official people of K'o Chen were lying close. It was not a nice time for them to go abroad. We had only not to walk within their reach. By the little stream which waters that country we found an inward-bound train of carts in camp. They were bringing down the cargo of several caravans, but were afraid to go on and had sent men ahead to scout. The men warned us of the points on our way where bandits or deserters had most recently been seen, and we went on. We were now well out in the open country, and the sun rose and shone with a hard clear light on strips of ploughed land and swards of sunburnt meadow; but the land had an empty look, because the people do not live scattered on their farms but, as in China, in villages. The camels sidled this way and that to get a bite at the crops, and the mules settled down to drag the cart along the deep ruts in the red earth. We could see blue and red and purple hills far away. The camel man shuffled almost briskly, and the carter cracked his whip like a man whose heart is in his job. "Now," they said to each other, "if we get to Larkland without meeting any Bad Men, then our luck is indeed not wrong."

We had still to travel something less than one hundred miles, to Pai-ling Miao on the edge of the chief camel pastures. The land nearer Kuei-hua is being steadily expropriated from the Mongols and allotted to Chinese colonists, so that it now retains almost nothing of its Mongolian character except the vigor of its air and the immense sweep of its distances. The Great Plain of North China is so uniform that it seems to have no edges, and the sense of distance is blunted. Coming from these flat leagues to the Mongolian uplands, one remembers with a shock the beauty of great distances; for the feeling of depth in a landscape that is added by mountain ranges brings home the realization of what distance is. Looking over the rounded country where the scant crops of a dry summer wavered in the morning wind, I was childishly thrilled to think that in a few days I should be traveling with a caravan into that great plateau of depth and color, with mountains in sight; mountains on whose far side lay strange country, where I might travel but the one time in my life, living for a few score days the life of men in other ages.

We lay up again over the noon hours, in a village of mud, and when the day cooled we took the road again, keeping on until after the moon set, when we stopped by Chao Ho, the Temple River. This is the open country that is full of bandits. It is easy to raid, and, while the ground is irregular enough to give cover, it is ideal for fast travel with ponies. There are villages where food can always be had, and in some of them there are informers who will bring news of likely caravans. If cavalry come out after the bandits, they can get away into the Ta Ch'ing Shan, where the pursuit, in fear of ambush, is at a hopeless disadvantage. Indeed, many of the bandits are villagers of the mountains. When dispersed, they are shabby crofters, scratching up a living out of a few stony fields, and herding a few sheep. Between raids, they hide their arms in roofs, or hollows in mud wall or k'ang.

To guard the caravans against these bandits the Kuei-hua Chamber of Commerce in 1917 raised a body of men called the Pao Shang T'uan, or Mercantile Guard. They sought out a rich Mongol to be the responsible head of it, and appointed another

Mongol, a sometime bandit, to be second in command and active leader. He has proved a successful captain and a determined fighter. The troopers themselves are a hard-bitten lot, some of them Chinese, most of them Mongols. Many have been bandits in their time, and almost all are men who would be bandits were they not paid to be bandit fighters. They are paid only a few dollars a month and have to bring their own ponies. Some of them make a little extra money by smuggling opium into Kuei-hua for their friends of the caravan — a safe game, since no tax collector would dare stop a man in uniform. Others, after serving for a few months, ride away to join the drifting scallywags and knights of opportunity who haunt the Border.

For the maintenance of the corps, the Chamber of Commerce collects from its members a small tax on every load of merchandise and a larger tax on every traveler they escort. One or two troopers accompany the caravans when no special danger is to be feared, but larger detachments go out if the bandits are active. The corps, of about four hundred men in all, has barracks at Kuei-hua, a mud fort at Chao Ho, where live also the chief and his second in command, and a smaller fort at Pai-ling Miao. Since this corps was raised, the caravans have hardly been troubled on the escorted stages. A similar force guards the caravans going and coming from Pao-t'ou.

When the caravans have entered the grasslands, the danger is much less. Large bands of robbers cannot find food enough for more than a few days beyond the farming country, while small parties would be roughly handled by the Mongols. When I passed by, however, the Mercantile Guard would provide no escorts. The greater danger was from bands of deserting soldiers, sometimes several hundred strong, most of whom were in search of a road of escape to Kan-su. They were too much for a patrol to handle and they were, in a way, brothers in arms with whom the Guard were in sympathy. Besides this, both of the Mongol chiefs of the force were much concerned for the safety of the temple, or rather monastery, from which Chao Ho takes its name, and were willing to abandon the countryside to the scattering soldiery if they could hold their own men together to keep the temple from harm.  This is the temple where lives the Khutukhtu or Living Buddha, the head of what was once the religious community of Kuei-hua.  The temple has been newly built on old foundations, and, as the Living Buddha prefers it to his city temple, it holds — at least in the popular belief — incredible treasures besides the sacred person.

What is nominally the main road goes past the fort and the temple, and at this point, before the Chinese had advanced so far into the hinterland, the road to Urga used to branch off.  In point of fact, however, there is no main road, but a general line of march, and carts can take any one of a number of roads leading in the same direction, which have been worn by carts taking grain from the villages either to Kuei-hua or towards the grasslands.  We stopped at a trader's hut several miles up the river from the fort, and early in the morning were on our way again.  It was all a matter of luck whether we were more likely to meet "bad men" on the main road or one of the village roads.  This time we did not halt at noon, but kept on through a belt of Mongol country where a few *yurts* were to be seen, until in the late afternoon we reached Ts'a-ts'a, the most outlying Chinese settlement.  It is in a small belt of cultivated land which has, as it were, overleaped the general front of the Chinese pioneers, being established like an island in Mongol country.  This way of encroaching on the pasture lands by groups and colonies makes it easier, after a few years, to take over the land behind the advanced villages, the Mongols preferring to move away rather than be isolated.

The different cart roads begin to converge near Ts'a-ts'a, which is about forty miles from Pai-ling Miao.  The hamlet is on the southern side of a strange boundary, the low ruins of a ditch and wall, covered with earth and grown with grass, running roughly east and west to an unknown distance.  This must be the same wall as that reported by Prjevalsky (apparently at a point farther to the east) in his journey of 1871.  All the Chinese whom I asked were sure that it was either a natural formation or an abandoned irrigation work.  All of them scoffed at my idea that it might be an old fortification.  The analogy with the Great Wall did not seem to them to have any force. Nevertheless, from the way it takes the contours of the country, it could not have been an irrigation work. It can only have been related to some ancient kingdom in the Kuei-hua plain (because it could not have been of use for protecting the open country to the north) which constructed it either to expand its territory or, more likely, to prevent nomad tribes from getting into the Ta Ch'ing Shan and from its gorges raiding the settled part of the Yellow River valley.

I believe it was the northern boundary or outwork of Marco Polo's "province of Tenduc." One of the problems dealt with by Yule and after him by Cordier [1] was that of squaring the region of Kuei-hua with the vassal Nestorian kingdom of Tenduc. Both Polo and John of Monte Corvino (who was in Peking at the very end of the thirteenth century), writing apparently of the same Nestorian kingdom, connect it with the legendary Prester John. Yule wrote a preface, with a commentary, for the English edition of Prjevalsky's book,[2] but neither he nor Cordier adverts to this ancient wall, as nice a piece of concrete archæological evidence as could be found. Cordier quotes the Archimandrite Palladius to show that Marco Polo and John of Monte Corvino may have attributed to the princes of Tenduc a descent from Prester John, through a confusion of names. One of the Central Asian prototypes of Prester John was called Aung Khan. A partly Chinese form of this name would be Wang Khan; and Wang Khan might easily lead to confusion with Wang Ku, which would be the natural Chinese form of Ongot. The Ongot were apparently a Tungusic tribe of Manchurian origin. "A Wang Ku family made its appearance as the ruling family of these tribes " — that is to say, north of Kuei-hua. "The Yn-shan Wang Ku guarded the northern borders of China belonging to the Kin, and watched their herds. When the Kin, as a protection against the inroads of the tribes of the desert, erected a rampart or new wall from the boundary of the Tangut Kingdom down to Manchuria, they entrusted the de-

[1] *The Book of Ser Marco Polo.*
[2] *Mongolia, the Tangut Country and the Solitudes of Northern Thibet*, translated by E. Delmar Morgan. London, 1876.

6. A CAIRN IN CENTIPEDE PASS (WU KUNG PA)
"They set up an *obo* or cairn in a high evident place and say, 'From here to the next *obo* . . . is the boundary between us and you.' " (p. 73).

7. MONGOL YURTS AT TEMPLE RIVER (CHAO HO)
"This is the open country that is full of bandits." (p. 40)

8. MERCANTILE GUARD, KUEI-HUA CHAMBER OF COMMERCE
"Almost all are men who would be bandits were they not paid to be
bandit fighters." (p. 41)

9. THE MAGISTRATE OF CHAO HO (TEMPLE RIVER)

10. WIFE OF THE MAGISTRATE (FA-KUAN) OF CHAO HO

11. CHAO HO: MONK MUSICIANS, DEVIL DANCERS
"The temple . . . holds—at least in the popular belief—incredible
treasures besides the sacred person." (p. 42)

12. CHAO HO: LIVING BUDDHA ON PALANQUIN
"This is the temple where lives the Khutukhtu or Living Buddha, the
head of what was once the religious community of Kuei-hua." (p. 42)

13. CHINESE PEOPLE AT A TEMPLE FAIR, CHAO HO

fense of the principal places of the Yn-shan portion to the Wang Ku."

This sounds to me like the wall I saw.  The Kin or Chin were a Tatar or Tungus dynasty ruling Northern China in the twelfth century.  The wall " from the boundary of the Tangut Kingdom " must have started from the Yellow River somewhere in its upper course, as the Tangut capital was at the modern Ning-hsia in Kan-su.  The Yn-shan are more correctly the Ta Ch'ing Shan. Now the Wang Ku became Nestorian Christians, and their kingdom is that which probably became the "province of Tenduc." What is more, it may be suggested that by the fusion of tribes at that meeting point of races the Wang Ku eventually became the Tumet Mongols.

It remains only to quote, on the subject of this vanished vassal kingdom of Nestorians, what Yule justly called " a curious but tantalizing communication " received by him from the mysterious Ney Elias, most of whose writings are not in print, though there are enough of them available to show that he must have been a fascinating traveler.

An old man called on me at Kuei-hua Ch'eng (Tenduc) who said he was neither Chinaman, Mongol, nor Mohammedan, and lived on ground a short distance to the north of the city, especially allotted to his ancestors by the Emperor, and where there now exist several families of the same origin.  He then mentioned the connection of his family with that of the Emperor, but in what way I am not clear, and said that he ought to be, or had been, a prince.  Other people coming in, he was interrupted and went away. . . . He was not with me more than ten minutes, and the incident is a specimen of the difficulty in obtaining interesting information, except by mere chance. . . . The idea that struck me was, that he was perhaps a descendant of King George of Tenduc: for I had your *Marco Polo* before me, and had been inquiring as much as I dared about subjects it suggested. . . . At Kuei-hua Ch'eng I was very closely spied, and my servant was frequently told to warn me against asking too many questions.

Some of the descendants of the ruling family of the Wang Ku became sons-in-law of the Mongol Khans, and it may be that Ney Elias's old man traced his lineage to the Wang Ku and claimed kin with the Emperor.  But this conversation was recorded when the Manchus ruled in China, who had no connection with the Mongol Empire hundreds of years before them. It is my opinion that the old man, if he were not a Manchu, was a Tumet with a family tradition of being descended from some other tribe. Whether Manchu or Mongol, his family might at some time have given a daughter to an Imperial household, thus acquiring the " Imperial " connection.

All these are matters which are never likely to be determined, unless by a good archæologist with a good spade. My chief reason for quoting Ney Elias is his last remark. That goes straight to my heart.

When we had passed the old wall, we had no more cultivated land before us. When we had gone about twenty miles the man in charge of the four camels carrying my baggage threatened to give trouble. He was far gone in opium, and only that morning had delayed our start because, paying more attention to his pipe during the night than to the grazing camels, he had lost them. Now he said suddenly but very mulishly that he would go no farther. He had finished his opium. He was exhausted and in misery. We must camp in the open. Had we done so, as we heard later, we should have been run on to by a party of deserters. Fortunately our man found two derelict camel herders by a marshy spring; all that they had for a camp was a tiny fire, and opium. He begged them for opium, but they would give him none; then a very heavy and cold shower broke over us and there was no more question of a halt. Wet weather has always a bad effect on opium smokers, and to be in wet clothes and thoroughly chilled must be torture. Our man, who had been ready to collapse, now insisted on going ahead. Pai-ling Miao was the nearest place where he could get opium, and he must smoke or die. Roweled by his desire, he kept on, finishing a forty-mile march. This brought us to Pai-ling Miao, one hundred and ten or one hundred and twenty miles from Kuei-hua, in four days and a bit, by day and by moonlight, dodging the whole way. That was noble going for the four broken-down and cruelly overloaded camels. When they knelt and the loads were eased off them, they could hardly get up. One more march would have been beyond them.

Their owner did not care.  He made straight for a fire, and warmth and opium.

The name Pai-ling Miao means Temple of the Larks.  This is what the Chinese call it, but the Mongol name I never heard.  It is one of the great lamaseries of which there are even more in Inner Mongolia than in Outer Mongolia.  It houses about fifteen hundred lamas; but when I was there the summer devil-dancing was not long over, and the majority of the lamas had either "gone on leave" to their homes or simply wandered off to beg and be lazy, since the begging of a lama is more in the way of command.  I did not go into the monastery, as Moses, returning from a private tour of his own, reported that all the main buildings were locked.  He had found almost no one but youngling lama novices, who were reciting the scriptures vigorously.  He asked them what it was all about, to which they replied that they were praying to keep looters away from the temple.  Moses, with the prompt Chinese contempt for barbarians, asked them if prayers had been of any use the last time looters came that way. The old monastery of Pai-ling Miao was looted and burned, apparently by insurgents from Outer Mongolia, and all the present buildings are new.  This burning was just after the Chinese Revolution, in 1911, when the Outer Mongolian tribes, under Russian encouragement, made a bid for their autonomy.  The Chinese were at that time most anxious to retain the goodwill of these Mongols about Pai-ling Miao, for fear they might also go against China, close the trade routes, and perhaps draw the rest of Inner Mongolia after them; and it is said that as an act of grace the money for rebuilding this lamasery was found by Yuan Shih-k'ai, the first President of the Republic.

"Anyhow," said Moses, with the finality and relief of a hardened tourist, "Pai-ling Miao counts as 'done.'"

This whole district is called by the Chinese Pai-ling Ti, the Land of the Larks.  The Mongolian larks, which nest on the rolling plains where the good pasture is, are famous throughout North China. They are especially in demand in Shan-tung, where fanciers pay high prices for them.  In the early summer, when the nestlings are old enough to be kept alive but not yet able to fly, the Chinese come in hundreds to catch them.   A bird market is opened in Kuei-hua, where a brisk trade is done in the very early mornings, before other markets have opened.   Before the time of the railway, men used to come all the way from Shan-tung on foot to catch larks; or buy them in the market, return-ing with as many as they could carry in two baskets slung from a pole.   The business has all the fascination of a gamble.   First the birds must be kept until the sexes can be distinguished.   The females are then set free, and the males carefully selected when beginning to sing.   Not all larks, even from these famous grounds, are equal in beauty of song; but sometimes a middling singer will improve when put near an old bird from which he can learn. An unproven lark is worth only a few cents, but the best natural singers fetch twenty or thirty dollars, even on the local market.

The Mongols hereabouts are of the Ulanchap League, which contains tribes of different origins.   I myself, I confess it, learned little about these Mongols.   I was, however, within their range until I reached Alashan territory, and as their tribal organization is not treated fully by either Prjevalsky[1] or Rockhill,[2] I will make free use of an article by the late G. C. Binsteed[3] whose lamentable death in Flanders cut short his work.   Binsteed, in addition to his own observations, drew largely on Russian sources not available in English translations, but his work was never published in book form.

In the Ulanchap League, then, there are four *Aimak*, divided as follows:—

1. The Durbet Huhet Aimak (Chinese Ssu Tzu Pu-lo) of one *hoshun*.
2. The Mao Mingan Aimak, of one *hoshun*.
3. The Oirat Aimak, of three *hoshun*, known as the Centre, Front, and Rear.
4. The Khalkha Right Wing Aimak, of one *hoshun*.

---

[1] *Mongolia, the Tangut Country and the Solitudes of Northern Thibet.*
[2] *Diary of a Journey through Mongolia and Tibet* 1891–2, by William Woodville Rockhill.  Washington: Smithsonian Institute, 1894.
[3] "The Tribal and Administrative System of Mongolia," by Lieutenant G. C. Binsteed, Essex Regiment.  The *Far Eastern Review*, Shanghai and Manila, July 1913.

Of these, the Durbet Huhet should, by their name, be Western Mongols by origin. The Mao Mingan may be genuine Inner Mongols, or they may be connected with the Mingan (sometimes also called the Mao Mingan) of Western Mongolia. Oirat is probably the same as the Mongol *oirat*, a confederacy. It would be easier to guess at their origin if the tribal names of the three *hoshun* were known, but I was never even able to determine properly which was the front, which the centre, or which the rear. Prjevalsky gives Barun-kung, Dundu-kung, and Tsun-kung. In these names the term *kung* seems to be the Chinese title commonly rendered " duke"; here, as often among the Mongols, applied to a minor hereditary prince or chief ruling a *hoshun*. *Barun* and *Tsun* are the Mongol words for West and East, and *Dundu* must mean Centre. Rockhill has the South, West, and Middle " dukes." I heard the terms Tung-kung (East Duke), Hsi-kung (West Duke), and Tung-ta-kung, which is obviously a Chinese form of the Dundu-kung of Prjevalsky. What struck me was that the order in which, apparently, they lay from East to West was East, West, Centre (Dundu or Tung-ta). Lastly, we have the Khalkha Right Wing, whose name shows that they migrated from Central Outer Mongolia.

The names of these tribal categories, though frequently used, are of little interest unless explained. Here again I rely in the main on Binsteed. The League (in Chinese *Meng*, in Mongol *Chigulgan, Chugulgan,* or *Chulgan*) is an artificial grouping imposed by the Manchus on top of the native Mongol system. It was an Imperial device for smothering the tribal interest and diverting power into the hands of Imperial officials, more usually Chinese than Manchu, nominated to share in the direction of League affairs. Among the Khalkhas, the central group of tribes of Outer Mongolia, to whom Imperial control was always least closely applied, the League coincided with the four *Aimak;* but the twenty-four *Aimak* of Inner Mongolia were arbitrarily grouped into six Leagues, of which the Ulanchap is the most westerly.

Under this extraneous grouping we have the native Mongol system.   The *aimak,* says Binsteed, quoting a Colonel Baranoff, is

an ancient Mongol name for the fief of a prince, being a group of one or more principalities, which form the inheritance of one princely family . . . bound together by singleness of descent and historical past as the former possession of a single prince, ancestor of the various present reigning princes of the *hoshun* forming the *aimak.*  With the course of time the *aimak* became divided up into several independent principalities; none the less the connection between the latter was not broken, and the prince senior in the family of the senior *hoshun* is still considered the head of the *aimak.*

The Chinese term for a Khalkha *aimak* was *pu,* and for an Inner Mongolian *aimak, pu-lo.*

Within the *aimak,* each integral *hoshun* (Chinese *ch'i,* the same term that is used for the "banner" organization of the Manchus) was the clan, so to speak, or inherited personal following of an hereditary ruling prince, the *Jassak.*  The term "prince" has always been used indifferently in English for the Jassak of a *hoshun* and the senior Jassak of an *aimak;* but perhaps the former would be better rendered as "duke."  There has also always been a swarm of chiefs who were princes by birth, but not ruling princes; exactly like a Highland chieftain without a "tail."  An irregular subdivision of the *hoshun* was the *somon.*  This was not so much a unit as an adaptable division, nominally for military but also for general administration.  A *somon* was supposed to be the number of families supplying one hundred and fifty mounted warriors.

As for the Mongols in the immediate region of Pai-ling Miao, I could never find out of what *hoshun* or *aimak* they were, but I suppose them to have been either the Durbet Huhet or the Khalkha.  The Chinese do not call them anything but the Lark Mongols, and their chief the Prince of Larks, and I think that good enough.  Any prince who would stand on being called the Prince of This or the Prince of That, when made free of the title of Prince of Larks, is no prince of feeling.

# IV

## PASTURES OF THE CARAVANS

ALL the roads of Mongolia seem to part at Pai-ling Miao. The Urga road is to the north, the Kalgan road to the east, the Uliassutai–Kobdo road to the northwest, while the two roads to Chinese Turkestan run in their beginning a little north of west. The old way, the established way during all the generations of Manchu rule, is divided for about the first half of the distance into the Great Western Road and the Small Western Road. They diverge at a few marches to the west of Pai-ling Miao. The Great Road goes to the north of a range for which I heard no general name, though the eastern spurs of it near Pai-ling Miao are called the Black Mountains.[1] This part of the road could also be used by caravans bound for Uliassutai. The Small Road takes the south of this range. After about forty marches the two roads, having overshot the western end of the range, come together again at a big Mongol trading centre called Kharaniuto. After this comes the most desert part of this route, until it strikes wells which tap the underground drainage from the Eastern Altai, running into the desert. These two roads, with their single continuation, are the natural way to the west. They only touch the northern lip of the Sandy Gobi and cross the Black Gobi in two stages. There is very little blank desert, and there are Mongols almost all the length of the road. They climb no mountain passes, but lie all the way at the foot of ranges which give them wells; indeed, the road is so easy that rich travelers commonly went by camel cart.

At the time of the Chinese Revolution, in 1911, the Mongols with Russian support secured a nominal autonomy in their own

[1] I heard also a Mongol name, Boyeh Bogdo.

affairs, the Chinese retaining an equally nominal control of Mongolian foreign affairs. This measure of Mongol independence did not at first damage the valuable Chinese trade in Mongolia, and through Mongolia with Chinese Turkestan. Russia had upheld Mongolian autonomy as a political measure expedient to Russian expansion; but in 1919, when Russia was weakened by civil wars, a Chinese adventurer attempted the reconquest of Mongolia. He was defeated by "White" Russian partisans and Mongols together. The Whites in turn were dispersed by the Reds, who had at last mastered the Counter-Revolution, and Mongolia again came under the domination of Russia, but of Russia under a new order.

Soviet influence effected a real change of front toward China. In order to bind Mongolia economically to Russia, all Mongol debts to Chinese traders (amounting to very great sums, for many of the debts had run at high compound interest for scores of years) were canceled, and a prohibitive discrimination against Chinese trade was enforced. This led to the almost complete abandonment of the Great and Small Roads. Caravans carrying tea and cloth for sale in Mongolia itself have continued a part of the trade, it is true, for these things are staples in Mongolia — tea being almost a currency. The transit trade with Chinese Turkestan was, however, straightway ruined. The Mongols at times refuse to let goods leave their country, and even business in general merchandise intended for sale in Mongolia has been made impossible. Sundry goods have never had a standard of value in Mongolia. Apart from his necessities the Mongol is a very capricious buyer. If a thing does not take his fancy, he will not have it at half its value; if it does take his fancy, he will pay whatever he can afford. The profits to the Chinese on this class of trade used to be reckoned in hundreds per cent, and it is this which has turned so disastrously against them. When the Customs officers, who are in reality men allowed a license of power in order to hinder trade, break open the boxes they run gloriously wild, having no standard of extortion to guide them. If they think a hat will bear a ten-dollar tax, it is no use arguing that the cost of the hat was only two dollars; the answer is, ten dollars or take it back to Kuei-hua. This kind of obstruction was especially applied to caravans going through to Chinese Turkestan.

The resulting breakdown of trade made it imperative to open a new road to Chinese Turkestan. It had to fulfill two conditions: to keep as far as possible from Chinese officials collecting *likin* or transit taxes, and far enough away from the independent Mongol tribes to escape confiscation. Such a road the caravans found, and called it the Jao Lu, or Winding Road. It stands in part for what must have been an ancient trade route through Alashan between Eastern Inner Mongolia and Khara-khoto on the Edsin Gol, when Khara-khoto was a city of the Tangut kingdom. From the Edsin Gol it crosses the Black Gobi and goes on through a No Man's Land, touching mountains that must be a southern extension of the Aji Bogdo, which themselves extend southward from the Altai. Then there comes a day when, from a certain lonely marsh, the mountains of perpetual snow can be seen, the outliers of the T'ien Shan. The important cities of Hami and Barköl lie to the south or astride of the T'ien Shan, but the Winding Road goes by them on the north, and joins the Great Road about a dozen marches from Ku Ch'eng-tze. Thus the Great, the Small, and the Winding Roads make together a noble entry into the ultimate city of Ku Ch'eng-tze.

The general line of the Winding Road has been known all through the history of the caravan trade. Indeed, it is of the first importance in the study of Mongolian trade routes to bear in mind that every one of them is more a direction for a journey than an absolute road. They all have variants or branches, followed at one time or another by traders for purposes of their own, or by Mongol caravans striking athwart the general east-and-west tendency of the lines of wells which are the key to travel, going southward to cultivated land in search of grain and flour supplies; or by families or tribes at war or in migration. One of the salient things about the line taken by Younghusband's guide in 1887, on one of the primary modern journeys in Mongolia, is the way in which it diverges from the courses in which the current of traffic became set in the last great period of the caravan trade, between the revival of Chinese power in the eighties, after the Mohammedan Rebellion, and the total collapse of Chinese power in Outer Mongolia about 1920.  At the present day many an old Mongol and many an old Chinese caravan master can, if put to it, find a "new" road to almost any important place, without going dangerously short of water or grazing.

There are several things, however, which tend to show that the line of the Jao Lu through Alashan is a very old route.  One is the number of legends attached to places along the road.  Unfortunately the men with the caravans know few of these legends, not having used the revived road for long enough.  A more striking proof is the situation of large monasteries in areas of the thinnest population.  Anyone who knows his Central Asia would be inclined to hazard that they carry on very old traditions of holy places, established when the areas of population were differently grouped; for the religious centres, not only of nomad races but of settled peoples living in oases divided by deserts, are founded naturally where the most people are going to and fro. A very slight climatic variation is enough to upset the economy of people who depend on the grazing to be found for their cattle; it is known that there have been such variations in Central Asia on the edge of our historical period, and it is arguable that most of the migratory wars of the barbaric hordes originated in the necessity so caused of finding new pastures.  In Mongolia, as in Eastern and Western Turkestan where the theory of desiccation, or rather of a recurrence or "pulsation"[1] of dry periods and their effects on the distribution of population has been most closely studied, most of the drainage falls inland rather than to the ocean.  The water supply in this series of regions depends either on the rain precipitated on the mountains or on the perpetual snow on their summits.  The water usually goes underground before it has flowed far, and beyond the limit of visible streams human life depends on wells dug to tap the underground drainage.

[1] For the study of "desiccation" see, *passim*, *The Pulse of Asia*, by Ellsworth Huntington.  Boston: Houghton Mifflin Company.

A small diminution in rainfall or the shrinkage of the snow cap on high mountains immediately affects the supply of subsoil water and curtails the zone of human habitation. A large part of Alashan comes within the scope of this argument; for though from a casual reference to the map it looks as if it would fall within the area of Pacific Ocean rainfall and drainage, represented by the Yellow River valley, it has actually more affinity with the basin of the Edsin Gol, which, deriving ultimately from the snow of the Nan Shan in Kan-su, flows into Mongolia to end in marshy inland lakes.

The capital relic in evidence of a greater population within historic times in what is now the most arid part of Inner Mongolia is the "dead city" of Khara-khoto on the Edsin Gol. A strongly walled and well-peopled city, founded in a region now almost empty of even a nomad population, where passed no trade of any importance until the recent revival under artificial pressure, which maintained its importance until after the period of the great migrations, for it was alive enough in Marco Polo's day, demands an historical background. There is only one way to sketch in this background. The Edsin Gol lands can never have been extensively cultivable. No city of importance could therefore have survived in such a position unless it throve on trade; and it follows that no trade could have come that way unless there were nomad tribes within reach. Sir Aurel Stein[1] mentions that the Edsin Gol provided a corridor for the invasion of Western China from Mongolia, followed by Jenghis Khan himself in his first assault of 1227. I believe that Khara-khoto, — or Etsina, as it was known to Marco Polo, — which was more than a mere garrisoned stronghold, was established not only to guard this corridor but to control a trade to the East, toward the richer regions of Inner Mongolia and Kuku-khoto, that Blue City which is now Kuei-hua.

This was the road on which I was bound for the Far West. It had been touched at different points by such great travelers as Prjevalsky, Younghusband, Kozloff, and Sir Aurel Stein, the latest visitor to Etsina being the American archæologist Langdon

[1] *Geographical Journal*, May 1925.

Warner, in 1923. Along it a few Russians, most of them White refugees who had passed through Chinese Turkestan, had come the whole way from Ku Ch'eng-tze; but I was the first to follow it throughout with a conscious interest in its history and its relation to the other great highways of Inner Asia by which the traders and warriors of obscure but momentous centuries passed up and down, fashioning their own histories and setting out to put their sign manual on the chronicles of Asia and Europe.

Pai-ling Miao, even in peaceful times, is the chief resort of the caravans and the nexus of all their roads, because it is in one of those regions of cheap, safe, and handy grazing without which a caravan trade is impossible. In the usual run of the business the camels are taken all the way into Kuei-hua to deliver their loads; but they start back on the same day for these pastures because the owners balk at the expense of feeding them even for a day in town. The men, though they may have been a year or more on the road out and back and though they pass the doors of their homes, must go with the camels.

The grazing grounds are mostly on the western side of Pai-ling Miao, in the Mao Mingan *hoshun*. A charge of twenty tael cents a month on each camel is collected by the Mongols as "grass and water money." There are no other charges, no supervision, and no interference, except that the Kuei-hua authorities demand a yearly tax of $1.60 for each camel. The few tiny streams are far apart and the water in them is not to be counted on in a dry season, but water can be found in almost any hollow at a depth of two or three feet. The caravans camp at wells, usually two or three of them in company. In spite of the lack of running water, the earth is moist enough to grow rich pasture; it is salt enough to suit the taste of camels and not too salt for sheep, the mutton here not being very fat, but well flavored. All the country under the climatic influence of the Ta Ch'ing Shan is unusually damp for Mongolia, and the cold in winter is therefore much more penetrating, rheumatic, and uncomfortable than in the true deserts.

When camels come in from the long journey they are always much worn down, and are seldom fit to start again until they have been rested on good pasture for at least two months. There is only one period in which they can really recuperate. This is in June and July, when they shed their hair. It is always held by Mongols, and usually by Chinese, that when a camel has cast his hair, which he does so completely that he is bald all over for a time, he is weak and unfit for work. This is not quite true. No Delilah ever ruined a caravan owner by pulling all the hair out of his camels. It is true, however, that a camel is then obnoxious to chills, and must be treated carefully when hot at the end of a march. It is also true that a camel kept in work over the summer will not grow a good coat and will be less fit for work in the winter; but caravans do travel in the summer, when freights are unusually high.

The seasons when caravans are dispatched from Kuei-hua in the greatest numbers are February, when there is time for them to reach the west before the grazing season, and August, just after the grazing. A caravan sent out in August, when the camels are at their very best, can sometimes make the round trip before the next grazing season. They reach Ku Ch'eng-tze in the winter; the weaker camels are left to keep alive as best they can on the winter grazing, and the stronger camels, after being fortified for a few weeks by a grain diet, are sent back to Kuei-hua, a very high percentage of them carrying grain for feed. It is, however, much more common for a caravan to start in August, make the journey in anything from three to eight months, wait for the grazing season, and start back again the following August, so that the owner in Kuei-hua cannot settle his profits and losses for about a year and a half. The best venture of all is that starting in the spring, grazing the camels at the other end, and returning in the autumn of the same year.

On the summer pastures the camel men look for the warmest hollows as well as the richest grass; dose their camels with salt and water them daily, instead of restricting the amount of water given, as is done on a journey. This makes them feel the heat more and shed their hair more quickly. After getting rid of the hair they begin to put on flesh rapidly; their humps get fat and firm and by the time the weather begins to turn, in August, there is a close, thick new coat which grows closer and thicker and longer as the winter sets in. Only during this period does a camel naturally put on first-class condition; indeed, they get so fat that before being taken on a journey they are often tied up and starved for a week or more, as a preliminary "hardening."

This happy eating for between two and three months will practically carry a camel through the rest of the year. Mongol-owned camels, which are lightly and irregularly worked, do not graze eagerly after the grass dries in the autumn, and, though they feed for only two or three hours a day, remain in splendid condition. Indeed, December is the rutting season. The colder the weather, the more rampageous the bull camels become. They are then very dangerous, eating nothing at all, impatient to roam in search of a harem, and showing fight toward anyone, whether man or camel, who interrupts them in their pleasures. Only an experienced man can handle a bull camel in the rutting season, and that gently, for if struck it is likely to be savage, turning on the herder with teeth and hoofs, throwing him, and kneeling or trampling on him. If a bull camel attacks a man it is hard to beat him off, as he is insensible to pain or fear. Bull camels are therefore rarely put to caravan work, and if they are, then at the approach of the rutting season they are starved and crushed with heavy loads to keep them in subjection.

The calves are carried for thirteen months, being dropped in January. A cow in calf is fit for work up to the very day she casts the calf. After that she becomes thin and weak if she suckles the calf, which remains with her about a year and a half. She calves, therefore, only about once in three years.

The idle weeks of the "herding camp," as it is called, are the best for the men as well as for the camels. The men are given leave in turn to go to their homes, and even in camp extra men are taken on to help with the herding, and the regular men do only one day's herding and one night on watch, followed by from five to seven days "easy." During this time they are busy with the curious pastime of knitting. The trade in camels' wool or hair, as it is indifferently called, is new, and has been developed entirely by the encouragement of foreign merchants.

Younghusband, in 1887, observed that the trade was just beginning. A *picul* of camel hair was then worth about taels 5.00 in Tientsin. It is now worth as much as taels 70.00 for a *picul* of 133 pounds. Before the foreign demand, the hair shed by camels used to be left to blow about the desert, sometimes rolling into huge balls. A camel sheds on the average about six pounds of hair, with another pound and a half or two pounds of coarser, less valuable hair from the mane and the bunches of hair above the knees, on the forelegs.

Knitting is a newer thing still. The caravan men say that they learned it from White Russian soldiers deported from Chinese Turkestan. Some hundreds of these men were sent down to the coast, divided into small parties traveling with different caravans, and their way of knitting and crocheting socks was eagerly learned by the camel men. All of the hair from the camel herd belongs, of course, prescriptively to the owner, but in fact he loses a great deal of this because it has become a perquisite of the men to use as much as they like for making socks for themselves. They never steal the hair to sell in town, but they do make a lot of extra things on the quiet, which they sell. Long scarfs knitted or crocheted by camel men were all the fashion among the richer Chinese at Kuei-hua when I was there. When we first started, many of the camels had not finished shedding, and it was an amazing thing to see men knitting on the march; if they ran out of yarn they would reach back to the first camel of the file they were leading, pluck a handful of hair from the neck, and roll it in their palms into the beginning of a length of yarn; a weight was attached to this, and given a twist to start it spinning, and the man went on feeding wool into the thread until he had spun enough yarn to continue his knitting.

While the caravan is in camp the owner, through his broker in Kuei-hua, arranges for outward freight. When the camels are ready and the loads in order, either the camels come in to town to take them up, or they are carted out to Pai-ling Miao. The border between the land directly administered by the Chinese and that still held by the Mongols is vague in many places, but Pai-ling Miao is held to be on strictly Mongol ground and therefore in some sense a sanctuary. Unless the need is desperate, the Chinese have always been careful of their conduct on tribal land. The Mongols are steadily exploited, but it is recognized that a certain dignity of procedure must be observed. The communication at this point between Inner and Outer Mongolia is so easy that the tribes under Chinese jurisdiction might, if incautiously pressed, go over to their kinsmen in successful revolt. Thus, when the military were in search of camels in the spring, Mongol camels found on Chinese ground were taken and not returned, but a Chinese patrol which rode to Pai-ling Miao to look for more was turned back by the Mongols, who refused to recognize their authority. Nor did the Chinese attempt to carry the point with a high hand. An indirect method was taken instead. The princes were asked for "loans" to aid in their own "protection" against the invading side in the civil war. They were allowed to understand that live stock would be accepted against part of the loan, and given enough time to shift the burden to their people. In this way, the Chinese administration got what it wanted, while maintaining the friendship and supporting the prestige of the princes. As for the princes, so long as the burden did not fall directly on them, they preferred to remain on the Chinese side. They were against any movement toward independence, well knowing that the princes in Outer Mongolia had almost entirely lost their wealth and power since the break with the Chinese and the substitution of Soviet influence.

In accordance with their policy of leaving the chiefs a great deal of power in affairs strictly Mongol, while continuing to dominate them from afar, the Chinese do not allow any of their own people except the men of the caravans and the traders to go freely among the Mongols. Were the Chinese allowed to settle freely, race hostility and border warfare would be inevitable. Thus the Mongols, though forced continually along what may be called their Chinese front to sell their land and move away, remain consciously their own masters in the lands left to them. One of the rules which they most jealously enforce is that no

Chinese are allowed to carry arms, much less to shoot game. Among the Mongols themselves there is an old muzzle-loader in almost every family. A few of them are better armed, and all are lovers of sport. In the mountains that break up the Pai-ling Ti pastures are many fine wild sheep — *ovis ammon*, or *argal*, as the Mongols call them. For some reason, not apparently connected with religion or the neighborhood of the temple, there is a ban on the shooting of them, even by Mongols. I was told of only one foreigner who had visited the grounds. He was not stopped. Good heads are to be found here. Even in places where the Mongols do shoot *argal*, they go mostly for the ewes and young rams, which are not quite so wary and better eating. The old rams with the big heads are more often killed by the wolves, which drive them in winter into deep snow, where they are hampered and easily slaughtered.

Few Mongols are to be seen in the immediate neighborhood of Pai-ling Miao, unless they ride in to buy gear or get drunk. Beside the monastery there is a group of *tze-hao*, the posts of traders in a large way who live permanently in small Chinese houses. These *tze-hao* sell spirits or cloth, boots, saddles, to-bacco, tea, or flour on the spot, in their "reception rooms," where the Mongol is given a seat on the brick sleeping platform, tea to drink, a brass pipe to smoke, an embroidered bag of to-bacco at his elbow, and friendly talk to hear. They also own small caravans, sometimes several caravans, which carry their goods on a round among more distant encampments. Both buying and selling for silver are not uncommon, but the greater part of the trade is still by barter. The Mongol even more than the Chinese hoards his silver, and the Chinese play nimbly on the Mongol's preference for giving twice over in goods or cattle rather than cash down in silver.

The traders exchange their wares for wool, cattle, ponies, camels, sheep, and a few hides and furs, and in every part of the business there is a great rivalry of fraud. In selling flour the Chinese use a small measure, but in buying wool they use a heavy weight. The Mongol in retaliation loads his wool with dirt, sometimes putting a little sugar in warm water and sprinkling it on the wool to make the dust adhere; but in the end the Chinese, who keeps accounts and charges interest, always wins. The wool he buys may be half sand, but then his one-catty weight is fully two catties, and as a beam balance is used, hung in a loop, deft handling will always give a little extra margin. The smaller the deal, the greater the profit, for a Mongol with only one lambskin or a couple of pounds of camel hair will not haggle overlong if given a little strong drink; whereas in selling a small quantity of flour the Chinese likes to do without a measure, giving it in bowlfuls with an apparently careless generosity. I have heard the Chinese accused of being shortsighted in business; but put a small deal just under his nose and no Jew could see it more clearly.

I stayed at a *tze-hao* while I was at Pai-ling Miao. All business was at an end, and the place was crowded with men who would in quiet times have been out trading among the Mongols. There was nothing to do, and men kept going to the door as if to look for an omen. Deserting soldiers had passed, but not within the last few days. No one came from the south and no one dared venture to the south, but other traders rode back and forth from east and west, bringing wild tales. The Chinese passed the day on the *k'ang,* talking and smoking. A few smoked opium, but most of them *tung-sheng* tobacco, greenish, dry, and dustily shredded, in long pipes with tiny bowls, while one man sucked and blew untiringly at a pipe made from one of the leg bones of an antelope. He had fitted it with a mouthpiece and bowl made of empty cartridge cases and smoked the tobacco commonly used in water pipes, a tobacco almost sweet compared with the acrid *tung-sheng.* It was of a red color, in thready, minute particles, but not dusty. To smoke it, a lighted taper must be held to the bowl of the pipe all the while that the smoke is being inhaled; two breaths are enough, and then the smoker must blow out the dottle and begin again.

All night they played *ma-chiang* by the light of red tallow candles. Like most of the miserly Shan-hsi breed, they played slowly, clumsily, and with avaricious hesitation. Even Shan-hsi men, however, get a certain swing to them when they take to the careless life of Mongolia.  After all, as one of them said when he lost, it was a good time to be devil-may-care; they were all playing with the paper notes of the Christian Army's provincial bank, which had gone to ruin with the defeat of the Army.

Staying at the same place there was a caravan owner, a western man from Ch'ing Ch'eng, near Hami.  Though a man of wealth, he was always known, according to the casual manners of his trade, as Ch'ing Ch'eng Li.  He at last told me what was the root of all the evil in my dealings with the fellow who held my contract.  He had been taken with a passion for a woman in a brothel in Kuei-hua.  On her and on opium he had spent every cent not invested in camels, and for her sake he had remained in Kuei-hua, evading my demands for fresh camels, when his own interest should have sent him scuttling away from that dangerous town.

One night, when the Chinese were yarning, the talk turned on the Mohammedans.  Someone said that their holy city was farther west of Turkestan than Turkestan was west of Peking, and that it was walled with brass.  Ch'ing Ch'eng Li, who had spoken Turki from his childhood, looked up from the lamp where he was preparing opium.  "Yes," he said, "I have heard the Turbaned-Heads speak of it.  It is called Roum."  With the hearing of that name, which is current throughout Central Asia for Constantinople, I knew that I was well beyond the Great Wall of China.

Ch'ing Ch'eng Li said from the first that my caravan owner would never show up.  Nor did he.  There came instead another man who said that he had been engaged to go with me.  I must review, as swiftly as may be, all the rogueries involved in my relations with this new man, as well as with the first contractor, because of the bearing they had on my journey.

The first man was well enough known to come from a sound family in Barköl.  They owned about seventy camels, which had started from Kuei-hua in February and escaped seizure.  The son of the family had waited in Kuei-hua with a few extra camels, which he had hired to me.  His intention was to overtake his main caravan, pick from it untired camels that had been traveling slowly, and go ahead by fast marches. Thus he had been able to contract to take me across Mongolia in the quick time of seventy days. When at last I had made him provide other camels, he had pretended, for some reason, that he was buying them. He did nothing of the sort. He hired them from the man who met me at Pai-ling Miao.

This man owned nine camels — two more than were called for in my contract. Owing to the way in which the market had fallen, he had been glad enough to accept the subcontract at taels 240 for nine camels, instead of the taels 350 for seven that I had paid out. He had not even been paid this money in full; the Barköl man had given him the hundred dollars advanced by me, and enough in ropes, packsaddles, and gear to make up half the amount. For the other half he, like me, had a lien on the camels owned by the Barköl family. In order, however, to clinch the low rate of hire, the first man, abetted by the conscienceless broker, had lied to him about the weights to be carried. He did not dispute that his nine camels were enough to carry everything, but argued that, having accepted a very low figure for the lesser weight, he ought not to be asked to carry a greater weight for the same sum. While he had been cheated in this, I had been cheated in another matter, for the original contractor had promised to go with me and to provide another man as well, thus leaving Moses and me entirely free of the work of road and camp. Still worse, the new man had never been over the Winding Road, and had relied on the other to guide him.

Thus we were both hipped. The Barköl man owed me a hundred dollars and my new camel man a hundred and twenty taels. He had promised both of us that he would go with us and pay us when he reached his family in the west. To both of us he had said that his camels would stand for security, and by failing to meet us it looked as though he meant to swindle us both. The matter of the difference in weights was the only thing that made it difficult for me and the new man to come to a good understanding; but this difficulty he made into a tremendous obstacle. I was ready enough to treat him generously, should he prove a good man on the journey; but he brooded so balefully on his wrongs that he became first morose, then almost unmanageable, and in the end so insanely savage that he threatened to murder both Moses and me.

While we waited, the rumors grew more alarming. Not a single traveler came out of Kuei-hua. We had been the last to get through. Then, on the third day, there came a foreigner in a motor car. It was Millar, the young Scotchman of the British sheep-buying firm. He had left Kuei-hua some days before me, and been traveling about the country on business. Only the day before, he had tried to send a messenger in to Kuei-hua. The man came back to him saying that the pass was closed and no one allowed to go toward the city. He had then driven to Pai-ling Miao to get clear of the trouble. Stopping at noon in a little village, he had seen about forty men ride into the other end of the village. Either they did not see his car, which was in a yard, or did not think he was their game; but they made the villagers bring them all the ponies they had, and a little food and money, and went off, taking with them a couple of men, perhaps as guides. On starting again he had run into three or four deserters. These men did not try to hold him up. They told him that they were scouting in advance of a much larger body, who were trying to get away from Kuei-hua and had just looted a trading post.

This decided both my new camel man and me to wait no longer, even though he did not know the way. Indeed, we should have run for it sooner. The first part of the road was plain to follow; after that we should have to go in company with some other caravan. The important thing was to get well away from the drums and tramplings of civil war; even with forced marches we should get clear none too quickly, and it was more than likely that we should have to dodge. A camel is the more companionable as a pet and the more decorative in a photograph, but when running away is the serious business of life a motor car has the wheels of him. Unfortunately my Scotch friend and I were running away in different directions. I was for the west, while he was for turning backhanded toward Kalgan, far to the east and south. He had a reserve of petrol and got there safely in the end, having made a prodigious tour to get round the rough and tumble of the retreat. More than three weeks later, on the day that my wife reached Kalgan, the first to get through from Kuei-hua by train, Millar came tumbling out of Mongolia on a worn-out car, and gave her a letter that I had written at Pai-ling Miao.

It is at least a pleasure to think how comforted my parents must have been when they heard that my foreign friend in the car was a Scotchman. There is nothing more reassuring in a letter home than to be able to say that there are Scotchmen about. People have all kinds of ideas about the terror and loneliness of travel in Mongolia, nourished by some of the recent books, but their minds are invariably set at rest, unless they are Irish, when one answers, "Oh, no; you see a Scotchman every now and then."

When a decision to run away has once been taken, it is astonishing how easy the rest becomes. All during our stay at Pai-ling Miao we had been disputing violently. The camel man made one last attempt, and a stout one, to get me to cast some of my loads. Then, without more talk except the indispensable swearing of handlers of freight all the world over, he led up his camels and made them kneel; the loads were heaved up and hitched on, and the camels stood up, snarling and threatening to spit slimy green cud. Cow camels are especially handy in spattering men with this cud, but all camels are free with it when they are fresh from pasture and have carried no loads for a long time. The stink of the mess is thrice wonderful and past all whooping, for there is not a smell in China, not even in the ooze-covered stone sewer streets of Ningpo, that approaches it in the reek of pestilence and corruption. When spattered, the only thing to do is to let the stuff dry, when it is easily brushed off.

We left at evening, in a misty drizzle that soon set to a steady rain. Fording the little stream — about thirty feet across after recent rains — which runs to the north, showing that this is the true Mongolia, divorced from the sea, we filed past the monastery and headed into a twilight vagueness of rolling pasture land, on which the darkness was rapidly gathering.  For an hour or two I sat my camel, waiting for two things of which I had been warned — camel sickness and camel boredom.  On either side of the load on which I sat were bags of clothing.  In the hollow formed between them and the camel's humps was my perch, with my legs hanging over his neck.  The ground looked far away, and I was a little puzzled by the thought that there is no manner of brake to use on a runaway camel, but I had no other worries.  About my stomach I had wound a very splendid purple sash, as a corseting against stitches; but as we went on through the night and the drumming rain I felt nor stitch nor boredom.  When I had caught on to the lurch and scramble of a camel's traveling gait, I got down to walk for a few miles.  Then I climbed up again, learning one of my first lessons.  When mounting a camel on the march, it is not the best of form to make him kneel; it is more tiring for him and halts and deranges the whole file.  One pulls down his head by the cord attached to a peg in his nose.  Left knee on his neck, just behind his head, and up it comes, swinging one lightly off the ground.  Right foot up to the bight of his neck, left knee up the next notch, at the top of his neck near the edge of the load, and with a heave and a scramble the thing is done.  After a little practice it can be done without even halting the camel.

I had yet to learn the knack of wandering through a labyrinth of dreams and memories and lazy half-thoughts, through the endless but sedately witching marching hours.  The mingled ache and eagerness of final departure, mixed with the thrill of being free of houses and wheeled things, died slowly in me.  I could see the ground shifting vaguely beneath me, and hear the soft impact of the camel's feet on the coarse sandy soil.  All about was the whispering hush of a night of ceaseless rain.  Now and again, far away to the side, Mongol dogs clamored at our passing.  Once the dim shape of a wolf crossed fifteen yards in front of us, and my camel, which was in the lead, snorted with fear.  The smell of the grasslands was damp and sweet.  The night was not so much an interval of time as an overflow of eternity, which did not bother one with beginning or end.

14. CAMEL OWNER

"The commonest ambition of a camel puller is to own a few camels which he can take along with him, while still working for his old master." (p. 124)

15. CARAVANS STARTING WESTWARD FROM PAI-LING MIAO
"This whole district is called by the Chinese Pai-ling Ti, the Land of
the Larks." (p. 46)

16. CARAVAN-LOADING NEAR PAI-LING MIAO
"Our neighbors were a *hu-la-mao'rh*—an expression meaning, more or less, jerrycummumble." (p. 68)

It was four in the morning when, after ten hours of steady plodding, a frontal charge by a pack of furious dogs showed that we had reached a camping ground and a caravan. The man on night watch came over; he knew my man and called off the dogs. In a few minutes the camels had knelt and the loads were slipped off; we got the tent up in the dark, spread felts on the wet grass, unrolled our sleeping bags, and, after a drink of hot tea from the pot on the night watchman's fire, turned in to sleep, at the end of the first full march on the road to Turkestan.

# V

## LANDS OF UNREST

THE next day we spent in drying out our camp, after the night's rain, and in making friends with the caravan already encamped. We were in little danger here, as we were in a big stretch of purely Mongol land, and most of the broken soldiery were keeping farther to the south, making for the Kan-su border. Our neighbors were a *hu-la-mao'rh* — an expression meaning, more or less, jerrycummumble. The *hu-la-mao'rh* are a recognized class among the Kuei-hua caravans. In this one there were more than two hundred camels, owned in sixes and sevens and twenties by a number of men, some of whom led their own camels while others were represented by hired men. Each owner provided food for himself or his man, and paid in proportion for the maintenance of the caravan master, his pony, and the camp dogs. The leader himself owned the tent, water butts, and other gear, and the camels carrying them. In addition to contributing to his expenses and his salary of taels 150 for the round trip to Ku Ch'eng-tze and back, the owners paid him a fee of taels 20 for each man living in the tent, to cover the hire of the commissariat camels. The leaders of such come-one-come-all caravans are often among the most able on the road, — men who have made a reputation for themselves through long years, and at last saved enough to set up on their own, — but these are not the best caravans by which to send goods. Though his authority is in most ways as absolute as that of any other caravan master, the leader is morally bound to consider the interests, not of one owner, but of a kind of traveling Soviet. If one man's five camels are worn out, the other two hundred or so must wait, if there is any pasturage at all, to give them a chance to recover.

In their mob of dogs I noticed one outstanding brute, which they told me was a stray. A dog is often lost from his own caravan, either because he has stopped too long by a dead camel to feed, or because he is footsore. If he can fight his way among the dogs of the next caravan that passes, he is taken on the strength; if not, he starves. This fellow, though he had won to the feeding basket with his teeth, was not yet on friendly terms with the pack. He was only two or three years old, by the whiteness and sharpness of his teeth, stood as high as a Saint Bernard, and was black in color with white forefeet and a splash of white on his chest. The most usual coloring is black with tan points and tan spots over the eyes. When I fed him from the hand, he at once moved over to my tent, and the caravan men, seeing that "my heart loved him," said I might keep him. That very night he savaged a man who came over to my tent, and the man, snatching up the stave of a camel pack, laid open his foreleg to the bone with a blow that would have broken the leg of any weaker dog.

I called him Suji, after the name of the camp. I learned afterward that *suji* is the Mongol word for the pelvis of a sheep, and that the camp came by its name because the shape of the little hollow where the well lay was like the shape of the bone. There was something fitting in the name for my dog, too, since he had been given to me, and the *suji* bone is a piece of honor which the Mongols offer to their guests. To have called a dog after the name of the place where I got him was, however, thought very comical by the men of every caravan with which I fell in company along the road. Everything goes by convention among simple people, and they have a conventional list of dog names of their own. Tiger, Lion, Black Ox, Red Ox, and Bastard are among their favorites, while the bitches are most often called by flower names, like Chinese girls. Suji was always called Leng-t'ou by one of the caravans with which I traveled later. A *leng-t'ou* is the kind of obstinate man who, if you tell him that a piece of iron is hot, will at once touch it to see if it really is; or who, if told that it is time to go softly and peacefully, will at once fight. They called him this because he broke the first rule of all dogs, that where a dog feeds, there he is on guard. Suji would take food heartily from any man, but he would savage the same man if he came to my tent, and though he pirated his food wherever food could be found, he returned always to guard my tent.

Caravan dogs are entered to the calling even younger than caravan men, for they are often born in camp. December and January pups are the best. When they are newly born the mother is allowed a place in the tent, but often the puppies are exposed for several hours in the snow, to kill off the weak ones. On the march, each puppy is carried in the breast of a man's coat, from which he is taken for his mother to give him a quick lunch during the short halts. When he gets a little stronger, he and the rest of his family are hung in a nose bag from a camel's load, and when they can run about they get their training from the other dogs of the pack.

The chief use of the dogs is to watch the camp at night. The place of the two men on watch is at the door of the tent, and the place of the dogs at the back, on the blind side. On the march they run always in advance. The man leading the first file of camels is the chief cook, whose voice they know because he has the charge of their feeding, and as the caravan starts he calls them together with a long, lilting cry — *lai, lai-lai-lai-lai-i-i-i!* They sometimes fight short battles when they meet the dogs of a caravan bound the other way, but more often each pack hangs together and goes warily by the other with hackles up. Even when two caravans are traveling in company it is a long time before the men can visit each other's tents without being attacked, for the dogs are slow to acknowledge anyone whose food they do not eat. Dogs belong nominally to the caravan owner, but because they help the men on night watch it is the men who cherish them and regard them as their own. If anything goes wrong with them it is the men who make trouble, and it is the men who steal good-looking puppies from other caravans.

"Small places for quarrelsome dogs," the Chinese say, "and big places for quarrelsome men." This is because the Chinese villager, with knowledge of no world bigger than his few fields or any civilization beyond the village temple, the village pawn-shop, and the village tea shop, is easily taken aback and put upon by *ya-men* runners, underling officials, or any stranger who can bluster and swagger. His dog, used to few people and kept to guard the house, is more valiant than he. This is not the way in cities, where men must of necessity hold their own against all kinds of roguery and learn to evade every sort of imposition; whereas the dog in a Chinese city becomes a cur, wanted by no one and kicked by everyone, whose principal business with men is the avoidance of their wrath.

The very best kinds of caravan dogs are said to come from the small Chinese border villages near Kalgan; big in bone, used to very hot summers and rigorous winters, and savage to the heart. Those mountains are never free from petty banditry, and the dogs, because they are the best defense of the villagers, are carefully tended and fed, so that they stand out from the general race of Mongol dogs to which they belong. Men who have been down toward Kalgan are proud if they can boast a dog stolen from one of these villages — for even the best of dogs is rarely bought or sold.

Above even these fine brutes, apart from all competition, is rated the strain of Ta Sheng K'uei. Because a herd of ponies belonging to Ta Sheng K'uei had gone by a day or two before Suji fought his way into the caravan from which I took him, and because of his build and size and style, all the caravan men I met put him down for a Ta Sheng K'uei dog. Now the firm of Ta Sheng K'uei has been established in Kuei-hua for more than two hundred years; it has a history that would stand well beside that of the Hudson's Bay Company, and its dogs have a unique breeding.

The firm never worked for others at the mere carrying of freight; it traded on its own, buying produce in Mongolia and carrying it back to Kuei-hua on its own camels. It had posts at all the important places, like Urga, Uliassutai, and Kobdo; it controlled ranches and bought live stock as well as raw produce, and its interests were so wide that it directed the affairs of Mongol princes and was the business agent of great lamaseries. Its caravan leaders were the picked men of their craft, its camels and dogs and ponies the best on the road, its agents the best business men, with the highest prestige. Only when the Chinese rule in Outer Mongolia was replaced by Russian influence was the weakness of its position made apparent. Its credits were secured on tribal lands and princely revenues, and many rich Mongols were deeply in its debt. When, under Soviet tutelage, the Mongols followed up their revolt from Chinese rule with a policy of hostility to Chinese traders, all these debts and obligations were canceled. The result was disastrous to the Chinese, and Ta Sheng K'uei, like all the firms in the group of great houses once dominating the Mongolian trade, have to-day only a remnant of their former wealth.

In the old days, before there was a telegraph in Mongolia, the dogs of Ta Sheng K'uei were trained to carry messages. Each dog had a home station; he would be taken out with a caravan, but so soon as released he would run back to his home. In this way Ta Sheng K'uei kept in touch with the buying and selling markets as no other firm could do. Traveling from one district to another, the caravans sent back word of prices and supplies, tied to a dog's collar. The dog would run amazing distances, without stopping, except to drink a little water or eat the flesh of a dead camel. When he reached his home station, the message would be relayed on to the head office at Kuei-hua. To keep up such a service, Ta Sheng K'uei had to breed dogs in far greater numbers and of a better strength and intelligence than any other firm or caravan company. To cover the extra expense, they adopted a practice that must be unique in the history of trade. They kept a special Dog Account in their books, to which was credited 10 per cent of the profit on every deal in which the dogs were engaged, and the money was spent in maintaining the number and improving the quality of their dogs. When the telegraph made the service obsolete, the old strain was preserved in their caravan dogs.

Ta Sheng K'uei are also said to have had a regular mounted courier service in the buying season, apart from the more erratic use of the dogs. The couriers rode ponies carefully trained into lean, hard condition — since a pony taken, as the Mongols take him, straight from the herd with a big grass belly on him and no grain in it, is good only for one long stage. Each man had two ponies, which he rode turn about, the led pony carrying a little dried bread for the man, a little grain for the ponies, and a little water when necessary. The man rode until he could no longer keep awake, then hobbled his ponies and slept for a few hours. The traveling gait was a trot. For comfort and show the Chinese, even more than the Mongol, Qazaq, and Turki, prefers an ambler, but when it comes to endurance and steady going he admits that the trotting pony holds up better.

Now it takes about two months for a caravan from Kuei-hua going stage-by-stage, as the Chinese say, — that is, without long halts, — to reach Uliassutai, so the distance may be anywhere between six hundred and nine hundred miles. As I heard the yarn, the courier, with only two mounts to change about, made it in six days. I think I should call this a legend. It is hardly kind, after sitting as a guest by the tent fire in the "ungirt hour" when men tell stories, to go back and note them down in one's diary as liars; but a legend this is, without doubt. I think it likely that over long desert stretches men rode something in this way; but once into the pasture lands of Outer Mongolia the message would be more swiftly carried on by Mongols on relays of fresh ponies. However that may be, the Mongol pony, who is at his best on a long ride, can do gallant things. Were I an Emperor, of the kind they used to have, I would summon the English Arab Horse Society to hold one of its endurance trials over the same course, with Mongol ponies in the running.

We marched in the afternoon of the second day from the pleasant camp at Suji-well. We were already in the Mao Mingan *hoshun*, having passed the *obo* that divides it from the range of the "Lark" Mongols. This is the way of Mongol boundaries; they set up an *obo* or cairn in a high evident place and say, "From here to the next *obo*, away there in those hills, along the ridge of these hills here between, is the boundary between us and you." They divide themselves by watersheds and not by valleys, because what they require is the delimitation of grazing grounds.

Our new camp, at a distance of about twelve miles, by a trickle of water flowing into a small marsh, was called Erlidsen-gegen (a *gegen* is a high rank of lama). We were about thirty miles north of the nearest cultivated land, but the Chinese were here driving a wedge into Mongolia. The ground on which we camped had already been appropriated; some of the settlers had moved in and next year would break the soil. We were at a point roughly north of Pao-t'ou, where the belt of Chinese-occupied land "behind the hills" is controlled from a small town called Ku-yang Hsien, standing in the same relation to Pao-t'ou that K'o Chen holds to Kuei-hua.

On the next day we parted company with our friendly caravan. We were nearing a point where the camel tax is checked, and they were for making a turn to the north of it, being short of passes. My man had tickets for all his camels, so we decided to take a risk and go straight through. We marched west for about fifteen miles and halted with low hilly country before us, after passing two small lakes called Bagan Nor and Ikki Nor. The next day, before we started, we were joined by a little old man on a stinking mass of boils which he called a camel. One side of it bulged with sores, the other side was caving in with hunger and age. He told us a yarn about having come from K'o Chen in three days, which would be in marches of about forty-five miles, and said that he was looking for company going to the west. He had nearly thirty camels at Ku Ch'eng-tze, entrusted to a nephew; but, owing to the troubles, his nephew had neither returned to K'o Chen nor sent him money, so he must go west again himself. He was fifty-one years old and had retired from business several years before, but had been in the caravan trade from his youth, and at one time had been an opium carrier. That was before opium was nominally under legal ban. Opium was then brought from Turkestan by the Outer Mongolian route. Cargoes had to be delivered, under guarantee, in thirty-five days. This was accomplished by arrangement with the owners of heavy caravans traveling slowly.

Every time that the carrier caught up a caravan, he would change his two or three camels for fresh ones and push ahead again by marches limited only by his own need for sleep and food. He drew a bonus for every day under the time limit, and would sometimes dismount in Kuei-hua on the twenty-ninth day.

The Old Man, as we came to call him, stopped at our tent to talk and eat. He went on talking until we started, helped us to load, and fell in at the end of our little caravan. Said he, looking at his own camel, "Yes, it is fourteen years old, or maybe fifteen, or sixteen, or even more; but it ought to get me there. As for being a dead bone, a dead bone it is, no doubt; but it will do." He had with him a few pounds of parched oatmeal, and a worn sheepskin suit in addition to his cotton clothes. According to his tale, he had been robbed of his few dollars, a small store of dried bread, and a greatcoat. Moses did not believe this at all. The man, he said, was looking for a cheap passage to the west, and hoped to live on the hospitality of the caravans. Still, we thought he would do. "First a dog and now a man," said Moses; "we are coming on." Because we were short a man, we had ourselves been helping to load, unload, and do the work about camp; but we had plenty of food, and it would be a good plan to take on the Old Man, making him work for his keep.

In three hours we had to camp, because it was raining hard, and in the murk among the confused hills we had gone off the trail. No sooner had we got the tent up than two men came along with a lantern. When we had rescued them from Suji, they said they had come to inspect our camel passes, but since we were not going on they would come again in the morning.

It was bad enough the next day packing up wet tent and wet felts, without having to face a row with a tax inspectorate. It was a nasty, unsatisfactory row. It was the first of September, and it turned out that the first of September was the due date, clearly marked on the passes, for the renewal of camel taxes. The tax, of $1.60, is collected under authority of the Northwestern Province, by officials posted in different places. Whenever or wherever the pass is bought, it is good until the next first of September. Our man, having bought his passes at some date which he remembered by the old Chinese lunar calendar, thought they were good for a year from purchase, and so landed us in this trouble.

Seeing that if we talked we might talk for a week, I led off the camels with Moses in attendance, leaving the camel man to debate lunar and solar calendars with the officials. After a mile or so, of course, he caught us up, under escort of several armed guards, who told us that we must pay because our man had no money. After some lurid talk, I bought the full number of passes for half the legal sum, and we went on. My man, of course, had money all the time in his waistband, but had not dared show it for fear he would be forced to pay the full sum and a "fine" in addition.

That we should have been allowed to pass on payment of half the tax, while the Old Man, who was obviously penniless, had franked himself through by the mere proof of that fact, was an adjustment showing in itself the rottenness of the tax-farming system. A tax like this is legal, and the passes issued are recognized within their validity; but the collection of the tax is farmed out to contractors who bid for the privilege. After they have sold the agreed number of passes, everything they collect goes to fill their own pockets, so that a pass can often be had for half the proper payment. Moreover, since the caravans naturally evade the inspectors whenever they can, each contractor is allowed to maintain an armed patrol to scout the countryside in search of taxable camel flesh. The men are armed with "government" rifles, but are in the private employ of the contractor; and the things that can be done by a private armed force among unarmed people are astonishing. It is no use appealing over the head of the tax collector, because the officials above him themselves draw a percentage on the tax. To go before a higher court means only the payment of a higher "squeeze." It is hardly a wonder that to the peasant the words "law" and "official" are expressions of terror. It is said that in England a man is innocent until he is proved guilty, in America and France guilty until he is proved innocent; but in China he can either be innocent or make another man guilty by cash payment. Even a government with genuine intentions of reform could not rid the country of this kind of abuse in less than two or three generations, because the people themselves are too acquiescent and their ideas of civil administration too hopelessly vitiated by centuries of similar misgovernment.

By reason of the long wrangling, we were late in getting on the march. Not long after dark we were again so hopelessly lost that we had to make camp. Again it was raining, and, as we had not had a chance to dry out our things before leaving the last camp, no one was happy. The name of this district of low hills was Yang-ch'ang-tze Kou, the Valleys of Sheep Stations. When traders in the live-stock business bring back sheep that are too poor in condition after long driving to be fit for city markets, they hold them over the winter in well-watered, sheltered valleys like these. In the spring, after the wool has been combed off them (in this part of Mongolia the sheep are combed in the spring for the best grade of wool and shorn in late summer for a lower grade), they are driven in to Pao-t'ou or Kuei-hua, where some of them are slaughtered and some sent on to the markets of Peking and Tientsin.

What with the wet and the chill, nobody slept well. The rain stopped, however, about midnight, and when the Chinese saw by the stars that it was near dawn we broke camp. By the time it was light enough to look for a road, the camels were loaded and we were moving off. Generally speaking, I have the grown man's wariness of this dawn business. The only thing more unwelcome than being routed out of bed to see an unpremeditated dawn is being unjustifiably routed out of bed to see the dawn as a matter of æsthetic duty. Perhaps the soundest dawn — I mean in cities — is that one sees when walking home after dancing all night with — well, anyone suitable. But this dawn was not an affair of civilized man; it was for the boy or the savage. I had been getting used to breaking camp at any hour of the day, and making camp at any time of the night, eating anything that came handy, and sleeping where I could lie down. It was the right approach, and I liked that dawn. I liked the clean chill that came with the light better than the damp chill of a makeshift camp.

I liked the live smell of earth that comes after rain; the almost English delicacy of coloring on the rain-washed hills, the scrubby growth on their flanks, and the scarfs of mist trailing from them.

In the night we had been puzzled by a shallow stream. It had a bed of soft, sliding sand into which we were lucky not to have fallen in the dark; but in the dawn my little caravan slouched sedately across — nine bored-looking camels mooching through a pastel morning of gray and soft green and rose and faint blue, followed by the wild-eyed, shapeless camel of the Old Man.

The mists were clearing away and we were making good time in the light of full morning when we saw five mounted men coming toward us. I could tell almost at once that they were armed. It is surprising how quickly one learns, when traveling in a dangerous country, to know whether a man carries arms or not, long before one can precisely see what he carries. " Bandits!" I thought. I felt that the top of a camel was a poor sort of place from which to do any shooting, and a remarkably silly place in which to be shot at. Luckily caravan men have an uncanny eye for telling people that are dangerous from people that are merely suspect. My camel man soon declared that the strangers were *t'u fan-tze*, opium runners, a class of traveler to be treated more with caution than with positive fear. As we got within hailing distance, both parties halted in an undecided way. Two of the opium runners dismounted, with rifles unslung and ready. My rifle was in a leather case, on a load. I thought it better to stay on my camel, after all, but I shrugged myself to bring nearer to the front the revolver under my sheepskin coat. In these attitudes we shouted politely at each other, as we gradually sidled closer.

All five men were Salars,[1] brown-skinned, strongly grown, hairy men of a Turkish stock settled around Ho Chou in Kan-su,

[1] Prjevalsky (*op. cit.*) gives a Mongol tradition, according to which there was once a tribe called the Yegur (this may be for Uighur) living about the Koko Nor. They were driven out by a Mongol invasion. (These Mongols still remain near the Koko Nor.) Those of the Yegur left on the Tibetan marches are known to the Mongols as "Black" Tangut; these may be the Golok, a modern robber tribe. Others, so Prjevalsky was told, escaped to the region of Ho Chou, where by racial fusion they became the Salars, differing by religion from the Khara-Tangut and now totally distinct from them. Western Kan-su was at various times overrun by Turkish tribes.

speaking an archaic Turkish dialect, though many of them can manage Chinese as well. They were dressed partly in uniform, and all carried what ought to have been government arms; a cavalry carbine, an infantry rifle, and a number of Mauser pistols, besides which two of them had field glasses. The Ho Chou Mohammedans made up a large part of Ma Fu-hsiang's cavalry when he was governor of the northwest, before the coming of the Christian Army. In those days, under the direction of their own officers, they brought down a great deal of opium from Kan-su, making a regular trade of it. They brought the opium through byways of the Mongolian border, and went back with cartloads of copper coins along the Pao-t'ou–Ning-hsia highway. Every part of China in touch with railways has been flooded with copper coins until they are everywhere at least 330 to the dollar; in Kan-su, however, where there is no mint and which is cut off by bandit areas from the nearest provinces where there are mints, fifty double coppers will in many places buy a silver dollar. The trade grew so brisk that it affected even Kuei-hua, which by the railway was usually in touch with the Tientsin mint. To steady exchange, an embargo had to be declared on the export of copper coins to the west. The embargo, however, could not be enforced against honest soldier-men, so that the only sufferers were still the greedy bankers and merchants.

When the Christian Army took over the northwest, they also took over the troops of Ma Fu-hsiang. Weighing their exchequer and their principles in a balance of expediency, the exchequer was found too light, so that a few principles had to be dropped. The Mohammedan cavalrymen "on leave" were therefore allowed to keep on with their traffic in opium. The traffic was even extended by the cultivation of opium in the northwest itself. Assessors were sent into the country districts to tax lands suitable for growing poppy, and the tax levied on these lands was so heavy that it could only be met by cultivating opium. The local crop, though superior in quality, was not enough to meet the demand, so that western opium did not fall very much in price. In 1926 opium was being bought in Kan-su

for about three Chinese ounces [1] to the dollar, and sold in Kuei-
hua for about $1.30 the ounce, including the tax levied by the
Christian Army.

Besides the opium they had on their saddles, the five Salars
led two pack ponies, so that they must have been convoying
several thousand dollars' worth of a drug that can be sold anywhere, is light to carry and easy to conceal. They looked like
fighting men; a look worth having in their way of life. Opium
runners have to be both reckless and resolute. Most of them
are men of better "bones," as the Chinese say, than common
bandits. They travel in smaller parties and run more risk, since
one of their handy consignments would make a pretty haul for
the bandits themselves. When carrying opium, therefore, they
are always anxious to avoid trouble; but if they are going back
to Kan-su empty-handed they are notoriously ready for the
minor kinds of devilment. On the way down from Kan-su they
usually turn into Mongolia from Ning-hsia, to avoid the Ko-lao
Huei or Elder Brethren bandits who are cocks of the walk
in the Ordos and Yellow River regions. They are splendidly
mounted and travel hard and fast along the unfrequented trails
of Alashan, keeping as far as possible to the cover of desert hills
and sand dunes. They get forage for their ponies, paying more
according to their own mood than the market price, from the
Chinese traders who sell grain to the Mongols.

The men we met were worried about getting their opium into
Kuei-hua. If the victorious armies had already arrived they
might have it confiscated — not to vindicate the law, but for the
benefit of the military. They questioned us eagerly about the
state of the road by which we had come, and told us in turn to
look out for a detachment of three hundred soldiers who were
reported to be collecting camel transport for the retreat of the
Christian Army. We were not in personal danger from the
Salars, though had they known that I had a first-class rifle and
a thousand rounds of ammunition they might not have been able
to refrain from borrowing such a nice toy. Chinese bandits like

---

[1] There are sixteen Chinese ounces in a catty (*chin*), which is equivalent to
one and one-third pounds. This is nominal; but local weights vary a great deal.

to do their work peacefully when they can. If a traveler is met by armed men who want to borrow his money or his pony, those men are bandits; but they will often use neither strong talk nor force, unless they are resisted. No courtesies of this kind passed between us and the hairy adventurers. When we had finished with questions and counter-questions, the Salars camped on the spot, sending one of their number ahead to reconnoitre. We went on our own way, talking over our chances of getting round the next danger point.

# VI

## THE WINDING ROAD

WHEN we had got well out of sight of the opium runners, we camped ourselves, to wait for dark before making the next move. We had passed several huts, and a man rode along from one of them to follow and take counsel with us. Everybody along the Border seemed to be looking for counsel in those days. He was an old man, and the bulk of his business was the selling of dried peas to winter caravans — a delightful kind of dealing which allows a man many months of almost complete idleness and brings in an excellent return.

The Winding Road is so desert that in winter even camels cannot glean a living in between marches, and its most damaging disadvantage, in comparison with the Small and Great Roads, is the heavy loss in camels. Caravans have to take about thirty loads of dried peas for every hundred loads of merchandise. Dried peas at the Kuei-hua end, or barley at the Ku Ch'eng-tze end, make the cheapest feed. The spare camels are loaded with these rations at the outset, and as they are used up the camels are released, so that other loads throughout the caravan can be divided and lightened. Rations have to be taken at all seasons, but winter is the time when the cost to the caravan owner is heaviest. He has then not only to carry feed, but to buy more from the dealers on the road, whose prices are high and who have no bowels of mercy.

Like all of these outlying traders with whom I spoke, this old man lived in resigned fear of the hungry companies of self-disbanded soldiery who might any day descend on him. The times were wrong, and the people must suffer. He told us that we were about a hundred miles north and somewhat west of

Pao-t'ou, and that the main road out of Pao-t'ou converged on our route. He told us also that we were only about ten miles from cultivated land, and that the whole of this rich district had been taken over from the Mongols. The settlers were to move in next year. I take it that the stream in the Valley of Sheep Stations is the Kundu-ling Gol of Prjevalsky, which he places near the boundary of the Dundu-kung (Tungta-kung) *hoshun*. The soil was rich, and the little brook, which passed for a river in Mongolia, made it all the more valuable. So the Mongols were to withdraw from the menace of fields and houses and a life they did not understand; the game would be scared from the pretty hills, and instead of ponies and sheep and white *yurts* there would be only a few squalid villages. To my way of thinking it was tragic.

Chinese encroachment in Mongolia is not a new thing by several centuries. In certain strategic areas it was encouraged by the Manchu Emperors, as when they dragooned the Tumet Mongols of Kuei-hua into subjection and planted there a Manchu garrison and Chinese merchants and peasants to secure that gate of trade and war. When the Christian Army and its militant politicians took over the northwest, a new forward policy was put in force. Its object was partly to shore up the Chinese strategic domination of the contiguous part of Inner Mongolia, all the way from Kalgan to Kan-su, which had been impaired by the loss of Outer Mongolia. The more immediate object, however, was to increase the revenues of the province by providing a new acreage of taxable land and a new tonnage of taxable grain.

According to what I was told by the peasants themselves, Mongol lands were being taken over, under the rule of Feng Yü-hsiang, at a flat rate of a dollar a *mu*.[1] All the land of Mongolia belongs, by one of the fundamental laws of a nomad society, not to any individuals, but to tribes. The only exception is in lands allotted to the upkeep of great monasteries, which have themselves, as it were, the status of tribes. The *shabi* or

---

[1] There are six and six-tenths *mu* to an acre, average measure; but the *mu* is not standardized.

serfs who look after temple herds are taken entirely out of the tribal system; they do not go by tribal names, nor are they subject to tribal authority or taxation.

Of the dollar a *mu*, I was told by different settlers that about eighty cents was kept by the officials through whose hands the money passed, and as all of the remaining twenty cents was probably kept by the Mongol chiefs, the tribe as a whole lost its lands for nothing. The provincial authorities then assessed and divided the land afresh. Good bottom lands were allotted to colonists at $1.60 a *mu*, while poor sandy soil might be rated as low as twenty or thirty cents. In a year or two after they have built their mud villages and broken the virgin soil, the settlers are raising full crops, of which the most important is a variety of oat called *yu-mai*. Oaten flour is the staple food all the year round, not even mitigated with a few fresh vegetables, of the northwestern peasantry and laborers. Even south of the Ta Ch'ing Shan, where a milder climate makes it possible to grow wheat and *kao-liang*, giant millet, these more valuable grains are exported, the peasants preferring the cheaper *yu-mai*.

The published reason for the forward policy in Inner Mongolia did not mention either finance or strategy — the kind of strategy I mean is only finance with a bayonet. A great talk was made of relieving the pressure of population in the interior provinces of China, and of giving the immigrants, who had lived under the shadow of famine, a fresh chance in a larger land. I believe, as I have said, that the process was fostered really because it meant a profit to the officials handling the Mongol negotiations, and to the provincial administration, which found it more satisfactory to collect taxes from settled Chinese than varying dues from a nomadic Mongol population. Although a good deal of notice was attracted by the pronouncement of the Christian General's policy, because it made good public reading, having the right modern and efficient cant, the policy will continue now that the Christian Army has been driven out of the northwest, under any succeeding administration. It is much easier for the officials to make a profit by extending the lowest form of Chinese civilization than by getting the best out of the Mongol civilization, with which they are not in sympathy and for which they recognize no kind of trust.

I call the whole thing a tragedy because it does not give either Chinese or Mongol a fair chance. The Mongols at present are, as a race, at a standstill, if they are not actually dying. Yet with wise treatment they would become again within two generations a proud and self-reliant people. The world needs more and more its pasture lands, to supply civilization with wool and meat and hides. The Mongols, with Russia on one side of them and China on the other, are powerless. As a nation they are unarmed and incoherent. Their political system was cunningly smothered by the Manchu Empire in China during more than two hundred and fifty years. At the same time their social system was atrophied by the artificially stimulated overgrowth of a pampered church. At the present time their ruin is not only being completed, but, in so far as they still come under Chinese influence and authority, they are being wasted. Properly understood and fortified, they would make, in their huge barrier country of mountains and deserts and pastures, the best political defense and buffer between Russians and Chinese, Europeans and Asiatics, on the only field where a dangerous racial contact could be feared.

Nor is it a wise policy to try to cure the economic disorder of China by extending, with the vain idea of thinning it out, the area of its operation. The Chinese who takes up land in Mongolia brings with him his old way of life intact, with all the inherent defects that are bound to produce the old economic depression and misery so soon as the population multiplies. Emigrants from the overcrowded areas of Europe to America, Canada, or Australia find that they have entered new worlds ruled by a higher standard of living. The Chinese does not raise his standard of living. He does not work quite so hard as in the interior provinces, nor is he so close to starvation, but his home is just as squalid, his diseases just as multifarious, his leisure just as empty. Above all, a safe investment for any money he may save is just as hard to find. In his old home, the pressure of crushing numbers is not perceptibly lessened by his emigration. In his new home, if he starts at the age of twenty he will find by the time he is sixty that the embarrassment of an overlarge family group of sons and grandsons, all refusing to abandon their interest in the original farm and all incapable of any kind of work except as farmers or the dullest kind of laborers, is just as harassing in kind, and almost in degree, as it would have been in Ho-nan or Chih-li.

That curious man and sympathetic student of the Orient, Lafcadio Hearn, saw a generation or more ago that the root cause of China's trouble is a low standard of living, caused by overpopulation. He set down in print his logical conviction that the Yellow Peril, then much and foolishly heralded, could never be military, but might exist as the economic danger of huge, unwieldy populations in the East, threatening to drag down the artificially nourished higher standards of the West. The prostration of the Chinese people is due to the almost superstitious veneration of the family, from the ancestral tomb to the newborn son, which is carried out in practice by reckless marrying and begetting. The fine philosophy of the classic Chinese civilization, when interpreted in its lowest terms by the most ignorant and numerous part of the nation, is a fatal thing. In his haste to found a family, attached forever to family land, the Chinese peasant simply cannot comprehend the idea of a fertile leisure, cautious marriage, and the fostering of his sons by enlarging the measure of their opportunities. This vice in Chinese political economy might be corrected by saner marriage customs; certainly never by merely expanding the area of their breeding grounds and burial grounds.

And as I thought these high thoughts I scratched myself, because I was a little raw from sitting on a camel in rain-soaked leather breeches, and wondered how my criticism of political philosophy would appear to the venerable, kindly, foolish, half-copper-saving old grain seller in front of me. In the meantime the Chinese are evicting the Mongols, as near as I can compute, at about the rate of ten miles a year, all along the edge of the red and blue and gold and purple Back Country, behind the Ta Ch'ing Shan.

After starting at dusk we soon emerged from the hills into what seemed, in the dark, to be a perfectly flat and eerily unlimited plain. The dew came down like a shower, and the night smelled cold and clean. It is very tiring to walk at the slow pace of a caravan, and after three or four hours each plodding step seems to jolt through the whole body; but in spite of that, and the subdued excitement in which we had started, the slow rhythm of marching soothed me until it seemed fantastic to think of danger. Once, while we were crossing a wide, shallow, dry river bed, we stampeded a herd of ponies. They fled squealing and snorting across our front, with a wild scramble of hoofs; but though they passed within a few yards I could not see them. The stars overhead were full and luminous, but on the plain the darkness seemed to hang close about us like an intangible curtain.

Then we struck a few small knolls, where we very thoroughly lost the way, though we all bent double as we quartered the ground, peering for a track. At last we made the stolid camels kneel, and off-loaded to wait for moonrise. I spread a felt, wrapped myself in my long Mongol coat, though it was soaked with dew, and seemed to float into sleep. When I woke it was with Moses tugging at my shoulder. Most of the camels had been loaded and were standing up, and the small moon was already high. Our man had found the track not far away, and, feeling chilled and stiff, I stumped along beside the camels, which looked uncanny, huge, and black in the greenish light of the worn-out moon. It was then half-past three, and within an hour I could smell the dawn coming.

We had run into countless antelope. Before it was light they had got up to feed, and we could hear them calling all about us — a queer quacking bleat. As the dawn broke we could see them everywhere, moving dimly through the ground mist; but by the time it was light enough to see the sights of a rifle they would not come within three hundred yards. I had heard of antelope running in vast numbers, but had never imagined the beauty of the sight in a noble dawn. There were a thousand or more of them, scampering away in scattered herds or wheeling into compact bands to turn and stare. Here and there one would buck-jump more than his own height into the air, to get a better view.

At half-past seven we camped. We were in a flat plain, stretching east and west to unbroken horizons, and perhaps fifteen or twenty miles wide. To the south was the blue wall of the Ta Ch'ing Shan, or rather their continuation which Prjevalsky calls the Munni-ola. To the north, four or five miles away, were hills of bare red earth or crumbling stone, which the Mongols called Khatei. We could see Mongol *yurts* scattered about in the distance. As we halted, several hundred unladen camels came up from the Pao-t'ou direction. They had dodged the patrols and were making for the safety of the hills. The soil was coarse and sandy, but there had been plenty of rain, bringing up a good growth of what the Chinese call "sand onions." They have a very delicate spring-oniony taste, with a captivating aroma of garlic. When plucked, no bulb comes up. We used to eat the tubular stems, or leaves, which grow in a bunch to the length of five inches or so, lying close along the ground. They were our only "greens," and we ate them in every kind of way until they were killed off by the frost; but they were most savory fried with brown lumps of mutton fat. All animals eat them greedily; they are considered better than grass pasture, and they give a body and a range to the ordinary stench of a camel that is phenomenal.

All over the plain were ponies; small, like all the ponies of Inner Mongolia, but shapely in build, being lighter in the shoulder than the ponies farther east. The prevailing colors were bays and browns, rather than grays. The Chinese do not care for them, as they rarely make good amblers and are not heavy enough to make good cart ponies. If carefully bred up a little in size, however, I think they would make a very handsome breed. Indeed, it would be an easy matter to improve the size and appearance of Mongol ponies generally, for the fault is not so much in the stock as in the handling they get. Mares' milk is not only a favorite drink of the Mongols, but is made into cheese for winter use, while all during the summer it is fermented to make *kumis*. The foals are therefore stinted of milk before they are able to graze for themselves, so that they are never properly fitted to face their first two winters. The lack of enough milk and the great cold together stunt their growth; the bones, instead of growing long and shapely, becoming thick and coarse.

Ponies, moreover, do not mature so rapidly as horses. They do not reach their full growth until between six and seven years; even an eight-year-old, if well fed and treated, will sometimes grow as much as an inch. The Mongols, however, begin to ride them when they are two years old, preferring the easier paces of a young pony. I fancy this may have something to do with the coarseness of the shoulders, because the Mongol puts his saddle right on the withers and then carries his weight well forward, in a way that is as hard as possible on the pony. Breeding is at random, neither stallions nor mares being under any control, with the result that mares mate in about their fourth year, which has also a bad effect on the breed. Ponies are gelded at three years. The Mongols hold that they are in their prime at seven, but the race is so hardy that ponies are fit for hard service up to and beyond twenty years.

Like all nomads except the Arabs, the Mongols pay no attention to mares, nor yet to stallions, but prefer geldings.[1] Their breeding stock also suffers from the way in which they allow the best and tallest mares to be bought out of the herds by Chinese, who use them for breeding mules. The Mongols themselves almost never breed mules, even where they have numbers of donkeys; but in China a big mule is always worth more than a big pony. A mule eats less, does more work either in the shafts or under a pack, and stands rougher usage. The full load for a pack mule is 320 pounds, against 375 to 400 for a camel, and the mule does the day's journey in not much more than half the time. It cannot, however, go much faster over a journey of

---

[1] The Arab regard for mares, and habit of tracing pedigree by the mare, is of commercial origin. Not having wide, free pastures, like the Central Asian nomads, they do not keep herds of untamed horses breeding uncontrolled. Most of the few horses owned by each Arab family are mares, from which they breed stock for sale. They are thus able to decide the mating of each mare, and to keep pedigrees.

many days, live quite so meagrely, nor suffer such extreme cold; and it must have water every day.

I spent about an hour in this kind of talk with two young Mongols who had ridden up to visit us. Then I went off with one of them (Moses insisted that the other stay in the tent, as a hostage, for fear something should happen to me) to try stalking antelope under cover of a led pony. This is a great trick with the Mongols; but the countless herds I had seen in the morning had vanished as if under a spell. We saw only one doe, with her kid, but she would have nothing to do with ponies. Most of the morning I had spent in a weary chase, but there was no cover at all, and even when the herds lay down, at about ten o'clock, having finished their feeding, there were always a few restless sentinels. The Mongol who was with me in the afternoon told me I might have known it was useless. From him, and others after him, I learned that by the Mongol way of thinking it is not right to fire at antelope, nor at wild asses, when they are in big herds. It may be that the soul of a saint or a Buddha has passed into the body of a wild animal, whose holiness gathers the others about it in great numbers. A Mongol will spend a great deal of time first breaking up a herd and then going after two or three evidently profane animals which have separated, rather than run the risk of shooting a "magic" creature.

From these two Mongols we heard that, of the three hundred soldiers of whom we had been warned, a detachment of about thirty had passed this way, gathering camels to take back to Pao-t'ou. Twenty of them had since gone back, with several hundred camels. The other ten had moved on, and were still ahead of us. The Mongols had driven away their own camels into the hills, but to no purpose. Their head men had been curtly ordered by the military to provide a stated number of camels, or stand the consequences. They had decided that the best thing for them to do was to part with some of their wealth, hoping to get rid of the trouble as quickly as might be; for these Mongols here were of the Hsi-kung, one of the *hoshun* of the Oirat, who have never been so independent as the Mao Mingan or the Mongols about Pai-ling Miao.

A little before sunset, therefore, we started on our final effort to get round the soldiers and leave the war behind us. We were to make a forced march, to get round a temple which the camel men, with their usual cheerful mixture of Chinese and Mongol, call Heiliutuho Miao. A number of the trails coming out of Kuei-hua and Pao-t'ou unite in this plain, in the Small Road, or southern branch of the Great Road. It leads along the base of the hills which we had on our north; a fine free road, marked by a dozen paths worn deep through the turf, trodden out by untold numbers of camels through untold scores of years. "This," said the camel men mournfully, "is what we should have the best part of the way to Ku Ch'eng-tze, did we not have to turn off along the Winding Road. Mongols every day, visitors, meat, milk — that was the good life. The road is plain in front of you with no passes to climb, and there is pasture stage by stage. A good road for camels and men; but wait till you see the Winding Road. Where it is not dunes it is stony Gobi; no people to see, and bitter water to drink."

As we were not sure where the soldiers might be, though we thought they would be near the monastery, we were to leave the main road for a more difficult way, taking us for a few miles through the northern hills. Then, if there were an alarm in passing the monastery, we might have time to hide in a side valley. First of all we held a rehearsal, at which everyone was primed with the right lies to tell if we should run into the soldiers. It was decided to rely on the waning but perhaps not altogether forgotten Christianity of the dispersing army. I was to be a missionary, bound for the conversion of the west. Moses, who never shirks an emergency, and whose vocabulary is universally geared, was my native preacher. All the camels had been specially furnished to me by the most Christian of the generals who had not yet run away from Kuei-hua.

Thus fortified, we commended ourselves to our fortune. Myself, I was ready to bluff the soldiery as the Living Corpse, or whatever else might most excite compassion. I had been on foot or on a pony from dawn to sunset, trying to get a shot at antelope, so that except for my brief nap under the lee of a

dew-drenched camel the night before I had been without sleep
for about thirty-six hours. First I tried to sit on the load on my
camel without falling asleep and falling off. Then I tried to
walk without falling asleep and falling down. At last, getting
on the camel again, I laid myself across the load with my feet
over his neck and my head over his rump (it is harder to sleep
on a camel with one's head to the front, because the balance is
wrong) and, twisting my arms among the cordage, entrusted
myself to sleep and luck.

I woke at two in the morning to hear the hounds of hell on the
camels' traces. We were passing the trading posts near the
monastery. Here Suji played up beautifully. Among caravan
dogs it is no shame for even the most truculent to be deprecatingly mild when they are on the ground of another pack; but
Suji took on all comers, even stopping to continue the debate
after we had passed, at a quickened pace, with much vain
s-s-s-sh-ing. The camel bell was muffled, and if we were near
the soldiers they must have thought it no more than a common
row among the local doggery. We did not camp until we had
marched the whole night through, to the verge of dawn.

We lay up for the daylight hours among low, smooth, utterly
barren hills of clay and sand. I heard several names for the
place, of which the most used was Gaidsegai-hutu. I should
have thought we were well hidden even from Mongol eyes, but
later in the morning we found the men of a large caravan squatting disconsolately among their loads a scant half-mile away.
They had been coming from the west, with only vague rumors
of the trouble about Kuei-hua, when the roving patrol from
which we were hiding had caught them, and taken every camel
away.

To my consternation, it looked like rain that day. There is
nothing that the Chinese hate more than rain. If it begins when
a caravan is on the march, they will sometimes hold on, hoping
that it will stop before they have to go into camp; but if there
is a threat of rain when they are in camp, it takes an Act of God
to make them move. My camel man refused to budge, preferring a dry capture to a wet march. As he had marched without

complaint during the rain of the first few days' journey, it may
have been that he was getting apathetic after all the alarms we
had had; or he may have thought the patrol would not come
back at once to a spot where they had made a good haul, and
where the caravan they had left sitting would certainly warn
everyone who passed. Perhaps, even, we were safe all the time,
by the rules of the game; for if a Chinese with valuable camels
to lose will not run in the rain, who would expect a Chinese
soldier to go out in the rain to catch him?

A little rain did fall, and it was six the next morning before
we started. Coming down after several hours on to the main
road again, we camped by a pool of water, brackish and rimmed
with white chemical deposits. There was a lamasery in distant
sight, to the south, which our men knew as Hoshatu Miao. *Miao*
is the Chinese for temple, and *hoshatu*, I was told, is a Mongol
word common in place names, meaning a *col* or hause between
two hills. From here there are caravan ways southeast to
Pao-t'ou and southwest to Alashan, and from this point I heard
the name of Ulangangan for the hills to the south of us.

We started again the same afternoon, and covered an honest
twenty-five miles before camping; but at the camp we reached
we spent three fretful days. My man was unwilling to turn off
on the Winding Road without a guide, yet no caravan came by.
It was not a pleasant camp. There was a high wind all the time,
and though there was plenty of water from a pool, it smelled
faintly but persistently of urine. Mongols were scattered about
near us, who came in the evening to water their ponies; but they
kept to themselves. They told us that most of their slow-moving
sheep had been driven farther away, and they were ready to
follow if things took a bad turn. My only comfort was that a
caravan passed, going slowly toward Kuei-hua and waiting for
a chance to get in safely. They took a mail for me which they
got into Kuei-hua (they refused payment), whence it was forwarded to my wife in Peking.

The rest of the time I spent in reading Yule's *Marco Polo*
and making a catalogue of my deficiencies from the *Hints to
Travellers* of the Royal Geographical Society. I think I had

bought it with the idea that it would be something in the same sort as a fascinating book, Galton's *Art of Travel*, frequently referred to in Shaw's *High Tartary and Yarkand*, which seems to have been full of Swiss Family Robinson tricks. I was sure that the *Hints* would at least tell me how to find the north from the hands of a watch, like a Boy Scout, and perhaps, like Galton, how to make gunpowder and such graver marvels. Instead, I found Isobaric Maps and the Minimum Requirements for Weather Observation. I learned also with chagrin that my cameras were inadequate and my armory of all the wrong calibres; but I must give the Royal Geographical Society a lot of marks for one thing on their list — a No. 1 Saloon Pistol, with dust shot, for shooting lizards. I should never have thought of that one.

On the other hand, some of their ideas on the best ways of killing the most things simply made me snigger, which in a Serious Traveler was wrong; I mean which phials and whatnots for insects I was to carry in each of my waistcoat pockets; which extra gun and kinds of ammunition were to be carried by the First Bearer, and which fishing rod and butterfly net by the Second Bearer. Moses, it was true, might have been funny as First Bearer; but to do the thing on the right scale I should have had to ape those sultans of modern travel who have motor transport and mobs of camp followers and as many auxiliaries as a Kaiserliches-Königliches Kriegspiel (old style). The only travelers of that brand who tried to get into Mongolia that year did not get farther than Kalgan. As for this business of being a Serious Traveler in Good Standing, I will, on reflection, resign all pretensions. *Conspuez* the First Bearer, the Second Bearer, the odds and ends and all the supernumerary ranks. The only thing I regret is the lizard shooting; but I prefer my own vagabondage, with plain Moses in support, who had a hankering to go forth and see the world with his master's son. "Can't curl, can swim, slow-stolid, that's him."

All the same, by the end of the three days that we spent at that pointless camp I was in a black depression. We were not making fast time toward Ku Ch'eng-tze, we were not sure of a guide for the most difficult part of the journey, and I was beginning to find out that my camel man was a thorough rogue. At last, however, we broke camp at a venture, and the march lifted my depression like a charm. I walked ahead of the caravan until dark, looking for antelope. The country was a little hilly, and when the sun set the afterglow lingered for a long half-hour, flaming through the gaps of a distant range on our front, the Lao-hu Shan. Then, against the sky line, I saw two antelope, feeding. It was already too dim to get the sights of my rifle on them, but I was trying for an approximate aim at the silhouette when they heard the far-away clank of the camel bell. One made a beautiful stiff-legged jump high up against the orange and saffron of the sky. Then the two of them trotted obliquely toward me and were blotted out as if by magic in the pool of darkness under the shoulder of the hill.

At last, in that glimmering light by which one learns to guess at things by night, I could see that there was a division of the trail. A caravan was camped not far away and when we had staved off the rush of their dogs their men told us that we must go to the south. In another mile or two we reached a camping ground among low barren hills, called Morhgujing. It was a decisive march. We were at the beginning of the Winding Road.

# VII

## OVER THE BORDERS OF ALASHAN

MORHGUJING is like a gate to the desert. We were encamped by a mass of low, barren hills, of some formation of compressed sand, which fills up the angle where the Winding Road deviates from the Small Road. This mass tailed off into a ridge running to the south, in which there was a gap about fifty yards wide and not more than a quarter of a mile long, between two little hills like fortresses; and in the little pass was a spring.

We were getting ready for the start when one of the Chinese called me out of the tent excitedly, asking me if my rifle would shoot wild sheep. Across the rock face of one of the hills guarding the gap five *argal* were advancing in echelon — all of them young rams. They must have traveled far to reach this water, because the hills out of which they had come looked too low for bighorn and were without any grass. The "heads" that they carried were not big, but they carried them with an insolent, challenging grace, walking not like silly sheep but with the sure freedom of deer. They stopped now and then to stare calmly down at the busy camps on the floor of the plain. The distance was well over three hundred yards, so I thought it better not to risk a shot, but to let them pass round the face of the hill on their way to the water. The last of them paused on a ledge, marked clearly against the sky, looking back to see if anyone were coming that way. Evidently that was not enough. Wild sheep are the most canny of game. They must have posted a sentry, for when I gained some rocks that commanded the water I heard, after a long wait, the faint sound of a stone tumbling down a hill, and with the glasses I saw the five rams, not so foolhardy as they had seemed, making fast into the barren hills.

We joined here a caravan from Pao-t'ou, which at last assured us of company on the road, and fell in behind them at the start. Passing through the narrow valley, we found on the far side a great sweep of open country going to the south, and small hills on our right front, extending from the knot of hills at Morhgujing. Here was a great cairn of rocks, with lines of small cairns leading up to it from the south and north. This was Ulangangan Obo, which marks roughly the end of the Ulangangan range that had lain to the south of us for several marches, showing that we had crossed over the western extremity of the range. Ulangangan Obo has attached to it a *verboten* that distinguishes, I am told, many important *obo* in Mongolia. No man may cover his feet,[1] as one of the more veiled phrases of the Authorized Version has it, with his face toward the *obo;* were he to face it, the Immanent Deity of the High Place would smite him with a paralysis.

There was a strong, warm, westerly wind blowing, which brought with it a dense haze which I suppose was dust, though it was so fine that it was not harsh to the skin. It is true that I found my ears full of dust that evening, but I am so unscientific an observer that I do not know whether it was the accumulation of those few hours or of the previous week. This dry mist was so thick that a man could look easily at the sun, which gleamed like a disk of white brass. My camel man said that it was the portent of dreadful times, for there had been nothing like it for twenty-six years — that is, not since the year of the Boxer Rising.

After going about ten miles through a hummocky country with a downward trend, covered with a creeping thorny growth, we camped with a range of mountains across our immediate front. These were the Lao-hu Shan or Tiger Mountains. We had seen them the day we left the Small Road, after which they had been hidden from sight by the low hills about Ulangangan Obo. Along the foot of the range the ground was more alive, with sparse grazing in between the hummocks. Here were

---

[1] The Mongols and Central Asian peoples do in practice cover their feet with their long gowns, being in this respect more modest than the Chinese.

Mongol ponies and camels, though no *yurts* were in sight, and I could see far away to the north, halfway up the ramp of the mountains, the white bulk of a monastery. There was a Chinese trader living in a *yurt* near our camp, from whom I tried to hire a lad to drive antelope for me the next morning. I had marked down a large herd, but the trader did not fall in with my way of thinking, because he wanted me to buy a sheep from him, and not a very large or fat sheep, for the outrageous price of ten dollars. This is the way along the Winding Road, in the few places where sheep can be bought; a sheep that would not bring three and a half dollars after being driven all the way to Kuei-hua sells on the spot for an average price of ten dollars. The caravans must have meat, or the men will get sulky, and they must pay the price or go without.

I set out by myself with a sigh, for I was by this time well aware of the difficulty of shooting antelope in a country without stalking cover. One of the surest ways of getting antelope is to have them driven, if the driving is properly done. The "beater" must not go at his work in a hurry, or the game will bolt wildly; but if he rides or strolls in a careless way, with due regard for the wind, he can put the antelope slowly up wind toward the man in ambush. My herd was right away in the open, so I went down resignedly on Napoleon's army's marching place. Two camels at once came over to see what I was doing, and nearly stepped where I prefer to sit. I could not scare them away with the yells I felt like uttering, because of the antelope. Nor could I catch one to use as a stalking horse, for, being Mongol-owned camels turned out to graze for an indefinite time, neither of them had a cord attached to the peg in his nose. I turned over therefore on my back and flipped bits of dung at them until they went away, snorting with a muffled subhumorous noise. I went on belly-hitching toward the antelope, but the hummocks were only about six inches high and they got restless while I was yet at an impossible range, getting up and making short, nervous runs until a peevish and useless bullet from me sent them off for good.

This would be a fine shooting ground to visit from Pao-t'ou, from which it could be reached in a week. It is far away from trouble, the lamasery to the north would certainly be worth a visit, and there is game in plenty which could be got at by any-one staying on the ground, though it is tantalizingly out of the reach of a traveler camping for half a day. The trader there had a lot of roebuck horns, which he said came from these mountains; these are a cheap substitute for the elk antlers for which Chinese medicine shops pay such high prices. Besides roebuck there are many wild sheep — the Inner Mongolian *ovis ammon*. Low down in the hills I found their winter lying-up places under sheltered rocks; I saw five rams through my glasses, and at pools in the pass I saw the slots of many. One, by the marks of him, must have been one of those huge old rams "bigger than a donkey" that so many Chinese and Mongol hunters like to talk about and so few foreigners have seen. The hills, in fact, are ideal sheep ground, and there is no reason why the finest kind of rams should not be found there.

Moreover, the range is new ground geographically. According to the Chinese it links up on the south with the Lang Shan, a western extension of the Ta Ch'ing Shan, overlooking the Yellow River; but of its northern continuation they are not certain. It would appear, however, from a comparison of the accounts of Prjevalsky[1] and Younghusband[2] that the Lao-hu Shan are an offshoot of the Lang Shan (the Khara-narin of Prjevalsky) and that they connect with the Hurku range of these two travelers, thus completing a rough arc from southeast to northwest or west-northwest. Prjevalsky sketches in the Hurku at the point where he crossed it from south to north, on his way from Alashan to Urga. He was told that it continued all the way to the Khara-narin on the south. He found that the range, which was about seven miles in depth, marked an important physical change from depressed sandy deserts on the southerly side to something more like true steppe country on the north. The next bearing is from Younghusband, who first crossed what he understood to be the eastern extremity of the Hurku and then had it

[1] *Mongolia, the Tangut Country and the Solitudes of Northern Thibet.*
[2] *The Heart of a Continent.* London: John Murray, 1896.

running on his north for many marches.  He made the crossing
on his twenty-third day out from Kuei-hua (I crossed the
Lao-hu Shan on my sixteenth march) and three days later
reached Prjevalsky's line of march at the Bortsum or Bortson
well.  Thus Prjevalsky's crossing of the Hurku was at a point
northwest of Younghusband's crossing, which again was northwest of my crossing of the Lao-hu Shan.  It seems probable
that what Younghusband calls the "Eastern extremity" of the
Hurku is more properly to be understood as a dip between the
Hurku proper and the Lao-hu Shan; but, since by a comparison
of accounts the Hurku seems to have a rather more desert character than the Lao-hu, it is perhaps better to distinguish the
names.

Our camp was at the foot of the pass, the Tiger Pass.  It is
easy, and the camels made almost as good going as if they had
been on the flat.  I saw one very old elm, the only tree.  The
hills were of some gray, living rock, not at all like the old decayed rock of the lower ranges that had lain parallel with our
route.  In three hours we had reached the top of the pass, a
small plateau grown with excellent sweet grass.  It was broken
by outcrops of the gray rock, curiously smoothed and hollowed
and covered with orange lichen.  The dogs, ahead of the caravan, put up a pair of antelope.

We came down the western declivity in the last glow of a
sunset colored so subtly and so demurely assembled that it took
me a long time to find the key that held it all together — the new
moon, in a pale, thin, shell-blue upper sky.  Under it, long and
low and even, was a far-away range of mountains: part of the
Lang Shan, in another tone of blue, soft and smoky.  Along
their crest, to one side, smoldered the tawny color of the sunset, fading to saffron under the moon.  I watched for a while
from some rocks, in a delicious melancholy, while Suji huddled
against my knees.  Then the caravan came up over the pass and
drifted down by me — one hundred and fifty camels at least,
mine at the end — with the clangor of their bells pulsing through
the pastel evening.  I climbed on my camel and swayed and
bobbed through the afterglow and the twilight, while the young

moon withdrew, leaving a sort of pervading reflected resplendence among the gleaming stars.

> *Un vaste et tendre apaisement*
> *Semble descendre du firmament*
> *Que l'astre irise. . . .*
> *C'est l'heure exquise.*

Sometimes, I think, what draws me more than anything else to travel is the melancholy of it — a winelike melancholy, tenuous but soft, like the delicate, plangent, muted syllables of Verlaine, fortuitously remembered in a Mongolian sunset.

The Lao-hu Shan stand out from the desert with vigor and life. Between them and the next hills there was a wide shallow, through which ran here and there the aimless channels of dry streams. We camped at a place called Chagan-erlegen, which, I was told, meant White Springs; but in spite of the name we had to dig for water. We found it in plenty, digging down only about a foot in the bed of a stream, but it was a little bitter and a little salty. The country was of a poor soil, sandy and coarse, through which the rains of summer drain quickly away. The commonest growth was a low desert plant with a leafage faintly like a miniature evergreen frond. The caravan men call it either *chien-ts'ao* — soda grass — or *hsien-ts'ao* — salt grass. It is good for camels if they do not have to go too long without water, and donkeys can stick it for a while; but it is poor stuff for ponies. The roots burn quickly with a bright hot flame, sometimes turning blue because of the salt impregnation. The plant is one of many which travelers call by the Tibetan name of *burtsa*. The genuine *burtsa* seems to be a kind of sage, though Shaw[1] calls it the "lavender plant"; but indeed the soda plant has a little the look of a savage and crude lavender.

We left in the afternoon of a windless, cloudless day and camped before midnight of a cloudless, windless night, after a stage of about sixteen miles, at a place called both Modaching (or Modajing) and Khara-terugen. The second name belongs more properly to the hill country we were about to enter than

---

[1] *Visits to High Tartary, Yarkand and Kashghar*, by Robert Shaw. London: John Murray, 1871.

17. CAMP AT MOHRGUJING
"It was a decisive march. We were at the beginning of the
Winding Road." (p. 95)

18. LAO-HU K'OU (TIGER PASS): CARAVAN WITH ITS
INSIGNIA SPEAR
"It means that the caravan . . . makes itself responsible for the safe arrival of
goods and travelers." (p. 153)

to this camping ground, and means, as I was told, Black Hill-tops.[1] The water was brackish, but it must have been as good as any other in the neighborhood, for near us were a few *yurts* and a Chinese trader. In the distance, on the slope of the hills away from our route, was a monastery. I remember the camp well because here Moses, having washed my socks to get his hands clean, made me some scones — without butter, eggs, or milk — with some of my little supply of baking powder.

Again there was neither wind nor cloud, all day long, though there was an angry claret sunset and the night sky was covered with clouds. Far away, to the south and southwest, was a last blue glimpse of the Ta Ch'ing Shan system, or rather of the Lang Shan, which we had seen laid out before us from the top of Lao-hu K'ou; but they were hidden soon after we started by the Khara-terugen, a mass of low, broken hills with outcrops of black rock. They are a northern excrescence of the Khara-narin or western Lang Shan.

The *lang* in the name of the Lang Shan is not from the word meaning wolf, but from an honorific title for young men of good birth. The mountains are associated with Chinese legends of the Pa Lang, eight brothers who are the heroes of a whole cycle of mythology, mostly concerned with the wars of defense and conquest between the Chinese and the border tribes. Erh Lang, the second brother, was the most celebrated of the eight, and the mountains are named for him.[2] The legend which recites this history explains that in the days when Kuei-hua was Kuku-khoto, and the power in that valley belonged to the Ta-tze,[3] the Chinese frontier was set at the mountains south of Kuei-hua,

---

[1] The name compares interestingly with Khara-narin, the name which Prjeval-sky heard for the Western Lang Shan and for which he was given the meaning "black pointed mountains."

[2] Younghusband heard the name Lang-lang-shan (*sc.* Liang-lang Shan) or Eurh-lang-shan (*sc.* Erh-lang Shan) much farther to the east, applied to the Sheiteng Ola, which are, properly speaking, intermediate between the Ta Ch'ing Shan and the Lang Shan and are more commonly called by the Chinese Wu-la Shan — *i.e.* Mountains of the Oirat. (Rockhill, *Diary*.) *Liang* is two and *erh* is second (also, in some uses, two). Evidently Younghusband's guide was trying to explain that these were the Mountains of the Second Lang.

[3] *Ta-tze* is probably equivalent to Tatar. In modern use it rarely means anything but Mongol, or sometimes Manchu, but in legend it includes the pre-Mongol nomad invaders. Most Mongol tribes resent the term, as do the Manchus; a few accept it.

which are in our day the northern boundary of Shan-hsi Province proper. The border wars, however, swept back and forth across these mountains; as is proved by the monuments of the fifth-century Wei Tatar kingdom at Ta-t'ung, and the fact that the Wu-t'ai Shan, even farther to the south, where the population is entirely Chinese, are still centres of Mongol pilgrimage.

At last the Chinese hosts, under Erh Lang, were so far successful that the barbarians were willing to settle the boundary afresh and make peace. The condition proposed by the wily Erh Lang was that he was to shoot an arrow to the north, and wherever the arrow fell all land to the south was to be ceded to the Chinese, and the nomads — Mongol or Tunguz or whatever they may have been at that time — were to withdraw to the north. This condition having been accepted by the barbarians (it is characteristic that in legends of this sort the barbarian is made to appear a terrible fellow in war and violence,[1] but always put down in the end by the address and guile of the Chinese, the only heir of the only authentic civilization), Erh Lang brought forth his mighty bow and shot an arrow. The arrow fell out of sight and the search for it then began; but in this Erh Lang had laid his plan for triumph. He sent a swift mounted messenger secretly, bearing the double of the arrow that had been shot, and this arrow the messenger planted, as some say, in the Ta Ch'ing Shan, or, as others say, in the Lang Shan — but at any rate somewhere in that linked chain of ranges that crowns the southern escarpment of the Mongolian plateau. The barbarians, once duped, were docile. They withdrew, and that, they say, is how the Chinese tide first began to overflow the wide gap between the Shan-hsi hills and what are now the confines of true Mongolia. In spite of growing Chinese domination, however, the Mongols never wholly evacuated the old dominions. They are still to be found well to the south of the Yellow River (notably in the Ordos), but, on the other hand, the choice lands

[1] Compare the legend of the Fifteenth of the Eighth Moon, concerning the downfall of the Yüan (Mongol) dynasty in North China; in which, as it is commonly told, the Mongols are said to have used the Chinese as riding cattle. Ten Chinese families (this is pure legend, not history) were allotted as helots to support each Mongol; but on the Fifteenth of the Eighth Moon, at a concerted signal they rose and slaughtered their oppressors.

between the Lang Shan and the Yellow River have long been penetrated by the Chinese, and the chief Mongol interest there now, though the land is of undeniably Mongolian character, is in the numerous and still wealthy lamaseries.[1]

At the beginning of the march we entered the Black Hilltops, and rising slowly into open plateau country, over greener and better pasture, we reached at about eight miles a valley in which there was running water. We crossed the stream, started up another valley, and camped at about nineteen miles; the valleys, after closing in, had opened out again, but we were still among the hills. A few Mongols were camped here, but they could give us no name for the camping ground, as they were strangers who had migrated from farther east because of the troubles. Their camels, though saved from the soldiery, had not been able to put on good condition. Our own camels, for several days, had not been able to get a bellyful during the few hours when they were turned out to feed. Throughout this part of the journey we were much at a loss for names, there not being a single veteran of the Winding Road among us. We depended for guidance on the leading camel puller of the Pao-t'ou caravan, who had been over the road several times; but though he knew his directions and distances he did not know the local names. The next march took us into much more broken country, where the gullies were so narrow that they made difficult the passage of laden camels, for the brutes at the end of each string, edging always to the side to look for grass, would bump and drag their loads against the rocks. We had to halt soon after the moon set, at ten o'clock.

We had a bad time pitching the tent because my camel man, stepping out to place a tent peg, fell over himself into a dry watercourse and thereafter nearly fell in again with a camel on top of him. His eyes had been giving him and the rest of us a

[1] From the Buddhist monastery temple of Ta Chüeh Ssu, in the Western Hills near Peking, a tower can be seen on the crest of a hill; it is called the tower of Erh Lang. It is of solid masonry construction and may have been a beacon tower built at a time when Peking itself was within striking distance of Mongol raiders.

I heard a fragment of a curious tradition relating to Liu Lang, the sixth brother; he is said in his old age to have feared death at the hands of the Mongols and to have turned monk and gone into a monastery or lamasery at Wu-t'ai Shan. The place is significant in view of its Mongol associations.

great deal of trouble. Throughout the journey they were apt to be obscured for a few days at a time with a faint rheumy film. I thought for a while he might have the beginnings of cataract, but Moses said that every man has in the pupils of his eyes two little men, the *t'ung-jen*. If you look in any man's eyes you can see them. If the two little men turn their backs, one goes blind. The trouble with the camel man, he said, was that his *t'ung-jen* were beginning to turn round — that is, the film made them less distinct. Whenever the affliction was on him, the man complained that, though he could still see distant objects plainly, everything near at hand was a blur, while at night he was almost totally blind. He would stumble and fall continually on the march, trip over loads and tent ropes in camp, and damage his shins, his hands, and his temper. I gave him a boracic acid wash, which he insisted on making into a paste with flour and applying to the undersides of his eyelids with a straw; afterwards complaining that it did him no good. Nor did he get any better after having his forehead shaved, though this is held by all Chinese to be a tonic treatment for the eyesight. The best strengthening diet for the eyes, however, and indeed for the whole system, is boiled liver; but especially the liver of a black goat, sheep, or cow. When I questioned them more closely about this they admitted that it was not always a direct cure; it was more like a preventive, a fortifying treatment — in fact, what they called a "slanting cure." Later I met a man who had been suffering from swollen legs; but he took a rest, riding as much as possible, and at the first opportunity he bought a black goat, for the sake of its liver. In a few days he was much better.

I was told later that somewhere in this region — probably in the main Lang Shan, south of our passage — there is a group of three holy peaks. On the central peak is a rock bearing the imprint of the face of a saint called Börhungwulu.[1] I say imprint

---

[1] I spell the name as nearly as possible as I heard it, from my Chen-fan Wa-wa. There is a curious resemblance between this name and the name of the peak given by Kozloff as Burkhan-Buddha, in the southeastern Altai, at about 46° N., 96° E. The Chen-fan Wa-wa spoke a soft, slurred southern Alashan dialect of Mongol. In some border districts the Mongol pronunciation seems to be softened until words are pronounced almost as the Chinese pronounce them — as, for instance, *hala* for *khara*.

rather than carving, because this appears to be connected with the very ancient legend of a saint sitting in meditation before a rock and impressing his image on it.  The approach to the peak is over a log laid across a chasm between it and the next height.  The crossing of this log is a test of the true piety of pilgrims.  Even lamas are not excepted; for a certain lama who got drunk, and took a woman up with him as well, fell off the log and became a warning to sinners.

The next day I lay out in the sun with my Homer before me, but very soon my thoughts drifted from

> heroes tall
> Dislodging pinnacle and parapet
> Upon the tortoise creeping to the wall,

by reason that it was the fifteenth of September and the birthday of a friend with whom I used to stay at Pei-tai Ho, that shoddy Simla-cum-Kendal-Revival by the Gulf of Pei Chih-li.  There Ministers of Legation from Peking hoist their flags for the summer, and the Diplomatic Body *in partibus infidelium* resting from the strict routine of dancing, scandal, and gambling, refreshes itself with swimming, gambling, and scandal.  There also come the women and children from Tientsin, because the " climate of Tientsin is so hard on Europeans."  There also the women take the children to the station to meet the evening train, if father is coming down; or go by themselves in something rather specially pretty if father is not coming down until next week-end.  There, moreover, the missionaries come for a " rest " — because missionaries never take an out-and-out holiday.  It is a snug little, smug little world, all complete with circulating libraries, a calling system, and revival meetings.  There is usually a gunboat in attendance, because of the diplomats and the flags, and there is a reassuring convention by which Chinese civil warriors usually leave it alone.

I remembered Pei-tai Ho with a great deal of pleasure.  I remembered my friend with a sudden vividness; I imagined the terraced garden going down to the sand, the moonlight on the calm bay, and maybe the lights of a gunboat full of polite

Italians in the — what d' you call it? — offing.   Probably I had my orders not to come to dinner without putting on shoes and stockings.   Anyhow, there would be cocktails in chilled frosty glasses, brought by the Olo Boy, and about the time that mosquitoes began to pay really earnest attention to one's ankles the children would come down from the verandah to say good night.   After that, in a screened-off corner of the verandah, as if under a monster mosquito net, would be served the Best Cooking in North China — an important memory, as I remembered it then.   Conscious of my integrity in wearing not only shoes, stocking, and white flannels, but even a tie; comfortably assured that my nails did not want cleaning, thank God, because I had been in the sea all day, I would watch in the glow of the candles the only Great Lady in North China. . . .

And then it was time to take down the tent, watch the camels being loaded and the loads cleverly hitched with a peg through two pairs of hinging loops, and take the road again.

The force of old memories revived had set me dreaming again, through a wonderful evening, out in front of the caravan in the dusk, the moonlight, and the starlight.   I balanced for the first time all the contrasts of the bastard treaty-port life; Tientsin, Peking, Pei-tai Ho, with Kuei-hua and the first glorious reconnoitring that my wife and I shared of the borderland behind the Kuei-hua hills; and then this drifting life of the caravans.   The feeling bore down on me like a wave that I was a long way off and going farther; that I had been in China so long that I had lost the feeling of Home, but that I was going Home all across Asia, by roads that men traveled before the sea roads were known.   The camels and the long road, with glimpses, before the sun set, of rolling country and a world without end, were the fulfillment of an old ambition, but they became suddenly tinged with the emotion of a new dream.

Those were high days for dreaming, before the cold began and the really arduous marches.   Part of the magic of Mongolia is in the satisfying physical joy of immersion in the life of monotonous fatigue and simple laziness; the shifting landscapes, the feeling of bodily exaltation in the proud distances and swinging marches. Part of it is in learning the tone and spirit of men whose crude but tradition-informed manners and society are only a rough balancing of physical needs : in long, idle talking not made brittle and false by thought, and in longer, idler silences. Part of it, for me, was in the luminous, dissevered hours when patches of dream and memory hung like a light, unreal veil between me and the more urgent potency of the desert world.

Moses and I, having outdistanced the camels, sat on our hunkers waiting for the caravan to overtake and pass us, that we might get on our own riding camels. Moses, good fellow, after saying bluntly that he wished my father could see me, did not talk. The caravan, overhauling us, seemed to fall into a stupendous rhythm, file after file striding by impressive with the great bulk and silent pace of camels. When at last our little caravan came up, and I settled myself on top of the load, I felt the sway of a new rhythm, with the clank and throbbing ring of one bell behind me and the mingled shaken clamor of many bells before me. Another night, another stage; all time seemed to beat like a pulse. The living light in the west withered and withdrew, the unreal moonlight shimmered in the southwest, and we headed boldly into that silver tide. The sound of the camel bells haunted all that march, for there was no wind beneath the stars and I could tell the overlapping tones of the several bells as the vibrant melody sped through the night, like successive stone-started ripples creeping across a pond.

We halted a little short of a great monastery called Shandan Miao, having cleared the Black Hilltops and completed the first major division of the journey to Turkestan. Shandan Miao is marked on Prjevalsky's map, so that from its position I can relate my route to those taken by other travelers, and sketch in the relation of the Great, the Small, and the Winding Roads. Unfortunately I was not able to study Prjevalsky before I left Peking. I had no adequate maps with me, nor was it possible to make the roughest kind of sketches as I went. I was often taken for a spy; had I been seen drawing lines on paper I should have been taken for a dangerous spy and reported to authorities who would almost certainly have impeded me. I can therefore take the geography between Kuei-hua and Shandan Miao only in its broad sweep.

Among the limited data available on the trade routes through Mongolia some of the most interesting are certain figures published by the Chinese Government Bureau of Economic Affairs, at Peking. According to these figures (stated in *li*, which I have converted into miles at the rough equivalent of three *li* to one mile) we have: —

1797 miles from Kuei-hua to Ku Ch'eng-tze by the Great Road; divided into 71 nominal stages of 60 to 100 *li*. (As a matter of fact heavy caravans regularly take as much as 120 days; "express" caravans carrying merchandise at a premium under guaranteed time limit take 90 days; and for travelers going very light and marching *k'ua-ch'i-ch'eng*, which may be rendered by "one forced march after another," 70 days is good quick time.)

923 miles by the Small Road from Chao Ho to Khara-niuto, where the Small Road merges again in the Great Road: taken as 35 stages. The difference in the distance by the two roads up to this point is given as about 46 miles. (I myself heard it stated that it was "about 40" stages by either Small or Great Road from Pailing Miao to Khara-niuto. This referred to heavy caravans.)

317 miles from Kuei-hua to Morhgujing, where the Winding Road turns off from the Small Road. No further details except that this road is more circuitous, desert, and difficult, and takes over 100 days. (By my own reckoning I made it 285 miles from Kuei-hua to Morhgujing.)

As a check to these figures which I suppose to have been taken from the estimates of caravan masters, we have Younghusband's estimate of his own journey from Kuei-hua to Hami at 1255 miles. Hami is, of course, not so far west as Ku Ch'eng-tze, but the check is of the highest importance because the Chinese tend to enhance distances in Mongolia. They all have the theory that the *li* beyond the Great Wall are long *li;* but, if anything, they are short, because for lack of civilized landmarks the Chinese traveler, obsessed and weary with the monotony of the country, is apt to multiply his count of *li*.

The Bureau of Economic Affairs takes Chao Ho (about fifty-five miles from Kuei-hua) as the point of divergence of the caravans. This may once have been the point, but owing to the advance of cultivation the "back-country" centre of the caravans is now Pai-ling Miao, say 110-120 miles from Kuei-hua. This makes a small difference in total calculations. It is interesting to note how the removal of the caravan centre is from temple to temple, and how great temples are placed always on convenient lines of travel.

I had no way of computing my own distances except by the traveling pace of camels. I took this to be at two and a half miles an hour, making allowance always for good or bad going. As both my compasses early went out of order, I was reduced to taking a sun direction by day and a star direction by night, and I would not back myself in an argument with anyone about them, because I am not even sure of my allowance for the deflection of the sun at sunset from true west. Lastly, my reckoning for the total distance to Ku Ch'eng-tze by my route, which is commonly said to be longer than the Great Road, is thrown out by my having turned aside in an unsuccessful attempt to reach Barköl; but by and large I make it not less than 1550 and not more than 1650 miles.

The great body of our information on Mongolia is compiled from Russian sources, and for this reason almost all the mapping that has been done has been from north to south. Thus the arterial caravan route from Kiakhta through Urga to Kalgan is well established, but the routes running from east to west are still imperfectly plotted, the Russian surveys only serving to give cross bearings at the points where they touch the caravan routes. The Great Road must have been followed in the main by Ney Elias in his journey of 1872, but he deviated from it to visit Uliassutai and Kobdo before going on to Ku Ch'eng-tze, and his accounts have never been published in full. The Small Road was followed by Younghusband in 1887, until on his sixtieth day out from Kuei-hua he bore away left-handed from the Ku Ch'eng-tze road to reach Hami, whence he traveled through Chinese Turkestan by cart. Of the Winding Road there has never been any account.

To recapitulate my own journey therefore as far as Shandan

Miao: From Pai-ling Miao I followed the Small Road to Morh-gujing, where the Winding Road branches off to the southwest. Two marches on the Winding Road took me across the Lao-hu K'ou, where there is another branching of roads, for a traverse can here be made to the south, joining the Kan-su Border Road south of the Lang Shan. This road, which is neither truly Mongolian nor truly Chinese in character, is one of the most ancient and important caravan routes. It is even less of a single road than are any of the Mongolian routes, being a number of parallel cart roads and camel tracks through the Ordos desert or along the basin of the Yellow River. Parts of it have been followed out by such travelers as Huc, Prjevalsky, and Rockhill, whose routes have sometimes coincided and sometimes diverged. Its most important section is from Pao-t'ou to Ning-hsia, after which it splits up into a number of roads leading to every part of Kan-su.

I am not very clear in my own mind about the arrangement of the mountain chains between Morhgujing and Shandan Miao, except that I was traversing a subsidiary system north of the Lang Shan, while the desert country both east and west of the Lao-hu Shan was probably a southern extension of the Galpin Gobi. Shandan Miao, however, is clearly placed by Prjevalsky's map, northwest of the Khara-narin or Lang Shan. On his return from his Alashan explorations toward Urga, Prjevalsky passed to the west of Shandan Miao, which he had previously visited. According to his account he passed into higher country, peopled by Oirat Mongols who extend here "like a wedge" between the Alashan and Khalkha Mongols; then descended into the depression of the Galpin Gobi and rose again to the Hurku range. Just before crossing the Hurku he halted at the Bortson well, where Younghusband later crossed his route, and he here indicates a radiation of routes toward Urga, Ku Ch'eng-tze–Hami, Kan-su, and Kuei-hua–Pao-t'ou.

This falls in with what I saw and heard at Shandan Miao, which stands between the part of Inner Mongolia administered from Kuei-hua and Pao-t'ou, and Alashan, where the relations of Chinese and Mongols are controlled from Kan-su. The descent from the territory of the Ulanchap League, through which I had passed from the east, with its more pronounced mountain systems, to the sandy deserts, is both geographical and political, for Alashan adheres rather than belongs to Inner Mongolia. The Alashan Mongols are Eleuths by origin, of the great western group of tribes which marks in all probability a primitive racial cleavage. The caravan men have some obscure idea of this, for they call the Eleuths "Black" Ta-tze and group other Mongols as "Yellow." This appears to be a distinction learned from the Mongols themselves.

Shandan Miao,[1] however old the present buildings may be, must occupy a very ancient site, for it is a natural junction of old trade routes radiating toward Outer Mongolia, Alashan, Kan-su, the Yellow River, and Kuei-hua. The route toward Outer Mongolia is important[2] because west of Morhgujing there is desert of a severe kind, the Galpin Gobi, between the Small Road and the Great Road, and whatever trade and travel passes between north and south is attracted to the easiest crossings.

West of Morhgujing there is a class of petty Chinese traders living in *yurts* and doing a small barter business with the Mongols, with grain and flour for capital. There is usually not more than one of these traders to be found in a day's travel, but at Shandan Miao there is a whole community, perhaps twenty establishments in all, forming a centre for fairs during the festal and social seasons at the monastery temple. They deal here not only in grain but in all the things that Mongols buy : pipes and knives and boots and silks, cotton cloth, tobacco, hats, and sad-

[1] *Shandan*, I was told, is Mongol for "a small brook," *miao* is Chinese for "a temple."

[2] Prjevalsky, in passing *west* of Shandan Miao on his way north, was following another route, that passing the temple of Tukomen Miao (his Bain tuhum), *q. v., infra.*
North of the Hurku, at eighty-seven miles, he crossed an arm of the Great Road; one hundred miles farther north he crossed another arm, maintained, he says, for mails and officials; I think the first to have been the true Great Road, the second to have been the Uliassutai Road. When Prjevalsky was traveling in this country the trade routes from north to south had fallen into desuetude, owing to the Mohammedan rebellion in Kan-su. He mentions that in 1873 the caravans setting out from Urga in search of a new Living Buddha crossed the Gobi in echelon, by *different routes.* Men were sent in advance along the high road, which apparently came down by Shandan Miao, to clear out the old wells and dig new; but there was a scarcity of water.

dlery.  The sign of the Alashan trader is the donkey, because on loose, sandy going the donkey is better than the pony, doing more work in proportion to his cost, and able to live on poorer grazing.  Even the Mongols in Alashan use them a great deal, and the number of donkeys at Shandan Miao is wonderful past all whooping.

# VIII

## CAMEL MEN ALL

THE extreme limit of control of the Northwestern Province is set at Shandan Miao, where there is a *likin* inspectorate to keep a check on the provincial revenue collected on goods in transit. On the morning after our arrival the Pao-t'ou caravan, with which I was in company, was visited by the tax officials. Although provided with passes exempting them from all taxation on the road, they paid a tip or squeeze to ensure good feeling. This is called "giving face to the officials" and is a mild example of what Chinese traders have to suffer. Most official documents are so loosely worded that they can be disputed at will by these *likin* inspectors. In order, therefore, to avoid delay and expense, carriers of merchandise who have paid good money down to get their passes must contribute a levy, for which there is no sort of warrant, to the upkeep of all the inspectorates they pass. At the Shandan Miao station were piled a number of bales, taken from a small caravan which had disputed some kind of imposition. These bales would be sold by auction, nominally for the benefit of government, actually to the profit of the officials.

Several days later I heard that the officials, while in the Pao-t'ou tent, had inquired about me. Having subscribed to their "face" in one way, the Pao-t'ou men were more than willing to make them lose it in another way. "That," they said, "is a foreign traveler of more than ordinary importance. You may inspect his *hu-chao* (passport) if you want to; but first you must collect some good dry dung for his fire. He always makes officials do that." I laughed with the men when I heard the story, for it went well with the malign humor of the caravans; but it set me wondering. I wondered how much of the foreign reputation for "frightfulness" with which such good play has been made in our time has been contributed by Chinese acting and speaking without authority in the name of foreigners.

We were tidying up before the start, and my camel man, who had been in a vile temper for days, had just said with disarming frankness that his eyes and therefore his humor were much better, when the Old Man came running in with bad news. Our camels had been herded with the big caravan, and the Old Man, with two of the Pao-t'ou men, was driving them in to camp when part of the herd stampeded for a few hundred yards, in the silly way that camels do. Scrambling across a dry water-course, one of them either stumbled or was jostled off its feet and came down, breaking a leg. It was one of our two very best camels, a cow. I went out with my camel man to look at her. The near foreleg had been broken so badly just below the shoulder that the bone stuck out of the flesh. There was nothing to be done.

Caravan men will grouse and quarrel over all the little things that go wrong, but it seems to be a point of honor with them to take lightly the loss of a camel. Were they to show how gravely the loss affected them, some vague power would jealously do a hurt to all their camels. It brings bad luck to talk about that kind of bad luck. The man laughed, turning his back. "She was good value for no money," he said; "the bandits gave her to me and I have worked her for six or seven years."

Mongolia-going caravan men never slaughter a camel dying of injury or starvation. They seem to think that taking the life of the animal prevents it being saved by a possible miracle. To kill it might make its troubled soul follow the other camels of the caravan, bringing them ill luck. The Chinese are capable of a callousness toward suffering that seems terrible to many Westerners. The truth is that they have the deep aversion of the East from the deliberate taking of life, which has become perverted until they would rather see an animal under torture than take the burden of its soul on themselves. Unless excited, they even prefer to use roundabout words for "dying" and "killing." "Our camels suffer for us all their lives," a man said to me; "is it not enough? If we did a violent thing at the end, would not the guilt be on our bodies?"

The Old Man, however, saw his chance of getting round the Custom of the Road. When we had started he ran over to one of the traders and sold him the camel for two packets of tobacco; a small price, for the trader, being free of caravan law, could slaughter it without scruple, eat its flesh, and sell the hide, which was in fine condition. One packet the Old Man "squeezed" for himself; the other he presented with a flourish to the camel man.

This camel man of mine had the narrow skull and long face of one of the Shan-hsi types. He had also a long, pointed nose, flinty in outward appearance but excessively mucous inside, from which in summer there hung a slimy drop and in winter an icicle. A pendulous, petulant underlip set off his appearance, and his only kind of humor was sneering and snarking. Coming of excellent folk, he had a long career and a bad reputation behind him. He had first been apprenticed to trade, and had learned to read and write a little, a thing most uncommon among caravan men; and as his firm sent out small ventures to Mongolia he rose to be a supercargo, traveling with their caravans in charge of buying and selling goods. Then the firm went bankrupt, which was not surprising if he had a free hand, and, failing of other employment, he had to begin afresh as a camel puller.

The men who go with the caravans are not all of them so very well traveled, for often they spend their lives on one of the greater roads, going to Ku Ch'eng-tze, Uliassutai, or Urga. This man had seen more than most. He had been with camels to almost every place that camels reach, not only by the chief Mongolian roads but over all the Kan-su routes, to Ning-hsia, Liang Chou, Lan Chou, Hsi-ning, and as far as Koko Nor-Tibet, as well as to Turfan in Chinese Turkestan and Chuguchak on the Siberian frontier. Between spells with the caravans he had tried many other shifts. He had lived much among the Mongols, trying to do a peddling trade, and I am pretty sure he knew a lot of Mongol bandit life. He had been a go-between for the Manchus who used to sell ponies by stealth from the old Imperial herds of Bar Köl and Ku Ch'eng-tze. Then for several years he had been a *p'ao-tueï'rh-ti*, which literally is a "leg runner," to the bandits of the Ta Ch'ing Shan who raid the Kuei-hua routes. Knowing as he did the ways of caravans and the look of the loads they carried, he would pick up in Kuei-hua news of the caravans about to start and carry word of them to the bandits. His chief in those days was the same man who is now the wealthy, respected, and very competent Mongol in active command of the Kuei-hua Mercantile Guard. The bandits rewarded him with the gift of a camel or a donkey now and then. This employment made him in the end a marked man, and after one of the periodical campaigns against the bandits he was forced to go into hiding for half a year. When he emerged again from the mountains, however, he set up unmolested in honest life as the owner of a few "honest" camels. Working with these, he engaged profitably in the business of carrying out loads on the short journey to Pai-ling Miao. During the past summer he had put his camels in hiding; but with the increasing danger when the Christian Army began to break up, he decided to take them himself to Chinese Turkestan, and that was how he had fallen in with the Barköl man who had fallen in with me and held my original contract.

Now almost all camel pullers are wild, if they are not bad. It is a favorite saying in their own mouths that there are no good camel pullers. They will fight at a look or a word, and they make it a matter of pride to do no service, even for a tip, for any "passenger" traveling with the caravans. They say they are servants to camels, not to men. They cheat and harry any man who is not strong enough to stand up for himself, but they will do no outright stealing except of food. Men who have had a turn at the bandit life are not uncommon among them, but they are all forthright rogues. Indeed, I always found that the worse a man's character, the better I got on with him. The most lawless men liked the idea of a young foreigner with no experience traveling alone among them. They took me in at once as a fellow adventurer, and a man could not have had better friends. The trouble with my own man was that he was not the real bold, bad villain. He had not even been a real bandit, but a sneak and informer to bandits, and the quality of sneaking malevolence showed in all his ill behavior.

He brooded over the wrong done him by the broker and the other man until he turned savage; then, instead of trying to gain my regard against the day when we should both have affairs to settle with the same man, he began to work off his savagery on Moses and me. The trouble he made was mostly of the underhanded kind that is hardest to fight against. He began by taking advantage of our ignorance, and had it not been for the friendliness of men in other caravans, who helped us to learn caravan ways, he would have made the whole journey uncomfortable. He tried always to fix the loads on our riding camels so that we could not ride in comfort, with the idea of making us get down and walk — even though of our own choice we used to walk a large part of each march. Then he would pitch the tent so that we got all the smoke of the fire, or try to spoil our food for us whenever he had been able to cadge a meal for himself in advance from some other caravan.

He had also a bad camel which, after going for days as peacefully as you please, would suddenly go frantic, struggling and bucking until it threw its load. He managed to get all my loads in succession thrown by this brute, with the hope of breaking as much as possible. He rarely went beyond little things, except in his talk; but little things on a long desert journey can be made very maddening. Moses tried his best to keep me from taking a strong line with the man, for Moses knew even better than I that, if it comes to an affair of blows between Chinese and foreigner, justice is lost in race feeling; the foreigner is always in the wrong. Moses wanted to leave our settlement to the end of the journey, but after suffering for a while from this petty bullying I found it best to make a row now and then. His worst habit was dark talk about "throwing us on the Gobi" and going off with the camels, and the only thing to do when he talked like that was to stand up to him. In China, if you manage your fierce talk properly, it need not lead to blows; to back down, after using fighting words, is no disgrace if you are within range of peace talkers, and so soon as we became friendly with other caravans there was no lack of peace talkers to take my side. One of my worst quarrels was on a day when we were thirty miles from the nearest water, and the fellow threatened to abandon me. Instead of doing anything high-handed, I made him carry out his threat. The other caravans had already started, and I taunted him into trying to follow them, but of course they forced him to turn back and take up my loads, the right and the moral advantage remaining on my side.

After a purging row of this kind he would be on his good behavior, sometimes for days. Then he would talk engagingly of the things he had seen and the men he had met in nearly thirty years between the frontiers of Tibet, Russia, and China — for with the exception of Kan-su, far to the west, he had never been in China proper, within the Great Wall. For the rest, the diversity of his life had made him cunning in the ways of Mongolia; a good cook, within the range of an iron pot and a dung fire, a good cobbler and mender of clothes, and skillful in the handling of camels.

Traveling from the time we entered the Winding Road with the Pao-t'ou people, I had begun to fall in with the ways of the men of the big caravans. From the first they made me free of their tent, passing me up to a seat beside the caravan master. They were one of the best-picked lots I met on the road, all of them youngsters and most of them owning a few camels of their own; and as during the months I had spent in the northwest I had got something of the turn of their dialect, and was drawn naturally toward their austere tradition, I soon came to pass almost unnoticed among them.

All of these men had a tan as dark as old wood, and wrinkles about the eyes from peering through wind and dust, the glare of the sun, the dark nights, and the smoke of fires in the tent. Yet some of them had the dull faces of men bound all their lives to plod in front of a string of camels, while others, the sort of men to become after their hard apprenticeship masters of caravans and owners of camels, had strong, resolute, enterprising faces

and sometimes heroically modeled skulls.  Among no other class
of men have I seen so many heads of such magnificent contour.
For one thing, their life of exposure wears down the flesh of
head and face, showing up the bony formation, and the effect
is heightened by the way they shave their heads.  Some shave
the whole head, others only the forehead, leaving either one long
queue or, more often, two pigtails at the back.

The queue is supposed to have been a mark of the Manchu
conquest, and has at different times been proscribed under the
Republic.  When the Christian Army occupied the northwest
they started a campaign against queues.  Many of the caravan
men had been captured and had their pigtails cut off by the
official "executioner" who patrolled the streets of Kuei-hua
with an armed guard.  They always grew them again.  The
peculiar fashion of wearing, not the formal queue, but two short
pigtails reaching to the shoulder, a fashion which prevails forth
from Kalgan through the northwest, and which has survived so
much persecution, seems to me to have nothing to do with the
Manchus.  It may be much older, a relic of some different racial
inheritance.

The men who lead camels through the *Hou-shan*, the Country
Behind the Mountains, never call themselves anything but *la
lo-t'o-ti*, which is to say "camel pullers."  They speak of much
of the routine of their lives in terms not of men but of camels.
"*Chin-t'ien ta-ta-ti la* (To-day we pull big and big)," they say,
when there is a long march ahead.  They are first of all men
of a common experience, for they are bound together by the
training of a great and hard school.  Often they come of families
that have been for generations in the caravan trade.  Always,
even if their families are well to do, they serve an exacting apprenticeship.  Because no man can make money out of caravans
unless he understands camels, they learn to know their camels
on the march and in camp, herding and drinking and resting,
by day and by night, full-humped and quarrelsome or worn-out
and staggering after scores of days on the road.  They learn
to know how a camel is standing up under his burden by loading
and unloading thirty-six camels a day in all weathers.  A camel

is the most foolish of all the beasts that do tasks for men, and, because there is no good doctoring known for him when he is sick, they must learn how to keep him well; how to find the best grazing, how much water to allow when he is road-weary, and how little when he is fat and likely to sweat. They learn where to park the camels, lying huddled in close rows so that they get all the shelter possible through midwinter nights when the wind is driving the snow, how to bleed blistered hoof pads and how to clean festered pack sores and pad them to take off the weight of the load.

When they have mastered their trade they can tell a camel with good solid flesh on him from one that has been fattened up to get him sold, just by plucking out a few hairs and looking at the roots. They know how to coax a few more marches out of beasts that have been worked beyond their strength, when there is no grazing and the ration of feed is running out; when to make the pace fast and when slow, and when a short march in the morning and another at night are better than one long stage.

While they master all these things they have also to become versed in the personal mysteries of their craft, and the jealously guarded privileges of the camel puller, with all the laws of the road, the tent, and the camp. Each thing in their knowledge must be got by experience, because the strictest of all the unwritten laws is that no man can expect help or advice from another. What he cannot learn by doing it himself, he must find out by watching others. There is no mercy.

Each man is in charge of a file of camels called a *lien*. The full number of a *lien* is eighteen camels, nor can any man be asked to look after more. If he does not speak of his work as pulling camels, the phrase he uses is *ting lien-tze;* and *ting* means more or less to hold down, or stop, or be equal to, as we speak of holding down a job. Every camel has his own place in the file, and on the march he is always in that place, carrying the same load; unless after consideration a change is made, for some camels when they are tired go better at the tail of the file than up in front. Two *lien* make a *pa,* and in camp these two *lien* lie either side by side or end-on. The two men, working on either side of the camels as they lie in a row between their packs, help each other to off-load and on-load. Except for this partnership they have nothing to do with each other, for in camp, when one of them is on duty herding camels or standing watch, the other must by custom be off duty.

The Chinese of all trades are fond of their jargon, their *hang-hua*, or talk of the craft. Camel pullers never talk of the exact number of camels a man owns. It is always a *lien* and a half, or two *pa*, or the nearest equivalent. Nor do they speak of "losing" a camel when it dies or is abandoned on the march; it is always "thrown away." In the same way they have their own phrases for the journeys they make. The outward road to Mongolia or Chinese Turkestan is always "up," while the homeward journey is "down." On the road up a man must walk the whole distance, unless he rides a camel of his own, no matter how footsore or sick he may be, even if he is leading several unladen camels. The only test of sickness is the inability to eat. If a man cannot eat, he is put on a camel and tied there if necessary, until either he can eat or he dies. On the other hand, when the caravan is going down, the employer is bound to let each man ride a camel, even if the camels are heavily loaded or weak from exposure and hunger.

At the head of the first string of camels on the march is the chief cook; his title is *kuo-t'ou,* or Head of the Pot. The man who leads the second string has no rank or title; he is there because he is the partner at loading and unloading of the Head of the Pot. Then, with the third string, comes the *erh-t'ou,* or Second Head, the assistant cook. Each caravan fully staffed has two mounted men, and the second mounted man and the second cook are in charge of the water supply. They must find the well, if it lies away from the track, and fill the big water butts, which make more than a standard load and must be carried by the very best camels. When a man is made second cook he is in the direct way of promotion, for he learns to know all the wells with their supply of water. From second cook he may become Head of the Pot, walking at the front of the caravan, setting the pace and learning the road so that with eyes shut he can tell when he is reaching the end of a stage. When he knows the wells and the road as a first-class man should know them, he can qualify as *hsien-sheng*, the second mounted man of a caravan, or even become directly caravan master, disposing absolutely of camels and camel pullers. Because, however, the Winding Road is still so new, there are some caravan masters who do not yet know it; thus the master of the Pao-t'ou caravan, though an able and experienced man, had for halts and distances to rely on his Head of the Pot. Custom retains its force for all that, among the caravans. This master lost no authority, nor did his Head of the Pot presume to do more than walk in the lead and answer when spoken to.

The standard wage of a camel puller is two silver taels a month; call it five shillings. This is not as much as the cost of his shoes and clothing, for he must have several pairs of shoes each journey and buy a new suit and greatcoat of sheepskin each time he leaves Ku Ch'eng-tze. He works less for his wage than for the privilege of carrying goods. Sometimes by special contract he is paid a higher wage, without right of carriage; but the best men go to the owners who allow the ancient privilege.

There is not an exact rule about the amount a man can *sao-che*, or take along; but usually he can bring as much as half a camel load without protest, and a full load on the homeward journey. Few, however, have the capital to buy in such quantity, unless it be cigarettes or brick tea. Usually they trade in small things — ankle bands, mirrors, belts, colored print cloth, tawdry jewelry, and women's trinkets; but often, if they are working for a tea caravan, they put all their money in tea. The profit is not so large as on a lucky speculation in fancy goods, but there is less risk. As the *likin* men — and this is the only kindly impulse of *likin* men — never bother about odd half-loads of bedding rolls and camel pullers' perquisites, they trade not only carriage-free but duty-free. In the west they either barter for skins or wool or gold dust or opium, or sell for cash, which they lay out in buying the same kinds of things. About 3.30 of the paper taels current at Ku Ch'eng-tze exchange for one silver tael; but one paper tael skillfully used in buying cargo is good for at least one silver tael when the cargo is sold again at Kuei-hua.

Indeed, were it not for his way of cutting a dash in Ku Ch'eng-tze, where men just "down from the Gobi," as they call it, like to swagger in restaurants, drink, gamble, and visit all the women of all the nationalities to be found in that town of many races and reckless spending, every camel man would soon grow rich. Before the boom days, when Ku Ch'eng-tze was a dreary little village, camel pullers could get credit in the Kuei-hua shops for fifty taels' worth or so of goods, without security; but now that Ku Ch'eng-tze is gay with all the lures that make easy money easy to spend, so many scatter every cent they have before getting away that they are no longer given credit in Kuei-hua.

The commonest ambition of a camel puller is to own a few camels which he can take along with him, while still working for his old master. One of his most valuable privileges is that when he has put aside enough to buy a camel he can place it with his owner's caravan. The owner assigns him a load, even if he has not a full complement for his own camels. The carriage money for this load belongs to the man, without deduction; but if he owns more than six camels he ceases to draw wages, doing his share of the caravan work in return for his food and the convenience of tent, water-carrying camels, and so on. In this way his camels may earn him several hundred taels a year, without expenses. When he owns about a full *lien-tze* he advances to a new status; he not only draws no wages, but pays his former employer, of whom he has become a kind of independent partner, twenty taels tent money for each round trip, to cover the cost of his food and a share in the commissariat camels.

Not all camel pullers, though some of them have been so long on the road that their names are known among all the caravans, come to be *ch'i-ma-ti* — mounted men. Only a few like responsibility or are fit for it. If a man is offered promotion he must usually serve first as *hsien-sheng*. The term means properly "elder born," an honorific only applied to literate men. He should therefore be the clerk of the caravan, but there are very

few among them who can read a character. Even a caravan
master spending comparatively large sums will sometimes per-
force carry accounts in his head for months.

From the time the caravan halts until it moves again the *hsien-
sheng* is in charge of the camp. He must watch the pasturing of
the camel herd and ride sometimes for several miles to look out
better grazing, and he must see to the watering of beasts and
the filling of the water butts for men. Between trips, when the
camels are at long pasture, he is also in charge. He works hard,
doing all the odd jobs, because no camel puller can be called on
for work out of the anciently established routine. His wages
are only six to eight taels a month, and he has not, nominally, the
prerogative of carriage, though if he owns camels he may put
them with the caravan in the usual way, and often goes shares
with one of the camel pullers in buying trade goods. Many
*hsien-sheng*, if they are not probationers waiting for the billet
of caravan master, are men who have worked for years under
the same owner, veterans who know the road and the usage of
camels thoroughly, but who have become too old for hard marching and have no money to keep them in retirement, as may often
happen either when a man has been shiftless or when he has laid
out all his earnings in the buying of camels, which through " the
business of the Gobi " have been " thrown away " without bringing him a profit.

Though the *hsien-sheng* may sometimes be no more than a
pensioner, the caravan master, emerging from the ranks, is always of the pick of the craft. He has not the privilege of carriage, but is often the owner of a few camels. He is not paid a
monthly wage, but a set fee for the journey up and down. He
has no expenses, and if the venture has been a success there is
always a bonus for him. The Chinese call him *ling-fang-tze-ti*,
which is Leader or Guide of the Caravan; but more currently
*chang-kuei-ti*, which is a commercial term for the manager of a
business, meaning " controller of the chest " — the till, that is,
and the accounts. Perhaps the best rendering is Caravan Master.
He must not only know the business of camels and the road, but
be able to handle the rowdy camel pullers, who demand dignity

without swank, and authority without discipline — a man, in short, to interpret the law of their binding customs for the benefit of camel owner and camel puller.  He must also be competent to deal with any Mongol or Chinese officials who may be met, and is responsible in full for the expenses of the journey, including the purchase of provisions for the men and feed for the camels.

If an owner does not accompany his own caravan he sends with it always a supercargo, a member, if possible, of his own family.  This man delivers the freight on arrival to the consignees, settles current accounts there with the caravan master, and buys fresh camels if he thinks the investment good.  For the return journey he may, according to his judgment, either contract to carry cargo or invest the money he has in hand in goods for "own account."  On the road, however, he has no say.  The caravan master is then alone answerable for expenses and the conduct of the caravan.  He may even, if he thinks it necessary in order to deliver his freight, hire or buy fresh camels.  I heard more than once on the way of disputes between owners or supercargoes and their caravan masters; but always it was the caravan master who had his way.  One dispute started in strong words used by the caravan master to his employer's son, who had imperiled the whole venture by coming out late from Kuei-hua when it was time to run for it from the soldiery.  The two men did not speak for months, but the caravan master said, "If you do not like the way I lead your caravan, I will hand it back to you at Ku Ch'eng-tze, and you may sack me there; but on the road it is not yours, — you are only a traveler, — it is mine."  Nor could the owner's son do anything, for the custom of the caravan is just as binding on master as on man.

In China, honest and competent servants can always be found, but men who will take responsibility and can work without orders are very rare indeed.  A chang-kuei-ti just good enough to get his caravan there and back is paid eighty or ninety taels for the double trip.  Some receive as much as one hundred and fifty, and it is even said that there have been men whose fee was three hundred taels.  One of the most famous caravan masters of recent times died only two or three years ago.  He had made a fortune for the family that employed him, but died poor himself. A canny trader as well as an admirable leader, he had such a prestige among the Mongols that even after they began to harry the Chinese traders he could take a full caravan into Outer Mongolia without risk. More than that, after his death a son of the family made a successful journey through the heart of the country, on the strength of the name of his father's servant. These things happen in the old, the magnificent Asia. The caravan master himself died of heartbreak, many marches from home, on hearing that his owners had sent out an extra caravan which, through bad leadership, lost half a hundred camels. The Mongols laid his body in state in a great lamasery and the owners sent all the way from Kuei-hua a splendid coffin and brought him back in a camel cart, with more honors than had ever been known in Mongolia.

These were the men who made me free of their tents and their talk, and whom I remember with a peculiar and intimate warmth. There are men of all nations who feel the fascination of a life unequally divided between months of hardship and short days of riot and spending; but in the end it is the hardship that holds them. The Chinese, taking them as they come, are not like this. They frankly detest hard work. A large belly among them is an honorable thing, because it means that the owner of it does not swink for his living. I never met a Chinese outside of the caravans who was what we should call sentimental about his work. Camel pullers alone have a different spirit, a queer spirit. Time and again when the men were talking around the fire and cursing the weather, the bad taste of the water, or the dust blown into their food, I have heard one ask, rhetorically, " What is a camel puller?" and answer himself with the blunt rhyme: —

> *Ch'ih-ti shih, ho-ti niao,*
> *Lan mao-k'ou-tai sui-har chiao.*

> He eats dung, he drinks urine,
> He lies down to sleep on a tattered sack.

Then another would say, " Yes, but this is the good life — do we not all come back to it?" and be approved in a chorus of grunts and oaths.   Once a veteran said the last word: "I put all my money into land in the newly opened country Behind the Hills, and my nephew farms it for me.   My old woman is there, so two years ago when they had the troubles on the Great Road and my legs hurt I thought I would finish with it all — defile its mother!  I thought I would sleep on a warm *k'ang* and gossip with the neighbors and maybe smoke a little opium, and not work hard any more.   But I am not far from the road, in my place, and after a while in the day and the night when I heard the bells of the *lien-tze* go by, *ting-lang, tang-lang*, there was a pain in my heart — *hsin-li nan-kuo*.   So I said, Dogs defile it!  I will go back on the Gobi one more time and pull camels."

## IX

## DUNES AND DESERTS OF ALASHAN

IT was late when we started from our camp near Shandan Miao, and twilight when, after a mile or so, we passed the white outer walls of the monastery. Then we entered sand dunes — the first great sand of the journey. We went heavily and slowly through them until midnight. The next morning I woke to find that we had camped by a little puddle in a flat stretch of reddish clay, encircled by the dunes. The name of the puddle was Ulan Nor, the Red Lake, all grown about with yellowing clumps of iris. It may be the same as the Engeri Nor of Prjevalsky's map, or Engeri Nor may be another pool among the dunes. It seems to be a characteristic of the Mongolian dunes that they tend to group themselves in amphitheatres about bare spaces like this, in which sometimes there are reeds or tamarisks, or sometimes a pool. Carruthers calls these circular pits by the name of *falj*. The secret of travel among widespread dunes is to find a way from one to another of them.

We were visited here by a begging pilgrim, a tall, gaunt, wild figure leading an undersized donkey. He was what the Chinese call a Hsi Fan-tze, or Western Tibetan from somewhere between Hsi-ning and the Koko Nor, blundering on his way to Wu-t'ai Shan, the five sacred mountains of Shan-hsi, in China Within the Wall. Though dressed, to my eyes, like a Mongol, he spoke not a word of Mongol. From Ning-hsia he had tried to get across Alashan by one of the ways the opium runners and the Mongols use, but had lost himself in the sands. For three days he had had no water, until he struck this brackish pool. He had seen no Mongols for so long that his little bit of food was nearly gone. He spoke fairly good Chinese, but that would help him

little until he reached Kuei-hua, so that he must look to the Mongols to pass him along from one lamasery to the next, through
their country.  Against the coming winter cold and the prospect
of sleeping many nights in the open, he had no protection but a
long sheepskin coat.  When he got to Wu-t'ai Shan he would
find lamas of his own people in the temples.  There he would stay
until the next warm weather, when he would beg his way back
toward Hsi-ning, having gathered enough merit for the rest of
his life.

We gave him a little flour and set him on his way to Shandan
Miao, leading his tired donkey — a strange figure of the wandering peoples of High Asia, who have been confused in blood and
religion since before the Dark Ages; at home without the use
of language in Lhasa, Urga, and Peking and all the deserts
between.  The Chinese call Fan-tze of Western Fan-tze most of
the races about the Koko Nor, except the Mongols, who are
Ta-tze; but he called himself a Tangut — one of those people
who ruled a kingdom, when Marco Polo passed on his way from
Europe, that included most of modern Kan-su, and against whom
Jenghis Khan made three expeditions before he conquered them;
indeed, he died on his last campaign.

We left Ulan Nor at half-past four in the afternoon, turning
at once into a winding track among big, bare dunes, from fifty
to seventy feet or more high.  After a couple of miles we reached
open, rolling country, still very sandy, but grown with round
bunches of thorn, and from this passed to a firmer soil of sandy
gravel, over which we marched, descending a little, until eleven
at night.  We had been taking a southerly direction, which I was
told would get us through the dunes at their narrowest.  The
next morning I could see them, away to the north and northwest,
a gleaming yellow desert of blank sand.  The caravans cannot go
round them to the north without trespassing in Outer Mongolia;
but the crossing of this desert on the Great Road, as I heard, is
a simple matter of about half a stage.  Moreover, by the Great
Road there is only the one belt of dunes to be traversed, while
we on the Winding Road had still the Big Sand Hollows, as the
men call them, before us.

Our camp was at a well in a little hollow at the foot of low rounded hills. We could see no *yurts*, but there must have been Mongols in the hills, for we saw several riding by during the day and a trough at the well, made of a hollowed elm brought from no small distance, showed that it was a drinking place for large numbers of animals. Not far beyond, the country became again very sandy, and the soil so loose that except about dawn the unflagging Mongolian winds kept the air always burdened with a haze. There was little growth but thorns, most of them *khara-mu* or *khara mun;* this must be what Rockhill calls *hara-ma-ku,* a berried thorn of which the fruit is edible, tasting something like whortleberries. We saw a surprising number of camels and ponies, with big flocks in which the goats far outnumbered the sheep — a sign of desert regions. The ponies were of a poor order, heavy in shoulder and head. It takes the sweet grass of rocky hills to bring out the best in the Mongol breeds of pony. Those of sandy districts are not only coarse in build, but have wide, spongy hoofs very different from the clean, hard hoofs and springy pasterns of the hill ponies.

Although one might think that the best camels for desert work would be bred in the sands, the dune-country camels are also inferior. They develop splayed hoofs, thinly padded, which keep them from sinking in soft sand but soon blister on the gravelly going which makes up such a great part of all the caravan roads. These camels also grow to much more than the common height. The Alashan breeds are distinct, and can be told by their height, their long thin muzzles, and their dark color, as brown sometimes as a very dark bearskin. Their height in itself is counted a fault, in spite of their rather greater absolute strength, because tall camels tire more quickly when carrying bulky loads against a strong wind. I have even heard it said that tall camels cannot feed so fast, because they have to reach farther to get their food! I found that undoubtedly, on an average, the lower and more thickset camels had more strength left at the end of the journey.

Another bad fault of Alashan camels is that they are notoriously savage. A much better breed comes from the mountains to the south, the Alashan range. For all-round work thickset, short-legged camels with small, round, thickly padded hoofs are the best. They can be picked from different hill districts. The finest of all are said to be those marketed at the Tushegun monastery in Outer Mongolia; they are of a striking reddish color, with a peculiar dark brown or blackish ring around the eyes. A superb type comes also from the Bar Köl mountains.

Alashan camels, perhaps partly because they are not in demand among the caravans, are the stock from which the camels in use about Peking are largely drawn; those debased camels which carry coal and lime, and sleep every night at an inn. They are bought in great numbers by Mohammedan dealers around Wang-yeh Fu, the Palace of the Prince, the "capital" of Alashan. This little city has, in addition to the Chinese traders dealing in wool and handling the Prince's salt monopoly, a population of Manchus, descended from the old Imperial garrison. The Mohammedans, some of them Salars and some of them Chinese from Ning-hsia, use the camels to transport wool to Teng-k'ou in Kan-su, for which reason Alashan wool is known on the China markets as Teng-k'ou wool. Here the Mohammedans sell both wool and camels, returning with silver loaded on Kan-su mules. Silver is always at a premium with Mongols, while there is a demand among the Chinese and Manchus of Wang-yeh Fu for cart mules, which the Mongols do not breed.

The camels and wool are bought at Teng-k'ou by Chinese from Pao-t'ou, who used in the old days to take them all the way to Kalgan and Peking. Now they usually sell the wool to merchants at railhead; but camels are still occasionally taken to Kalgan, and thence to Peking, sometimes with loads of some inferior cargo like soda. The tradition of dealing in camels lingers with all the Pao-t'ou caravans, and is the great distinction between them and the caravans of Kuei-hua. A Kuei-hua man buys camels as he needs them, and uses them until they drop out and die. A Pao-t'ou man buys always in the hope of a deal. He includes more extra camels in a caravan, shifting loads more frequently in order to avoid pack sores. It seems to be definitely accepted that a young camel which has been hardened by carrying loads under caravan conditions is more valuable than one which has

never been in work until it is more than full-grown.  The Pao-
t'ou man conditions his camel carefully, so that it becomes fit for
long, hard journeys with little water and poor grazing, but does
not show the blemish of patches of white hair over healed pack
galls.  When he can sell it, he buys another and starts in again.
As might be expected among Chinese, there is little love wasted
between the Pao-t'ou men, who accuse the men of Kuei-hua of
having no brains for anything beyond the carrying trade, and the
men of the Kuei-hua caravans, who despise those of Pao-t'ou
as camel peddlers.

A camel is not fit for hard work until he is about four years
of age.  Even then he must be gradually broken in with half-
loads.  At first he is a lot of trouble, shying and flinging his
load when scared by things that do not worry his elders.  Yet
they also panic frequently, though they recover quickly.  They
are not frightened so much by things they see, unless it be strange
things near the road at night, as by things they hear.  A pony
galloping up from behind will stampede a whole caravan, for
which reason the trick is often used by bandits.  Both ponies
and dogs which belong to the caravans wear bells, to the sound
of which the camels are accustomed.

Young camels, however, are much the best for riding, as they
are not only faster but softer-gaited.  The Mongols set much
store by pacing or ambling camels, which can, it is said, carry
a man for as much as a hundred miles at a march; and it is
added that they can do this for six or seven marches on end,
which I take leave to doubt.  It is true, though, that the Mongols
prefer a fast camel to a pony for a long journey in haste, if they
cannot get relays on the road.  The camel is starved for several
days as a preparation, to get its belly "tucked up" and so prevent
colic from overheating followed by a chill, and allowed next to
no food during the journey.

When first being broken, learning to kneel and to carry loads,
a camel is usually haltered.  Its nose is pierced in the third year.
This is done, by the Chinese and Mongols, below the opening of
the nostrils and well back.  The Qazaqs and Kirghiz do it above
the level of the nostrils, where the cartilage is much weaker.  The

peg then almost always causes chafing and bleeding, and if the camel attempts to bolt it is often torn right out, causing a hideous wound. It is curious that the Qazaqs, though in many regions they mix a great deal with the Mongols, have never acquired the same understanding of camels. They do not breed so many, nor do they know how to get the best work out of them.

The Turki buy more camels than they breed, and one can see all kinds of nose piercings among their camels, besides which they often bridle and bit them, a thing never seen among the nomads. The piercing of the nose is done with a pointed stake, hardened in the fire. Edged or iron tools are never used; it is said that the wound would heal less quickly. A wooden peg is then put in, to which is attached the cord by which the camel is led and handled. One can tell by the whittling and shape of this peg the district from which the owner comes. Some of them are very neatly finished, with little cuplike wooden "washers" to prevent chafing, while others have leather washers.

Camels are gelded usually at the age of four or five, but this may be done without risk when they are much older. They reach their full strength at about seven years, and are in their prime until at least twelve. After about the twelfth year the teeth begin to wear down badly, and it is difficult to tell their age. By the time they are sixteen or seventeen the teeth hardly show above the gums. They keep up their strength if fed out of nose bags, but rapidly weaken if they have to shift for themselves where the grazing is short, being no longer able to crop close. If grain fed, it is said that they can carry full loads for full marches when as much as thirty years old.

I heard talk about camels in plenty from the men of the Pao-t'ou caravan. The Chinese workingman, like the Chinese merchant, likes to talk shop because he has no mental history to interest him in anything else. I became very friendly with the caravan master, though he was a man of few words; a solid, grave, brown-faced man of about forty, with a small square chin and a broad blunt nose. He had been once as a lad to Peking, with a caravan of camels which, when their loads had been delivered, were sold at Feng-t'ai to carry coal from the western hills. That was before the railway. He had spent half a day inside the walls of Peking, and I asked him slyly if he had seen the Temple of Heaven. "No," he answered; "I bought clothes in the shops and walked up and down the streets to stare." Which, after all, is in the ancient spirit of travel.

It was a fine morning at our camp by the well in the hollow. Moses washed my stockings, a striving toward cleanliness which made me suggest that I go down to the well and have him throw a few buckets of water over me. The idea horrified him as well as all the people who had come to sit in the tent. Water from below the surface of the earth, they explained, which had not been shone on by the sun, was full of the dangerous *yin*, or dark, or cold, or deadly female principle. It would almost certainly cause sickness. Water from which part of the *yin* had been driven by the life-giving *yang* or male principle of sunlight would not have been so bad. Which argument so delighted me that I gladly limited myself to a little splashing of the face and hands.

It would not have been much use getting clean. As the day grew warmer a dusty sultry wind began to blow, clouding all horizons. Thin, flat clouds formed at sunset and we marched at night beneath a moon with a wide ring around it. It was a slow, tiring stage, again to the south, through thorn-grown sand; but it brought us once more to a community of Chinese traders living in *yurts* hidden among low clay hills at a place called Hasa-buchi. We were told that there was cultivated land, formerly Mongol, about forty miles to the east, under the administration of Pao-t'ou. This must have been the area of "thick Chinese population" marked on Prjevalsky's map between the Khara-narin (Lang Shan) and the Yellow River. I could not make out hills to the east; probably on account of the prevalent haze. Climbing to an *obo* that overlooked the *yurts*, I could see, the next morning, dunes to the south and southwest, backed by a blue range of hills which must have been the extension of the Khara-narin in that direction. To the north were more dunes. To the northwest I could see the line of our next march, lying toward the gleam of a salt marsh in flat, sandy country grown with spear grass and thorn.

We made only a short stage of about thirteen miles, because at ten a light rain began to fall. No one was anxious to break the rule of not camping in wet clothes on wet ground if it can be helped. Moreover, the track was worn down through the sand to a clay subsoil; this was thickly impregnated with all kinds of salts and, immediately the rain began to fall, became so slippery for camels that they floundered about in a distressing way. We camped on the north of the salt mere, for which I could get no name. " It is a salt marsh," said everyone patiently. I found there the next morning scattered pools of water, some of which seemed to be solidly crusted with salt and soda. The crystals had a bitter flavor, suggestive of purgative mineral salts. Any child would have said they were " medicine." There are a great number of these meres in Alashan, with deposits of salt and soda. Some of them are worked under monopolies let to Chinese merchants, providing the Prince with a handsome revenue on which he lives in Peking, keeping up a style that few Mongol princes can rival. The tax revenue from the same source assures him of the continued friendship of Chinese officials.

There were many wild fowl about, but it was the migrating season and they were flying early and flying high. The plain that bordered the marshes was thick with soda grass whose autumnal color was burnished by the cloudy morning sunlight to a red-russet sombre glory like that of Cumberland bracken. On the south were sinuous ranks of dunes, but on our side one or two elms struggled against the salty earth — the first trees we had seen since the solitary elm in Lao-hu K'ou, at least eighty miles to the east.

When we camped, in the night, we resumed a great uproar begun before leaving the last camp; and all because I had lost my eyeglass. Just before starting, I had been taking a nap. I had taken out the glass and gone to sleep with it clutched in my fist. When I woke it was gone. We had searched all over that camping ground, scratching about with tent pegs and bits of fuel (the scrub kind, not the dung), and finally, seeing nowhere else the glass could have gone, I had taken off my belt and shaken all my clothes. In vain. However, when we had camped again my camel man, who always took an interest in helping people to keep their minds on their troubles, admonished me to take off my breeches carefully. " I 've lost all kinds of things in my time," said he, " and found them in my trousers." As he was speaking, I did find the glass — in the crook of my knee, though how it could have lodged there unbeknownst, deponent knoweth not. Probably I had scratched myself in my sleep — a knack that one gets — and dropped it in my shirt.

"There you are!" said the camel man, a little disappointed that I had found my glass, but pleased with the justification of his own theories of treasure seeking. "Everything appears (*lou ch'u-lai*) when you take off your trousers." "Like your backside," murmured the Old Man from his nest of sheepskins and felts.

We started as usual in the afternoon, it being the twentieth of September, 1926, and we a month out from Kuei-hua. We had soon to pass a *likin* station, maintained on Mongol territory by the Kan-su authorities; but they gave us no trouble. At the head of the marshes we crossed the course of a dried-out stream which had once fed a living lake. It was marked by a row of fine big elms, of which none looked to be less than fifty years old at the very least; showing perhaps that in the last generation or so the region has become slightly drier — dry enough to impede a growth of new trees, but not to kill off deep-rooted veterans. From this point we climbed slowly for ten miles out of the hollow between the sand ranges where the marshes lie, until we saw wan white temple buildings gleaming in the obscure moonlight. As far as I could see, they were grouped about a central square, with flanking wings of cloisters.

This was the monastery called Tukomen Miao. It is curious that all lama temples in Kuei-hua are called *chao,* which I was told was the regular Mongol word;[1] but that Kuei-hua men when in Mongolia always use the Chinese word *miao,* a temple. There is a *ya-men* here to collect a "grass and water" tax of

[1] *Chao,* according to Rockhill (*Diary*), is the Tibetan word *jo,* meaning "Lord," and refers to images of the Buddha said to have been made during his lifetime by sculptors who had seen his divine person. There are three in existence; but wherever there are copies of the original they are also called *jo* or *chao.*

20 tael cents on each camel passing through Alashan territory. No one can object to a small tax like this, the only one levied by the Mongols, in Inner Mongolia, on all the trade in transit through their territories.    It is the sending of Chinese officials to chase and mulct Chinese trade in Mongolia for the benefit of Chinese tax farmers that is damaging to Chinese interests.

The collector of the grass and water tax is himself a Chinese (I did not see him), said to be an opium-smoking Peking crony of the Prince, who has farmed out to him the right of collection. More probably he is represented by an agent; and the agent, at all events, is watched by a Mongol official.    The tax is in taels, but is of course collected in dollars.    The Mongols of Alashan, like most other Mongols, will not accept the "dragon" dollars minted under the Empire.    The dragon, they argue, was the emblem of the Manchus, the Ta Ch'ing Dynasty.    If the dynasty has passed, how can its coins be legal tender?    Hong-Kong dollars, which, from the figure of Britannia, are called "standing man," are accepted, but the most popular is the Republican coinage of "head" dollars, so called from the head of Yuan Shih-k'ai.

Although my usual custom was to walk in front, I had lagged behind on this march.    When I caught up I found the caravan halted in front of the monastery.    The Pao-t'ou caravan master was having an argument about head dollars and dragon dollars, while my camel man and the Old Man were lying valiantly to get out of the tax altogether.    The camels belonged to the foreigner.    No, the foreigner could talk neither Mongol nor Chinese. He was a very great foreigner — an official.    As the lying had gone so far, I thought it better not to interfere; had I done so, there would have been much more trouble.    Someone would have thought I was yielding; therefore that I was afraid; therefore that there was something wrong about me.    We might have been there all night.

"Foreigners do not buy camels," said a shrewd old Mongol, who carried a Chinese nickel-plated cane for a badge of rank and fashion, and spoke so charmingly like a Peking man that I wished I could pass the time of night with him.    "You are hired camel men, trying to get past on the foreigner's 'face' because he does not know what you are saying." With that the Old Man was haled to the *ya-men* to explain. My own man promptly marched us all on. It was a long time before the Old Man caught us up, puffing in the moonlight. He said he had been ordered to bring back the "interpreter,"—to which rank he had advanced Moses,—but he had said that the interpreter was very proud and would not get off his camel. The Mongols had better send a mounted man to visit us at our camp and see my credentials. Of course no one ever came.

Judging by the direction of my march from Shandan Miao (visited by Prjevalsky in the first part of his travels of 1872–73), the temple or monastery or lamasery of Tukomen Miao is almost certainly his Bain-tuhum. This indeed sounds more like a correct Mongol name, though I give it as I heard it from the Chinese. He fixes its position as 40° 43' 9" north, 106° 0' 0" east. He reached it on his thirteenth march north from Wang-yeh Fu in roughly a straight line, on August 7, 1873, and describes it as 4352 feet above sea level, and seven miles south of the northern boundary of Alashan. Continuing his march, he crossed the Galpin Gobi. It was eighteen miles wide at that point, but he makes no end of a fuss about it, as is the way of travelers. He then crossed the Hurku hills and the Kuei-hua-Uliassutai road on his way to Urga, which he reached on September 17. Thus Bain-tuhum would be roughly a third of the way between Wang-yeh Fu and Urga. Kozloff marks another place called Bain-tuhum, farther to the north and west, without, apparently, a temple.

From Shandan Miao, for a distance of more than three hundred miles to the west, as far as the Edsin Gol, my route had been touched only in two points; once by Prjevalsky going from south to north, and once by Kozloff going from north to south. Between their routes their maps leave white blanks, so that my journey from east to west, across the widest part of Alashan, was through country previously unknown.

Some miles beyond the temple we camped under huge dunes of sand, bordering on arid clay. At the edge of the dunes was a pool of brackish water, where I shot the next morning two teal. The camp, or the pool, was called Jagasatai. Far away to the north were barren clay bluffs with a few trees below them, probably following the bed of a stream; or still more probably a dead stream represented by a line of wells. Along this line were scattered a few *yurts*. Nearer to us a band of hinted or suggested green showed water nearer the surface. I climbed the steep northern scarp of a dune, to find that it was the outer ramp of a confusion of dunes filling up the southern distance, with the blue range behind them that I had seen before. The dunes ran roughly east and west. A solitary track near by showed that a man had either crossed the sands or gone into them after antelope or strayed stock. Gritty bluffs near camp showed the nature of the subsoil; it was like a kind of half-petrified or strongly compressed clay, friable and conspicuously wind-eroded in exposed places, of the color of old yellow-gray brick. I suppose that the wind, wearing down these bluffs of sandy clay, produces the loose sand of the dunes.

I was told that at a day's march to the south of Tukomen, in the hills, — probably the same hills that I saw over the dunes, — there is a rock carving which the Mongols say is not a carving at all, but the relic of a saint called Laoyingjingwo. (The name, like so many of the Mongol names I heard, is obviously modified by a Chinese pronunciation.) The saint, as the story was told to me, was on a journey when he felt his death at hand. He therefore dismounted from the bull camel he was riding and let loose the two white cow camels he was leading. Of these two one ran to the west, reaching the land of some kind of foreigners, but the other ran to the east, as far as Liaotung, where it became a holy animal of the Manchus. The bull camel the old saint hobbled with a rope. Then, sitting in a hollow in a cliff, he composed himself to death and "grew into stone," and the bull camel, with his hobbling rope and all, also turned into stone. In front of the cliff there opened a chasm, so that no man may approach the saint in his shrine; and before him there is a spring of running water. In midwinter, at the rutting season, the camel comes to life and foams at the mouth.

No bull camels may then be led in sight of him, for fear they be stricken and die. The expected corollary to this "magic" of the stone camel would naturally be that cow camels led before him at the rutting time would be fertilized and bring forth excellent young. I could not confirm this, unfortunately. I might, of course, have asked a direct question; but, in examining people with primitive minds about folklore, this is a silly thing to do. They either get frightened or uneasy and lie, or guess at the answer they think is desired and lie to please.

From Shandan Miao to Hasa-buchi we had gone south, with a kind of drift to the west; then we turned northwest to reach Tukomen, and afterwards kept pretty well due west. The first march from Jagasatai was through low dunes, the fringe of the great sands now to our south. There was a thick tamarisk jungle, owing probably to water from the southern range that had disappeared under the sands and was tending toward the surface again. This was the first tamarisk we had seen; a weird jungle of gloomy, heavy green with a sort of shifting gray under-color, against the staring yellow of the higher bare sands. Then we went on over flat sand. The night came down warm and oppressive, forgetting the sharp Mongolian chill. It was cloudy, but there was a suffusion of moonlight. In the west, at intervals of about a minute, there were regular flares of lightning; not in flashes, but as if spreading from an explosion. There was no thunder. We camped near a Chinese trader, at a well called Shihni-usu, in a sterile plain seemingly as far as possible from any Mongols. It did not look as though anything could live in such country; there was nothing but grit, sometimes harder and sometimes softer, but signs of antelope were plentiful.

Another march took us well past the dunes and the distant range to the south, while on the north a small barren range appeared. We crossed a shallow, dried-out swamp, about three miles wide, where soda grass grew thickly. The disappearing moisture had left a hummocky formation in the depth of it. Here we saw a large herd of camels belonging to Mongols, but no *yurts*. Then, after a long tramp through the moonlight, we came to some outcrops of a rubbly formation, making hills less than a hundred feet high. I scrambled to the crest of them and watched the caravan going through, minute but magnificent. We went on another mile, to a camp called either Hayir-khutu — Twin Wells — or Dir-usu, which I believe means Bad Water.

Here we overtook a Barköl caravan on its way home, and were ourselves overtaken by two caravans. We had halted at about one in the morning and had already drunk tea and rolled up in our bedding when, in the deep hush, we heard far away the faint throbbing beat of camel bells. As they drew nearer the sound swelled slowly until the caravans were almost up with our camp, when it broke into the jangling of many different bells. It was over an hour after we heard the most distant pulsation that the first files of silent-footed camels began to go by us, their bulky shadows seeming to darken the night as one watched from the door of the tent. I got up to watch. A caravan master had ridden up first. At the position he took, the camels wheeled left and right in alternate files and then wheeled inward again until they were head-on in pairs of files. Each halted in a straight line; the camels gurgled and screamed as they knelt; the two-foot bell on the last camel of each file clanked as it was slipped and thrown to the ground, the clamor was over, and the caravan lay in two compact squares, facing each other across a clear space. As the men finished unloading they led the camels out and made them kneel again in ranks in this space, their park for the rest of the night; the tent was put up behind, with the door overlooking the loads and the camels, and a fire was lit. The other caravan camped two hundred yards beyond.

Some of the men came over to talk while their tea was boiling. They claimed to have made two forced marches of about forty miles. Behind them, they said, were five or six caravans, numbering more than a thousand camels in all — the final assembly of all that had got away from Kuei-hua and Pao-t'ou. They had all converged on the road after their individual dodgings and circlings, but, as no well could water so many camels, they were stringing out. With the Barköl caravan we had overtaken, the Pao-t'ou caravan, and the newcomers, we were still too many — more than six hundred camels. The newcomers said that they would make yet another long march, to get the lead. I was glad to go with them, and luckily there was no fight with my camel man about it, as he was anxious to leave the Pao-t'ou men as soon as he had a chance of Kuei-hua company.

Taking stock of the country next day, I found it about as arid as any to be seen in Mongolia, though we were away from dunes. The water in the wells was not enough for all the camels, and there was only a bit of the worst kind of grazing — shriveled, sparse desert plants of a woody kind. There was not a hint of Mongols, but the usual grain seller was there. The track lay along almost level ground of hard clay covered thinly with gravel. On our north were low hills of red rubble, running east and west. A miniature range like it went off to the south, and near the gap between the two was our camp. Much farther to the south, blue in the distance, was a much bigger range, said to mark the borders of Kan-su. They may have been the hills marked Yabarai on Kozloff's map, but are much more likely to have been a range filling in the gap between the Yabarai and the Alashan range. The country masking the frontier of Kan-su along the line Ning-hsia–Chen-fan–Liang Chou–Kan Chou–Su Chou appears to be an indeterminate region of sands, if anything more Mongolian than Chinese in character. These sands thin out northward into the deserts of Alashan, recurring occasionally in dune-encumbered areas. There is a general slope to the north. Prjevalsky describes the Galpin Gobi as a depression, and Kozloff stresses the depression of Goitso, as he calls it; Kuai-tze Hu, as I heard it called. In fact the whole region is a vast lowering of the Mongolian plateau, which, though previously crossed from north to south and now from east to west, still requires a survey before it can be comprehended as a whole. The land rises again in the north to the Altai and the Hurku, but small ranges have been indicated running east and west in the depression itself.

Marching from Dir-usu (Hayir-khutu), we kept on for seven steady hours, in a gritty haze that by afternoon occluded even the nearer hills. At last, in the night, we heard an uproar of dogs ahead; one of the caravans had camped, and their dogs were challenging the caravans that went by.  We camped also, because in the dark hazy night my camel man, whose eyes were bad again, kept stumbling and falling; but at half-past four in the morning we picked up and started out again to catch whatever caravan was in the lead.  The people camped nearest us were the Pao-t'ou lot, and thus we ended our partnership with them.

The night had cleared; the dawn was coming up and the moon going down; the light was unreal, and it was sharply cold, though the day before had been oppressively sultry.  In a couple of miles we passed a grain dealer's camp, with a big caravan said to have come out from Kan-su with supplies.  Then we passed the Barköl caravan, which had also made a bid for the lead, but given up. They were near another dealer, living not in a *yurt* but in a mud house.  He had a big well, less than ten feet deep, from which he watered a tiny garden in that uncompromising wilderness; *chiu-ts'ai* (a plant of an oniony-garlicky kind), turnips, and a huge sunflower, which last was grown for the delicate eating of the seeds.  At about four miles we saw the caravans in the lead, the same two that had overtaken us, and camped within a mile of them.

A little family group of Chinese passed us here.  They were refugees from a famine district near Chen-fan, making for Pao-t'ou, where they had relatives.  They sold some watermelons at two for a dollar [1] to one of the caravans ahead, and the man who bought them gave me half of one.  It would have been worth a few cents in Kuei-hua and the shadow of a fraction of that in Turkestan; but melons at two for a dollar are delectable eating in the desert.

We started once more that same afternoon, in the tail now of the two Kuei-hua caravans.  We turned into the rubbly hills to the north, where in a waterless watercourse were a few elms, the biggest and finest we had seen.  Getting out of the hills, we camped in a big circular plain.  There was a large flock of blue-rock pigeons here, the only ones I saw between Kuei-hua and Turkestan.  A newly arrived trader was building himself a mud

[1] The dollar meant here, as throughout the book, is the silver Chinese dollar, worth about two shillings, or about seven tenths of a silver tael.

house.  The number of traders in this region bore out their statement that there are Mongols to be found, though the ragged hills and sere plains did not seem to promise any life at all; but they say that more water and a little grass can be found along the foot of the hills.  The traders have undoubtedly multiplied in the last few years, owing to the profits to be made out of the caravans in winter.  It is hard to estimate comparative prices in China, because of the variation in measures — Kan-su measures, as used by these traders, being especially confusing.  They charge, however, literally famine prices, for they bring all their grain from regions that are constantly suffering from famine; and the caravans have to suffer commensurately in the rates they pay.

We made two further marches, through an even more silent and empty country, without even traders.  Bearing to the north to get round a hilly mass, we came up on to a kind of irregular plateau, with a tilt to the north.  It was much cut up by dry rifts, and the soil was hard and dry, of a coarse sandy clay, overlaid with black gravel in thin flat pieces.  This gravel came from outcrops of black rock, all of them shattered by alternate heat and frost into sheaves of flat slaty pieces, ready to be diminished further into the prevalent gravel.  A great deal of sand must be blown off from exposed clay highlands like this.  The last well we had passed had been filled in with blown sand, and in places the hard soil gave way to looser sand, yellow overlaid with black. Wherever the sand was looser grew gnarled and withered desert plants, sometimes standing to a height of six struggling inches, sometimes hugging the ground even closer.

This is the region called Khara-jagang, or the Black Tamarisks.  Everywhere there is tamarisk scrub, and everywhere it seems to be dead except for a very few bushes.  They get their name from their black deadness, and they have a height sometimes of four or five feet, but they never grow so thickly that they stop the view.  Here once more there are traders, because there is a route coming up from Chen-fan and because of the trade in liquorice root.  This plant, as is well known, is at its best when wild; and the most valuable roots on the market have always come from the western territories of China — from parts of

Kan-su, the Ordos, and Alashan. It is one of the most valuable products of Alashan. The Mongols themselves do not deal in it any more than they deal in any other produce of the soil. It is collected by the Chinese. During the short season when the roots are fit for drying and cleaning, thousands of laborers from Kan-su, employed by the traders, swarm into Mongolia. In the last two or three years, however, the Mongols, not wishing to have any influx of Chinese made desperate by both famine and political oppression, have managed to put a ban on the trade in Alashan; nor have the Chinese, owing to lack of continuity in official policy, debated the question.

## X

## SPEARS AND TRADITIONS

AFTER taking up with the two Kuei-hua caravans, I soon became even more friendly with them than I had been with the Pao-t'ou people. One of them, numbering three and a half *pa* with consignments of general merchandise, belonged to the House of Liang, a Mohammedan family of Kuei-hua. The other, which numbered five *pa*, — that is, five double files of about eighteen camels to the file, — carrying brick tea, belonged to the House of Chou, a family of the Great Faith. Although caravan-owning families all have a trading style or firm name, this name is never applied to their caravans. Even caravans belonging to firms or partnerships are always known under the personal name of the caravan master, while it is a matter of pride with the old families, whose business has always gone from father to son, to have their caravans known by the "house" or family name rather than by the trading style.

Each of these caravans was in the charge of a caravan master, while the owning family was represented by a son, traveling in charge of the cargo. One of them I had met at an inn near the top of the pass leading from Kuei-hua to the plateau. We recognized each other at once, and he said that he must have "borrowed my luck" to get out of Kuei-hua. He had been scared away from the pass on two successive days by the sound of firing, but got off at last on the same day that I did. He was the Eldest Son of the House of Chou, and he proved himself the best of all the friends I made on the road. He was of the fourth generation in the trade. The family was of Shan-hsi origin, and had long been settled near Ku Ch'eng-tze, where a junior branch still owned wide lands; but his grandfather had fled to Kuei-hua during the Mohammedan revolt of the seventies. His own father had retired early from an active share in the business in order to devote himself to the opium pipe, with which he was a famous performer. The original wealth of the clan had at that time been divided, so that there were now three House of Chou caravans on the road, two of them belonging to cousins. My friend's father was not yet fifty, and he himself at the age of thirty had a son of fourteen, so that with his seven brothers, the youngest not older than his own son, he represented a stock of admirable vigor.

In early youth he had started with the family caravan as a camel puller, in order to learn the business of which he would one day be head. A younger brother was now serving the same apprenticeship under him, receiving no better treatment than any hired servant, nor even drawing wages; except that, being weak in health, he was allowed to ride a camel for part of the time on long marches. He had first been articled to a business firm, but when his health broke down his father, having sons to spare, ordered him out to the Gobi "to see if he would get better or die." He had already made one trip and was getting stronger.

My own friend was known to everyone by his child name of Liu-tze or his nickname of Ta-t'ou, which is Bighead. He was the friend of everyone up and down the whole road, except his own cousins, whom he considered purse-proud, and had no particular care for anything except opium. He would have nothing to do with anyone who put on any kind of side, but was cherished by all camel pullers; and he liked me, he said, because I was not like either a foreigner or a merchant, but would have made a good caravan man. "It is as well," he would say in a slightly snuffling voice; "we can be friends. I am not at my ease with anything but an opium pipe or a camel puller."

Short-legged, pot-bellied, and big-headed, with features like a well-fed pig, I do not know if I can make plain the charm of the man. I only know that I had a never-failing pleasure in seeing his paunchy little figure coming along on top of a camel, and that inside his dirty sheepskins and under his round felt cap he was as good a gentleman as could be found in Mongolia. He spoke like a camel puller, but his lurid language was slowly, lazily, and humorously uttered, in a snuffy-puffy voice, and his chuckling laughter accented his charm. Indeed, everything he did had a subcomic flavor. He was not on the best of terms with his caravan master, a worried little man; and the caravan master, according to custom, was in charge of all supplies. Therefore when he found that I was short of *ts'ao mien* and passionately given to the eating of it, he would take advantage of the confusion when camp was being made in the dark to steal that which he really owned, and would sneak over to give it to me privily, grinning and snorting.

When he was not in my tent, I was usually in his, and both his men and those of the House of Liang were cheery fellows. They had at first a forced and wary politeness not natural to their own habits, but before long this wore off and they began to accept me without reserve as an understandable person of their own kind. This was in part because I had smoothed out my own awkwardnesses. I had fallen into the way of gossiping with them, instead of asking questions point-blank about things I did not understand. There is nothing that shuts off the speech of simple men like the suspicion that they are being pumped for information; while if they get over the feeling of strangeness they will yarn as they do among themselves. Then in their talk there comes out the rich rough ore of what they themselves accept as the truth about their lives and beliefs, not spoiled in trying to refine it unskillfully by suiting the words to the listener.

The Chinese have a whole series of formal questions to be asked of foreigners: Do we have snow in our land? Or coal? Do we plough the land or do we make our food by machinery? Do we bury our dead like the Chinese in coffins, or like the Mohammedans in a winding sheet only, or like the Mongols by simply exposing the body in a waste place? There is no end to such questions, but I got rid of them by telling yarns myself. I soon found that interest in wireless and skyscrapers was only perfunctory. They asked about these things because they thought I was a millionaire trader who only knew about the lives of rich and incredible foreigners; but the answers could not hold their interest for long, being too far removed from the world of their own realities. There was nothing about them to be visualized, whereas all their own talk is in words like pictures, simple and vivid.

One day I said, simplifying my own idea of Alaska, that we not only had snow in our land but a kind of outer land (as Mongolia to the Chinese is an outer land) where so much snow fell that no farms could be tilled. Most of the food was brought from outside, except for fish caught in the summer; men went there only to trap fur-bearing animals and to find gold, and for most of the year transport was by dog sled. They brightened up at that. They were transport men, they liked to talk about transport; but what they thought to be the foreign ways of getting about were too unnatural for them to understand. Many of them had a vague idea that a motor car, though run by machinery indeed, was a kind of mechanical animal fed on *ch'i-yu* — aerated oil, or steam oil, or gas oil being the meaning conveyed to them by this neologism. They had much the same ideas about railway engines; in fact, there was a legend current among them about an engine which had "gone mad" at Kuei-hua — refusing to go forward, they said, it had bolted backward, killing several people. Dogs were different, and my rendering of all I could remember of *The Call of the Wild* became a borrowed saga of the caravans.

One thing it took me a long time to learn. I had wanted to know from the first why a spear is carried on the leading camel of all caravans that have any pride or swagger. It is a long spear, with a tassel of red hair below the blade, and sometimes a small white pennon, with the name and style of the caravan owners and the name of the town from which they hail. When marching it is lashed on the first load, usually with the banner furled, but in camp it is little regarded. It is not, as one might think, set up by the tent, but thrown down on the ground. Big Mongol caravans carry the same kind of spear. Among them it seems to be a sign either that a man of high rank is traveling, or that the caravan is going on the business of some prince, thus making it free from seizure for tributary service by any other chief.

When I asked directly about the flag, no one would say more than that it was "an old custom." Then I fished, but for a long time was baffled. At last the talk came round to it by a side channel of talk about something else. The use of the spear, it seems, may be partly in imitation of the Mongol style, but in the present custom there is also the memory of another origin.

Before the time of modern bank remittances in China there existed a class of treasure carriers, the *pao-piao-ti*. They were often men who, after making a reputation for courage as bandits, turned honest and made fortunes as carriers of bullion remittances. A percentage was charged on the silver, in return for which the *pao-piao-ti* deposited security or provided guarantors bound to make good any loss in transit. He gathered a band of men to convoy the treasure in carts or by mule train or camel caravan, according to the nature of the country. He sometimes took travelers under his protection and in many regions the only express travel known was under his escort. He traveled fast, but, contrary to what one might expect, as openly as possible. He and his men wore a costume modeled on an ancient military style. The head was bound with a black turban, or in summer a straw hat might be worn, with a very wide, loose brim caught up to the crown by ribands. Over the wide-sleeved tunic a sleeveless jacket was worn; the loose breeches were secured at the ankle with ankle bands, and half boots were worn reaching to the calf. The color of the uniform, which was nominally of leather, was either black with red facings or white with black facings; black being the traditional military color, while pure white would never have done because it was the ill-omened color of mourning. The whole was set off by a sash about the waist. Stuck in the back of his sash the leader carried a little banner, which set forth his name and pretensions.

On approaching a city the men shouted out to clear the road. They declared the name of their leader, the nature of their convoy, and by implication challenged anyone to fight for it. This must usually have been nothing but eyewash of the good old histrionic kind. The captain would be an ex-bandit who had set up in the country where his name was best known and where by paying any bandits a percentage on his own percentage he could easily avoid trouble. When, on completing the journey, he reached the house or firm to which the silver was consigned, he would fix the metal-shod haft of his little banner into the wood of the door, from which it might not be removed until the silver was weighed over and found correct.

Ts'ang Chou, in Chih-li near the Shan-tung border, was noted for the bad men and *pao-piao-ti* it turned out. It was the home of *pa-shih*, the ancient Chinese system from which the Japanese *jiu-jitsu* was derived. So many were the robbers bred about Ts'ang Chou that it was said of a village in the prefecture that not a corpse in the village graveyard had its head on tight. The last bow that all of them had made had been to the executioner. "To this day," said Moses (for this part of the tale is his; he comes from thereabouts), "all the men of that place are scamps. If you ask them why they do not have a try at an honest living, they tell you that many of them have tried; but that they are all born bad, and it will out." Moreover, in our own time many of the swarming bandits of Manchuria and Eastern Inner Mongolia are emigrants from the Ts'ang Chou country, so that it is said that the best passport "beyond the Eastern gate" (of the Great Wall) is a Ts'ang Chou accent. Moses had what he thought was a Moral Tale about a good little Ts'ang Chou boy who went to Manchuria to seek an honest fortune; but when he got there he found himself plucked by the elbow by a mysterious stranger who said, in effect, "You talk like a Ts'ang Chou man; come, let me enlist you among the bandits." Moses then exploded the moral by adding "and thus, in Manchuria, no Ts'ang Chou man has to work."

In the days of the *pao-piao-ti*, Ts'ang Chou took a manly pride in its original sin. The custom was jealously upheld that no treasure carrier might utter his professional challenge within forty *li* of Ts'ang Chou walls. Were he to do so, then "What!" the wrathful people of the countryside would say; "do you come to the home of fighting men to boast that you are a fighter?" and they would rise up to overwhelm him.

All this by the way; but then, most of the talk that goes back and forth across the tent fire is rambling talk.    It is very good talk, at that.    The *pao-piao-ti* has not survived the posts and the telegraph; he is no longer known on the Ku Ch'eng-tze road, but his banner, so they say, has become the emblem of the caravans. The men are more attached to the prideful spear than are the owners, who grudge it a little because, tugging and swaying, it exhausts even the stoutest camels.    It is the men who keep the old custom from dying out; to them it stands for the tradition of the *pao-piao-ti*.    It means that the caravan is not afraid of the distant desert stages, but makes itself responsible for the safe arrival of goods and travelers.

Another thing which I learned through the same diffuse but vigorous talk was a truer respect for Chinese swearing, which I had always thought thin and poor, a short range of expressions based on one obscenity.    These men had a much richer vocabulary and more varied turn of phrase; but it is true that the oath of the heaviest calibre I ever heard in Chinese was discharged by a foreigner.    He was a man with a naturally Elizabethan command of the vernacular, but I sorrow to this day because I never made sure whether he compounded that phrase for himself or heard it from some genius of the people.    "Go tell that man," he said, "that I am coming to-morrow to defile eight generations of his grave-buried ancestors."

It is a pity that even in this age of experiment a treatise on swearing would have to be privately printed, because language that is robustly and originally foul is almost always achieved by startling combinations of words that look so disgusting.    It is a still greater pity that the disguised use of swearing in print should have led to all kinds of sham.    I do not mean so much things in the style of "d——!" or "The captain swore a frightful oath. 'Confound you!' he said, turning on his heel."    I mean a serious and active falsity in our literature, which was revealed to me while pondering an attempt to Bowdlerize the strong talk of the Kuei-hua camel men without emasculating it.    What I cannot away with is the spurious ornament and gingerbread "picturesqueness" of our versions of Persian, Egyptian, Arabic, Hindu, and Oriental cursing generally.    In that hour of mental exertion it was forced on my understanding that the ruck of those rococo expressions must be not only related in kind but identical in word with many of the raw formulæ of the caravan men. They have, I can only suppose, very little of that artful sophistication they have assumed in English. What is *ko-p'ao! jih ta tsu-tsu!* (a favorite address to a camel) but "O base-born son of a shameless ancestry!" Yet literally (and, except for the comparatively little-known dialect of the northwest, I have selected an Easy Example for Beginners) it is "Bastard!—— his ancestors!"

It is at that word in blank that we all stick. "Defile" is in some measure a version; but it is not a full rendering, not a flat-footed, absolute translation. On the one hand, "defile" implies a suavity that is not there; it implies a use of metaphor and allegory present to excess in all our Orientalized English, but not justified, I am persuaded, by most of the original tongues. On the other hand, that original word in blank would not be justified were we to render it by the equally curt word in English. Undeniably it does have in the vernacular a more resonant quality, some sort of overtone, a fuller content, a proleptic versatility—but I give it up. I can only suggest that by corollary the late James Elroy Flecker ought, though with sorrow, to be moved a long way down the class, and that by presumption there is no prophet but Burton, with the private printers for his apostles.

But what a keen grief it is to think that my knowledge must perish with me!

Thus,. eating and sleeping, walking and talking, we drifted on through the deserts of Alashan, seeing scarcely a soul, with "every bloomin' camping ground exactly like the last." Yet, arid and poor as the country was, we found almost every day a trader's encampment, and sometimes there were Mongol *yurts* at a distance. The camel pullers complained bitterly of the shy hostility of the Mongols on the Winding Road, who never sought out the caravans for gossip or trade. The people of Alashan, they said, are well enough to do. There is plenty of money brought into their country by the Chinese trade. Also they are not outrageously taxed by their prince, who draws a sufficient revenue from the salt monopoly, and they suffer less from the burden of monasteries than do other tribes. Yet they live in squalor, not even showing off their wealth in fine if dirty clothes as other Mongols do. This may be because they do not belong ethnologically to the tribes of Inner Mongolia, but are Eleuths [1] or Western Mongols by origin, of a group differing somewhat in racial characteristics. The Western Mongols, as I found later, enjoy at least as easy a life as most nomads, while some of them have their lines cast in the pleasantest places of the earth; but all of them live in conspicuous filth, not caring to make any demonstration of their wealth.

Everywhere in Mongolia there have always been Chinese traders. The Mongols will not stoop to manage a business in person, though some of the Chinese firms are run wholly or in part on the capital of rich Mongols, or backed by the prerogatives of Mongol princes. Except, however, for the traders and the caravan men, who are under some sort of check because all the entries to Mongolia are watched by Chinese officials, no Chinese are allowed to go among the Mongols. Those who do, like all Chinese who live among foreign peoples, become more than half Mongol in manners, dress, and speech. The result is to confirm the stubborn conservatism of the Mongols. Their boots and hats and most of their clothes not made of leather have for centuries been manufactured in China and brought to them by Chinese merchants; but they show no tendency to adopt Chinese fashions. The boots and hats and clothes must be made to the Mongol pattern.

In language they have the same conservatism. In the border territories, especially, many Mongols can speak Chinese fluently, but they do not like to use the language, nor will they have anything to do with a Chinese on Mongol ground unless he speaks Mongol. In fact, despite centuries of contact, despite the many

[1] The spelling *Eleuth*, according to Couling (*Encyclopædia Sinica*, Oxford University Press, 1917) is due to French missionaries. The original sound is more like Ölöt. The sound becomes, in the official Chinese name, *Nge-lu-te;* another Chinese pronunciation of the Mongol name is probably responsible for *Alashan*, "the mountains of the Ölöt."

Chinese who go among them, the scores of Mongols who go to Peking every year on government business and the thousands who go to Wu-t'ai Shan on the still more urgent business of pilgrimage, there is a point at which the Mongol recoils from the Chinese. This aversion has been stimulated recently, among the tribes still under Chinese dominion, by the increased activity in expropriating land.

Furthermore, the Mongols of Alashan resent the new arrival of the caravans among them. They have long been separated from Outer Mongolia by well-defined desert barriers, and have in the past more or less controlled the terms of the Chinese commerce in their country. They recognize only Ning-hsia merchants in Wang-yeh Fu, Chen-fan men in the deserts, and Mohammedan camel buyers who do not wander among them, but only travel between their chief markets. I passed throughout the length of Alashan, traversing a country that, although so desert to the eye, held a surprising number of Mongols with their cattle, thinly dispersed. Everywhere they stood clear of the caravans as it were in fearful dislike, nor would the few men we met on the road speak with us. It seemed as though they were taken aback by the new turn of affairs in both Mongolia and China, being in dread of entanglement on one side with the changing world of Outer Mongolia, and on the other with the civil wars in Kan-su, which might bring down on them an invasion of escaping Chinese. The caravans that in growing numbers tramp and camp through the golden sunshine and lowering hazes of their deserts, though, seen from Peking, they look to be dwindling down the perspective of history, loom up to them like the forerunners of a trade they do not want and politics that for them threaten all the decencies of life.

The caravan men speak with disgust of the new lonely years in which they have used the Winding Road, and longingly of the old fat years on the Great Road, where through generations of usage Mongol and Chinese had come to friendly terms. There, at every camp, Mongols would come riding up to look for a little trade — which meant even more to the camel puller, with his "perquisites," than to the caravan owner. It was the

custom of the road that every Mongol, rich or poor, should be
given a bowl or two of flour or *ts'ao mien*.  In return for this
they would often patch worn shoes or sheepskin clothes, and
there were even tinkers who could mend broken grates and cooking pots.  After the formal gift of flour, trade would begin.
The Mongols exchanged wool and camel hair and lambskins not
only for trinkets and brummagem stuff, but for the staples they
needed; cotton cloth and thread, brick tea, pipes and tobacco;
while for flour they would give milk and cheese and mutton, or
the meat of antelope and wild ass.

Toward Uliassutai, flour was worth several times its weight
in meat.  There grew up a curious system by which caravans
took out extra flour from Ku Ch'eng-tze, where it was even
cheaper than at Kuei-hua, and left it with Mongols, to be collected as supplies on the next journey to the west.  For keeping
the flour, the Mongols were allowed to take a percentage of it
for their own use.  With a stock in hand they could feed themselves free, by taking full weight from well-plenished caravans,
to which they returned short weight, and supplying short weight
to caravans short of food, who had to return them overweight
on the way back.

The relations between Chinese and Mongols are supposed to
have been fixed for all time by K'ang Hsi, the second Manchu
Emperor, who in clamping together all the Manchu conquests
made tours of observation as well as of invasion in Mongolia.
His name must have been a terror to the Mongols which the
Chinese invoked to improve their own standing.  As the Manchus in China treated the Chinese cavalierly, so the Chinese in
Mongolia treated the Mongols with a high hand.  I often heard
men regret the fine spirit of the old swaggering days when any
Chinese could strike any Mongol with a light heart, " even if he
wore a blue button on his cap " — a sign of noble rank.  There
is said to be a rock at some place on the Great Road where the
hoofprints of K'ang Hsi's horse can still be seen,[1] and his voice

[1] There is a comparable legend, concerning not K'ang Hsi but Ch'ien Lung,
localized at the lamasery at Ma-t'i (Horse's Hoof) about forty miles south of
Kan Chou; related in *Through Jade Gate and Central Asia*, by Mildred Cable
and Francesca French. London: Constable, 1927.

is said to have decreed every practice of the caravans which is different from Chinese procedure. He is even put forward as the inventor of the caravan tent (really an adaptation of a Western Mongol form), basing it on the *pa kua* or Eight Trigrams, a very ancient Chinese symbol; though this is a little difficult to understand, seeing that the tent has not eight sides or panels, but ten.

The truth is that the Chinese, after their superiority over the Mongols had been made clear by the harsh decrees of their Manchu rulers, set themselves to build bridges between themselves and the barbarians. Most of the customs they recognize, though fathered on K'ang Hsi, are obviously concessions to the customs of a nomad society. Before the disasters that confounded the Chinese in Mongolia, when they no longer had behind them a Dragon Throne but a catch-as-catch-can Republic, there had grown up friendships between Mongol and Chinese families that sometimes endured for generations. The caravans of families well known in Mongolia could even hire or buy camels without paying cash. If a hired camel died on the road, the Mongol could either claim an agreed price for him or take his pick from the caravan of the borrower. With one of the caravans I knew were two camels that had been hired from a Mongol two years before. Both had been commandeered for military use a season before the current civil war, and had been returned in shocking condition. Both were taken on the journey to the west only to save them from being commandeered again, and both died on the road. The owner shrugged his shoulders and said that he would have to pay a hundred and twenty silver taels for each of them, for they had been picked camels, hired when the market was high. I asked how he could pay when it was impossible for him to take his caravan through Outer Mongolia. He replied that he was going to send a messenger *t'ou-t'ou'rh-ti* — like a thief — about certain other of his affairs, and this man would carry the silver to the Mongol. That was the old Chinese honesty, on which, in spite of the outrageous profits they made, the Chinese built up such vast businesses in Mongolia.

*Tsou hou-ti, sui hou li*, say the men of the caravans — when traveling in the Back Country, follow back customs. Thus, not only the universal nomad law of hospitality, but the law of the tent has been taken over from the Mongols. In a caravan tent, as in a *yurt*, the cooking things are on the right as you enter, while water butts, wicker buckets for hauling water from wells, camel whips, and other gear are on the left. It is the worst kind of discourtesy to enter a *yurt* carrying a whip; it should be stuck in one of the ropes that bind the *yurt* down on the outside. As there are no such ropes on a tent, the whip is thrown into the tent before a man enters. These camel whips are only used while herding; they have a wooden handle a foot and a half in length, and a lash of braided camel hide ten or twelve feet long. It is dangerous for an unskilled man to crack one, for it might easily blind him or take off an ear.

In the tent itself no one may cross between the fire, which is between the two tent poles, and the back pole. This is because the pole represents the back of the round Mongol *yurt*, where opposite the door and in line with the fire is the family shrine, with butter lamps burning before it. Fire itself is holy, for before the introduction of matches it must have been as precious to the nomad as it was mysterious. When a new fire has been lit, after the tent has been newly pitched, a little of the first tea or food prepared must be thrown on it for an offering, and a little as an offering out of the door, for the hungry spirits of the void, the guardians of the place, who may have been disturbed by the arrival of men. The sanctity of fire carries even beyond itself, entering into the iron fire grate and tongs. They must be kept strictly for the fire, whose house and servant they are. It is sacrilegious to knock out a pipe against them, for the indwelling spirit will be enraged. As he is mute, he can only express his resentment by making the heads of all those who sleep in the tent ache as if they had themselves been hit.

Although they are so strict in Mongolia about these observances, I never found a caravan man who seemed to understand that they might be imitations of Mongol customs. If one suggested it, they said it was not so; all of these customs were decreed by K'ang Hsi. Yet the Chinese not only do not take these rites home with them, but seem to have nothing similar of their own — a delightful illustration of a principle taken so much for granted in primitive religious relations that it is never specifically mentioned. This double practice is a survival from the days before history when the Chinese in his heart recognized that his gods could no longer protect him when he left China, and that in Mongolia he came under the tabus of the Mongol gods. A man in this standing, when he says "Thy gods are not my gods," does not mean to hint that there are no other gods than his own, or even that they are less powerful. His is the attitude recognized in the Old Testament, where we find admissions, though no undiplomatically bald statement, that Jahweh was originally not a universal but a tribal god, hostile to the gods of Moab and Philistia, but a little uneasy when encroaching on their territory. The gods which were afterwards declared to be false in the sense of not existing at all were in the first place believed to be real enough, and false in the sense only of being alien.

The principle is so elementary and easily understood that it is not felt to be incongruous for the Chinese who live a quasi-nomadic life trading in Mongolia to have a code different from that of the caravans, whose men make their living in a different way. Thus a trader may eat camel flesh and buy and sell camel skins, which are tabu to a caravan man. An injured camel may be fat and young, but caravan men may not eat it, though they say they will eat wild camels. To make money out of a dead camel, even to save the price of a sheep by eating it, is to insult the souls of those who give them their living. A camel skin is worth from six to twelve dollars in Kuei-hua, — as much as a man gets in wages for the whole journey to Turkestan, — but camels left by the road are never skinned any more than they are ever slaughtered. The most that the men will do is to take a strip of hide for patching their shoes from a dead camel left by some other caravan.

The trader, however, because he deals in sheep, comes under the sheep tabus. He must be as scrupulous as a Mongol in picking a bone clean. To waste mutton is to esteem lightly the soul of a sheep whose life one has taken to feed one's own life;

therefore the soul of the sheep might visit the flocks with wrath. It is also the custom to break certain of the bones, notably the shoulder blade. The idea informing this custom appears to be that a soul proceeding from intact bones, even if the bones are dissevered, is a whole soul, capable of motion; but if an important bone is broken the soul also is lamed and cannot follow the killer of its body.

All of these customs become so much a habit that I myself was startled at the free behavior of the men about me when I first sat in the tent of a Mohammedan caravan. The Moslem, like the Christian, has always endeavored to take his own tabus with him, and to overrule the Books of Etiquette of the local godlings. To a Mohammedan, fire is not sacred. Some Mohammedans are even bold enough to take the life of a cast camel, instead of leaving it to die naturally. Moreover, they do it to put the animal out of pain, not for the sake of the flesh or the hide, which they leave. The Salars, who travel armed, shoot it, instead of cutting the throat to make it pure eating. I believe that the camel, by strict law, is not a clean animal, but that on the Mecca road it is frequently given the *halal* to make it as fit as possible for starving pilgrims to eat. Central Asian Mohammedans, however, do not stress the point of cleanliness with camels any more than they do when it comes to eating horseflesh. Though in a Mohammedan-owned caravan there are rarely more than one or two Mohammedan camel pullers, the non-Moslem Chinese serving with them take their time from Islam just as unaffectedly as they follow Mongol usage in their own caravans.

Chinese Mohammedans, under the Koranic law, slaughter a sheep by cutting the throat. The Mongol way is to make a slit in the stomach, thrust in a hand, and seize the heart. When skillfully done scarcely any blood is shed, and the custom may be due to an awkward evasion of the letter of the Buddhist law against shedding blood. It is more likely, however, that the intention is to make the meat more warming and nourishing. Mutton so killed, owing to the blood not having been drained out, has a full, gamy flavor. The caravan men used once to slaughter their sheep in this way, but it is one of the customs that are dying out, sad to say, since the caravans took to the Winding Road and lost close touch with Mongol life.

One of the Tales for Newcomers is that when men consider they have not been given enough meat they will bring camel flesh into the tent, scorch it at the fire, and pretend to eat it, to shame the caravan master. It is true that the meat ration is not so strictly regulated by custom as are other details of caravan usage. At the beginning of the journey several sheep or perhaps an ox must be slaughtered, to give the men good meat meals for a few days and to provide fat for mixing into sauce. On the Great Road sheep could be bought almost anywhere, but on the Winding Road there are only a few places where they can be had, and usually at each of these places one is killed.

Meat, however, which is a necessity to the Mongol, is a luxury even to Mongolia-going Chinese. They demand flour for a staple. The steady ration is white flour, *ts'ao mi,* and *ts'ao mien.* The white flour is rolled and kneaded into dough, then either cut into crude spaghetti or pinched between finger and thumb into flat pieces called *chiu-p'ien'rh.* In either form it is cooked very simply. Sometimes a little chopped meat is first fried in the pan; then water is added and brought to a boil. When it is boiling fast the dough is thrown in, and in two or three minutes ladled out again. With each bowl of this the men are given a spoonful of *chiang,* the standard sauce. This is carried in a half-solid, concentrated form like pemmican. The base of it is bread, which has been first fermented and then allowed to mildew. The rest is made of chopped meat, mutton fat, and whatever the generosity of the provider has furnished — beans, bean curd, ginger, green peppers, spice pepper, and a great quantity of salt, to preserve it.

This is the capital meal of the day, taken in the early afternoon. Before and after it the men can have *ts'ao mi* and *ts'ao mien* at their discretion. *Ts'ao mi* is a kind of millet, parched well so that it is always ready to eat. *Ts'ao mien* is oaten flour, ground very fine and then parched. Both of these are mixed into bowls of tea. The *ts'ao mien* is highly glutinous, absorbing moisture with reluctance and slowly, but when stirred with tea into a porridgy consistency it is very good, and, like porridge, the taste of it never palls. These two things take the place of bread on the upward journey. On the way down from Turkestan, where little oats or millet is grown and white flour is cheaper than anywhere in China, enough of it is taken to make bread. Only caravans hailing from the west, where men are pampered, are provisioned with bread for the journey both ways. Kuei-hua men themselves also prefer bread, so much so that they call the great snow peak of Bogdo Ola, which can be seen a hundred miles out from Ku Ch'eng-tze, Bread Mountain — Mo-mo Shan, or Man-t'ou Shan, or still more affectionately Ta Man-t'ou Shan, Big Loaf Mountain; and all because it is a symbol of the fat lands of the west, where men eat their fill of the noble white-flour bread and are happy. On the day that they deliver their loads in Ku Ch'eng-tze they joyfully throw away what is left of their rations of the road, demanding bread as by right. What is Paradise if it is not a country where food can be thrown away?

For the matter of that, few Chinese, unless they have been bred in the northwest, will admit that *ts'ao mi* and *ts'ao mien* are fit for human food. They use the words as if they were an expression tantamount to "privation and suffering"; and I have heard men say that they were "going to eat parched millet and oatmeal" when they meant that they were going to make the caravan journey through Mongolia. In point of justice it needs to be said that both these things are honest foods; the *ts'ao mien* nourishes and invigorates, while the *ts'ao mi*, as the Chinese have it, is "cooling." This is recognized under the caravan rule under which vinegar, which mitigates the effect on the blood of a heavy cereal diet, is only provided on the downward journey, when there is no millet.

When at the beginning of the year I had made a reconnaissance to Kuei-hua to arrange for camels, every Chinese I met and all the foreigners who knew anything of life in Mongolia told me that it would be insane (and the foreigners added that it would be insanitary) to try to live on the food supplied to Chinese travelers by the caravans, which is no more than the rations that the camel pullers get. Even Chinese travelers take with them a few extra things to eat, more as necessities than as luxuries. When I submitted that traveling in China I had always eaten anything that came to hand, and, living on donkey men's food and muleteers' food, had always been able to keep up with donkey men and muleteers, they ceased not to dissuade me. China was different. You could always get to a train and reach a doctor in a few days. Camel men, they said, had stomachs little more human than camels.

Now my stomach is a prideful organ that has always urged me to let it try anything once, and has usually liked it. Nevertheless, when I returned to Peking, I took that same stomach to a friend of mine who was a doctor with Mongolian experience and asked him what I should put into it. The doctor thought of a lot of things. He drew up a wonderful list in which the proportions of the proteins and the carbohydrates and the what-nots were superbly balanced. Then he checked it by the dietary of the American Navy (for he was versed in many things besides Mongolia), saw that it was good, and made some additions. Afterward I checked it with a check book and made some subtractions. Finally we arrived at a *modus edendi*. Of the original theory on which the regimen was based I seem to remember only that the American Navy can keep afloat (if pushed, as the saying goes) on baked beans and what are Americonautically called "canned" tomatoes.

Although a layman, I take a really intelligent interest in my gastric juices. Therefore, when the doctor had squared his idea of what I should buy with my idea of what I should pay, and announced that the calories, at any rate, would be no disgrace to the American Navy, I made bold to ask him how I stood on vitamins, the A and the B, or both, or either. I told him roundly that tinned vegetables were deficient in vitamins. Nor could he deny it. We pondered the vitamins with silent gloom and a whiskey-soda. At last the doctor said: "Well, anyway, America was largely civilized by the canned tomato." To which I answered . . . but no matter. The American Navy has been getting very large of late.

When I opened the first tin of tomatoes I was relieved to find that I could not taste the lack of vitamins.   This mood passed. I found that the food I was eating did not give my stomach the required feeling after meals of having a man's job in hand.   I began to suffer from headaches; I felt tired and listless and my gums were sore and tender.   At last I remembered that, to point my argument with the doctor about vitamins, I had bought some dried fruits, free of tin.   I set to work earnestly on prunes, and within a day or two felt better.   The caravan men told me that they regularly suffered at the beginning of a journey from the same discomforts, of which the soreness of the gums is the worst. They attributed it to the lack of fresh vegetables and to the " overheating " or costive effect of a flour diet.   I wished I knew the Chinese for vitamins, that I might tell them what it really was that they were missing.

Even I, however, with prunes for my prop and apricots for my stay, had to listen to the protests of a stomach which maintained that a steady diet of tinned food was no go.   I thought I would try, for one day, the horrors of the camel puller's diet.

After that I used no other.

Immediately the men wake, before dawn, when the camels must be started off to pasture, it is the duty of the first cook to make tea.   Brick tea, unlike any other China tea, ought to be stewed to get all the juices out of it.   The Chinese say that the virtues of this tea are that it is " warming " and that therefore it can be drunk in harmony with meat.   It is made of mid-Yang-tze leaf, and the inferior kinds include tea dust, twigs, and the refuse of the warehouses pressed into bricks at Hankow. The southern teas, more delicate in aroma, are " cooling " and upset Chinese stomachs if taken before meat, causing diarrhœa. The barbarian foreigner never seems to have heard of this, much less to have noticed it for himself.   In the morning, then, the camel pullers drink a few bowls of tea.   Then they take a few more bowls, mixing in their parched cereals, which are the *tsamba* of Tibetan travelers, though the grains used vary according to the region; after which they send down a few more bowls of clear tea.

About noon the second cook comes on duty and prepares the one really distending meal of the day, that made with white flour. At this meal each camel puller eats the equivalent of at least a pound of dry flour. The colder the weather, the faster they eat, bringing out a profuse sweat as their stomachs strain at the task. Thereafter they make more tea for themselves, one canister after another. At last the caravan master, seated in order on his felt at the head of the tent, knocks out his pipe and says in a chatty way, "Let us drink tea." This by convention is the order to break camp. All the men take up the long howling cry, "Dri-i-i-ink te-e-e-e-e-ea!" The *hsien-sheng* has already been out to turn the camel herd toward camp; each man rushes out, collects his own camels, and leads them to their places, where they kneel between the loads. The weaker camels are then given their ration of dried peas in a nose bag, while the men, as fast as they can work, sling on the loads. They get so hot at this that even in the coldest weather they often strip to the waist; for with each half-load a man has to swing about a hundred and seventy pounds on to his knee and steady it there against the side of the camel while he slips a peg through the loops that hold it to the other half-load on the off side, where his partner is working.

The first to finish turn to with the caravan master and the *hsien-sheng,* getting down and packing the tent and loading the water butts; a tent to shelter a score of men makes a handsome camel load. Then the caravan gathers in a massed formation for the start, all the files abreast. The canisters or billies in which the last tea has been brewed have been left standing on the embers of the fire. The Head of the Pot picks them up; anyone who is thirsty comes for a last swig, and then, solemnly pouring out the dregs, he leads off his file, calling the dogs. The others follow in their order, and the caravan is on the march. A little fuel is carried along, so that as soon as camp is made there need be no delay in brewing tea. Different men take turns in gathering fuel while in camp, but the cooks do not have to do this fatigue. In a tamarisk country fuel is easily had, and of the best; but in the barest countries, if an old camp is passed, the men fall out in turn to gather each a sack of dry camel dung from the parking square.

The Head of the Pot is on duty again at night, after the halt, to tend the fire and make tea. With their tea the men eat once more as much *ts'ao mi* and *ts'ao mien* as they like, and when that is done the two men on night watch pull up their little stools to the fire (but they must be between the fire and the door); and the others, after smoking a few pipes and drinking at leisure a few more bowls of meditative or recreational tea, unroll their felts, cover themselves with their greatcoats, and without any more fuss are asleep.

Each caravan carries two stools, about five inches high and wide enough for a man who is not in soft condition. During the morning only the Head of the Pot may sit on one. During the afternoon only the Second Head may sit on one. At night, or at one or two or three in the morning or however it may be, when the march is finished, only the two watchmen may sit on them. When they fetch out the stools and sit down between the fire and the door, the long day is over.

## XI

## MERES IN THE SAND

THE name of Khara-jagang is applied to a wide region in which
the tamarisks have died off through increasing aridity; but we
traversed in about eighteen miles what seemed to be the core of it.
The plateau, sloping toward the north, but rimmed at the northern edge with hills, is dominated from the west by a massif of
those irremediably sterile hills which attain a peculiar grandeur in
Mongolia.   This massif culminates in three sharp peaks and a
little one at their side.   The outline of the whole is like an exaggerated tooth, and I was told that the Mongol name for them is
Soya-kheilikhun [1] or Overlapping Teeth; but this name must not
be uttered in the presence of the mountain, or it will bring a
sand storm to overwhelm the utterer.   All along the south there
appeared to be bad sandy country, embayed among hills of decaying rock.   A valley opening plainly from these hills on to our
road was said to be a well-used road to Chen-fan.

We met here a caravan handled by bearded Turkis from Hami.
A few of them reach Kuei-hua or Pao-t'ou every year, competing
with the Chinese for the carrying trade.   The caravan owners
belong to a limited ring of merchants acting as trade agents for
the Khan of Qomul (Hami, that is), who is the ruler of a "native
state" within the Chinese province of Hsin-chiang.   These men
had with them a few camels of the single-humped kind, found
occasionally in Chinese Central Asia, though bred from a stock
that comes from farther to the west.   Great gaunt beasts they
were, taller than our Bactrians, and with a foreign look about
them, because of the different way a pack has to be adjusted over

---

[1] For the last three syllables of this name, compare *Khairkhan*, of frequent
occurrence in Kozloff's map, in *La Géographie*, vol. V (1902), pp. 273–8, with maps.

the one hump. Most of them were haltered and bitted, instead of having their noses pierced; and whereas in a Chinese caravan only the camel at the end of each file wears a bell, a big cylinder a foot and a half long or more, many of these were belled, some of them carrying a cluster or collar of small bells. Halters and bell straps, again, had a look that was not Chinese, being of carpet work, gay red and yellow and green, hung with red and yellow tassels and pompoms. The strange and far-come appearance of the caravan was touched off by the caravan master, a fellow whiskered to the eyes, with an antique sword strapped to the saddle under his leg. According to our men, the single-humped camels can carry a heavier load than the two-humped, but cannot make such a good shift for themselves on the real desert feeding and are far more vulnerable to the cold. Those we saw had nothing like the maned and tufted hairiness of our own Bactrians.

Our road entered the hills across our front to the west, after rounding the Overlapping Teeth by a small pass. We had marched thus far before the end of daylight, having made a very early start, but had to continue for some miles after dark. It seemed that at last we entered a dry watercourse, scrambling into it by a gap through which loaded camels passed very awkwardly. As the watercourse widened out, the caravan masters began searching for four cairns; and when they had seen one of them against the sky and ridden over and proved the mark, we turned off into a kind of hidden pocket.

I found the next day that this camping place was thoroughly masked and would never be guessed from the line of march were it not for the four guiding cairns on a clay and rubble bluff. Farther up in the pocket there was a tiny marsh, nearly smothered by sand. Bits of water showed here and there, but they stank of rotting tamarisk root and sour vegetation. Still farther up was deep sand, cradled between the hills and overlying the source of the springs. The best water was to be had by digging small trenches at the side of the marsh and allowing water to filter into them; but even this was thick, yellow, and horribly bitter. We had to take enough to carry us through the next march, where, though it was said a well existed, it lay at some distance from the trail and was very salt.

From the marsh, the camping ground was called Sharahulasu [1] or Yellow Reeds. I saw a few duck, probably lingerers between stages on migration. We were now on the northern edge of a sprawling confusion of hills mixed with sand. So far as I could see, by climbing to a small height, dunes had collected wherever the valleys were wide enough — partly of sand worn from the dry crumbling hills themselves, partly no doubt of sand dropped by the wind. On the outer flanks of the hills, toward the plains on the north, were fringes of moving dunes.

Before we drank the tea of starting in the afternoon, there approached my tent a pitiful figure dressed in rags, a lad of about twenty, with a broad, childish face and elf-locks hanging about his ears. When I had rescued him from the dog Suji, we sat him down in front of the tent and gave him food without question, as is the custom. Thereafter he began to talk, but broke down into weeping and asked if I would give him work and take him to Ku Ch'eng-tze. He said that he was from the country of famine and poverty around Chen-fan, so that he had set out to look for a living, and, being used to work with camels, he wanted to become a camel puller on the Ku Ch'eng-tze road. He claimed to have a brother in Ku Ch'eng-tze who would help him, if we would only take him through the desert. Then he wept more, with every appearance of terror. He had come up from the south, he said, a forgotten number of days, through great mountains,[2] where the wild sheep looked down at him unafraid.

He had started with a little food, but this was finished by the time he came to the Black Tamarisks. There he tried to get work with the traders; they were all Chen-fan men, of his own neighborhood, but Kan-su men of those parts have no bowels of mercy — they have been skirmishing with famine for too many

---

[1] I could not make sure of the Mongol word for a reed; the name may be Shara-khur-usu, Yellow Reed Water. The reeds (Chinese *wei-tze*) are of the tall kind which grow in masses in the Zungarian swamps and the Tarim basin, as well as in Mongolia and China.

[2] Undoubtedly the Yabarai mountains of Kozloff's map.

generations. He might have known better than to expect pity from men whose living is in taking grain from famine districts to sell in the desert at more than famine prices. They gave him food by the half-handful and told him to go farther. He had therefore set out in a panic desperation to walk to Ku Ch'eng-tze, but had been mazed in this desert of rock and sand. Then a caravan had passed, two days before we came. He followed them for half a night, knowing better than to approach them in the dark; but they found out his presence in some way and were as badly frightened as he, thinking a bandit spy had fastened on to them. The next morning he came to their tents; but the caravan master, though he gave him his fill to eat and an old coat to wear, told him he must keep away. After that, he said, he had " squatted in the hills, waiting to die." In the night he did not know which to fear most, devils or wolves. Then he heard our caravan bells, but again waited for the day before coming near us; moreover, he had waited the whole day before his fear of the night became stronger than his fear of being roughly handled. That was the end of his coherent talk; he began to weep and rave.

My camel man showed a surprising interest in this chance for doing good. He had been quarreling savagely for days with the Old Man, whom he had wanted several times to drive away, but that I would not allow it in such a desert. The Old Man, true enough, had been slandering him with every caravan we met, and had an old reputation for speaking evil; he was a *yü-tsuei* or Jade Mouth — very hard. I heard that he had once got so far as being *hsien-sheng* of a large caravan, but had come down in the world entirely because of a two-edged tongue. For the matter of that, the two of them were rogues at odds. The vile-tempered camel man made no effort to get on good terms with the Old Man, who was living on my food and helping him in his work for nothing; while the Old Man, as if it were not his good luck to be fed all the way to Ku Ch'eng-tze in return for doing a little caravan work, must go making extra mischief with his deadly old tongue.

Now the caravan in front of us, which had turned away the

poor waif, was from K'o Chen, the town of the Old Man himself, who knew some of the people with it. My caravan man therefore thought it expedient that we should dispatch the Old Man as soon as we could, to join his townsfolk, taking on in his stead the refugee, who was young and manageable. If, said the camel man, I would feed the youngster, he would make him a small promise of wages to be paid at the end of the journey. The arrangement was thus made; but it was a much more unorthodox thing to do than had been the gathering in of the Old Man, who needed succor less, since he had at least a few pounds of food and a camel of his own. If I had not passed, the sobbing refugee would probably have died in the desert. He would have got a meal on the spot from any caravan, even though suspected of being a bandit spy, because that is the custom; but there was probably not a caravan in Mongolia that would have taken him on the strength. Every camel puller, no matter how meanly paid, gets his job only on a guarantee from himself, if he has any money, or under a bond from a friend or relative; otherwise he might be tempted to desert, some night, taking a few camels with him. The refugee was only a beggar boy, but nowhere in Asia can gratitude be expected from a beggar one has fed. Therefore, as the Chinese said plainly, this lad might decamp at any time with some of somebody's camels. However, when it was made plain that any evil which might come of rescuing a frightened stray in the desert was to be on my head (or on my body, in the Chinese phrase) the Chou caravan came forward with some flour and the Mohammedans with some millet to bolster what they were ready to praise in someone else as a Good Deed; the matter was settled for the time, and we struck tents and made ready for the march.

It would not have been easy for a stranger to get himself on the right way of that march. Though we were almost on the edge of the hills, it was hard to get out from our hidden place on to the plains, because of the sand driven into the opening valleys. This had caused the trail to be changed at least once in recent years, the dunes having swept over it in an easterly direction. It took our caravans more than an hour, part of which they spent

in going to the northeast, before they got round the sands and
back to the point where the way now used coincides with the faint
abandoned trail.    Once clear, we were still in sandy country,
with a view of a group of high peaks on our southwest front,
apparently the umbilical point of the desert of sand and rock.
The highest of these peaks must be treated, so the Mongols say,
with the greatest deference, as bad language uttered near it brings
sand storms.

In the night, after we had camped, there passed us a strange
caravan laden with thousands of taels' worth of raw jade, from
Khotan in the ancient Kingdom of Jade.    It had been bought
by a group of merchants as a speculation, and had already been
over a year on the road, traveling by laborious stages from
Khotan to Ku Ch'eng-tze.    Jade from the rivers, especially the
Qara Qash, running out of the K'un Lun mountains toward
the Lop deserts, used to be sent to Peking as Imperial tribute.    It
is probably a good many hundred years, however, since any of it
has reached China, except in small pieces, because of the difficulty
of transport.    In modern times only the most accessible jade,
which is of a poor color, has been worked at Khotan itself, because Khotan workmanship is poor and the local market cannot
afford the finer grades of stone, which are more difficult to
find.

Amateurs of jade have been prone to assume — gratuitously,
as it seems to me — that because certain qualities and colors of
the stone have not been in evidence since certain periods, therefore the supply has been exhausted.    In Peking, for instance,
a striking kind of reddish-brown jade is commonly called " Han
jade."    It is assumed that a piece in this color and quality is
necessarily a Han piece, worthy of a Han price.    It is much more
probable, having in mind the history of the Han dynasty, that
this peculiar jade was worked with great difficulty in some hardly
accessible part of the K'un Lun, and that, Chinese power in the
West never again having reached the height of Han times, no
one saw fit to bribe or force men into the depth of the K'un Lun
to bring out this jade again in large quantities.    It is still more
probable that, in the more splendid periods, like the full tide of

the Ta Ch'ing power, this jade was again available, but the color had gone out of fashion.

After the Chinese Revolution, almost incredible stores of raw jade came into the hands of the Peking dealers, the loot of Imperial treasure houses in the Forbidden City, where some of it had been kept for unknown periods. Only in recent years, however, with the rise in price of Chinese antiquities, did it become worth the while of the Chinese dealers to bring to the working of these jades the scholarly study and highly paid workmanship which they demanded. Then, the foreign fashion in Chinese art having swung from the seventeenth and eighteenth centuries toward more remote periods, there began to appear in " Jade Street " an astonishing profusion of Han jade — the right stone, the right color, the right designs. The dealers said that to meet the demand they had sent agents into the interior, who had returned with what they smilingly assured the buyer to be the select pilferings from tombs of the most respectable antiquity. In point of fact, it is worked in Peking, from Han and other ancient designs, diamond drills being used to emulate the superb polish of the ancient craftsmen. I suppose that all of the skilled buyers, even the honest ones, have tumbled to it by this time ; but I doubt not that before they did a number of pieces were acquired by the best-regulated museums.

The point about this jade that was being taken through the desert by the ancient way, with something of the ancient lavishness of cost and effort, was that most of it was in pieces of a size previously unknown. If, in Peking, some of these pieces should prove unflawed and the working of them could be kept quiet, no buyer, however skilled, would doubt for a moment that they came from the tombs of genuine but unknown early kings. It is a canon of the trade that if anything is only superb enough in conception and execution it must be genuine, because the cost in modern times of transporting the raw material and financing the work would be prohibitive. It is very sad that when this lot did at last get to the railway and Peking the times must have been so unsettled that it could not be exploited; but it will turn up some day, and I should like to be there. Some of it was in huge raw masses too heavy for a camel load. The owners had been afraid to take it through China by cart along the old Imperial Road, because its high taxable value would have laid them open to unmerciful robbery at one *likin* tax office after another. The only thing to be done was to take it by camel cart; but the Winding Road has always been held too difficult for camel carts. One caravan that had attempted to carry this freight had already been forced to admit defeat. Now it was being taken on by the House of Ts'ao, one of the proudest Mohammedan families of Kuei-hua, whose orchards near the city are like a memory of Turkestan. The big pieces were being hauled in carts wherever possible. Even over good going three camels had to be tallied on to one cart; while over passes or through heavy sand they had to make shift to load each piece on a camel, carrying it by short relays. I was told that in settling the price of the contract it had been assumed that some enormous number of camels would have to be "thrown on the Gobi."

It was hot the next day, before we moved on, but I could drink nothing because the only water we had was the bitter stuff we had brought from Shara-hulasu. On this march we fetched up once more against dunes, through which we entered tortuously the last oasis of Alashan that we were to see, and having passed two wells, not far apart, camped at a third. I was here once more (though I did not know it at the time) in a region that had been traversed by previous explorers, the great depression of Kuai-tze Hu. Kozloff, in his expedition of 1899,[1] had crossed it from north to south on his way from the extreme eastern Altai to Chen-fan; and Kaznakoff, a member of his expedition traveling independently from the Edsin Gol to Wangyeh Fu, had penetrated it in a southeasterly line roughly coincident with my own route but in the opposite direction. Kozloff calls it the depression of Goïtso, evidently from a mishearing of the same Mongol word that has been adapted to the Chinese Kuai-tze Hu.[2]

---

[1] Summary in *La Géographie*, vol. V (1902), pp. 273-8, with maps.

[2] I am sure from the sound of it that "Goïtso" does not represent a pure Mongol sound; even though this spelling is in the French version, through the

Kuai-tze Hu, as I saw it, was a long, narrow marshy tract, extending roughly east and west for about sixty miles. To the north a wide belt of reeds ran parallel with it and beyond that, as I was told, the land rose again to bare gravel Gobi, where hilly country is indicated by Kozloff's map. On the south were heavy dunes, buttressed on barren mountains. The more fertile strip of the oasis was on the southern rim of a hollow, which declined slowly to the north, and into it there seeped apparently a drainage from the hills, passing beneath the dunes. To the east was the desert of sand, clay, and occasional rock through which we had made our entry, while the west was closed by dunes. I heard from the caravan men that there were other reed beds and marshes scattered among the dunes, and even a big expanse of water. I was not inclined to believe this, so completely did the dunes mask the appearance of any more living country near at hand; but it is confirmed by the findings of Kozloff, who visited, still farther to the south, a small lake called Kuku-burdon. It has a circumference of ten kilometers, a depth of from one and one half to three meters, and the spring-fed water is sweet; and he remarks that the site is marked on Chinese maps as "an enormous lake" called Yü Hai. South of it are the Yabarai mountains, dividing this part of Mongolia from the half-Mongol region of Chen-fan. The lake is thus at the southeastern corner of the Kuai-tze Hu depression,[1] which Kozloff defines as "the fringe of the great desert of Badain-Jarenghi-Ilisu"—the dune country. He found the water-logged level to be from thirty to sixty centimeters in thickness. I am almost sure that the well (or wells) marked Kudo-Khuduk on Kozloff's map, north of Kuku-burdon, is the point where I entered Kuai-tze Hu; it sticks in my mind that I heard the name of Khutu-Khuduk somewhere in this region, but—I confess it

Russian. (I have since seen, I forget where, that the name is from a Mongol word meaning "pleasant.")

The *hu* of Kuai-tze Hu is Chinese for "lake." In the west this word is used exactly like the Mongol *nor;* it can be a lake (though more often a lake is advanced to the rank of a *hai* or sea), a marsh, or even the dry bed of an ancient lake or marsh.

[1] Kozloff is quoted in *La Géographie* (*loc. cit.*) as having determined that the depression is below sea level; but his figure of four hundred meters is questioned by the editor, who suspects a possible misprint in the original Russian.

—I never wrote it down, nor have I a record of the wells we passed that night.

It is true I was preoccupied at the time. On that very day I had made the Great Discovery. Although the days were still hot, especially when we were sheltered by dunes, the nights were sharp, and with sullen reluctance I had just added to my clothing a suit of all-wool underwear, stamped all over with offensive trade-marks. How I hated them! In making the change I noticed a whole colony of insects on my shirt. I had seen one of the same kind only the day before; it had tumbled out of the front of my shirt, and with the most Buddhistic courtesy I had put it on the ground to let it pursue its own destiny. Now, seeing so many others, a sickening thought took hold of me. I handed one to Moses. "A louse, to be sure," said Moses, brightening up. "I thought you must have them, the way you've been scratching." He was right about that. For weeks I had been treating myself to a long, satisfying scratchment all over every night when I got into my sleeping bag. I had begun to grow uncomfortable a few days after the start from Pai-ling Miao, from what I thought was a dry and irritated skin, the result of a dry climate, a still drier washing programme, and rough clothing. It was not so. It was lice. I must have picked up the pioneers while sleeping at inns on the way out from Kuei-hua.

For all my years in China, my traveling third class on railways and sleeping with muleteers and donkey drivers at mountain inns, I had never even seen a louse. I thought in a panic of typhus and shuddered as I stripped, handing my trouserings to Moses while I searched my shirt in horror and despair. We waded in slaughter, killing scores and scores. I had always thought that lice were little wriggling black bacilli, but that is not the right of it. They are minute, pale, boat-shaped animalcula, and if there is a dark spot in the middle of one it means that you have recently stood him a meal. Their bite does not look like that of a bedbug or flea, but like a faint rash. In the weeks that followed I learned to know them so well that I became even skillful at gathering their eggs, or embryos, or whatever they may be. We of the Great Open Spaces call them nits. They go off with a pop against the thumbnail just like the adults, but not so loud.

I began at once to put my clothes out of the tent at night, and I found that it was cold enough to slow down their breeding, though the camel pullers did not promise me much success. They themselves, because they wear sheepskins next to the flesh, in which the lice can fortify themselves, are resigned to the belief that it is impossible to get rid of them until the really cold weather, when the lice are so numbed after a night of exposure that they can be thrashed out of their coverts with a small stick. Washing, even with boiling water, is of no use, for the unhatched nits are incredibly hardy. The men, I found, were not even sure that lice and nits were the same thing. Nits, according to the Old Man, come out of your skin when you sweat. Lice, by the general verdict, are a plague sent upon those who drink many kinds of water. On a journey, they pointed out, one drinks every day water from a different source. On a journey, lice always flourish. *Post hoc, propter hoc.* Bad water breeds lice, but snow water, which is the purest of all, breeds them more than any.

I kept to my treatment: a nightly exposure of my clothes and a daily hunt, and after a long war, in which I learned to use my thumbnails by way of laundry at least once a day, I got myself louse-free even before the coldest weather. It was very much like the Boer War: an initial period of frontal attacks against a mobile enemy, in which I was the more harassed; a gradually established domination, and then the famous "sweeping operations" to deal with scattered guerrilla bands. A war like this requires subtlety as well as assiduity. Even the strongest frosts in the depth of winter will not account for nits. Therefore the crafty traveler will put on his clothes again, encouraging the nits to grow up into brave little lice, like their daddies, and then at the first bite, before they have time to celebrate weddings in the new generation, their bodies can be committed to the frost.

During the first campaigns of the Louse War we made four marches through the length of Kuai-tze Hu. The range of temperature between noon and night was astonishing, owing to the way that the dunes, which were almost always in sight on our left, took up the heat of the sun. It was so warm during the day that I went about naked to the waist. About four o'clock, when we were getting ready to march, I would dress, and by eight I would be wearing my sheepskin greatcoat, even while walking. There must have been a population of two-score families at least scattered along the way we went, with sheep, goats, cows, camels, and ponies, and, most remarkable, mules, which the Mongols are not accustomed to breed and which I saw nowhere else in Mongolia. All of the animals were of a poor quality, having little grazing but reeds. The Mongols were dirty and unfriendly even for Alashan.

At about the center of the oasis there was a remarkable spring called Obo-ch'üan, the Spring of the Obo. The water here appeared on the top of a small mound — a thing that could not fail to excite the superstitious interest of the camel pullers. A large *obo* of sods was built beside it, to commemorate the phenomenon, and this was one of the *obo* where the camel pullers joined with the Mongols in making offerings of incense, when they had it, and rags tied on sticks. It looked to me as though the spring had originally been a mere bubbling up of water to the low surface, but that in the effort to keep it clear of wind-blown sand it had gradually come to be a small pool depressed in the middle of a sandy mound. It was by no means for lack of other wells that this place had come to be specially regarded, however; wells were to be found every mile or so, and water could be tapped almost anywhere by digging three or four feet. There were also occasionally small abortive streams appearing from springs and disappearing into marshes, and not far beyond the Spring of the Obo was the largest stretch of open water that I saw. It was not larger than a generous horse pond, but the thick reeds crowding about it may have hid other pools.

Undoubtedly the Mongols camp here in far greater numbers in the winter, the shelter from wind offered by reeds and dunes being exactly the kind of thing they look for for winter quarters. The marshes were swarming with geese and duck, gathering for the flight south, but very wild. Some of them are said to

19. KUAI-TZE HU DEPRESSION: SAND AND TAMARISKS
"With the third string comes the *erh-t'ou* . . . the assistant cook." (p. 122)

20. KUAI-TZE HU: THE GREAT LOUSE WAR
"They go off with a pop against the thumbnail." (p. 178)

spend the whole winter, however. Only once, creeping through some reeds, I got a chance at a small party of duck; whereupon, giving them no license of flight, I shot three of them severely in the neck, so that they became good for food. There are also numbers of antelope, which spend most of the day in the dunes but come in to the marshes to drink.

Coming to the western end of the oasis, we brought up before the high dunes that bar the way to the Edsin Gol; the high dunes that are one of the greatest monuments of the Winding Road. The men call them the Great Sand Hollows, for the Chinese term refers not to the dunes but to the hollows between. The reason for which they dread the crossing of them is that in a few hours any strong wind can erase every track made by caravans that have gone before, leaving only the tall yellow hills of sand and the swathes of tamarisk, springing unnaturally green in the shifting, rainless desolation.

Our last halt — the last in Kuai-tze Hu and the last in Alashan — was at a well where the supply of water seemed illimitable, since not only the several hundred camels of our group of caravans but a Mongol herd of at least a hundred were all watered on the one day. This was the poorer end of Kuai-tze Hu, a small plain of soft earth, grown thickly with reeds, most of which had been cropped short by the Mongol camels. On our immediate front and on the south the dunes huddled most closely, sweeping away to the northwest in a lower but deeper belt. The line of march of the caravans is the shortest way through; the men said that both north and south the sands were wider, but that among them were a few reed beds and pools.

A few minutes after starting we were among the dunes, hidden from all sight of everything but sand; a maze of long-backed sand hills running sometimes nearly up to a hundred feet and averaging at least sixty, with a rough direction of southwest to northeast. Some of them were bare and were probably moving dunes, while others were anchored down by tamarisks, the finest I ever saw, growing like trees with a heavy, drooping frondage. At about two miles we passed a small well and met a caravan headed for Kuei-hua; at ten miles we encountered huge bare dunes, and in an hour more, having reached a belt of strong tamarisk growth, we camped. We had kept a general westerly direction, but the caravans were led all hither and about in order to climb the dunes where they were lowest, so that at times we were going northeast, or south, or anywhere in between. The pressure of the prevailing wind must drive the dunes in on Kuai-tze Hu, so that we had always to plunge up the shorter, steeper slopes, from which we slouched ponderously down the longer southerly declivities.

Our camp was at a huge *obo,* stacked together out of gnarled tamarisk boughs, like a tepee. In the hollow centre was a small god, flanked by two lions and attended by a number of figures, a few of them obscene. All of them had been modeled out of clay by caravan men, and though some seemed to have been made in a spirit of lewd mockery, many burn incense before them, hoping vaguely to propitiate some undetermined power that may save them from winds during the passage of the dunes. The *obo* was the mark of a large well, giving water that was yellowish and a little bitter with the taste of tamarisk roots; but the men said it was better than usual, as the water had been constantly drawn out by recent caravans, instead of being allowed to steep.

The Eldest Son of the House of Chou, whose regard for tradition showed itself in bursts of piety at all the well-established shrines along the road, waddled over to the *obo* with a few amiable oaths to burn a bundle of incense sticks; but in spite of that there was a high wind the next morning, laden with stinging sand. My tent sagged, because the iron tent pegs would not hold well in the loose sand, and from waking time to marching time everything was filth and grit and misery. The wind fell a little toward noon, and because it was a following wind, and because the caravan masters did not like to linger in the dunes, we bundled up and shuffled off a little after noon. The air cleared during the afternoon and I could see that the dunes rose bigger than the day before. We dodged most of the time from belt to belt of tamarisks, because the going was firmer, but both north and south I could see the sweeping lines of much higher dunes, a fulvous desert barren of any growth, while the buttressing rock mountains toward the south were hidden, or else we had overpassed them. The sand was heaped on a clay soil, which now and again, in the deeper hollows, could be seen in small bare patches, with a few tall reeds growing. Antelope tracks crossed here and there, but there was never a sight of anything alive. The men said that in the deep hollows water could be found at from two to four feet, some of it bad, but some of it tolerable. We heaved on and on, pushing gradually through to lower dunes, and when we camped we had put the most formidable sands behind us. We had marched in the two days a total distance of perhaps thirty miles, the direct distance being between say fifteen and twenty miles. There was no well at this camp, but before us there stretched only a declining prospect of lower and lower hummocks.

When we had gone into camp another caravan from the west went by. They confirmed that the caravan of the Old Man's townsfolk was only just ahead, and thereupon we cast him off to go ahead and join them; but it was not done so crudely as all that. All these things have their due process. First the Eldest Son of the House of Chou came over to yarn by my fire, and my camel man made that the occasion to entertain him with a startling catalogue of his own version of the major crimes and lesser villainies of the Old Man. By way of summing up he said that it was perfectly certain that the camel he had lost had had its leg maliciously broken by the Old Man, with a large stone, and that he was going to have the law of the Old Man when we got to Ku Ch'eng-tze. During this recital the Old Man lay doggo, wrapped in felts near the door of the tent. He knew better than to wake up.

On the next morning it was his turn to move. He arose very early and made a speech to Moses. He said that a sad conviction had come over him that we were traveling too slowly. He must hurry along to Ku Ch'eng-tze to find his nephew and his camels. He asked Moses not to wake me, but to inspect his few belongings to make sure that he was leaving us in an honorable manner. Moses forbore the inspection, knowing perfectly well that the Old Man had been laying in a provision of flat cakes of

bread, made with my flour, but not wishing to spoil his " face."
Thus the Old Man went away — a doleful figure on a lopsided
camel, slouching away into the sands; fifty-one years old, and a
rogue and adventurer still. As for me, I always liked that
runagate villain. He had one formula which never failed to
make my own scoundrelly camel man wince and rage. If *he*
were taking me to Turkestan, he would say, he would not wait
on the slow caravans just because he did not know the road.
"What is this talk of roads? Good camel pullers in the years
when I went on the Gobi did not talk of roads. I do not go by
roads. I go by dung — camel dung. If there is a country in
which caravans travel, there you will find camel dung. That's
all there is to it. Show me camel dung, and I will go anywhere."

I do not think I have heard a more superb boast.

# XII

## THE FAR SIDE OF ALASHAN

WHEN I woke, the Old Man had been gone several hours; in fact, what woke me was a gathering of visitors in the tent to hear the comminatory triumph of my camel man, who had thought of a lot of things to do to the Old Man when they met again in Ku Ch'eng-tze. Thus we were left with our stray of the desert — the Chen-fan Wa-wa, as everybody called him — to do the work of assistant camel puller. A *wa-wa*, in Tientsin, is a dolly, but as they use the word from Kuei-hua to the west it means anything from a babe in arms to a squalling brat, to a boy half-grown, to a young man past twenty, not yet married. It is a grand word. The Chen-fan Wa-wa told his story in different ways, a native caution about telling the truth hampering his boyish desire to tell his troubles; for he knew as well as any camel puller the sound old rule that a man who travels ought never to give the true reason for it. This, in the main, was the way he told his tale.

When he was a child his father was a trader in a small way at Ku Ch'eng-tze. Having made enough money there to return to his home, he started with several other Chen-fan men, all of them carrying their savings in silver. At the start they were joined by a party of Mohammedans, who suggested that it would be safer for all to travel together. Taking the mountain road between Ku Ch'eng-tze and Barköl, they came to a place called Ta Shih-t'ou, the Big Stones. It was then the season of the Chinese New Year, and the Mohammedans, who do not keep the same festival, invited the Chinese to make merry, saying that they would stand the night watch. The Chen-fan men drank enough Chinese spirits to make them sleep heavily, and in the night the Mohammedans rose up, pulled their tent down on them, and beat them to death under it. Then they threw the bodies into a dry well and made off with the silver. The murder was not discovered until the next spring. It made a great stir, being one of the most savage crimes ever committed in the region, and there is already a definite legend about it. They say that it was discovered by a Chinese official who was traveling that way. His pony refused to pass the abandoned well and at last the official caused his escort to make a search. They found the bodies in the well, with a dead wolf on top of them, which had leaped down to feed and died in the end of thirst. By the orthodox interpretation of the story, the official's pony did not stop because it smelled a wolf smell; nay, but far otherwise — the official was a Virtuous Official whose virtue, passing into his pony, made it able to detect untoward things. This is a recognized process. Nevertheless, neither the official nor his pony ever caught the murderers.

The Chen-fan Wa-wa, having thus lost his father, soon lost his mother also, and became dependent on an elder brother, who beat him, until at the age of eight he ran away. He was picked up by some travelers who were going to Liang Chou in a cart. When he got there, he was set to herding sheep to earn his food and clothes. The wolves in the Nan Shan, the great range to the south of Liang Chou, are so bold that they take sheep in the broad of day. To guard the flocks, the shepherds of those parts keep great savage dogs which are trained to circle about the feeding sheep, keeping them close together. This is the only report I have ever heard of dogs trained to herd sheep by Chinese or Mongols or any Central Asian people.

Another marvelous thing to be related of the Nan Shan concerns the Hairy Wild Men to be found there. I asked at once if this were not the *jen-hsiung,* the Man-bear of which the Chinese have legends. The Man-bear is enamored of human beings. When he sees a man he will walk up to him, put his forepaws on his shoulders and lick his face for pure love; but his tongue is so rough that it takes off the man's face. The only way to escape from a Man-bear is to charm it with music and dancing. To ensure safety the dancer should take off all his clothes — a kind of dancing by which not only bears are charmed.

But no, said the Wa-wa; the Hairy Wild Men are neither Man-bears nor yet any kind of ape. They are covered with white hair five or six inches long, so thick that they are invulnerable to bullets from Chinese muskets unless hit in the belly, where less hair grows. They live in caves and holes in the hills, from before which they clear away trees, brush, and boulders by the enormous power of their hands. Their food is the raw flesh of animals, which they kill with their hands, often wantonly. After killing a horse they will first taste the shoulder. If it does not please them, they will leave the carcass; but if they like it they will gorge full, afterward sleeping for several days. Occasionally they are seen by woodcutters or by hunters; but the hunters do not dare fire on them unless they find them asleep.

I met later in Urumchi a veteran missionary who had heard the tale of the Hairy Wild Men when passing by Liang Chou, but it was long after that I found the yarn had been heard by Prjevalsky, who proved that the beast was a bear. He saw one in the mountains and another stuffed, in a temple. According to his description, it had the head and forepart of the body a dirty white color, the back darker, and the paws almost black.

By his employers in the Nan Shan, said the Wa-wa, he was also well beaten; but he did not dare run away again. When he was about fourteen, however, he fell very sick, and his employers, not wanting to have him die on their hands, sent him away as soon as he could walk. He begged his way to Ninghsia, and from there ventured among the Mongols of Alashan, with whom he took service. They set him once more to herding, at a wage of one tael a month, paid in kind, with plenty of beating also, because he was usually beaten for the cattle which the Mongol herd boys allowed to stray. When he grew old enough he was advanced from this to work as a camel puller for a firm of Alashan traders — Chinese working on Mongol capital. Thus he went up and down and back and across the whole of Alashan and learned to speak Mongol fluently.

He it was who told me that on the forested slopes of the

Alashan range, south of Wang-yeh Fu, there is a sanctuary of wapiti (Asiatic elk) where white elk may be found. On these mountains there are three Kings of the Spruces, trees of enormous girth and age. They grew originally on the Nan Shan, near Liang Chou, whence they ran away to Alashan. On the Liang Chou mountains remain two Kings of the Spruces, which were bound with chains to keep them from deserting. These, he said, he had himself seen; but the chains were so old and rotten that they flaked to the touch. It is possible that this story dates from a period of desiccation when the tree line on the Nan Shan began to recede. It may be that the people of the mountains thought the trees were dying because holiness had departed from among them, and that therefore they selected certain trees, declared them holy, and bound them down to prevent the escape, not so much of themselves as of their magical influence. If at the same time they had heard that the trees of the Alashan were still flourishing, they might have supposed that the virtue of their own forests had gone from them into Alashan, thus completing the legend with the story of the three runaway Kings of the Spruces.

With the camel pullers of Alashan, almost all of them Chen-fan Chinese, the Wa-wa had been put to a hard training. Their whole practice is different from that of the caravans on the great trade routes. They do not have a caravan master, nor even a Head of the Pot to lead the first file of camels. Each man cooks for one day in turn. On leaving camp the men pair off to load, and then whoever is first ready is first to start. If a load is cast on the road, no man will help another to get it on again; he must look out for himself. The distance of each march is settled in common council, and, once the camels have stood up from the loading lines, each man must get his camels, his loads, and himself to the next camp in his own time.

The camels are Mongol-owned, picked from the herd and returned to it after one rapid journey. Because of this, because the loads are much lighter than the standard trade-route load, being seldom more than about 270 pounds, and also because every man is given a camel to ride, the marches are very long.

At dawn the camels are turned out to graze while the men cook and eat and break camp. A little after sunrise the march is begun, and they keep going until about sunset. Then they camp, and the two men whose turn it is graze the herd until about midnight, when the camels are made to kneel for a few hours. The interesting part of this is its flat contradiction of the vigorous myth that camels will not feed after dark — a myth originating in the way in which, along the trade routes, the marching hours are in the late afternoon and the first half of the night and the grazing hours from dawn until after noon. Undoubtedly the origin of this practice is in the difficulty of looking after large numbers of camels turned loose to graze in the dark. So far, however, from refusing to eat at night, hungry camels will frequently get up from the kneeling lines and start off in search of some supper, and the men on watch have therefore to keep fully awake all night.

A few months before I picked him up, this waif of the desert had returned to his home near Chen-fan with twenty-six taels (about three pounds), the savings of a boyhood of bitter hard work between the ages of eight and nineteen. This would be a tempting sum in Chen-fan, where, as the other Chinese say, the price of a wife is enough raw cotton to make her a winter suit of wadded clothes. His brother at once arranged his marriage to a girl two years older, to whom he had been betrothed by his parents in his babyhood. She, however, hated him, for she loved another man (here again, say other Chinese, is a Chen-fan barbarity — the frowardness of its women, to wit), and after four days of marriage he ran away to the Mongols again. After a few months he heard that his brother was looking for him, to bring him back, whereupon in desperation he ran away farther, to the edge of the desert where the caravans pass, hoping to get to Ku Ch'eng-tze, where he had another brother, working as a camel puller.

I heard several committees or juries of the Chinese discussing the story of the Wa-wa. They all said that undoubtedly he had run away after killing either his wife or her lover, or the two of them together. Not that they held that against him. The Chinese

West is full of men who do not go by their own names, and still
fuller of men who have a different story of their past every time
you ask. Nobody minds that. A man is expected to keep his
own eye on his own interests and to sleep lightly among strangers.
Beyond that, he can say what he likes, hear what he likes, and
believe what he likes; but if he expects anything other than direct
lies in answer to direct questions, he is a fool. As for the Wa-wa,
I never was sure. Sometimes the story sounded as though he
were afraid because of something he had done. I only know that
he was a mild kid, terrified of physical violence. When my camel
man began to bully him, he did not dare stand up to him until
he found that I was on his side. Even then he would not fight.
" Since I was eight," he said, " I have been running away from
my brother because he beat me, and been getting beaten by
strangers instead." On the other hand, Chen-fan people are a
queer lot, and a Chen-fan man who would not fight might well
stick a knife into his enemy in the dark and then run.

As for the Wa-wa's other brother, he never found him. In
a very bleak desert we passed a grave (not the only one along
that road) — a mound of stones in which had been set a stave
of birchwood from a camel's packsaddle. It was painted with
characters, but the name was already illegible. Hundreds of
miles to the west of that we fell in with a man who had known
the Wa-wa's brother. "Why, don't you know?" he asked.
" He died a year and more ago, out on the Gobi, in such and such
a moon, between this well and that other." Then we remembered the grave.

Short of an Old Man, we resumed our march in the sands —
our last march through the Great Sand Hollows. A few more
miles and the going was not so heavy; then we came out of the
tamarisks into hummocky ground covered with the earth-hugging
plants which I remembered well from the harder desert soil
farther to the east. Then a few low dunes, with the sunset
flaring on them, and we were beyond the sand, with the night
coming down on us. At about half-past seven there was a burst-
ing star of startling brilliance. It left a trail as wide as the Milky
Way, and a little to one side of it, the blaze enduring half a

21. A MONGOL BIVOUAC IN THE GREAT SAND HOLLOWS
"Goods and gear hung from stacked camel pack saddles to keep them out of
the sand."

22. THE GREAT SAND HOLLOWS: MOSES AND THE OLD MAN ON
CAMEL-BACK
"A little old man on a stinking mass of boils which he called
a camel." (p. 74)

23. A CARAVAN MASTER ON HIS PONY IN THE GREAT
SAND HOLLOWS
"He must . . . be able to handle the rowdy camel pullers." (p. 125)

minute or more. All the men muttered uneasily about this, taking it for an evil portent. One man, however, argued good from it; he said that it was the star of Feng Yü-hsiang (the Christian General) and that the way it headed into the northeast meant that the Christian Army, driven out of the Northwest Province, had not made for the provinces of Kan-su and Hsin-chiang, but had tried to get to Urga and would therefore not be in our way.

I was surprised at the chatter and argument among the men before they determined the true north. Inquiring later, I found that very few of them knew even the Great Bear, and still fewer the North Star, though it stands for a saint who is invoked by builders when a house is begun. In fact, though these men have a phenomenal sense of direction, they never know the points of the compass except generally; nor can they describe any direction between west and north except as northwest — unless by saying, for example, that "the west is big and the north small," which may be anywhere between west and northwest. This is the more surprising because they always use the points of the compass instead of "left" and "right" in everyday matters; a man will even say that his bed roll is on the west side of the tent door. They call the Great Bear the North-*tou*, which corresponds neatly with our Dipper, a *tou* being a wicker basket for drawing water from a well.

The country that we saw when the morning broke was of a new character. Scattered, steep-faced buttes of clay overlooked sunken, soft plains of cropped-off reeds. A good deal of soda efflorescence showed in the soil. The country was intermediate between the Kuai-tze Hu depression and the Edsin Gol, an ill-defined valley depression. The reedy plains represented, in all probability, ancient overflow areas of the river (or of ancient rivers of the same system, of which only the Edsin Gol survives), which tends like the "shorn and parcell'd Oxus" to ramify and scatter, "forgetting its high cradle" in the snowy Nan Shan as it struggles to a strangling death in the desert. A few trees, all *wu-t'ung shu*, were to be seen in straggling lines, the last evidence of old water channels.

There is a division of the route here. By bearing to the southwest, the Edsin Gol may be crossed near the point where it leaves the vague borders of Kan-su, which are more an area than a frontier, and one may continue by the Coal Mine Road. This lies " inside," as the Chinese put it, or on the southerly side of the Pei Shan (the North Mountains, in opposition to the Nan Shan or South Mountains, the great snow range of Western Kan-su), a sketchily mapped system extending southeastward from the Qarliq Tagh or easterly buttress of the T'ien Shan, towards the upper course of the Edsin Gol. It goes through a border region between the Pacific drainage represented by the Nan Shan and the inland Mongolian drainage of the northern versant of the Pei Shan. Different fragmentary drainage or seepage systems from either the Nan Shan or the Pei Shan support a few poor oases divided by deserts of clay and gravel. The Mei-yao or Coal Mine Road is named from what are probably primitive surface workings from which the city of Hsü Chou is supplied. It can be used by carts, and leads to Ch'ing Ch'eng and Hami. Thus it is a kind of outer alternative to the main cart road, the extension of the Imperial High Road coming up from China through Shen-hsi and Kan-su, which advances across the desert from Ngan-hsi to Hami. Its disadvantage is that it is much harried by Kan-su tax collectors and sometimes by Mohammedan bandits.

The alternative is to bear northwest, crossing the Edsin Gol farther north on its lower course; then west, over the magnificent Black Gobi crossing, leading to No Man's Land and the fringes of Mongolia between the Altai and the T'ien Shan. This road goes first all along the north of the Pei Shan. When it comes abreast of the T'ien Shan, there are passes to the south, first to Ch'ing Ch'eng, then to Hami, then to Barköl. The main route, having overshot Barköl, turns more directly west, joining the last stages of the Great Road, and in the end attains Ku Ch'eng-tze and the grand convergence of all the cart and caravan roads that, setting out from China and going by the Chinese provinces or Inner or Outer Mongolia, come to the Gates of the West.

The Edsin Gol is an aberrant from the Pacific drainage of the

Nan Shan; for though the Nan Shan stand for the ultimate climatic influence of the moisture borne inland from the Pacific and condensed on its high ranges, yet the Edsin Gol does not flow back to the Pacific, but escapes northward, to an obscure end in the hedged-off inland deserts of Mongolia. The position of the Edsin Gol in Mongolian geography is important. The distinction between Inner and Outer Mongolia is rarely defined with sufficient accuracy according to the available canons. Inner Mongolia physically is the part of the Mongolian plateau isolated by the great barrier of the main Gobi, running east and west. The political distinction between Inner and Outer Mongolia originates in the fact that the tribes south of the barrier have always been affected more immediately by a strong rule in China than those on their north, segregated by the additional defense of the Gobi.

The Inner Mongolian tribes are therefore those which were given a distinct political shape and received a direct social influence from the Manchu dynasty in China. Farther west, but still in geographical Inner Mongolia, comes Alashan, though tribally the people are Western Mongols by origin. They came into the Manchu Empire on a backwash, owing to their unwillingness to adhere to the Imperial movement of the Western Mongols under a succession of fighting Khans who were contemporary with the early Manchu Emperors and at one time threatened to rival them.

Still farther west and still more isolated is the flat valley of the Edsin Gol. The name of the river comes from Etsina, the Black City, translated by the Mongols as Khara Khoto. Etsina, of which the ruins have been visited by Kozloff, Sir Aurel Stein, and Langdon Warner, was a city not of the Mongols but of the Tanguts, whose kingdom, based on the Nan Shan, once commanded Western China and Western Tibet. It defended the approach from Mongolia by which, in the end, Jenghis Khan came down to attack the Tanguts. The city survived in the time of Marco Polo, in the thirteenth century, when the Tangut kingdom had become a feudatory of the Mongol Empire; but the walls of Etsina are now invaded with sand, and the Tanguts, their kingdom utterly swept away, survive as a despised remnant of tribes cast far off in the wilderness of the Koko Nor.

West of the Edsin Gol the term Inner Mongolia should not be applied, though the hesitant dotted line of the boundary between Inner and Outer Mongolia is usually projected into it in a supposititious way. The Great Gobi here cants to the south, sweeping across the vaguely named Pei Shan and extending west and south until it abuts on the Quruq Tagh, the boundary of that other great desert, the Taklamakan. Going west from the Edsin Gol and crossing the Black Gobi, a widespread but confused system of oases is to be found. They are cradled between the Altai–Aji Bogdo systems and the Pei-Shan–Qarliq Tagh ranges, coming to an apex at the Black Gobi and expanding as one goes west. They were probably at one time more habitable and formed part of the ranges of the Huns who centred at Barköl, but apparently for generations they have not been much sought by the tribes of Outer Mongolia, and the name of No Man's Land, which is used by the caravan men for the central part of the district, might well be applied to the whole territory.

I never knew how near I might have been to Etsina, owing to my lack of maps. None of the caravan men had ever heard of any dead city. I must have passed somewhat to the south, since I did not see the "sandy hummocks, some of them fifty feet in height," described by Mr. Warner,[1] — who can hardly have meant the huge dune ranges that I had just crossed from Kuaitze Hu, — nor "a labyrinth of dead forest, in which all the trees were lying prone," nor "a dry lake bed with stems of reeds fully nine feet tall." It seemed to me a little hard that I should have had only this one chance of seeing one of the remotest places of the earth, and, passing almost within hail, yet pass it sight unseen. It made me wonder how much more I might have seen and learned, had I been but a Competent Traveler, with all the assistance of lavish funds and the cordial regard of legations. As it was, the fortune I followed was no more than the fortune of travel in company with the trading caravans — the haphazard

[1] *The Long Old Road in China*, by Langdon Warner. Garden City: Doubleday, Page, 1926.

life among men whose very going forth and coming in is a survival from forgotten ages, and is as regardless of outer things;
men sometimes close-lipped and sometimes free-spoken, whose
fragmentary legends of immemorial tradition are like dim lights
flickering down long corridors of ignorance.

We were not only going to take the northerly road, but, having
heard from the last few caravans we had met that trouble was
to be feared from a tax collectorate newly established on the
river, we had it in mind to cross still farther to the north.  Our
camp was at three wells, called in Chinese fashion Po'rh-ch'üan
or, with a more nearly Mongol pronunciation, Bolo-ch'üan, of
which the *ch'üan* is Chinese for a spring.  The water was good,
but by an oversight we did not take on a supply when we left,
and the butts had to be filled at another well on the way, where
the water was salty.  We had gone about five miles in a north-
westerly direction over beds of dry reeds, all of them cropped
short and overlooked at a distance by flat clay buttes, when we
reached this well.  I was watching the men fill the water butts,
as the caravan went on by, when we saw a tall man and a short
man coming from the west.  They both rode donkeys, which
carried their bedding rolls and provisions as well.  The short man
rode a high donkey, and had a carbine and a cloth bandolier full
of cartridges.  The tall man rode a low donkey and had a sword
of antique pattern strapped on the load under his thigh.  He was
also distinguished by a white straw hat, of a kind made in Tientsin in the shape of a foreign felt hat.  By this alone he might
have been a small trader, of a kind literate enough to keep accounts; but, taken with his armory and his company, it meant that
he was an official in petty authority, for such are the signs that
one reads along the road.

The tall man dismounted — in itself a courtesy and an indication of respect — by putting one foot to the ground, lifting the
other leg, and letting the donkey walk out from under.  They
addressed us cautiously, seeing that I was armed and that we
were in numbers.  At a look of appeal from one of the caravan
masters, I forgot my Chinese completely and smiled a bleak smile.
Evidently the caravan master had a first wild hope of passing

under my protection. Then the Chinese began to fence with each other, the strangers trying to make us admit our standing, while the caravan men tried to make them show their character and warrantry. As neither side would give a lead, the two men said politely that they were not going anywhere in particular and might as well accompany us. Knowing that they had been nabbed by the taxation officials, the caravan masters abandoned the idea of going farther to the north, and we held for the Edsin Gol fords.

Near the camp we reached that night was a clump of *wu-t'ung* trees, the first I had seen closely, though we had passed a few in the dark on one of the marches through Kuai-tze Hu — their most easterly range, so far as I know it. The caravan men call them " false " *wu-t'ung* for some reason of their own. The true *wu-t'ung* is the *Dryandra* of the upper Yang-tze, the tree from which is obtained wood oil, one of the most valuable exports of Hankow.[1] The *Dryandra* may have been originally a sacred tree of the aborigines of the Yang-tze valley, judging from the legends with which the later-coming Chinese adorned it. They say that the first fall of its leaf is the undeniable beginning of autumn — a fitting symbolism for a holy tree. It is yet more venerable because it is the only tree on which the phœnix will alight when it visits the earth. I have never seen the true *wu-t'ung*, nor do I know how the " false " *wu-t'ung* got its name, since I have heard Chinese say that it has not much resemblance to the *Dryandra;* the caravan men explain very simply that it is false because no phœnixes ever perch on it. The masquerading *wu-t'ung* is the *toghraq* or wild poplar of the Tarim desert. It is found throughout the half-deserts and desert fringes of Chinese Turkestan and Zungaria, and also, I am told, in India. One of its peculiarities is that parasitic willow shoots are often found growing in the notches of old trees; another is the great variation in the form of the leaf. On the Edsin Gol the leaf is fairly uniform, but in the Tarim basin it is sometimes very nearly round, with slightly serrated edges, and sometimes almost as deeply in-

---

[1] I now find that, according to Giles (*Dictionary*), the *wu-t'ung* associated with the phœnix is not the *Dryandra* but *Sterculia platanifolia*, while the oil-producing tree also is not *Dryandra* but *Aleurites cordata* (*t'ung-yu-shu*).

24. "FALSE" WU-TUNG ON THE EAST EDSIN GOL
"It is false because no phoenixes ever perch on it." (p. 195)

dented as a maple leaf. The wood is of no use for any carpentry, and burns rather weakly without giving an intense heat. It is impregnated, apparently, with the salts of the deserts where it grows. A plentiful sap or pitch oozes out of it when burning, which is used like soda or yeast to raise bread; the camel men call it "*wu-t'ung* soda."

During the morning the Mohammedans and the House of Chou held furtive councils, mostly in my tent, to light on a way of dealing with the tax foragers. The Mohammedans were for bribing them to let us go away to the north, the Chou for facing it out. Both of them gave up the idea of claiming to belong to me. I told them I should be glad to continue in my ignorance of Chinese, and that they could say what they liked; but I pointed out that their documents would have to be shown, and would not bear out fantastic talk. My own man, bold in the knowledge that he would almost certainly pass free under my name, recommended that the men be beaten and chased away. He cited with relish yarns of the old smuggling days when freights used to be delivered among sand dunes not far from Ku Ch'eng-tze. It seems that the trade in brick tea, or certain grades of it, used to be let out to monopolies, which forced up the price until successful smugglers could make a good profit. They say that in those days the agents of the revenue and the monopolists, if caught in inferior numbers, were apt to be roasted on a fire of tamarisk boughs.

The Eldest Son of the House of Chou had nothing to say but that we might have known something nasty was going to happen. At the last camp two of his camels had howled all night — not the ordinary camelious gurgle or snarl, but a prolonged moaning. Everybody agreed that this was known from of old for a bad sign. The last time it had happened to the Chou caravan they had had both their ponies taken by a Qazaq thief.

The two strangers behaved very circumspectly, with a lack of confidence which showed their position to be at best but semi-legal. When one of them called at my tent, I allowed him to watch me writing up my journal. Then, through Moses, I asked his name, which I wrote down, and took his photograph — all of which made him uneasy. When we started, one of them rode off in advance, saying that he was going to advise the *ssu-yeh* or official in charge. The other, after accompanying us until it was evident that we should make no attempt to run for it, also went scuttling before us on his donkey.

On this march we passed through a splendid desert, which had, as it were, a commanding presence about it. We crossed a table-land seamed with abrupt gulfs, running from south to north. These must all have been extra channels of the Edsin Gol, serving to carry away flood water in long-ago periods when still greater snows melted on the Nan Shan. In the rifts were low mounds of sand, and a few willows and phœnix trees that set off the savage bareness of the plains above them. The table-land was of solid clay, the tops of the plains being almost dead flat and sprinkled with fragments of black gravel. I walked a long way ahead, until I could see the whole spectacle of the severe desert; the hundreds of camels strung out for a mile or so, the head of the thin column going down into one of the rifts while the main body was still on the table-land above and the last camels not yet in sight; the warm color of golden phœnix-tree leaves down below, and a slight dazzle from the black gravel where I stood. I felt as if transported to a great distance, looking down on both the ancient spectacle and the lonely spectator, all fixed as in a magic medium in the drenching sunshine — the strange Mongolian sunshine, thin, strong, and heady.

We kept on for about fifteen miles, until after dark we left the high desert, descending to a sandy belt of willow scrub, tall bunch grass, and phœnix trees. When we came out of the dark thickets there was a kind of void before us and a band of black. We stumbled down into the void, turned and twisted past the dim glint of starlight on a few pools of water, and, coming up through a line of tall trees, made camp, having crossed the Eastern Edsin Gol on sand.

The next day, in a horrible dust storm, came the reckoning with the tax collectors. I watched the whole comedy with interest, because it was the fullest illustration I had yet seen of the collapse of civil administration in China. Foreign trade in China owes its growth and prosperity in great measure to the shield of a treaty-controlled tariff, but at the Tariff Conference at Peking in 1925 the Sovereign Chinese Republic claimed that foreign trade should be put on an equal footing with Chinese; that is, that the foreign Governments should surrender their treaty control, and foreign trade be subject to Chinese taxes at the Chinese discretion.    Foreign merchants in China knew what this would mean, but foreign public opinion, which has in late years been much exercised about the "sovereign rights of China," is influenced strongly by what appear to be appeals to pure reason, and dangerously prone to the assumption that a well-stated vindication of rights is a valid guaranty that they will be competently administered.

The "official in charge" proved to be none other than the man in the white hat who had presided at our capture.    He must have wished that we had been bluffed the day before into paying a bribe to be allowed to escape.    He had told us then that there were thirty men at the crossing of the river; but his tall-donkey-riding and carbine-carrying bravo, questioned apart, had said that there were seven or eight.    There were, in fact, no more than White Hat himself, who was a Chen-fan Chinese, and three hairy Ho Chou half-bred Salars in his pay.    The man did not even enter my tent, but when he confronted the Chinese everything was soon clear enough.    The whole ramp was a backwash of the civil war, which I had thought to have escaped when I got clear of Kuei-hua.

My friends explained to me that they knew the Winding Road also as the Borrowed Road, because it was "borrowed" tax-free from the Kan-su authorities.    When Outer Mongolia was closed to the Chinese caravans the Governor of Chinese Turkestan, anxious to preserve so far as he could the trade of his own province, interested himself in the development of the Winding Road.    Because it lay in part in Inner Mongolian districts under the supervision of the Chinese authorities in Kan-su, he initiated an arrangement by which caravans provided with agreed documents from either Kuei-hua or Ku Ch'eng-tze were to go free of Kan-su *likin* or internal transit tax.

This arrangement had broken down as a result of the civil war. The "Christian Army" had, the year before, extended its power over Kan-su by a sudden raid; with the defeat of the Army the Governor of Chinese Turkestan was afraid that they would fall back from their position in the northwest and, passing through Kan-su, attempt to occupy his own province. He had therefore broken off relations, and ceased to issue documents to caravans going out from Ku Ch'eng-tze. Kan-su itself being in disorder after the shock to the Christian Army, the lower officials had begun to act independently. The district collector of revenue (or rather the tax farmer) of Chin-t'a, an oasis in Kan-su on the upper Edsin Gol, had sold to White Hat the privilege of calling himelf a *likin* collector and trying his luck in Mongolia. He could not even read a caravan's list of goods carried, nor had he any kind of document to prove his own pretensions. He was, in fact, a pure filibuster, with no credentials but his three armed ruffians.

While White Hat and his gang were in one tent, a Mongol came to the other, asking us not to recognize them. The Mongols, he said, resented their presence, but did not dare try to run them out. They had been camping on the Edsin Gol for several weeks, terrorizing small caravans and begging from big ones. From one small caravan they had exacted both a camel tax and an *ad valorem* tax on goods, at their own estimate. As the caravan had not enough silver to pay this exaction, they took in settlement forty-eight pieces of cloth — which, of course, the owner of the caravan would have to make good to the consignee — without giving even a receipt. When faced out, however, as my friends faced them out, they changed their tune. They became poor subordinates, badly paid, who would be grateful for a little something "to give them face."

It is a proof of what I mean by the "collapse of civil administration" that these two big caravans, even when they had proved the imposture, did not dare treat the rogues roughly. They gave them altogether two bricks of tea and two packets of tobacco — a comic remission of "taxes" that would have amounted to about a hundred pounds. More than this, we had heard ourselves from the jade-carrying caravan that they had paid a bribe of eighty dollars to be allowed to escape. This money had fallen to one of the Mohammedans who had been out prowling by himself. We got one of the Mohammedans alone and started asking him about this. He turned out to be the very man, and begged us not to split on him to the others, as he had been able so far to keep all the money for himself. I thought that at least the caravan men would not miss a chance like this of making trouble among the thieves; but they kept quiet. In short, to treat these masquerading scallywags roughly or make trouble among them would only have been to draw the attention of bigger thieves, who would bleed the caravan trade more thoroughly.

This indeed happened later, as I was told. The marauding patrol was replaced by a strong armed party, under a man with something more like real official power, who began to enforce the tax on camels and a duty on goods as well. This move threw the whole caravan trade out of balance. It meant that caravans must carry big sums in silver with them (since bank notes are nowhere recognized in the far interior), thus becoming an immediate lure to bandits. In doing this the Kan-su officials encroached on the lands of a few isolated and weak Mongols, to bleed a trade that has no connection with their own province except that of passing within plundering distance — a transit trade between the coast and Chinese Turkestan. The caravans have no alternative route. Nor can the Governor of Chinese Turkestan, who did so much to establish the road, negotiate a fresh understanding, because Kan-su and Kuei-hua are no longer under a unified authority. A trade of millions of dollars a year is being killed to provide a few thousands in ready cash for greedy officials. More than that, the Chinese trade of Chinese Turkestan is thus wantonly turned away to Russia by Chinese folly, and the Treaty Power merchants at the coast, who fostered the business, are penalized in competition against the power which in recent years has done the most damage to order and normal development in China.

# XIII

## THE EDSIN GOL

W HEN the harrowing business of the tax marauders was done with I went out to see as much of the world as I could through the harsh whirling veils of the dust storm, which turned the sky sallow and made the things of the earth formless and monstrous. I soon found the river, the river of obscure fame — a long channel barred with drifts of sand between which were a few pools. It was bordered by a few meads, shielded by thickets and overhung by big phœnix trees. Taking casts back and forth as well as I could through the wind and dust, I found that the river bed widened in places to as much as half a mile, but was usually much narrower. In many sheltered bays among dunes there were beds of reeds; but in general, taking river, meads, trees, and reeds all together, the whole of the life supported by the Edsin Gol could be spanned within a mile. Beyond that, on either side, rose the yellow clay and black gravel plains of the Gobi.

Evidently the summer range of the Edsin Gol Mongols extends through the meagre reedy oases that we had seen to the east on our way from the high dunes; but they were now in winter quarters and I did not see a single *yurt*, so closely were they hidden in the lowest hollows. "In summer," say the caravan men, "camp on a slope" (because of the rains) ; "in winter, down in a hollow" (because of the winds). I did see a number of cattle — sheep and goats, camels and ponies of inferior kinds, and more horned cattle in proportion than are to be seen anywhere in Alashan.

When I got back I found that the caravans, unable to march against the wind and dust, through which bursts of rain and hail had begun to fail, were declaring a holiday. They had already bought sheep, at the price of seven dollars each, the skin to be returned to the Mongol. This was not usual, for the skin should belong to the buyer. By the Custom of the Caravans, seven out of ten of the skins of sheep bought by the caravan owner go to the caravan master, the other three to the *hsien-sheng*; but of sheep bought by travelers seven skins go to the Head of the Pot and three to the Second Head. Even when there are many passengers, or " guests," as they call them, each one in turn buys a sheep during the journey, so that the men feed high and there are nice perquisites for the cooks.

Sheep buying is done by Mongol usage. There is first a bargaining for quality — small sheep, good sheep, or pick of the flock, at different prices. It is usual to agree that good sheep are in question, at so much a head. The Mongol then turns out about a score, which he says are good. The buyer disputes this with scorn, making the Mongol change as many of them as he can. When at last the goodness of the herd as a whole has been admitted, the Mongol plunges among the sheep, seizes one, and cries "This is it!" "Not so," says the buyer; "it is the worst of a poor lot." The buyer is here in the right, for I never saw a nomad, whether Mongol, Qazaq, or Kirghiz, who failed to tackle the worst sheep with speed and skill. The Mongol protests and argues, but after a while he seizes another; the argument then begins afresh, but after several have been rejected the buyer in the upshot gets the mathematically average sheep of a mathematically average lot, the whole deal, with words and antics, having taken from half an hour to half a day.

The way of a caravan cook with a sheep is very straightforward. He cuts it up haphazard, roughly stripping the bones. Chops, for instance, are not recognized, but each rib is taken off separately and the backbone in small sections. Bones and meat are boiled for hours in a great cauldron. The men do not care for the soup except in winter, and then only if specially prepared with a liberal allowance of fat; it is drunk in savory bowlfuls, with the addition of a peculiarly aromatic pepper, which I have tasted only on the caravan road and in Chinese Turkestan

—I think that it is, in fact, an adulterated pepper considered inferior to the sort used in China.

At the first eating, a little of the meat, with the head, stomach, entrails, liver, heart, and other offal, is served. The small bowel, which has a thick internal coating of fat, is considered a great delicacy, as are the cheeks and the bits from behind the ears. A very delicate soup can be made by boiling the stomach separately, but this is never drunk. A large share of the meat is then set aside to go with the flour ration, or chopped finely and put into the big wicker crate of sauce. The bones, with plenty of meat still on them, are fairly divided among the men, the Head of the Pot seeing to it that the best pieces do not fall to the same man every time. Usually two men share a little bag in which they stow their meat, taking out a bone whenever they feel like it to warm up at the fire and eat. A dozen men can remove all traces of two fat sheep in a very short time.

I went over to watch the young Mohammedan, the Son of the House of Liang, kill his own sheep ceremonially. First he washed his hands and face, then blew his nose with his fingers, doing the whole business of purification in a sketchy way that would have offended a Moslem from nearer Mecca. Then, putting on a little round cap, since a ceremonial slaughtering may not be done bareheaded, he went out of the tent with a knife in his hand. The sheep was laid with its head to the west, the neck being over a trough scooped in the earth to receive the blood. He felt and kneaded it about the throat, under the ears, clearing away the wool a little; then, muttering something that was not Chinese and must, I suppose, have been a garbled Arabic, he cut the throat, and the rite was accomplished.

All that afternoon there was a great cooking, followed in the evening by a great eating. Both caravans entertained me to as much as I could stow, because they said my presence, my notebook, my camera, and my rifle had been a valuable support to them in the face of the tax collectors. Also the Eldest Son of the House of Chou, having inquired of Moses with great courtesy to know what mutton was a piece of honor among foreigners, and having been told that I was a renowned eater of livers,

25. TUR KÖL: SHEEP BOUGHT BY CAMEL MEN
" 'Not so,' says the buyer, 'it is the worst of a poor lot.' " (p. 202)

presented me with liver.   I garnished this with a tin of beans, Moses cooked the whole in foreign style with an addition of garlic, and the Eldest Son of the House of Chou, with other distinguished guests (the Mohammedan, unluckily, could not eat infidel cooking in public [1]), assisted me in the final and most distending feed of all.

On the next day we set out from the East Edsin Gol to reach the West Edsin Gol.   Before we had gone five miles Moses had a bad spill.   My camel man, after he had had every load in turn thrown by his ill-behaved camel, had assigned it to Moses to ride. I wanted to protest against this, but Moses was confident he would be all right, and even a little pleased with himself as a camel buster.   The camel man swore that the brute was now tired and docile, since it had given no trouble for days.   Then, on this march, something fell from one of the loads in front, and the camel broke away at once and began bucking.   Moses was all right, sprawling over the load and clinging fast, until it came off and he fell eight or ten feet, with everything landing on his chest.   Luckily it was only his own bedding and sack of clothes, but it knocked the breath out of him and he had a pain in his chest for days.   He squatted for a moment on the flat desert, looking for all the world like a large frog that has been picked up and put down and does n't know where its pond has gone.   My Mohammedan friend rushed up and started to walk him about slowly, "to keep the blood from congealing in his

---

[1] Like all Chinese Mohammedans he dropped his formal prejudices when in private — say with only Moses and me. He once ate my tinned beans, which were prepared with pork, though naturally I did not affront him with a statement of the fact. The Chinese have a shrewd proverb about the difference between Chinese Mohammedans when taken together and taken separately: "Three Mohammedans are one Mohammedan; two Mohammedans are half a Mohammedan; one Mohammedan is no Mohammedan." This proverb has been quoted before. The following yarn, however, I had from my father, who had it from Dr. Tenney, sometime First Chinese Secretary and for a while Chargé d'Affaires at the American Legation in Peking: A Mohammedan traveler reached a town late at night; as usual, there was no one abroad but a night-hawking food seller with a charcoal stove and a tray of hot meat patties. "What meat have you there?" asked the traveler. "Pork," said the Chinese. "Ah," said the Mohammedan, "and what is in these?" — pointing to another row of the same patties on the same tray. "Pork, of course," said the Chinese. "And in these?" the traveler persisted, pointing to a third row. The food seller tumbled to it at last. "These are mutton," he said. "Well, why did n't you say that before!" quoth the Mohammedan, beginning to eat heartily.

chest," which appeared sound enough counsel to me. I turned back to have it out with the camel man, who, paying no attention to Moses, had gone after his camel. I gave him a dressing down, but he talked back with an impudent swagger and even said roundly that Moses must go on riding the same camel. It rested with him, he said, to assign the camels as he pleased. I forced him to give way on that and then the two caravan masters, riding up, intervened as peacemakers, in the Chinese manner. This was the first trouble that the fellow had given since he had got his way in turning off the Old Man; but I could see that there was going to be more and worse.

We marched, as it seemed to me, about twenty miles due west, camping in the night at the western river. The desert in between was not quite so sterile as the general sweep of the Black Gobi to which it belongs. It was mitigated here and there with tiny patches of reeds and even a few wild *tsao'rh* or jujube trees — a kind of thorn bearing "an edible berry-like drupe."

The Edsin Gol springs from two sources, in the Kan Chou and Hsü Chou oases at the foot of the Nan Shan. After watering several minor oases, of which the chief is Chin-t'a (the Golden Pagoda), they unite near Mao-mei, off the southeastern extremity of the Pei Shan. Thence they flow somewhat east of north, as the Hei Shui or Black Water, crossing the indeterminate borders of Kan-su and entering Inner Mongolia. The Hei Shui then separates into the Eastern and Western Edsin Gol, which, after reaching Outer Mongolia, end in two communicating lakes or meres, Gashun Nor and Sokho Nor.

According to the account I heard, the water in this curious system is drawn off throughout the summer and autumn to irrigate the Kan-su oases. No water then reaches Mongolia, and the two branches of the Edsin Gol decline into successions of pools. In the winter, after enough water has been laid on to the fields to freeze and supply an early moistening at the spring thaw, the dikes are closed and the water comes north. This, however, does not appear to fit precisely the descriptions of Mr. Warner,[1] who was in the region in November and December,

[1] *The Long Old Road in China.*

and does not report living streams.  At any rate, the chief flow of water is in the spring.  There is a light fall of snow between the Nan Shan and the desert.  This melts in the spring, whereas the snow of the Nan Shan, the true supply of the rivers, does not melt until early summer, by which time it is all needed by the farmers in the oases.  During this first melting, the Edsin Gol is in spate.  It is said that each branch is then a quarter of a mile wide, waist deep, and very tricky to ford; more because of the bottom of shifting sand than because of the strength of the stream.  When the caravans have to face this water, the mounted men first ride in to make sure of the ford.  This they stake with willow wands, and after a few unladen camels have been led across and back as a trial, and to tread down the sand a little, the caravan is taken over.

Along the restricted pastures by these two rivers live the Edsin Gol " Old " Torguts — called Old, as I infer, because they were excepted from the Torgut tribal system as reconstituted and confirmed under Ch'ien Lung.  " The story of the foundation of this principality," says Binsteed, " and its adherence to the Ta Ch'ing Empire, is so interesting and illustrates so much of the history of the Eleuths or Western Mongols and their extraordinary migrations, that it is worth narrating . . . in spite of the comparative unimportance of this *aimak*, which only contains some five hundred people." [1]

In the course of the wars of the Western Mongols, which resulted in the seventeenth century in the rise and brief power of the Zungarian Empire, the whole of the Torgut tribe, unwilling to submit to the Zungars,[2] migrated from the district now called Tarbagatai across Siberia to the Volga.  About eighty years later the Manchu Emperor of China, Ch'ien Lung, after he had defeated the Zungars and practically wiped them out by massacre, invited the Torguts to return.  In 1770 the main body of them made the prodigious journey back from the Volga, though losing

[1] " The Tribal and Administrative System of Mongolia."  The *Far Eastern Review*, July 1913.  Cf. also *Unknown Mongolia*, by Douglas Carruthers.  London: Hutchinson, 1913.
[2] Zungars and Torguts both belonged to the confederation of related tribes called Eleuth.

great numbers from the severity of the winter and the hostility of other nomad tribes like the Qazaqs. They settled partly on their old lands, partly along the Altai and in Chinese Turkestan.

The story of the Edsin Gol Torguts begins, however, before the great return. While they were on the Volga a Torgut prince called Arabjur took with him a band of followers, traveling in the Mongol way with wives and children, to go on a pilgrimage to Lhasa. He must have made this journey during a period of truce; but when he was on his return he found the way barred by Tsevan Rapadu, the lord of the Zungars and the rest of the Eleuths, who was again at odds with the Torguts. Unable to rejoin his kinsmen, he therefore went in 1705 to Peking, where, having tendered homage to the Emperor, he was given a Manchu title and granted lands for himself and his followers. His son and successor, about 1732, was allotted the present lands on the Edsin Gol, and in 1783 the family received the title of Pei-le.

Here the tribe still remains, ranging also to the eastward through a few starveling patches of reeds and coarse grass in the desert. Cut off from effective contact with other Mongols to the west and north by the black gravel Gobi and from the outlying oases of Alashan by the high dunes, they are at the mercy of the Chinese to the south of them. However, they are not poor, and though so small a community they support a lamasery on the Western Edsin Gol, at some point south of where I crossed. In quiet years they must have as contented a life as any Mongol tribe, but when they are threatened with the unpredictable consequences of unintelligible Chinese politics and civil wars, their isolation seems to make them uneasy with a vague dread.

Though so few in numbers, they show, like other Mongols, divergent physical types, proving that the Mongols are not of unmixed blood. With them, moreover, there is probably a good deal of recent admixture, from the Tangut strain that survives along the borders of Western Kan-su. There are also differences of costume and in the way the women dress their hair which distinguish them from the Alashan Mongols, who are of another branch of the Eleuths, as well as from the true Inner Mongolian tribes. Fine-looking men appear among them, combining the wide-set Mongol eyes with an almost Central Asian haughtiness of nose; but they ride about so meekly on donkeys that no one would associate them at the first blush with those high-hearted nomads who, from their Russian exile by the Volga, voyaged incredibly to Lhasa, to Peking, and at last to these flat quiet valleys where the Edsin Gol, flowing northward in a double stream, attains the limbo of a region of salt tarns and meres.

I remember the day I spent at the West Edsin Gol — it was the eleventh of October, 1926 — as the most magnificent of all my journey through Mongolia: a day of sonorous beauty. I strolled for a while in the morning through meadows covered with the short, close growth of wild liquorice, then returned to camp, stripped to the waist, and sweltered indolently. At first I was only hot and slothful, but after the turn of noon a sense of the beauty of the place rose slowly in me, like a strong tide — the brown of the meadow flats along the empty stream, the russet of the willow scrub, and the coppery red of the phœnix trees. In a warm late afternoon of windless melancholy I read the XVIIIth *Iliad,* the Making of the Armor, because it happened to begin where I had left off many days before. When we started I was still reading, and turned to the story of Nausicaa in the VIth *Odyssey,* because I like it best of anything in Homer and because it is an amazingly beautiful thing to read on the top of a camel at the fading end of a glowing autumn afternoon. In the *Iliad,* after all, it is at times a strain to hold in perspective the mighty proportions of the whole, while the mesmeric repetition of detail seems to parody itself into an endless knock-down and drag-out of gods and prize fighters. I lean to the variety and humanity of the *Odyssey,* and the sixth book has, for me, a serenity sweet but piercing that is more lyric than heroic, or rather fuses the two in enchantment. It seems to prophesy that late reflowering of the Greek spirit which once in a while astonishes and enraptures one in English literature. Then, reading it in that way, on that afternoon, there seemed also a far-away reflection or prefiguration in its beginning, where the story of the wandering Phæacians is so swiftly told, of the heroic legend of the wandering of the Torguts who settled finally on the Edsin Gol.

Only a thin fringe of flat water meads, phœnix trees, liquorice, willow scrub, and thorny wild jujube marks off the West Edsin Gol and its flood channels from the gravel and tamarisks of the Gobi. At the point where the caravan trail enters the desert after climbing a long, faint slope, a great *obo* of tamarisk boughs has been set up for a sign; it is the last or first point from which the valley of the Edsin Gol can be seen. We traveled on, into a cloudless sunset of orange and yellow and smoky red, and just as it was falling into embers we met two caravans from Ku Ch'eng-tze. Their camels marched slowly and wearily, with extended necks. Like all camels coming from the west that season, they were in poor condition, because for lack of rain the grass at both Bar Köl and Ku Ch'eng-tze had been scant.

We halted after a twenty-mile march, but the Mohammedans kept on, to camp somewhere ahead of us. For all that the day had been so hot, the night was sharply cold. A little tea left in a wooden bowl in my tent froze solid before morning; but the morning was hot again. There was a shimmer of mirage dancing all over the plain of black gravel, distorting the lean tamarisks and the occasional mounds of sand that were all there was to break the bleak levels of the Gobi. This mirage was not the sweet illusion of cool groves and pleasant waters of library travel in Arabia Litterata, but an obvious refraction of light. In places it twisted the sky line into bays and inlets of what only one of those Warburtonian travelers in the reign of the Dear Queen could have imagined to be water; or within a few score feet cast pools of glassy light between the tamarisks. A number of birds, like small crows with gray heads, came to scavenge about the tents, getting almost under men's feet or perching on the camels to pick at their saddle galls.

We started early in the afternoon, along a yellow trail worn down through the black gravel to the clay beneath, and marked now and then by small *obo* of stacked tamarisk. Just before sunset we passed several more caravans from the west. They carried a great many loads of elk antlers. These were only the dry antlers cast by the elk; the "blood horns," taken from elk killed in the velvet in early summer, are far more valuable.

They bring in Kuei-hua from eighty to a hundred and twenty taels the head. To secure these horns in perfect condition is very difficult; they say that the way used in the Bar Köl mountains is to drive the elk from the forest into the open before shooting him, a chase that may last for days. If shot in the forest he will do his best to wreck his antlers against the trees before dying, in order to break the velvet, let out the blood and spoil the profit of the hunters. This is a legend which must have grown out of what one would think the obvious danger that a wounded elk, thrashing among the thickets, is likely to damage the velvet; but it is of a kind with legends that the Chinese tell about other wild animals which produce something more than ordinarily valuable. Thus they say that the Manchurian sable, if not killed outright by bullet or trap, will turn on himself, trying to spoil his pelt with biting and scratching.

When the elk has been brought down, the antlers must be carefully sawn off at the boss and sealed, in order to preserve the blood. They are hung to dry slowly in a dark room, while the blood congeals in swellings at the tips of the tines.[1] As a large part of their value is lost if they are not in perfect condition, they are skillfully padded and crated before being committed to the Mongolian transit, and the caravan owner must give a guaranty under indemnity to deliver them sound and unscratched. Blood horns are a very " hot" drug, according to the traditional medicine which diagnoses all sickness as hot or cold, moist or dry humors. Elk velvet[2] is a *fu-yang* or nourishing aphrodisiac for men of decayed virility who wish to beget last-moment sons, and a tonic for old men whose natural heat is abating but who, because virgins in these latter days seem to be even scarcer than elks, are unable to foster themselves, like King David, in the bosom of an Abishag.

There were also many travelers with these caravans, some

---

[1] A different description is given by Stephen Graham. Writing of the elk farms where elk are kept for the sake of their horns, which are sawn off yearly and sold to Chinese merchants, he says that the horns are first dipped in boiling brine and then dried in the open air. These elk farms are kept by Russians in the Russian Altai and along the Russian border of Chinese Turkestan. *Through Russian Central Asia*, by Stephen Graham. London: Cassell, 1916.

[2] The Chinese term, *jung*, corresponds exactly with our "velvet."

perched on loads of bedding high on their camels, wrapped in long sheepskin coats, opening down the front, with the huge collars that distinguish the men of Central Asia from the Mongols, whose fur collars are small and close-fitting and whose coats button down the side; while others were huddled in camel sedans, little wooden hutches like dog kennels that are slung one on each side of a camel. The camel pullers shouted greetings to each other, with bits of news about friends on the road or in Ku Ch'eng-tze or Kuei-hua; the passengers stared at us out of their sheepskins, and the mounted caravan masters rode to meet each other in little groups, talking for a few moments gravely of high matters like the state of the road and conditions of pasture and water, military requisitions, disbanded soldiery, and tax collectors. A brother going east would run over to speak with his brother bound for the west, and after a few words with each other for perhaps the first time in a year they would plod away again to the west and the east, each with his file of camels, not to meet for another year or so. The camels turned their heads to stare like the men as the long files drew past each other, with a vast mingling of the slow, reluctant tones of camel bells; and in no more time than it takes for a good long stare the meeting and parting in the red and yellow smoldering sunset, in the black desert among the thinly scattered gray tamarisks, was over.

At fifteen miles we camped in a small oasis called White Earth Well or White Mound Well, with a few bushes, phœnix trees, and beds of dry reeds. A battered Mongol visited us the next morning who said that he was not a Torgut of the Edsin Gol, but belonged to a group of two or three families which had taken refuge in this wilderness to escape the heavy taxation that is crushing the tribes of Outer Mongolia. They had come down, perhaps, by the ancient road of "forty days without an inn" which, according to Marco Polo, led from Etsina to the old Mongol capital of Karakoram, and of which, according to Palladius, "traces are still noticeable, but it is no more used."[1]

The well had been nearly exhausted by the many caravans

[1] Quoted in *The Book of Ser Marco Polo*, edited by Sir Henry Yule and Henri Cordier.

going both east and west within a few days, so we moved on the morrow five or six miles to the very last water before the crossing of the Black Gobi. This was at the Reed Grass Well (Lu-ts'ao Ching), in a faint depression on the edge of the main swell of the Gobi. By the well there is the strangest temple in all Mongolia, the Lao-yeh Miao, built of tamarisk boughs. It is a temple in the size of a shrine, only a few strides long and a few paces wide. In the innermost recess, where the roof is not high enough for a man to stand, there is a colored picture, a print made probably in Peking and bought in Kuei-hua, of the Lao-yeh. He holds in one hand his black beard and in the other the frankest gospel I have ever seen, a book such as ought to belong to all of the gods of which I know anything much. It is a very nice book, and it lies open; but there are no characters on the page.

The temple is full of blue and red cotton rags (among which I saw one gaudy flowered chintz), many of them roughly painted with a few characters, but others hung up in wordless devotion. There is also an array of inscriptions on boards from packing cases, notably one in Arabic character, left, I suppose, by some Turki from Hami, whose Mohammedanism unbent in this desolation to acknowledge the inchoate piety enshrined in this monument of the infidels. There are even lanterns, hastily made of wooden slats and paper, with earthenware oil bottles in them, to give the intention of light if not light itself, while an old soap box in front of the Lao-yeh, with its gaudy side to the fore, serves for incense trough. There is also a forecourt of the temple, all in the best style, fenced with tamarisk boughs and birchen packsaddle staves. In it are wooden halberds held upright by strings, and hung by the temple door are a camel bell (for what temple is complete without a drum and a bell?) and a miniature drum of hollowed phœnix-tree wood and camel hide.

This temple is partly in commemoration of a famous Lao-yeh Miao, more than a dozen marches out from Ku Ch'eng-tze, at the place where the Great Road finishes the crossing of the Gobi in two stages. There the caravan men used to butcher sheep, bought from the priests, just before or after making the desert traverse. Being bought of the temple and slaughtered in the temple precincts, the sheep had sacrificial rank, though they were eaten by the men of the caravans. That older temple was an undeniable Institution, built of brick and wood and served by Taoist priests with their long hair bound up in the sacerdotal style; but they say that since the years of disorder it has been pillaged by the Kirei-Qazaq and the Tao *Shih-fu* either killed or driven away. The irreligious camel pullers held it in high regard, for they were its only parishioners, and they still celebrate its memory with affection, in their tamarisk temple on the lip of a greater desert and a more dangerous crossing. The mixture of superstition, reverence, and mocking blasphemy with which they treat this little makeshift tabernacle of tamarisk and camp wreckage, made by themselves and tended by no priest, is delightful. There is a spirit about their observances that has been almost lost to Europe since the Middle Ages — the free and adventuring spirit that got a stunning whack on the head at the Reformation, when a desolate and cranky kind of prophet rose up, thinking to ensure salvation by unfettering dogma and shackling emotion instead; a spirit in which there is a fine realization, without any articulate opinion, that piety has nothing to do with sinlessness.

And now, I wonder — did I discover a Great Truth in the Desert and Make a Note of it in my Journal? How like a Traveler!

The water in the Reed Grass Well lay three or four feet below the surface, in a hollow that might have been an old stream bed or an old spring, and the name of the well was from the ancient reeds, long cropped off, whose roots remain in the soil. As usual, a pool had been dug by the well into which the water could be poured to let the camels drink. Two caravans from Barköl, just down off the desert, were camped on the ground when we arrived, but they very courteously surrendered to us the privilege of watering our camels first, though it is one of the strictest customs of the road that the first caravan on the spot has an inalienable right to first water for its camels. Water for men, dogs, and ponies may be taken in any order, but no matter how

26. WEST EDSIN GOL TORGUTS ON THEIR DONKEYS
"The tribe still remains, ranging . . . through a few starveling patches of reeds and coarse grass." (p. 207)

27. FORECOURT OF THE "STRANGEST TEMPLE IN MONGOLIA"
"In it are wooden halberds held upright by strings." (p. 212)

urgent the need of the camels they must wait on the caravan before.

With these caravans I first saw the splendid white dogs which Barköl men love.    They are not a special breed, but there seems to be a strain in the blood which often brings out dogs of a pure white color that are not albinos.    Kuei-hua caravans never have them.    The men say that the white shapes moving at night would scare the camels.    In the Barköl caravans, where the camels are used to white dogs, there is no complaint about this. I think the real objection of the Kuei-hua men is superstitious, but I never could get at the rights of the matter.    Their dislike for white dogs is patent, but it seems to be an ancient distaste of which the reasons have become obscure; unless it should be that they think it unlucky because it is the color of mourning. This would be a purely Chinese aversion, and it might have been forgotten in Barköl, especially if white dogs were once prized, say, among the Huns whom the Chinese supplanted in those mountains.

I took my own dog over to the well just as the camels were starting, to make sure that he had a last drink, and while there I somehow found myself washing my face.    It may have been that I was imitating the camel men, who often wash, with some half-understood idea of purifying themselves, before starting on a bad stage of the journey, like the high dunes or the Black Gobi. It was so long since I had done this that I had even forgotten whether it was in the same month; but there is this at any rate to be said for face washing: you don't know that you have missed it until you do it again, and then you find it really a most refreshing operation.

The blankness of the plain we had been crossing on our way west from the Edsin Gol had been relieved the day before by the sight of tiny hilltops floating in the mirage above the horizon. Now there was a desert range in sight, to the northwest, and, keeping a little to the west of these hills, we set out on the crossing of the Khara Gobi by the Four Dry Stages.

# XIV

## THE BLACK GOBI

FOR many days all the talk among the men had been of this crossing, the *han tsan,* the Four Dry Stages and the Three Dry Stages. "These are the Big Sand Hollows," they had said among the dunes that we crossed from Kuai-tze Hu; "they can be bad enough when the wind blows and the road is covered, and evidently they are not easy walking: but still, it is the Dry Stages that are bad. There you will see men worn out and camels thrown away."

The main Gobi, as I have indicated, is a desert running, on its longer axis, east and west between Outer and Inner Monoglia; but west of the Edsin Gol it takes an incline south and west, spreading on until it reaches the limits of the Taklamakan. This region west of the Edsin Gol is the Khara Gobi or desert of black gravel, in which the confused ranges of the Pei Shan stand up like barren islands in a desolate sea. We were to cross the desert in its broadest and most waterless part, following a route not only unmapped but utterly unknown. Absolutely nothing is known of the country I crossed for two hundred miles or more between the West Edsin Gol and the route taken from north to south, between the Altai and Hsü Chou in Kan-su, by Ladighin, a member of Kozloff's expedition of 1900.

We left the softer soil and reliquary growth of reeds about the Lu-ts'ao Ching almost immediately, ascending to the plain of the full Gobi at a higher level. The character of the desert was constant throughout, giving a weird but superb impression; it was of flat fragments of black gravel, like shattered slate in formation, laid thickly over yellow sandy clay of an unknown depth. After slugging for twelve miles at least across this plain, we dropped off the flat into a gully that ran across our front, and began winding confusedly among low hills, as the night fell with a keen chill after the heat of the day. We continued through these hills until one in the morning, when we finished a march of well over thirty miles.

Kuai-tze Hu, the dune belt, and the Edsin Gol valleys are depressions where the average temperature, to judge not only from my own experience but from what I heard in the descriptions of the caravan men, is much higher than in Mongolia generally. We were now, however, back in plateau country, and in October the plateaus of Mongolia are cold at the moment the sun goes or a wind begins. The cold of the next day was an abrupt contrast to the easy warmth of the low-lying countries. There was a thin leaden band of cloud across a sky that even in mid-morning had a pale, enameled, lucid brilliance like the dawn, and a cutting wind blew from the northwest.

Our camp, beside a big *obo*, was in a wide, flat, circular black plain, walled in by smooth black hills of a suavely grim outline. The hills appeared to be of exactly the same formation as the plains — deep yellow clay covered with black gravel. The manner in which the flat stone fragments ever came to be scattered so widely and uniformly is a mystery to me. There were very few outcrops of the stone from which it came, and no loose pieces of larger size. Wherever the stone could be seen, at the sides of hills, it was thoroughly shattered, cleaving always in flat pieces; I thought it, rather hesitantly, to be of volcanic origin.[1] As for the hills, as far as I could detect any scheme in this part of the desert, they tended to run from southeast to northwest.

From the *obo* a more northerly road branches off, presenting an alternative to the Four Dry Stages and known as the Two Dry Stages. The two roads form an ellipse, rejoining only after the Three Dry Stages as well as the Four Dry Stages have been passed. The northerly road has better camel pasture, but though only one stretch of two stages is altogether without water, there is not enough in the wells for a group of caravans in company. Apparently it is the older way, long known to the Mon-

[1] I am now told it was more probably slate.

gols, while the Four Dry Stages make a forced crossing only undertaken since traders came this way in numbers. The old way is said to pass through the chief country of the wild camels. I was told this by several caravan masters, and one young Mohammedan camel puller told me that he had seen one which was shot by a Turki caravan master. It was of a grayish color, of about the same height as an ordinary caravan camel, but slender in build and with very small humps "like a woman's breasts." [1]

Wild camels are also found nearer to the Edsin Gol. I was told that a Mongol, the year before, had caught a very young one, but when I passed it had already escaped to the desert again. They say that on the Two Dry Stages the wild camels come sometimes out of the hills to look at the caravan herds at pasture, but that even so they seldom come at all near and are shy and almost impossible to shoot. There are men who say that even when caught extremely young they can never be tamed; but a Hami man told me he had known an Edsin Gol Mongol who used one for riding, and that the wild camel is considered a very fast and a most distinguished mount for a Mongol who fancies himself. Reliable information about wild camels collected by modern travelers remains incomplete, but there seems to be a general agreement that they can be tamed for riding, though never for carrying loads; and everybody who has been told that they can be ridden has been told fantastic tales of the distances they can cover. It seems to be evident that it is a rare and startling thing even for a Mongol to catch and tame one. [2]

On the second day we marched again more than thirty miles, keeping our westerly direction, though turning in and out among the black hills. The growth, even of plants found in the most arid deserts, was more scarce than I had ever seen. Scoring the flanks of the slow-curving hills were faint depressions, in which were a few tamarisks of small size. They say that little

---

[1] The simile would be most extraordinary from a Chinese of the Great Faith, but the Mohammedan Chinese have to some extent a vocabulary, and always a style and manner of speech, all their own.

[2] Prjevalsky gathered more information about wild camels than any other modern traveler, in his journey of 1876. In fact, not much has been added since. Prjevalsky's notes and speculations are in his *From Kulja Across the Tian Shan to Lob-Nor*, translated by E. Delmar Morgan. London, 1879.

snow falls on the Khara Gobi, but what there is must run down
these channels at the thaw.    In the same runnels were a very
few tiny, close-growing, shrubby plants.    None of them seemed
alive and none of them mitigated the profound and sombre desolation of the dominant Gobi.    I remember that at the time it
seemed to me more magnificent than fearful; but then I was
exhilarated by the effort of the forced marches.    Now, in re-
membering, I seem to look down at it from a height and watch
the thin caravan crawling through the black scene, and to admit
the deathliness of it.    Still, it is not as though that desert has
an active threat, like the threat of shifting dunes, and I think
that the horror of it which the Chinese have is perhaps in the
main a practical dread of losing their camels, heightened by the
effect on their minds of the monotony and the fatigue; for it
takes a full twelve hours to cover thirty miles, and putting one
foot in front of the other for twelve hours at the lagging gait
of traveling camels is weariness to the body and crippling to the
spirit.

Our third day in the Khara Gobi was full of happenings.
Both Moses and I had suffered from the cold the night before,
so I discarded the socks I was wearing (the first time I had
changed them since Kuei-hua) for a very heavy pair of camel
hair, knitted for me on the journey by a camel puller, and
though I still wore a battered old pair of shoes while marching,
I got out a pair of thigh boots of antelope skin, lined with felt,
to wear while riding.

While we were marching, I suffered my first casualty in eye-
glasses.    I had stooped down to mend a shoelace, and the wind
blew the glass out of my eye on to the gravel, where it perished
with a tinkle.    I had worn it for months and months, and it had
an honorable history and more than one chip on the rim, where
I had dropped it before on stone floors and bricks and a variety
of things.    It was the same glass I had worn in the very beginning of the year, when on a shooting trip in the Ta Ch'ing Shan
I had had my ears frozen.    That time also the wind — but a
real wind, not a silly gust — had blown it out of my eye into
a snowdrift, whence I had been at some pains to recover it.    It

was a more than ordinary eyeglass; the Eyeglass Inordinate.
The assembled caravans mourned over it. They had never seen
one before; but what capped all their previous amazements was
my fetching out of another one the next day.

We left at half-past one, and five hours after that I saw a
camel die; in fact, I killed it. There are many dead camels on
the Khara Gobi. The caravan men say that they lie end to end,
all across, and it is a fact that there is hardly a place on that
narrow yellow track from which, if you look, like Shelley, before and after, you cannot see dead camels. The Dry Stages
are in the middle section of the Winding Road, and the camels
must make the biggest effort of the journey when they have
worn off their pride of condition. Simple exhaustion accounts
for many in the cool months, but it must be worse when the
weather is hot and the camels feel the lack of both food and
water. The dead lie thickest at the two edges of the desert,
many of them only a few hundred yards from the wells, proving
that the four-march distance, with almost no feeding and no
water at all, is just too much for laden camels that have traveled
at least a month without feeding full. Over and above these,
many are killed by the Khara Gobi that do not die until a week
or two later — those that have been so knocked up by the crossing
that their weariness is too much for their power of recuperation.

This camel, however, died of an outright sickness, which had
started the day that we left the West River. The nearest account of the sickness that the Chinese could give was that a
*hsich feng*, which I take to be a slantwise or malicious kind of
wind, had got into the animal's throat; though some of them did
admit that it might have eaten something not meant even for
camels. It suffered a paralysis of the jaws and throat which
must have come on suddenly, for its cheeks were puffed out with
a large cud it could neither swallow nor chew nor spit out.
After six days with neither food nor water it was terribly weakened. Its legs grew rigid so that it could hardly walk, and its
eyes bulged as though it were choking. At last it stumbled while we
were on the march; it toppled over flat on its side and was quite
unable to get up, as its legs would no longer bend at the joints.

The young owner was the son of a former caravan master of the House of Chou, traveling in their company with a full double file of camels. He was badly cut up by the loss, for it was the first time that he had been sent out independently, and he had counted youthfully on a triumphant journey. He and I lifted up the lips of the sick camel and got the tongue out behind the back teeth. It was covered with nasty pustules. Undoubtedly it was poisoned. There are well-known poison grasses, of which one kind grows in the Hsi-ning district, and two in the desert near Barköl, not to mention those of the Karakoram and Kashmir. The effects of these grasses are well known to the camel men, who said that the sickness of this camel was something else again. I heard of another camel in a different caravan which died of the same sickness in the same region, so that there must be yet another poison plant growing by the Edsin Gol, strange as yet to the caravan men.

The caravans had gone on, for no one stops in the Gobi (unless he is an Elephant's Child of a foreigner, full of "'Satiable Curtiosity'") for another man's business. Then the *hsiensheng* of the House of Chou rode back and delivered the Funeral Oration for Camels About to be Dead, in a very cross voice. "For what are you waiting?" he shouted. "Do you not know that this is the Business of the Gobi? We buy camels with silver and throw them on the Gobi. There is no way out." Still we lingered for a moment, because I asked the owner to let me shoot his camel. It was the only time on the whole journey that I interfered with this law of the caravans, and obtained a swift mercy. The owner agreed because he was a boy after all and, in spite of his despondency, curious to know how big a bang my revolver would make and how big a hole. There was, however, a good deal of head-wagging in camp, and after that I left the camels bought with silver to be thrown on the Gobi according to the business of the Gobi.

The weariness of those marches across the black gap between water and water was cumulative, and I remember that I was heartily tired and heavy-footed in the last night hours. Hills and darkness had begun to close in on us at the same time; thus far we had been rising slowly, but now we crossed a low divide. The descent was just as gradual, almost imperceptible; but at last, at two in the morning, after slugging away for twelve and a half hours, or about thirty-one miles, we struck into a knot of hills. Then we dropped into a pit of more agglomerate gloom and camped. We had achieved the Lien Ssu Han, the Four Drys Together, in three stages. The distance is at least ninety, perhaps nearly a hundred miles. Even if four days are taken it means four swinging marches, but the four-march division is more usually made in winter. Water can then be poured out in pools at the last well, allowed to freeze, and carried in lumps of ice, a sack or two on every camel. They say that once a caravan started on the Four Dry Stages without enough spare camels and all of them weak. By the second march so many camels had been "thrown away" that the caravan master had to abandon a lot of loads. Two men were left with the dump, and they lived there for at least two months on flour and ice given them by passing caravans, before spare camels could be sent back for them.

Although we had camped so late and so tired, I could not let the pitching of the tent close the day's business. It was my turn to force a row with my camel man. The fatigue and monotony had given an extra edge of savageness to his temper, and he had been turning it on the Chen-fan Wa-wa. He had been cock-a-whoop ever since getting rid of the Old Man, and had begun to bully the Wa-wa without mercy. It was not that he used violence, but he threatened and cursed him and harried him unremittingly. Badly shod and not yet used to the long marches, the Wa-wa was footsore and lagged on the march, but the brute gave him no respite, making him do all the herding and the gathering of fuel. I had not interfered, because nominally the Wa-wa was under his "protection"; moreover, he must make his own way in this hard school or drop out. Lately, however, he had begun to threaten, with his fiendish snarl, to drive the Wa-wa out of camp altogether — without food, without even a camel or friends within reach, as the Old Man had had. On this day when the Chou men came in from camel herding they reported that the Wa-wa had collapsed; that his feet were raw and that he was worn-out.    I was out of camp at the time, prospecting for a view from a low hill.    When the Wa-wa struggled in to eat, just before the start, my camel man set his food before him.    The Wa-wa was too weary to eat fast enough for the pleasure of his lord, who in a fury took the food from him and threw it to the camp dogs.

I did not know of this until I joined the caravan on the march. Then I gave the Wa-wa my camel to ride for a while, and after I got up to ride myself the kind-hearted Eldest Son of the House of Chou wrapped the Wa-wa up in his own sheepskin coat and put him on his own camel, though he was not much of a walker himself, and waddled along, leading it for miles.

I had expected the camel man to start a row when I let the Wa-wa ride my camel, thinking he would say that I might ride because I had paid for it, but the Wa-wa must walk because he was earning his living, but he did not accept the challenge. At last, in camp, when we had made a pot of tea, the camel man first helped himself and then put the pot back on the fire.    I reached over, emptied his bowl, poured out one for myself, and passed the pot to Moses and the Wa-wa.    The man took that challenge all right.    He began to rage about the Privilege of Equality in the Tent.    It is in fact a privilege jealously maintained by camel pullers, for neither caravan master nor caravan owner, in eating or drinking or anything out of the routine of duty, puts himself in the slightest way above any camel puller, and Chinese travelers with the caravans must recognize the same level footing.    I had always observed it myself, except when eating tinned food.

I told the man now, however, that I was a foreigner and had my own laws.    I recognized the caravan laws only by courtesy, and if he did not give courtesy in return he could get out of my tent.    The tent was mine and the food was mine; he had no right to my food because in my contract it was written that I should feed myself and Moses, but not him.    This stung him to an insane retort.    He said that if he did not sleep in my tent he would not carry my tent, and if he did not eat my food he would not carry my food.  This was an open repudiation of the whole spirit and letter of caravan law, which is ruled by the convention that at any cost goods and travelers must be furthered to the end of the journey.  Had I been in a position to take up this counter-challenge I could have broken the man and broken with him, with complete justification in Chinese eyes.  As it was, I could only bluff; but I remembered the quarrel with a memory that was getting a very Asiatic turn to it, to be brought up later when it could be put to an Asiatic use.

He realized himself that he had gone too far, and began to back down.  We got to bed at last at five in the morning.  There had been some point to the shindy, though, and for many weeks he behaved himself and the Wa-wa was given something like a fair chance.  For one thing, the man had turned public opinion against himself.  Though the Chinese had sympathized with me, they had been loath to take my part too openly against a fellow Chinese and a fellow caravan man.  They had thought that perhaps I had erred in giving overmuch protection to the evil-tongued Old Man.  Now at last they came over in groups to my tent; they said that I must keep an eye on the camel man, whose grudge was set and sharpened against me, but that he was a disgrace to their kind and they would support me to the full.

The well, or rather pair of wells, marking the end of our last long stage was known as the Shih-pan Ching — the Stone Slab Wells.  To me the place seemed much more sinister than all the desert through which we had been traveling, for we were camped in a straitened pocket among the everlasting black hills, which here, from the way they crowded about us, looked much more steep and menacing.  There were also a few big pieces of black rock, which gave the place its name.  At the foot of the highest hill, in the crotch of a dry watercourse, was a pair of wells ten or at the most fifteen feet deep, — a good deal deeper than most Mongolian wells, — giving an unlimited supply of water that was a little salt, but clear and drinkable.

The legend is that these wells were dug by a pioneer Barköl caravan that had lost its way perhaps from the Two Dry Stages, in the days when the Winding Road was not yet a known route and the Four Dry Stages had not yet been "opened," as the phrase goes, by that strange figure of unwritten history, the False Lama. The Barköl men, after several days without water, would have been in a bad way had not the Lao T'ien-yeh [1] sent them a heavy rain. They caught enough on felts not only for themselves but for their camels also; nay, but yet again, the shower was a genuine miracle, for it fell truly on top of them but nowhere else in the desert. Not unreasonably accepting this for a sign, they dug these wells, which it had not occurred to them to do before. Therefore to this day there is a little shrine above the wells, of slabs of the flat black rock. It is one of those nobler shrines in which there is no figure, only a sliver of wood on which is the name of the Lao-t'ien; and beside it an inscription on a board warns all caravans that they are entering on the most dreadful of all the Gobis, where it is imperative to take enough water.

Here we caught up with the Mohammedan House of Liang, which had raced away ahead of us from the West River, to be beforehand with the water both at the near and the far edge of the Khara Gobi. The Chinese cursed them heartily, there being little affection between the Great and Little Faiths, saying that they had gone ahead when it was to their advantage, but would cling to us from now on, for the sake of company through the chancy country of No Man's Land, where there is danger of raiders.

Though the other Chinese cordially extended their dislike to the whole caravan, it contained only two Mohammedans — the owner's son who represented the "house," and one camel puller to do the cooking that it might be "clean." Mohammedans prefer to employ a majority of Chinese, because their own people are touchy and undependable and will leave their jobs for a whim or a fancied slight. Like most foreigners, I rather warmed to the Mohammedans, and liked especially the young

[1] This is a beautiful vernacular name, with a tang hard to preserve in translation. Could Uncle Remus be consulted, he might render it "Old Man God." I once heard of a beggar in Peking, an ancient more boil-ridden than Job, but more cheerful, who remarked with a grin when he was received at a foreign hospital, "*Lao T'ien-yeh chen ya-chu wo-ti nao-tai* — Old Man God is certainly squashing my head."

Son of the House of Liang. He was a fine lad of twenty-three or -four, of one of the Mohammedan types which show traces of other than Chinese blood. He may well have been a descendant of the "Argoons,"[1] a people of some Central Asian stock whose men had taken Chinese wives, described by Marco Polo at Tenduc, the city which modern scholars think to have been at Kuei-hua or in that region. Ney Elias[2] noticed that the Mohammedans of Kuei-hua had certain reminiscences of Turkestan in their surroundings, and these memories remain in their orchards and gardens especially.

This young Mohammedan employed a Chinese caravan master, but himself took far more than the usual initiative in handling the affairs of the road. He seemed to me more prompt and energetic in his measures and decisions than the Chinese. The Mohammedans are credited by the Chinese with courage and enterprise and are said to be persuasive in talk and in blarney, but they are debited with being undependable in business. "Eat the food of a Mohammedan," they say, "but do not listen to his talk"—take, that is, what he offers but do not believe in what he promises. Indeed, they talk about the way the Mohammedans talk much as the English talk about the way the Irish talk; and there is something in it at that.

It is also recognized that a Mohammedan Chinese is cleaner than a pagan Chinese. Even with a Mohammedan Chinese, however, cleanliness has nothing to do with godliness—only with churchliness. Now this is one of the sundering differences between the Asiatic and the European. If a man says to you, "Of course his house (or his tent) is cleaner than mine; he is a Mohammedan," you know that you are indisputably listening to an Asiatic. It does not matter what kind of Asiatic he may be or what kind of European you are; the broad difference is there. Only the Asiatic is inherently unable to detect that different ways of life are admirable or imitable or attainable in different degrees. His way of life is to him something to be accepted. He may despise a man born to a different way of life,

---

[1] A term sufficiently explained by Yule (*The Book of Ser Marco Polo*) as meaning "half-caste."

[2] Cited by Yule.

but he does not necessarily despise that way of life. Although most of the Mohammedan communities in China proper have become almost entirely Chinese in blood, a Mohammedan is no less among aliens when he is among Chinese. Nor do the Chinese necessarily regard him as an alien because of his pork tabu. For the matter of that, he might well, and in the laxer places more or less often does, forget his prejudice against pork without the Chinese in the least forgetting their prejudice against his birth. This is that Asiatic attitude toward a man's destiny which can under particular conditions, as in India, be formulated in a code, like the rule of caste; but as a general prejudice or predisposition it is one of the decisive spiritual tests of the Asiatic mind. You have only to apply it to any individual Russian, for instance, to determine whether his Oriental or his Occidental inheritance predominates.

Of the names for Mohammedans that can be used in Mohammedan hearing there are *Hsiao chiao*, the Little Faith (opposed to the great majority of the Chinese);[1] *Chieh chiao,* the Faith Apart or the Different Faith, and *Hui-hui.* The etymology of this last term has been in high dispute. The Chinese characters mean "return-return." I have heard the explanation advanced that this goes back to the use of Moslem mercenaries from countries west of China proper. Some of these mercenaries, according to the argument, must have settled down with Chinese wives while on their way home, and, being foreigners, became known to neighboring communities as "the people who were on their returning way." The reduplication of the word *hui,* in elevating it into a proper noun, would be in accord with colloquial usage. It seems to me, however, that it is just this colloquial simplicity which makes the explanation too easy to be true.

Chinese etymologies are in the main an impenetrable mystery, because changing pronunciations and borrowed words have left no mark on an ideographic writing, as they would on alphabet-

---

[1] Seeing that even at this day the terms Buddhist (which is silly) and Confucianist (which is ignorant) are sometimes sweepingly applied to the Chinese as if they were organized in definite churches, it is wiser to state that the Chinese of the Great Faith are so called rather because they do not belong to the Small Faith (Islam) than because they do belong to any other faith.

ical spelling; but, having regard to the sharp cleavage between spoken and written use and the ponderous respectability enshrouding the latter, there is a *prima facie* justification for doubting that *Hui-hui*, were it of true colloquial origin, would have come into quasi-official use. I even think that a wilder guess would be safer; that it may be a corruption of an old tribal name — perhaps even the name of a barbarian tribe once known to the Chinese, which they later transferred in error to a Moslem people.[1]

Chinese Mohammedans, though more in some districts than in others, are prone to be affronted by the name *Hui-hui*, which proves that it did not originate with them but with their unbelieving neighbors. It is, however, made much more dignified if the adjective *lao,* old, is prefixed. The most formal Chinese title, written up over the gates of mosques and used in courtesy of the people who worship there, is *Ch'ing-chen,* indicating that the belief is Clear and True. Almost all of the names not to be used to the face of a Mohammedan harp on the awkward subject of the pig, as thus: *p'ing-tsui,* Vase Mouth, from the shape of a hoggish snout, which I think rather clever; *hsiao i-pa,* Little Tail, which comes back to the pig once more, but from the other end; or more bluntly *chu-wa,* Pig's Baby. The name I like best, however, I heard uttered by the Eldest Son of the House of Chou, who in a moment of spleen referred to his colleague of the House of Liang as *hsiao chu-tan,* the Little Pig's Egg.

Curiously enough the Chinese Moslems, who usually speak of pigs as "black animals," will use the direct word when swearing at each other, saying "pig-defiled" where Kuei-hua men would say "dog-defiled" or Tientsin men "defile your younger sister" or Shan-tung men "defile your grandmother." Why the pig should be ultimately abominable seems to puzzle the Chinese. I knew one, and even among caravan men he passed for no sluggard at swearing, who had spent all his youth among the Mohammedans and had their little turns of speech so neatly mastered that they always took him for one of themselves; but

---

[1] I find, on later reading, that it was once applied to the Uighurs. (Bretschneider, cited in Rockhill's edition of William of Rubruck, Hakluyt Society.)

even he did not know. I have heard it put forward that pigs must be abhorrent to the cleanly Mohammedans because they eat human ordure; only to be countered with the argument that the sight of chickens fattening on the same diet has never been known to make a Moslem blush.

As usual when facts cannot be made to fit, legend is brought in to adjust matters. The most straightforward of these ætiological yarns is that a certain Mohammedan Emperor (or, as some say, the Prophet), being imprisoned by his enemies, was released by a pig which rooted a way through a wall. As the wall must therefore have been of mud, this is most probably a pure Chinese invention. Other Chinese go so far as to say that the Mohammedan holy animal, or god (totem would come nearer to the idea behind this tale), is a pig. This last idea is the most interesting of all, for it points to a lingering tradition among the Chinese of a time — obviously much older than Islam — when they were familiar with the very primitive religious conception that the thing accursed, or more precisely the thing tabooed, can be the holy thing as well.

There is another well, but of inferior water, a few miles beyond the Stone Slab Wells, in a small drift of sandy country. Overpassing this, we camped in blank desert and the next day passed through narrowing valleys choking us at last into a gorge, to Yeh-ma Ching, the Wild Horse Well. Taking up water here for ourselves, but leaving the camels still without, we camped a mile or two beyond. These marches took us through the same kind of Khara Gobi country, but with higher hills, a pasture rather better or at least not quite so bad, and at times an outlook southward to a distant red desert. They say that on this fringe of the Khara Gobi there are wild horses (*equus prjevalskii*) and wild asses.

On these two marches all the camels were reviewed for sore hoof pads. The gravel surface of the Four Dry Stages had done them more damage than any rocky going; for, being tired by the long marches and made lazy by the level trail, they would not lift their feet properly, as they do when they are among stones, but dragged them at every step, causing blood blisters and fevered pads. The treatment is to keep the camels at least one day without water. (Cold water is said to make horses lame, as well as inducing blisters in men and camels, and caravan men will rarely drink anything but hot tea, especially just before or after the march.) They are then set on the road long enough to start the circulation working well through their hoof pads. After this the sore pads are attacked with a small flat lancet. The blisters are not opened and drained from the surface, but the lancet thrust in at the side of the pad to a depth of two and three inches, the object being not to deal with the immediate blister, for fear of making the pad tender, but to ease and cool the whole foot by bloodletting. Water blisters are let alone, only blood blisters being held serious. The result is buckets of blood all over the trail, as the camels stamp wildly, squirting blood each time. When a camel has a pad that hurts him he does not go tenderly on it as any other animal would, but stamps impatiently on it every few steps, with disastrous effects if it has picked up a nail or a thorn. Sometimes the forehoofs, though never the hind, are bled from a vein in the joint just above the hoof.

It was also at this time that we began to have the first miscarriages among the cow camels in calf. A camel, if well fed, and above all if watered regularly, can remain in full work up to the day that the calf is born; but the hard marches and poor feeding in the Khara Gobi, followed of necessity by a big drink at the first well, had caused these miscarriages. Yet even so the camel would only be delayed for a few moments before resuming the march, still carrying her full load. Kuei-hua men indeed, unless they are near the end of the journey or at pasture between journeys, will rarely try to save even a normally born calf. With a calf at suck the camel would become too thin for work, but if the calf is abandoned at once she will remain as fit as ever. Only she must never be allowed to see the calf, or she will moan and pine for it. If she never sees it the poor brute thinks she has suffered, to use that phrase of the caravan men which stands for so much suffering callously seen or stoically borne, only one more mischance of "the Business of the Gobi."

## XV

## THE HOUSE OF THE FALSE LAMA

The Wild Horse Well is on the very brink of the central plateau of the Black Gobi. From it we had descended so gently into a deep, wide valley, which declined with a gentle pitch toward the north, that only looking back the next morning over the last part of the ground covered in the night could it be seen that we had come down from a wild table-land, with ramparts of barren hills buttressed by long sweeping slopes of detritus. On the other side of the valley or basin we ascended to another lower plateau to undertake the Lien San Han, the Three Drys Together or Three Dry Stages, which complete the crossing of the capital desert of Mongolia. Caravans often force the crossing in two marches, though it is reckoned at three regular stages; but we took the full three, because at the end of the first, unusual rains in the summer had formed a mere, of which a few pools and mudholes remained where the camels could be watered.

At the very start we met a caravan traveling in the come-one come-all fashion of the Mongols, so different from the orderly line of march of the Chinese traders. They were Torguts of Qara Shahr, in the depths of Hsin-chiang, on the road from Urumchi to Kashgar, where they herd their famous ponies between the valleys of the T'ien Shan and the skirts of the Takla-makan. They were going in the train of a relative of the Han Wang, their Prince, on pilgrimage to Peking to adore the Pan-ch'an Lama, the great ecclesiastic and quasi-divinity of Western Tibet, who was supposed to be the head of an anti-Lhasa and anti-British party and to have left Tibet for political reasons.

Be it said that I have a high regard for most religious motives, especially if they be grossly superstitious or mixed with art magic or resplendent with ritual, and the Mongols on their fantastically pious journeys always stir my blood.   There was something stupendous in the march of these tribesmen from Central Asia, from one of the most outlying Mongol communities, with their women and children, their camel loads of treasure and offerings, their gowns of yellow and purple, red and green, their bold, determined faces, their assured carriage, their mixed armory of matchlocks and breech-loading rifles, swords and assorted pistols, bound across the desert for China to acquire merit by abasing themselves in the presence of the holiest of the Incarnate Divinities of Tibet — for the Pan-ch'an Lama is nearer to God than the Ta-lai Lama, though not so high above men. Evidently they were traveling at their ease, for many of their camels carried the felts and framework of *yurts* in bulging loads, over which were draped old carpets of Turki weaving from Khotan, glowing softly with worn reds and faded yellows.

In the Three Dry Stages the character of the desert changes gradually to a grittier kind of sand, overlaid not with the unbroken glossy black of the Four Dry Stages, but with what seemed to me fragments of quartz, red, brown, and white (though the black stone was also present), melting at a distance into a gray tinge.   Nor is the desert quite so bleakly barren as the central Khara Gobi, for there is more variety and a little more abundance of desert scrub.   By the third day there were even a few wild onions, which caused almost a stampede among the camels, which for days, as the men said, had been chewing nothing but firewood.   They were so difficult for the herders to control that we had to break camp much earlier than usual, in spite of a high wind.   By that day we could see far off toward the southwest the blue beginnings of the Ma-tsung Shan.   From the east the country of the Three Dry Stages can be seen as a plateau, but on the west it subsides gradually to lower levels.   When, coming down from it, we struck the first well, we had left behind the greater deserts and were engaged among the oases of No Man's Land.   The name of this well is significant: it is Ho-shao Ching, which means the Well of the Hoshun.   "Going the *hos-*

28. CAMEL FEEDING FROM NOSEBAG

"Dried peas at the Kuei-hua end, or barley at the Ku Ch'eng-tze end." (p. 82)

29. DONKEY RIDER, TORGUT MONGOL CARAVAN (BLACK GOBI)
"They were going . . . on pilgrimage to Peking to adore the
Pan-ch'an Lama." (p. 230)

*hun*" is one of the caravan phrases for traveling in Mongolia; it means to travel as a trader and dealer, not as a carrier of goods. This well is on a variant of an ancient route, now fallen into some desuetude, between Hsü Chou in Kan-su and Yunbeize, an important lamasery and trading centre under the slopes of the Altai.

One stage more to the west from this well is a half-dry mere called Kung-p'o Ch'üan, the strategic point of the region which the caravan men call the San Pu-Kuan. Moses, a little depressed in spite of himself by so many days in a desert to which he always referred by the stock Chinese phrase of "savage hills and wild land," where there was no one with whom he could chatter but tired-out camel pullers, cheered himself with mild jokes about the name; for is there not a San Pu-kuan in Tientsin? It is the quarter which, they say, was once set aside to be an American Concession; but, the Americans deciding not to have a concession, it lay for many years a dirty bit of swamp between the Japanese Concession and the Chinese city. Then as the waste land ceded to the foreigners was drained and filled and built up into a clean and prosperous Treaty Port, the mud and water which had been refused by the Americans and not claimed in reversion by either Japanese or Chinese began to be more valuable and to be occupied from both the Chinese and the Japanese sides. By the time it was all built over it was time to determine the boundary afresh — or so the popular story goes; and indeed to this day it runs in some places through brick and mortar, instead of keeping, like orthodox metes and bounds, to streets and gutters.

Because in the beginning the land had been despised and rejected of three nations it was called the San Pu-kuan — the Three Don't Cares, as one might say. In the days of its unregeneration it had been a sort of thieves' kitchen, an ungoverned Alsatia. By the same token all the more tinny wickedness of the city still flourishes there, in cinemas and brothels, theatres, billiard rooms, and those remarkable Western style restaurants which serve nothing but beefsteaks and the weirder brands of Worcestershire sauce, to the sole end that shipping clerks and students with glossy hair may exercise their familiarity with knives, forks, and

the mystic formula "God damn." Those foreigners who know
the Three Don't Cares are mostly insurance agents who hurtle
in motor cars down the dinginess of its daytime streets to appraise
the sprawling brothel quarters, replete with bathhouses and
theatres, owned by Chinese generals and insured for impressive
sums.

Occasionally a foreigner does stray down there at night to sit
in one of those theatres where the ageless events of ancient battles
are represented by acrobats and made fashionable with electric
light; where also attendants with rapt, passionless faces throw
hot face towels for the sweating audience to amazing distances
with uncanny accuracy, howling the while like jackals. As for
me, however, when I remember the Three Don't Cares, I remember always those restaurants where they of the glossy hair
eat the amorphous beefsteaks garnished with the startling sauces
and say "God damn" at the behest of Conscience. Then — for
these things must be, in order that China may awake — they pass
from the electric light of the restaurant through the electric light
of the garbage-laden streets to the electric light of the billiard
rooms, there to lean on their cues in the latest foreign attitude
dictated by Shanghai and say "God damn" some more.

Charming memories! There is fun to be had in Tientsin if
you know the passwords. But in this San Pu-kuan between
desert and desert the discouraged wit of Moses was all unwinged
words to me. Here was a Three Don't Cares for which I would
fuse and confound all the electric light of the Five Continents,
might I but pass the one time through it with the camel caravans,
as camels are meant to travel, with a red-tasseled spear swaying
over the leading camel, the long, awkward cylindrical bell clang-
ing dolorously under the shaggy sweep of mane of the last camel
in each file, the men trudging through afternoon, dusk, and unreal moonlight without speech, except now and then for the warning hail *chüeh-lo-o-o-o-o-o!* when a nose string breaks and the
released camel with all his mates behind him stops to feed.

At Kung-p'o Ch'üan the way of the Two Dry Stages joins
again that of the Four and the Three. Moreover, there comes
into the same oasis the main trail from the north, coming from

Yunbeize and going to Hsü Chou, through an easy pass of the main range of the Ma-tsung Shan. It is important to remember, as I have said before, that any Mongol road is more a direction of march than a set route; but I take it that this is the point where I crossed the line of Ladighin, of Kozloff's 1900–1 expedition, whose march was from north to south, though he made lateral excursions at points much farther to the north. His most important excursion was eastward, to the Kuku-tumurtu-ola (the Ati Bogdo of Carruthers), which he found to be related, as a life zone, to the Altai; well watered, wooded, and "pullulating" with game. This range, he says, links with the Noin Bogdo to the east, north of the terminal basin of the Edsin Gol. It is isolated on the north by a desert, the Charghin Gobi, from the Altai, and on the south by the great deserts in which I had been engaged. The Tumurtu hills are apparently about three hundred kilometres from the Altai, where Ladighin struck them, and the rest of his route to Hsü Chou covered about eight hundred kilometres — excluding, I assume, the two hundred kilometres traveled in the Tumurtu. Rather more than halfway between the Tumurtu and Hsü Chou he indicates a portion of a range called "Madzi-shan."[1] This is undoubtedly the Ma-tsung Shan. "Madzi" is in fact such a classical example of the Russian way of corrupting Chinese pronunciations that, without having heard the correct pronunciation, anyone who has a slight acquaintance with the invincible Russian clumsiness over Chinese names might guess that "Ma-tsung" was meant. They are approximately 42° N., 98° E.

In a depression beginning at the Well of the Hoshun, deepest at Kung-p'o Ch'üan and running from southeast to northwest, is a series of marshes, half dried out at the end of October, but kept alive by unfailing springs. To the northwest is a sterile gathering of low hills, waterless and seamed with waterless gullies. They are, as near as I can hit it off, the Sertsinghin-nuru of Ladighin, and I suppose that they run up to the Aji Bogdo, yet farther back in the north and west. On the south and running

---

[1] Madzi-chan on the map attached to the summary of Kozloff's accounts in *La Géographie*, vol. V (1902), pp. 273–8. *Chan*, by the French system of transcribing Chinese, is *shan*, a mountain.

to the west is the blue main range of the Ma-tsung Shan, distant
perhaps thirty or perhaps fifty miles. The whole is one of the
most lightly mapped provinces in the world — a big, empty, un-
crossed country full of uncertainties.

In the depth of it is an unknown oasis, and there, on a knot of
reddish rubbly hills, looking to Outer Mongolia over the yellow
reed beds of the largest mere, are the strangest ruins I ever saw.
They might in all seeming be " half as old as time," yet many who
had a hand at their building are still alive. This deserted citadel
in the vacant domain of the Three Don't Cares is all that stands,
except the confused story that is on the tongues of a few men
who spend their lives tramping up and down the desert, of the
works of the False Lama. It is from these ruins that the mere
is called Kung-p'o Ch'üan — the Spring of the Hillside of the
Duke.[1]

Already the legend of the False Lama has been elaborated
beside the tent fires into many versions, but from the choice
of details it is possible to throw together a picture with life in it,
of an adventurer who, during those years when Mongolia echoed
again for a while with the drums and tramplings of its mediæval
turbulence, proved himself a valiant heir in his day to all the
Asiatic soldiers of fortune from Jenghis Khan to Yakub Beg of
Kashgar.

I have heard men say that the False Lama was a Russian.
Certainly the thing they remember most vividly about him, next
to his harem, is the habit he had of changing his clothes every
day or so, dressing at different times like a Russian, a Chinese,
or a Mongol. Others maintain that he was true Mongol, so it
may have been that he was a Buriat, a Russianized Siberian
Mongol. The most substantial story of all is that he was a
Chinese from Manchuria who had served in Mongolia as a herder
of ponies for the princely firm of Ta Sheng K'uei. In this employment he learned the language and customs of the Mongols.
They say that he rose suddenly to power and notoriety during the
violent period about 1920-1 when first the White and then the

---

[1] I am not quite sure of myself here. Any Chinese name in Mongolia may be a
Mongol name given a Chinese twist to save the Chinese trouble.

Red Russian "Partisans" overran Mongolia. He began by proclaiming himself a Lama, and a lama of high rank, a Bogdo or Great or Holy One, taking a title that belongs only to the several degrees of Living Buddhas.

While winning his early successes he got himself the repute of being immune from fire and invulnerable to bullets. It is declared positively that he was captured by White Russians at Kobdo who burned him for three days, but to no purpose. Escaping from them, he led the Mongols back to the sack of Kobdo, the massacre of the Chinese, and the eviction of the Whites. The caravan men never seem to have counted it against the False Lama that he gave over their countrymen at Kobdo to a Mongol massacre. For one thing, the men of their calling never had much feeling of kinship with traders sitting on their hams, in privileged marts like Kobdo, Uliassutai, and Urga. For another, their simple realism accepted the fact that the adventurer was playing for power. They know that buying a camel and working a camel are things that admit different attitudes and different words.

The detail of those wars in Mongolia is a confusion of murder and riot, but their main course is plain enough. At the collapse of the Russian Empire, which had in latter years exercised a powerful indirect control over Mongolian affairs, the country was invaded by a Chinese military adventurer, whose ambition was to reassert the nominal Chinese suzerainty and to create in fact a satrapy for himself. He was defeated with great massacre by White Russians, a broken soldiery from the Imperial armies, together with Mongol levies. The Whites, who under the wolfish leadership of the "Mad Baron" Ungern-Sternberg had swept over a kingdom with wolfish ferocity and courage, were quite incapable of rule. They lost their ascendancy over the Mongols, who turned to the Red Russians, and the Whites in their turn were overwhelmed. The idea of Chinese domination had gone by the board, but the Mongol chiefs were not equal to their chance of fortune and the Red Russians were not yet collected and organized enough to take over the country. An uneasy period followed in which the Living Buddha at Urga was declared the

Spiritual and Temporal Sovereign of the Mongols, under ten-
tative Soviet guidance.

This period only lasted until the death of the Khutukhtu or
Living Buddha.  By a peculiar fortune it was known in his lifetime that he was to be the last of his succession.  A Living
Buddha is only the vehicle, generation by generation, of a cycle
of incarnations; it is decreed at the beginning of each cycle that
it shall last for a stated number of generations, after which the
spirit which informed it is caught up to a higher plane.  The
Urga cycle came to an end with this Khutukhtu, so that after
his death the Mongols were left under scattered hereditary
chieftains with no central figure on which to rally.  The Soviets
in the meantime had confirmed their own power and were able to
carry out their own designs.  They took over Mongolia, working
on the young men in order to discredit and disestablish the
princely families; and that is how Mongolia stands to-day, except
for the Inner Mongolian tribes, which have remained under
Chinese rule.

When the Urga Khutukhtu was acclaimed ruler of all Mongolia, with the title of Bogdo Khan, he gave to the False Lama
— or so it is said — large territories in Western Mongolia for a
fief, including Kobdo, the Altai country, the *hoshun* of Mingan,
and the temple trading centres of Yunbeize and Dabeize.  The
False Lama, however, afraid either of intrigues against him or
of the recoil of his own intrigues against others, fled westward
and stopped for a while near Ku Ch'eng-tze, representing himself
in a friendly way to the Governor of Hsin-chiang.  Later, probably on an understanding with the Governor, he moved again to
these oases in what for many years had been a No Man's Land.

This No Man's Land is the country that I have indicated before as not adhering clearly to either Inner or Outer Mongolia.
It came by its name of San Pu-kuan or Three Don't Cares because none of the big Mongol groups, nor yet the Chinese
provinces of Hsin-chiang or Kan-su, had cared to push a claim
to it.  It was too remote and too inaccessible.  When the Huns
in the fifth and sixth centuries were centred about Bar Köl, it
may have been one of their outer ranges, but there is hardly

30. THE HOUSE OF THE FALSE LAMA
"He got himself the repute of being . . . invulnerable
to bullets." (p. 236)

reason to think that at any time since then it has been much in use.  The few Mongols of the Ma-tsung Shan are mostly Torguts, of that portion of the tribe whose proper range is in the Zungarian trough, between the Altai and the T'ien Shan, dividing Western Mongolia and Chinese Turkestan proper.  Although the False Lama had been in touch with their kinsmen near Ku Ch'eng-tze he did not attempt to lead them as a tribe or in any large numbers to the new principality he was marking out for himself in the Three Don't Cares.  His followers were a mixed lot, lifted from all over Western Mongolia, some of them his own fighting retainers, the rest whole families that he had swept up on his way in order to establish a population about him.  This was in the end the weakness of his position, for not only had a large number of his subjects not come with him willingly, but they did not like his high-handed way of keeping all the men at call for service under arms and seizing women at his will for the harem that was his especial princely recreation.

For a year at least he ruled boldly and successfully at Kungp'o Ch'üan.  He must have been a man of vision and energy, for the caravan men say that it was he more than anyone else who pieced together the Winding Road, linking little-used Mongol routes to the byways of the opium runners.  His masterwork was in establishing the crossing of the Khara Gobi by the Three and the Four Dry Stages, thus making it possible for large caravans to travel from Ku Ch'eng-tze to Kuei-hua in a zone protected by the desert from all but the boldest marauders from Outer Mongolia, and offering, then at any rate, little temptation to tax farmers on the Chinese borders.  The digging of the "miraculous" Stone Slab Wells had shown that it was possible to find water in the Khara Gobi at no great depth; the only trouble was that in the ordinary way no caravan would care to spend the necessary time digging wells.  It was his intention, therefore, to improve the crossing still further by digging another well in the Four Dry Stages.

Whether or not he was a Chinese, and however many Chinese he may have slaughtered in his Kobdo days, he made it the forefront of his policy, from the time he set up in No Man's Land,

to encourage Chinese trade. Until his time, it is said, no regular
Ku Ch'eng-tze heavy caravan had been over this road. He not
only invited one (with the approval of the Governor of Hsin-
chiang, who wanted the trade of his province to recuperate from
the loss of the Great Road) but escorted it through the Gobi.
Thereafter he kept patrols out in the direction of the Two Dry
Stages and the most dangerous approach from Outer Mongolia
and gave armed safe-conduct free of charge across his domain.

These were the days of his pride, remembered by the caravan
masters who used to be invited to sit with him in his high room
overlooking his stronghold, to smoke decorously and talk of
roads and travel and the growth of trade. The caravan men admitted the full measure of his enterprise, his vision and energy;
but with the shrewdness of their kind they never forgot his beginnings. Though he was "duke" (*kung*) and Holy One
(*Bogdo*) of that conquest of the desert, they remember him
always as the False Lama, the False Bogdo. Also, being full-
blooded men, they dwell more on the memory of his harem than
on the help he gave them. They speak always of his women as
his *hao k'ou-k'ou-tze*. *K'ou-k'ou* is a version of some Mongol
word for a woman or girl; it is the regular word for the Mongol
lights-o'-love that the men pick up about Ku Ch'eng-tze, and they
utter it with an indescribable toothy relish that always delighted me.

The False Lama was more than an opener of roads. To encourage traffic he hired and sold camels at cheap rates to caravans whose cattle were worn out by the desert stages. He drafted
off some of his disgruntled Mongols to cultivate crops in the
better oases to feed his own people and planned to establish a
constant supply of grain and flour for the caravans by finding
touch with Hsü Chou on the other side of the Ma-tsung Shan.
For the Mongol side of his enterprise they say that he talked of
founding a fair, for the full scope of his ambition was to build
up a whole trading city, fed by the new road, about his fortalice.

At the height of his power he had more than two hundred
*yurts* on permanent foundations of stamped clay under the
shadow of his walls, while other families herded his thousand

head of camels, his hundreds of ponies, and his many thousand sheep, dispersed through the central chain of oases and over the slopes of the Ma-tsung Shan.    His road, however, was not more than well founded and his fortress well built about him when the wrath of Urga sought him out; in the year 1923 or 1924, as I understand it.    Ten men rode out of the desert to his north saying that they were lamas of the Bogdo Khan, sent to invite him to council at Urga on matters of high policy.    Three of them, as chiefs of the mission, were admitted to his chamber in the central keep, from which he could overlook almost all the frontiers of the kingdom he had brought into being as if out of a vision.    When they were brought before his face, in the same moment that they saluted him they shot him with automatics, thus ending a legend with murder and the vulgar proof that his invulnerability was not equal to his incombustibility.

Other ways of telling the story are that the emissaries from Urga came in one or two motor cars; that the False Lama was taken out and shot before his people; that he was taken to Urga and shot; that his head was cut off and his body bound down with chains to make sure of him; and that he was never captured at all, but another man in his stead, and that he is yet alive, an outlaw in hiding.    However these things may be, it is certain that such a raid on this man of violence and craft could never have been pushed to an end without the sympathy of some at least among his Mongols.    It is also evident that whoever planned the raid from Urga struck shrewdly.    Without any strong point to guard the approach from Outer Mongolia, the caravan road is always under a threat, and without any ruler in No Man's Land it has become a sanctuary of thieves.

After the wiping out of the False Lama his following soon broke up, returning for the most part to their own *hoshun* except for those who were carried away to Urga.    A few of his people are said to be still in the region, but their *yurts* are not within eyeshot of that ruin and that marsh where the caravans pass, but pass without talking and hurriedly, and never camp. The rough buildings are rapidly falling down, and soon there will be little trace of the House of the False Lama to stand for a monument of one of the strangest episodes of that period, so recent and yet so remote, when history was swiftly acted and never written down.

We camped about five miles beyond the Chia-lama Pan'rh at the next group of springs. I walked back the next morning to see the ruins, taking one man with me, a favorite of mine from the House of Chou, because it was a bad country, no place for a man alone. I think the caravan men were as much afraid of ghosts as of men in the flesh, but they were sure that plenty of both were about.

The fortified quarter is built partly of mud bricks, partly of mud and stones, and partly of uncemented boulders and slabs of rock. On the easy hillside just under it are the foundations of a temple, because men do not build in a wilderness without making a house either for the spirit of the place or for the gods they bring with them. This temple has been utterly razed, because it would never have done to allow the ghost of so dangerous a man as the False Lama to come back to a house ready prepared and the converse of assembled spiritual powers. The main gate of the fortress is entered sideways by a ramp, and opens into a wide lower court with stabling, or rather shelter yards, and garrison quarters. This is overlooked from one of the side walls by a tower which, with a gallery connecting it with the upper works and the keep, was designed for the central defense. The crown of the knoll is a rats' delight of a place, a maze of passages like tunnels and stairways like wells, and rooms and cells locked and piled and nested one within another without any regularity or plan. From the look of things the man who planned this place was a Mongol, with no idea of how to go about the making of walls and roofs.

The core of the whole is the keep where lived the False Lama himself. This room, which was furnished with the luxury of a sleeping *k'ang* heated by flues, has been wildly knocked about, even the brick and stone *k'ang* having been pulled to pieces in the search for the tyrant's treasure. All the buildings have been unroofed and most of the floors in buildings of more than one story have been destroyed, partly in the search for treasure and partly to free any spirits that might have gathered in the living places of men. The weakness of the position is that it is commanded at barely more than a stone's throw from another hill. This is guarded by an isolated tower, but it would have been hard to keep the garrison in food and water.

From the keep one looks down on the whole mass, with the ground plan of the temple before the gate, the mud *yurt* foundations laid out in ranks in front of the fort and in groups all about the sides, and northward over the sloping marshes to the narrow trail, looking like a footpath, trodden by camels coming from the Two Dry Stages and Yunbeize. In the fortress itself there is a cramped and sinister feeling. I did not feel happy. Withered in the light of the noonday sun almost to the dingy color of the hill on which they stood, and lying so empty and quiet in that utter emptiness of marsh and hill, brief patches of living land and long stretches of desolation, the rifled ruins seemed to be oppressed by something uncanny. I did not wonder that the few frequenters of the wilderness should avoid them and whatever ghost they harbor.

On our way to the ruins my camel-pulling friend had seen a wild sheep. When I got my glasses on him I could see that he had a superb head. Standing nearly a mile away on the ridge of the low hills of rotten rock behind the House of the False Lama, he gazed down for a long time on the plain across which we were walking before he trotted away toward the distant mountains. I was told that it was a very dry autumn after a dry summer, which perhaps accounted for the wandering of a ram of his many years — for by the curl of his horns and his loneliness he must have been a very old and very lordly ram — so far from the higher hills, with swards of turfy grass between the rocks, which are the proper haunt of wild sheep.

When we got to the ridge we looked for his spoor, somewhat idly, but did not find it among the stones. I thought nothing of this until we got back. After my friend had told of the lonely wild ram the men began to fidget and mutter. The general finding was that we had seen the spirit of the Chia Lama, departing after a visit to the castle of his former power.

Our own camp, all night, was in an uproar of frantic dogs. To this whole series of springs there come at night antelope, wild asses, and, they say, wild camels. Their unseen presence kept the dogs awake and later, when a wolf howled here and there, they went into pure frenzy. In the daytime there was not a glimpse of anything alive, except sand grouse flying furiously overhead, several hundred together. At a little distance from the trampled margins of the drinking pools one could see the narrow paths by which the desert animals approached the water. The tracks which were pointed out to me as those of wild camels were frequent. They were more than half the size of the tracks of a caravan camel, and more elliptical in shape. Nor, at least as it seemed to me, were the toe prints quite so deep — perhaps because the wild camel, whose gait is not affected by the carrying of loads, places his weight differently. The caravan men were positive that the tracks were not made by half-grown camels belonging to Mongols.

This camp was called T'iao Hu. When we got there we found an enterprising Barköl trader in camp. He had brought out flour for men and barley or dried peas for camels, and was prepared to hire the camels that had carried them to caravans in need of fresh transport. We halted here for a whole day, to let our camels rest their gravel-fevered feet in the soft soil. The great quantity of soda in the soil healed them amazingly. There is also saltpetre, and large pits filled with water show where it was dug and washed for making crude gunpowder in the time of the False Lama. The big caravans were running out of *ts'ao-mi* and *ts'ao-mien*, so the men spent the day in baking bread, to their great joy. They made ovens by digging small pits near to steep clay banks. When the pit was dug a boring into it from the bank would be made, in order to give a draft. Then fuel was lit in the bottom of the pit. When it had burned to red ash the draft bore was stopped, the bread put on the coals to bake, and covered. By putting crude soda in the dough they raised it very creditably. My own camel man made bread for us occasionally as a luxury. It is a simple trick, but needs knack, and few even among the caravan cooks can do it neatly. Dough is made in the ordinary way and hung up in a damp cloth to the ridgepole of the tent, where it gets the warmth of the fire, which ferments it overnight. The knack is in judging the heat and time required for the fermentation. The next day this sour dough is rolled out into pancakes, which are baked in the bottom of a dry cooking pot. It rises very fairly, and at the same time the sourness is baked out of it. This kind of pancake bread is best eaten after being fried in mutton fat.

As usual after a day off, the men sat talking late around the fires, visitors going the round from tent to tent. In my tent the talk ran on cinemas, or "electric shadows." It was agreed that they are all about brothels, though adorned with other humorous matter. Even to the Kuei-hua camel pullers, whose women have far more freedom than most Chinese, pictures that have so many women in them going about publicly must be indecent — to say nothing of their joy over the love-makings. These pictures, by general admission, can do anything but talk, and even then no one has any bother in supplying the talk. Thus one man had seen a cinema in which a foreigner had ridden up to a brothel on a horse — I suppose in the original he was courting a Pure Flower of Womanhood. There was a good-for-nothing opium smoker outside to whom he gave his horse to hold. The opium smoker (tramp), going to sleep, let the horse run away. When the man came out of the brothel after some gay business with a girl inside, he said to the opium smoker, "Curse your——! Where is my horse?" "—— —— — ——," said the opium smoker. Then they both went to a policeman, who said, "May dogs defile him! I haven't seen him!" and so on. This reminded another man of a picture which began with a policeman who saw a ladder leaning against a house. He said at once, "Defile his mother! This is a thief, may dogs defile his ancestors, curse his——!"

And that was the way we went to bed, five miles from the House of the False Lama, where ghosts walk.

31. TIAO HU: SHAVING DAY, MOHAMMEDAN CARAVAN
"In a Mohammedan-owned caravan there are rarely more than one or two
Mohammedan camel pullers." (p. 161)

32. MOSES WITH BRICK TEA (RIGHT), CHEN-FAN WA-WA
"You must have a safe man behind your back." (p. 14)

# XVI

## CORPSE CARAVANS AND GHOSTS

WE moved on for three marches to a camp called Salt Pool Wells, a group of stingy spring-fed pools in the hollows of a soil permeated with salt and soda. That was some of the worst stuff we drank on all the road, more bitter than salt — bitter as the Waters of Separation. The weather was much colder, with prevailing high winds from the north and northwest, so strong that on one day the caravans would not break camp, saying that such a head wind was too much for camels with bulky loads. On the twenty-sixth of October our first snow came flurrying down on a stinging wind. We were now in the heart of the Ma-tsung Shan, though most of the time we were out of sight of what had appeared from the House of the False Lama to be a single, well-distinguished range. On every march we passed in and out of small flat plains, crossing over one low semicircular range after another. The men told me the hills are called Ma-tsung Shan — the "horse-hoofprint hills," or Horseshoe Hills, as we should say.

In these Ma-tsung Shan or jumbled hills lying off the extreme southward-reaching spurs of the Altai, we began to see Mongols again. Most of them were renegade Western Torguts, who had set up in No Man's Land to be free of all government control and the authority of their own tribal rulers as well, thus escaping both Chinese taxes and the levies of their own chiefs. Among them were also Mingan and other tribesmen from Outer Mongolia, driven out of their own country by the crushing taxation under the new Russian- and Buriat-directed régime. As things go in that part of the world a man makes himself an outlaw by moving away from his own tribal region — a grave crime in the eyes of the rulers who tax him. I found strong differences

between the Western Torguts and their kinsmen of the Edsin Gol
—a difference enhanced by costume, for these people here had
already gone into winter dress.  They wore felt stockings reaching to the knee, soled with the hide of wild asses and bound from
ankle to knee with leather thongs.  Then they wore loose sheepskin trousers with the fleece inside, and either a short sheepskin
jacket or a full-length coat.  Some of them had a light coat of
antelope skin over all, but for the most part they were lightly
furred, being the hardiest men I ever saw, even among the Mongols.  Their long coats were often dashingly set off by a border
of red cotton, running from the collar under the arm, down the
side and around the hem.  For headgear some of them wore a
bonnet lined with lambskin, carried down to shield the neck (a
sign of Qazaq influence), but others had only a kerchief bound or
knotted into a kind of light turban, in a style often affected by
the T'ung-kan in Turkestan and the Kuei-hua camel pullers.

In their Zungarian range the Torgut live, though often with
a good deal of hostility, in constant touch with the Kirei-Qazaq,
whose Turkish dialect many of them speak freely.  I fancy that
mixtures of Qazaq blood account for the hazel eyes, reddish hair,
and light moustaches which are common among them.  The men
I saw in the Three Don't Cares were of good stature, with a
free, bold carriage.  They were cleaner than most Mongols and
a cut above those of their own tribe who live more timidly and
lawfully under Chinese surveillance.  The cleanliness is easily
understood, because the more truly nomadic a nomad is, the finer
fellow you find him.  These people are kept on the move by
scanty pasture and their own reiving habits, so that they do not
have time for sloth and filth.  It is the half-nomad, whether
Qazaq or Mongol, who splits the year between summer and winter
quarters, who lives pig-dirty and without pride.

Mr. Carruthers, who had a wide and intelligent experience of
the tribes of Western Mongolia and Hsin-chiang, described the
Ku Ch'-eng-tze Torguts as degenerate, plumping for the Kirei-
Qazaq as a better lot.[1]  It is largely a matter of feeling.  In the

---

[1] He had, however, the advantage of meeting first the Kirei-Qazaq of the
Altai, a superior division of the tribe.

first place, Englishmen are commonly prejudiced in favor of
Moslems and are repelled by what they call the "Buddhism"
of the Mongols, which they find dark and loathsome. The real
religion of the Mongols is magic, and all I can say about that is
that it is magic to them and magical to me. Also it is fatal to
approach the Mongols from the Russian side, as is shown by Mr.
Carruthers's own innocent assumption in 1911 that Russian influence in Mongolia would bring enlightenment and salvation.[1]
In point of fact the Siberian Russian who deals with the Mongols
is a hopeless barbarian who begins by looking down on the Mongols because he believes that at last he has found people more
barbarous than himself. The only way to go among the Mongols
is as an equal, and the only sound approach to the country is
from the Chinese side. A Westerner going through Siberia or
even Turkestan to Mongolia feels that he is passing from alien
to still more alien people; but the average Westerner entering
Mongolia from China feels that he has emerged from a totally
incomprehensible race among a race with whom good-fellowship
is understood in equal terms. Finally, it should be remembered
that any Moslem people are found more superficially sympathetic
and understandable by the stranger than are the Mongols or the
Chinese, who are overwhelmingly different from us in the ele-
ments of their civilizations. Beyond the outward courtesies
which are shown to a stranger by any nomad, it is impossible to
get on terms with the Mongol unless you deal with him in his
own language, or through a first-rate interpreter. But when you
have got on terms with him, you can trust him behind your back,
which is more than you can do with the fair-spoken Qazaq.
As for the Qazaq tribes, it is my opinion that, after all the milling and swirling and campaigning and countermarching in
the centuries of the great migrations, God let the whole stew
simmer for a while, and when the scum came up he called it
Qazaq.

[1] In criticizing a common type of Russian (Red or White) to be found in
Mongolia and Chinese Turkestan, I do not wish to imply utter condemnation of
the Soviet influence in Outer Mongolia. As far as that goes, in the first place I
do not know enough to judge, and in the second place, if I were to judge, as an
outsider, I should be inclined to say that a very strong case can be made out for
the Soviet position.

In No Man's Land your law is in your own right hand. Elsewhere in Mongolia a man does not ride armed as a matter of course unless he is hunting. Here no man who has arms would think of riding without them, and they even come armed when they call on the caravans. The men treated these masterless Mongols with caution and respect. They said that the very men who came to our tents as visitors might call on us again as thieves. Not, be it understood, while we were within a short range of their *yurts* and the gracious law of hospitality. Like the Qazaqs, who sometimes from the slopes of the main Altai and the Baitik Bogdo push their raids even as far as this, they never go harrying within two or three marches of home. Thus, if they do make a successful raid, they can lie up for a while in the hills, so that it is useless to return to their homes to try to prove the robbery on them.

Qazaq and Torgut raid alike. Sometimes they dash up from the rear on a caravan marching at night, stampeding the camels and cutting out a few in the confusion. Anywhere in Mongolia it is a discourtesy to ride near to a caravan at night. In No Man's Land it can only be done at the risk of a bullet. Then a favorite exploit of young men who want to prove their daring and skill is to rob in pairs, by stealth. In the small dark hours of the morning they creep up to a caravan camp, where the herd lies in orderly rows in front of the tent. Attaching a long cord to the nose peg of one of the camels, the thief crawls away again. Then he twitches the cord, making the camel get up, and draws it slowly away as if it were straying. In the meantime his companion lies in wait at the other side, ready to make a diversion if there should be an alarm. If the watchmen are drowsy the thieves may even return to carry away a half-load of goods. In this kind of thieving the approach must be made from the front, where the watchmen are, because the blind side of the tent is guarded by the dogs.

Reiving and thieving of this order, though it keeps the caravan men watchful and nervous, is a very different matter from the wholesale capture of men, camels, and loads by large bodies of outlaws, as the thing is done near Kuei-hua and Pao-t'ou.

We heard later of a much more serious raid that had been carried out within striking distance of us. This was the waylaying of the caravan of Ts'ung I Ho, one of the very oldest and most celebrated firms (they have since gone into bankruptcy), in the Two Dry Stages. They must have been at the time exactly parallel to our position in the Three Dry Stages, as it was only by an accident that I had not accompanied them.

The camels were at pasture one morning, a mile or more from camp, herded as usual by two men, when they were cut off by eight armed Mongols. The captured herders were beaten to make them tell whether there were any arms in camp, then tied and left on the ground. While six of the raiders made good their start in driving off the whole herd, two kept watch over the Chinese from a distance, closing in and circling within hearing of the tent all night. The next morning, seeing that they were gone, the mounted men of the caravan, whose ponies are always staked near the tent while the camel herd is grazing, rode cautiously out. After a few miles they found about sixty of the camels, but more than fifty — all that were fit to be taken in forced marches to Outer Mongolia — had been driven on. The caravan was now unable even to carry on all its loads. Abandoning what they could not take, they moved on to Kung-p'o Ch'üan, from which a few of the better camels were taken back to recover the loads; but when they reached the place they found that the raiders had been beforehand with them and taken their choice.

Among the raiders were several well-known "bad men" of Yunbeize. A week or two later they impudently camped in No Man's Land, to barter stolen brick tea for trade goods with caravans which, following on, knew nothing of the robbery until they were told by the Torguts. The affair made a great stir among the men who carry on "the business of the Gobi," for its audacious success meant that they would stand in future in danger of raids from Outer Mongolia as well as from the Torgut and Qazaq camel lifters.

At one good march from Salt Pool Wells we reached Ming Shui, the first place "on the map," with the exception of Ladighin's line of march, since we had left the Edsin Gol seventeen days before. Ming Shui, by my reckoning, is the place where Younghusband in 1887 cut across what is now the Winding Road. From Kuei-hua he had followed the Small Road, carrying on past its coincidence with the Great Road. Then, striking off from the wells and springs fed by drainage from the Altai which define the course of the Great Road, he crossed over by Ming Shui, rounding the eastern end of the Qarliq Tagh, and reached Hami. This is a little-used variant from the established roads, but for the study of trade routes it is of the first importance, because Hami is the most easterly point on the arterial cart roads of Chinese Turkestan. Under the special conditions of the caravan trade, camel traffic usually overshoots Hami, going on all the way to Ku Ch'eng-tze. This is partly because the pastures near Ku Ch'eng-tze are more adequate to caravan needs, but still more because, transport being cheaper by camel than by cart, it is to the advantage of merchants to have their goods carried as far as possible by caravan.

Ming Shui stands boldly on some of the maps, being a useful name to fill up the prevailing blankness in that region. It deserves its ink, though the place is no more than a buttress of hills with a well below. The name of it means Clear Water. There is neither tree nor tilth nor habitation in sight, but over beyond another hill, or it may be two, is a group of small cairns, marking a nexus of trails leading to Hami, to Hsü Chou in Kan-su by way of the Pei Shan oases (the Coal Mine Road can be reached from here), to the Winding Road whether east or west, and to Outer Mongolia. We took on water at the well, but camped at a distance beyond, because at Ming Shui was the bivouac of thirty or forty refugees, fleeing to Hami from some famine district in Kan-su.

Famine refugees are classed locally as *t'ao-huang-ti* and *t'ao-nan-ti,* both meaning "refugee." By a distinction in usage the first class are people with a little money, transport, and provision, who are getting away in good time. The second are the totally destitute, desperate, and like a horde of locusts on the march, taking food wherever they can find it. In bad famine years they are feared by the caravans, because, issuing on to the caravan roads from places like Ming Shui, they overwhelm by numbers anyone they meet, devouring and carrying away provisions. By that curious consensus of opinion which in China so largely stands in the place of law, it not only is not criminal for the starving to take food by force, but something like an inverted kind of robbery to stand them off by force. If you are a good man it is not absolutely expected of you to provide the starving with food at your own inconvenience. On the other hand, you are not expected to deny them when they come to take it. In the upshot the only way to maintain your integrity is to avoid them. Rich Chinese are uncommonly nippy at this.

The camp we passed was luckily not of the ravening kind of refugee; but there was no reason for us to risk our standing in virtue by camping beside them. When we came on them in the night I went over toward the firelight. The first thing to be seen was an old woman in the lee of a tattered windbreak of cloth, smoking opium. Thereupon the caravan master, who was with me, realizing that here were neither Mongols nor traders, hustled me away, and both caravans were rushed by in quick order. The next day we saw them at a distance, on the diverging trail to Ch'ing Ch'eng and Hami, the women and children on camels and the men walking.

To our camp that day there came riding a Mongol, who had followed us for two marches to sell the hinder half of a wild ass that he had shot in the Mongol way from a pit near the drinking place. He was hailed with joy, because one of the ponies of the House of Chou was taken with a colic. The Mongol closed his bargain at two bricks of tea for the half of an ass, on condition that he doctored the pony.

To begin with, he slit both nostrils, inside the opening, on the upper edge. Then with an awl he lifted a fragment of cartilage from each incision, which he cut off. The pony, which was in a stupor of pain, stood quite still for the operation. The man did this just to show that he had the science, for it is one of the central mysteries of Central Asian horse doctoring, in use by Mongols, Kirghiz, Qazaqs, Turkis, and Chinese. Men who can do it skillfully are in high demand.    There is no imaginable sense in it.

Then the Mongol, tightening his belt and grinning, demanded a long rope.    He fetched a clove hitch with it around the pony's belly, well back.    He took a hold on one end, giving the other to a camel puller, and both heaved away.    This was too much even for a sick pony, and the patient at once bucked, in a hearty, natural, and pleasing manner.    The doctor and the nurse held on like terriers, the crowd howled and danced, and the pony bucked grimly until, slewing both men on to the same side, he loosed the rope and freed himself.    He walked off slowly, cured. The violent exertion had made him break wind, thus easing the colic.    By the time we started he was able to walk, and long before the end of the march he was being ridden.

About due west of Ming Shui we looked up into bigger hills than any of the Ma-tsung Shan, the final bastions of the Qarliq Tagh; but, sheering away to the northwest, we marched for twenty miles to Tuei'rh Shan or Twin Mountains, an isolated double peak, where we cast the Ma-tsung Shan magnificently behind us.    Here the camel herders in the dawn reported a herd of wild asses.    It was the only sight of them that I ever had, but by the time I got out they were already so well away that even through the glasses they looked just like antelope, which they resemble in color.    Their skins make first-class clothing, with much more wear than antelope skin.    I have heard that there is a Turki proverb that wild asses are so hard to kill that even when you get the skin of one safely spread out on your sleeping platform it wiggles.    The meat is something like beef, but a sublime beef.    It is very dry, with a coarse grain and a strange aromatic sweetness.    Chinese and Mongols put it above any other game, and it undoubtedly ranks with the noblest venison.

At this camp I saw more doctoring — the famous operation, to wit, of cobbling a camel's hoof.    A tiny but deep hole had eaten into the pad after a badly healed blister, and grit working into it was setting up an irritation.    The camel was made to squat in the loading position, in which the forelegs are doubled up with most of the weight of the forepart of the body over them. A rope was then lashed round the neck and one of the forelegs, making it quite impossible for the camel to get up or even struggle with its forelegs. The hind legs are also gathered well under the camel in the lying or squatting position, but another rope was made fast just above the near hind hoof, the one to be treated, and two men, hauling mightily and swearing not a little, got the leg stretched out straight behind — a thing which looked as if it would lame the beast, but possible with a universally jointed and almost indestructible brute like a camel. A good strong man kept a steady strain on the rope, holding the leg stretched out while the *hsien-sheng* of the House of Chou, a toothless old devil with a face like a hymn-singing Roundhead and a profound command of worse language than ever came out of Flanders, did the cobbling, being well skilled in these matters. First he picked the hole clean with a sailmaker's needle, such as is used for sewing tents and felts, and then he clouted the pad with a piece of hide stripped from a dead camel a day or two before (which was not against any tabu or law of the craft), sewing it with camel-hair twine into the edges of the pad where they are most callous. When the job was done all holds were cast off and the camel stood up, a bit sore in the temper because, having had a miscarriage a few days before, she was in no mood for chiropody. By the time that the stitching of the rawhide clout had worn through, her pad was healed.

From Tuei'rh Shan there swoops away downward a long even slope, the skirts or glacis of this redan of the Ma-tsung Shan. All evening and half the night we trundled down it, and at the foot we found a marsh with springs. When I woke the next morning there soared above the ground mist, as faintly but as surely and serenely drawn as a Japanese print, the outline of the Snow Mountains, the T'ien Shan, the Heavenly Mountains, the Ten-thousand *li* East-by-South Mountains, the ramparts of Chinese Turkestan and the goal of the desert road. I do not know how often I may have pondered over pictures of those mountains, seeing my visions and dreaming my dreams, until the sudden sight of them was like a prophecy fulfilled. We had yet to cross a trough to enter their outer foothills, through and past which we should work our course on an arc, overpassing Hami and Bar Köl, which lay away from us on the southern versants; but I felt with the camel pullers something of the exultation of journey's end. The many tens of days spun away in Mongolia were nothing like the weariness to me, it is true, that they were to them. I was not so much eager to be shot of the caravan life as lusting for the new life beyond the ranges. Indeed and indeed, I could not put away without a pang all those swinging days in Mongolia, of which certain passages, like the Lao-hu Shan, the sandy countries, the Khara Gobi, the Three Don't Cares, and some other things yet lying before me, of which I was unaware, like Dead Mongol Pass which gave me defeat, and the final staggering days in the snow, must mark a man forever.

Just before we started, at the time when the frost begins to prevail against the sun of a late afternoon, a huge skein of many hundreds of geese drifted across the sky, — to my amazement, for I thought they must all have gone long ago, — and their calling fell through the air to us like a good omen and an encouragement from voyagers as stout-hearted as any. No traveler could ask a better omen than the bugling of wild geese, but I do not quite know what to make of corpses. We had met caravans carrying corpses on the march from Tuei'rh Shan, and again on this march we spoke a caravan carrying about forty dead passengers, twenty alive and one dying fast. He had been started off from Ku Ch'eng-tze in a camel cart, this last one, because he was an old man who wanted to see home and die. The cart had been battered to pieces in the pass called the Great Stones, and the old man was now lashed on a camel, where he was expected to die without much more botheration.

Corpses bound for China from Turkestan are mostly freighted by the Shan-hsi guilds, of which the Ta-t'ung, Tai Chou, and Kuei-hua are the most important. The Shan-hsi guilds never forget that they are rooted in the caravan trade. Of other guilds the most important are those of the Tientsin merchants; but Tientsin men prefer to establish permanent cemeteries, and in many a shambling brink-of-perdition town in Turkestan the most splendid buildings and noble grounds are those of the Tientsin guilds. The Shan-hsi guilds are not of much importance except at Ku Ch'eng-tze, their capital. There, in their economical way, they maintain left-till-called-for or corpse-curing cemeteries, where bodies are buried in light coffins, usually for about three years, while the flesh consumes away and they arrive at a handier weight. When they can be conveniently carried four in a camel load, the guild starts them off for their family graveyards. Camel pullers are not keen about this kind of cargo, but they do not balk outright at the custom, and corpse freight, though higher than most, is not exorbitant.

One of these caravans belonged to one of the junior Houses of Chou. The Eldest Son of our own House of Chou turned back, not with them, but with the caravan in their company. He took his pig-faced pleasure in thus insulting his purse-proud cousins. For more than a week he had been below his usual mark, because he had smoked himself out of opium. He got all he wanted from this friendly caravan, and did not rejoin us till the next day, riding up red-eyed, whacking a disgusted camel. "No sleep. Opium. Talk," he puffed as he bounced to the ground. Like the good fellow he was, he had not looked after himself alone, but had brought sheepskins for Moses and me. We had been feeling the cold, being a little under-fitted against the winter. Moses had a sheepskin jacket and breeches, but no greatcoat, while I had a Mongol-cut sheepskin greatcoat and racoon-skin-lined horsehide breeches, but no jacket. I had now a sleeveless vest of heavy western sheepskin to complete my turn-out, and Moses a huge coat in which he could sit comfortably all night on a camel. This coat was in the Turki style, opening down the front instead of under the arm and down the side, and with a wide, head-muffling collar. Such coats are called *ch'ia-p'an'rh,* a word current only in the west, being a corruption from the Turki.

It seemed that with the sight of the Snow Mountains the Kuei-hua men began to lard their talk with western jargon, a slang rich in hybrid Turki words, and began also to swear in the Ku

Ch'eng-tze terms. My ear was now so well set that within a few days I was abreast of them, to their huge joy, and there was a fresh impetus to the smacking wit flung back and forth across the fires.

The inimitable Chou, because his first care after we made camp was not sleep, but opium, was fond of snoozing on the march. He did not sit on top of a big soft load, like Moses and me, but astride a packsaddle. Sometimes he would doze as he sat, and sometimes, turning round, he would sprawl over the camel's back hump and hindquarters. This is a lordly pleasure only to be enjoyed by rich camel owners or passengers who pay handsomely to travel with the caravans. Most desert-bred men grudge themselves the luxury because the ill-found weight of a sleeping man wears out a camel after a few marches. While the Eldest Son of the House of Chou indulged himself thus, his camel would lag until it was out of sight. At last the fat young man would wake up to the terror of loneliness in the bedeviled desert — a terror that haunts the desert-going man — and come scuttling after us for company, like a cat trying to get out of the rain. Our first news that he was awake would be a mournful squalling far away behind. That would be the Eldest Son of the House of Chou keeping up his heart with song. At last he would overhaul us, beating time with a stick on his camel to make it hasten until its moaning blended with his ballad.

Jolly once more, he would start a little pleasantry with the Wa-wa, of whom he had become very fond, to divert the marching hours; but his humor was of the heavy-handed camel-pulling kind. "Mouse of the Sand Hollows," he would begin, using the name that is tacked on to Chen-fan people throughout the west; "Little Mouse of the Sand Hollows! Squeak, squeak! How old are you? Twenty? Are you married, Mouse? Have you a woman? Is your woman lots of fun? How many babies? Not married long enough? Ah, it is more fun, then! Didn't you like it with your wife, on the *k'ang*, more than suffering evil on the Gobi? And now who puts your wife on the *k'ang*, when you have run away to pull camels?" By this time the Wa-wa, skirmishing in wretched retreat through evasive and contradictory answers into unhappy silence, would begin to snivel. Then the fat Chou would ease off. He would begin to tease him about his unintelligible "mouse-talk" dialect until the Wa-wa, reviving, threw camel dung at him. Then he must slide down the neck of his camel to put the neck of the Wa-wa in chancery, and all was well.

One wind-ridden stage from the Marsh of the Vision of the Ultimate Mountains took us into broken, waterless country. It was so cold that every time I put out my hands from their long protecting furry sleeves to light a cigarette they went helplessly numb. The next day was the first of November, and evilly cold. The caravan masters would not have moved against the wind but that we were out of water. We marched only to the nearest water, on the fringe of the outer range which now barred the snow mountains from sight. The camp was called the Two Phœnix Trees, from a clump of them we passed, though the trees were out of sight from the well. These were the first trees west of the Black Gobi. The name was curious: Erh-chia Wu-t'ung, *chia* being properly not the numerative of trees but a colloquial numerative of vines. There was a half-panic after we had camped, the House of Chou finding that their tent was pitched close up against the fresh grave of a camel puller who had died while traveling with a homeward-bound caravan. His ghostly neighborhood kept them nervous all night, and but for the high wind and the misery that cowed us all they would have moved.

The next day we worked, not westward, but northward through these foothills. We overshot a camping place called the Small Stones and reached the Great Stones, named not for the place of the well but for the stage beyond. We had here climbed high enough to sight the snow range again, but it had lost the splendid unity of the distant vision from below Tuei'rh Shan. The men knew of birchwoods near this camp, but though I went out with a small party who wanted birch poles for making pack-saddles we failed to see anything from the lesser heights we climbed but scree slopes and a little tufted grass and far prospects into the mightier hills where the snow lay.

34. THE ELDEST SON
(MOUNTED) TEASES
THE WA-WA
"And now who puts your
wife on the *k'ang*, when
you have run away to
pull camels?" (p. 256)

33. MING SHUI:
DOCTORING A
CAMEL'S HOOF
"A good strong man
kept a steady strain on
the rope." (p. 253)

Then we broke camp and started and fell all unbeknownst into the pass of the Great Stones.[1] I had not understood that we were to go *down* a pass, and it took me with astonishment.

The name of the stage is from the ponderous masses of rock and sheer-run sandstone cliffs that cramp the edges of the gorge. The hills are not great, but the pass is as noble, or so I found it in the dark, as any I have ever traveled. Taking off from rounded hills at a plateau level, we plunged for half a night down a narrowing valley that twisted in every direction but due east. As we sank step under step the rims of the hills reached higher until the stumbling caravan dwindled and was lost at their bases. I looked upward to a far sky where the stars hung big as lamps. Most of all I remember a steeple rock, about three sides of which we turned, that soared blackly toward the glowing stars. At last, more suddenly even than we had tumbled into this enchantment, the march ended. The cliffs fell away all at once, and we were almost on top of an encampment, low bulky loads in the gloom and firelight half occluded by tent walls. Dogs came at us ferociously, but we passed them in a running skirmish, broke out of the hills on to an edgeless plain where the unconfined darkness flowed over us, and file by file wheeled into camp.

Morning showed us newly oriented, with the snow range on our south and a different rank of foothills below them. From the foothills the plain where we were camped pitched northward at a slow tilt toward a yellow gleaming hollow, where I was told there was a settlement of Turki, cultivating irrigated land. This, as near as I can make it, was Bai. A faint track showed a way on which carts had been in use, going south, I suppose, to Mogoi or to round the end of the Qarliq Tagh in making for Ch'ing Ch'eng and Hami. By this orientation our northward course through the foothills and our pass of the night showed that we had been engaged in turning the Emir Tagh, a quasi-independent massif off the snout of the Qarliq Tagh. We were thus once more in a known country, or at least a country sighted

---

[1] Nothing to do with the Great Stones (Ta Shih-t'ou) where the roads going from Hami and Barköl to Ku Ch'eng-tze converge.

by earlier travelers, where the running of several good surveys has determined the main geography.

Having witnessed the doctoring of a pony first and then a camel within the last few days, I was now to be in at the doctoring of a man, and for devil possession at that. We had been working up to this for some time. First there was the corpse talk that grew out of our meeting the corpse-carrying caravans. Then there was the camp where the House of Chou had all but sat itself on a new grave. That began another stir of talk. A fresh corpse in the desert is a thing to dread. Tales were told over of how whole caravans, when a man died in the tent, had simply cut and run. It is a chancy business to take a hand at a desert burial. The men are afraid that the newly evicted spirit will try to seize one of them; for what could be more lonely than a spirit hovering about a new grave in the Gobi, with the sound of the camel bells departing through the night? The more seasoned ghosts that are being sent back in decency by the guilds to join their ancestors are not so likely to make trouble, but even so they must be spoken of respectfully. Now at this camp the men herding camels on the dawn shift came running back with a report of an unburied corpse. The men did not like it. They began to talk among themselves in twos, instead of bringing their speech out noisily and in public. A bad sign. They were reassured when I proposed to go out to photograph the corpse; several came with me, and after a search we found there was nothing but a bundle of clothes. It had probably been thrown away by a traveler on foot who was caught by a storm in the last winter, trying to follow the cart track. Any storm that had made him throw away his bundle had probably ended in his death; but at least the body was nowhere about. The men felt better.

Then, while the others were making ready to start, I went back with the *hsien-sheng* of the House of Chou and the Mohammedan caravan to fill the water butts. The spring was at the place where we had passed a camp in the night, but had not been able to halt ourselves because the narrow ground was taken up by three caravans from the west. The spring is called Ts'u-mei Ch'üan, the Spring of the Wild Rose, and it is one of those watering places by the road that the caravan men hold in especial affection; not only on account of the sweet water, but because the spring, instead of being in the bed of a dry watercourse, is well up on a hillside; an unnatural thing, and probably holy. By it there are two of the little shrines, with black characters on red paper in them wishing a prosperous journey to men and beasts, such as are found only at one or two favorite waters or at the beginning and end of such awe-regarded marches as those of the Khara Gobi. The spring issues clean and sweet from a crevice in the rock; it is only a small flow, but pools have been dug below it in terraces for the camels to drink. A few yards away there is an even tinier spring. Beside it there is a single wild rose bush, which even in that bleak month, with neither flower nor leaf, nor any company but a little desert scrub, sprang with a light forlorn grace in its loneliness. I am sure that it had been carried from one of the rose-filled gorges farther to the west and planted there by a camel puller.

Truly sweet water is thrice-rare on the Winding Road, but you get it at the Spring of the Wild Rose. The men spoke of it with nothing less than ardor. In spite of their coarse diet, smoke-tainted cooking, and crude tobacco, they retained the Chinese palate, the palate of the tea drinker, which discriminates minutely the grades of drinking water. I never could learn to pronounce like them between, say, fairly good water and passable water; the strength of the brick tea smudged out for me every difference except that between the bad and the vile. It is not as if the camel pullers were alone among lowly Chinese. They all have this delicacy. The endless argument of the men at their tea drinking used to remind me of a turn of traveler's luck at Pao-ting Fu, the capital of the metropolitan province of Chih-li, a well-watered and heavily farmed region. I had wanted to walk on the city wall, but it was forbidden, because the general then in occupation had notions. Strolling past a guardhouse near one of the gates, to have a look at the ramps leading up to the wall, I heard a soldier cast a remark at the strange foreigner. I countered at once with a remark of my own, which brought a laugh and an invitation to sit down and have a cup of tea.

Now, though I am not fit to judge between one well and the next, yet so far as talking goes I can bandy terms of merits and shortcomings as well as the next man, if given a lead. So I gargled on my tongue and sucked in my breath and wagged my head and said in sorrow that the water in Pao-ting Fu was not so good as some. Thereupon four or five soldiers of the worst sweepings of Asia began to talk like lords and princes of their likes and dislikes in the water with which they had made tea in the manner of life of a Chinese mercenary, running away or following after, from Manchuria to Ssu-ch'üan, with all the provinces between. I kept the talk going, and they bit into the subject with gusto. When they had all become well pleased with themselves I suggested, as one who would put up a little entertainment for good fellows, that they come up on the wall with me and let me show them how my camera worked. And they made it so.

When we got back from the Spring of the Wild Rose the caravans had already moved off; but by the trail, with a morose camel standing over him, lay a groaning camel puller. I did not know what to make of him at first, for his clothes were covered with blood; but when at last I got the man to talk I found that this was only from thumb pricking.[1] The man was in a mortal agony, which gave me at first ghastly thoughts of appendicitis,

---

[1] Thumb pricking is the major part of all the doctoring that is practised forth from Kuei-hua. The arm is first massaged all the way down from the shoulder, to force as much blood as possible first into the hand and then into the thumb. When well done the ball of the thumb can be made to swell distinctly. The thumb is then pricked with a needle, not on the ball, but at the base of the nail. Sometimes a surprising flow of blood results. This treatment is given to relieve any pain between the toes and the crown of the head, or any general indisposition. Experts claim to tell the state of the patient by the color of the blood. If he is in a bad way the same treatment is given to the other thumb.

Evidently we have here an association with the more recondite Chinese needle doctoring, which at its best (but it is very seldom found at its best) is based on an empirical knowledge of the nerve system. In theory a pain at any given place can be relieved by a needle prick at another point, known to those who are versed in the art, which causes a neutralizing sensory reaction between related nerve centres. In theory, again, relief of the symptomatic pain is accepted as removal of the cause. Needle-doctoring charts can be bought for a small sum at fairs.

In the grosser thumb-pricking cure-all we have either a degeneration of the complicated practice, or an association with some primitive Mongol idea, or a relapse towards a primitive Chinese idea, or a mixture of all of these. I am quite sure that the makeshift surgical idea is tainted with a thought, or perhaps only a feeling, that an evil spirit in the man's blood is coaxed down the arm and into the thumb and then squeezed out through the puncture.

35. THE SPRING OF THE WILD ROSE
"Truly sweet water is thrice-rare on the Winding Road." (p. 260)

lying curled up as tightly as if in the last spasms of cholera, and far gone in the delirium of rank terror. "*Ai-ya*, my mother!" he wailed; "*ai-ya*, my old mother, I shall not see you again, I shall die here! *Ai-ya-ya*, Old Man God, can this yet be suffered? *Ai-i-i-ya-ya-ya*, my mother, this is waiting for death!"

In the upshot I found out that this was what had happened. The poor devil had been taken with a vast bellyache just after the loading was finished. The most skillful man at hand was called over to prick his thumbs for him, and they would doubtless have put him on a camel and carried him along all in order had not the starting files run across an empty coffin lying only a couple of hundred yards beyond our camp. That did it. The coffin had not been seen before because the camels had been pastured in the other direction. When it was found it made a culmination for all the horror talk that had been going on and had only been partially stilled after the eerie finding of the castaway clothes that morning. When the men saw the coffin they all jumped at the same thought: the coffin had been shaken and bumped to bits in the passage from Ku Ch'eng-tze, and probably the shriveled corpse had been stuffed in with another in a stouter coffin. The ghost, still hovering about its body on the journey, but disgruntled by this treatment, had cast loose and was now trying to effect a lodgment in more roomy quarters in a live camel puller. That was enough. Off they all went, as hard as they could peg. They left a camel with the afflicted man. If he could fight it out with the ghost, so much the better. The others would not stop until they were well beyond ghost-reach, and then they might send back to see what had happened. What would have happened, had I not taken it into my head to see the Spring of the Wild Rose by daylight, would have been the death of the camel puller from pain, his own fear, and the hypnotic fear left behind by his stampeding fellows.

After my first scare at seeing a man with blood spots all over his clothes rolling about under the nose of an uninterested camel I began to suspect that there was nothing wrong but a severe colic. When I got him steadied up enough to answer questions, he admitted that, after the very common habit of Two-fisted

He-men living in the Great Open Spaces, he had been constipated for a couple of days. Then, indulging in one of the simple pleasures of his way of life, he had eaten a large meal, as hot as he could take it, at an amazing speed; this induced a profuse sweat, whereupon, throwing open his sheepskin coat, he had caught a chill on his distended belly. Nothing showed until after the loading of the camels, which brought on another sweat, another chill, and turned the trick.

I took the *hsien-sheng* of the House of Chou (who, not being party yet to the ghost fright, was feeling humane and sympathetic) off his pony, and, mounting the sick man's camel, he sped it howling dismally after the caravans, to urge them to camp, saying that I would get out Foreign Medicine — words of power. Then I unfolded the unwilling camel puller, laying him out as flat as I could, and massaged him strongly from the navel downward, where the grime of months was channeled by the sweat of honest eating. When he felt better I hoisted him on the pony and led him until at the next paroxysm he wept loudly that he would fall off, invoking again his Old Mother and Old Man God. Then I did some more stomach kneading. Then the *hsien-sheng* came back with word that the caravans did not like to stop; so I left him with the sick man (neither of them felt happy about that) and galloped after the caravans on the pony. The assembled caravan masters wanted to know whether the man would die. They did not seem to think it right to stop for a man who would die anyway, especially if he were going to release a double ghost in their midst. I told them that he would surely live, there being nothing but a swelling of wind in his bowels. It was agreed then to halt, and about two hours later the sick man staggered into camp on his own feet, saying he felt better when he could walk all doubled up. I dosed him with Dover's powder and delivered *cursim* an Abracadabra lecture on bellyaches, which soothed his companions until they ceased to mutter about ghosts. I believe I even tabulated the symptoms of true ghost possession, to convince them that this was something different.

The stricken man was rather a pal of mine, for he was a

buffoon by nature, and I admit without shame that I am ready
to drop any business to listen to a fellow who can recite all the
patter of all the peddlers, pimps, quacks, ballad-mongers, tale
reciters, and jesting vagabonds who haunt the forecourts of
temples on feast days and fair days.    My friend, I remember,
had a gorgeous nickname which implied that he was fortunate
in the achievement of his love affairs, but not so lucky in the
effect they had on his health.    Like most Chinese of his standing, he was capable of bearing great pain stoically, as with his
chronic disease, but broke down when attacked by a sudden,
awful pain that he did not understand.    As for the mother on
whom he called so pitifully, he had probably not so much as
thought of her since leaving Kuei-hua.    From that time forward
I had only to groan in the tent of the House of Chou " *Ai-ya-ya!*
My old mother, how can this be borne!" to put everyone in
good humor.    After all, the proverb supports me : —

*Erh hsing ch'ien li, mu tan yu;*
*Mu hsing ch'ien li, erh pu ts'ou.*

When the son journeys a thousand *li* the mother is ill at ease;
When the mother journeys a thousand *li* the son does not (turn his
head to) look.

All of which is a part of "the Business of the Gobi."

# XVII

## DEAD MONGOL PASS

WE were still settling into camp after our little excitement when we heard a camel bell, and after a while two men came up to us with about twenty camels. One of them was a junior partner in the ownership of a caravanserai in Ku Ch'eng-tze, well known to the Eldest Son of the House of Chou, who always put up there. He was on his way to meet his own caravan, with relief camels and spare provisions. He and his men were more than glad to fall in with us, for they had been followed all during their march by three or four Mongols, and, not daring to halt, had kept on until they struck our camp. This set up a new nervousness among our tents, and before we turned in and the night watch was set the Chou caravan master fired his indescribably rust-fouled carbine as a warning at large. The carbine had been hidden in the straw stuffing of a camel saddle while we were near Kuei-hua, where neither the Chinese authorities nor the Mongols like to see armed caravans, fearing that the arms may be sold to or taken by the bandits of the Ta Ch'ing Shan, but had been taken out after crossing the Black Gobi, to conduct us like a talisman through No Man's Land. I argued that if we were going to make a demonstration like this it would be better to give the carbine to one of the men on watch, to fire about midnight, the time when any bandits or thieves would be likely to start edging in on us, in order to warn them that we were armed and wakeful. Not so. The answer was that the caravan weapon is always discharged by the caravan master, and, as the caravan master has the privilege of sleeping all night, it would be inconvenient to shoot after his bedtime. After that everyone slept peacefully until the watchmen saw by the stars that the dawn was about to show, when they woke the Head of the Pot, who made tea and roused out the rest of the men, and when they had eaten, stirring parched oaten flour or millet into their tea, the camels were sent out to graze, all before the east was fully light.    The Mongols had vanished.

That afternoon we set out on one of the longest marches of the whole journey, because for the sake of the sick man we had camped short, without water, so that we had a stage and a half to make.    I walked until dark, past the slowly shifting contours of the Mongolian landscape.    We were on the çamber of a curved "Gobi" of black gravel, sprinkled with gray and red, scattered over dun clay, descending from the foothills.    It was rifted with shallow dry flood channels, down which I suppose the water races at the spring melting of the snows, which for the rest do not lie deep outside of the mountains.    There was a scanty tamarisk growth, and we saw a few antelope.    On the right, to our north, were the unchanging Mongolian ranges, the Aji Bogdo — blue, red, gray, and purple, skirted with long slopes of piedmont gravel and mercilessly barren, at least in their visible lower reaches; but at the foot of our slope was the new yellow gleam of reed beds about invisible cultivated fields, while to our left stood up living hills, the hills topped with snow which the caravans hail so eagerly.

It was after midnight when, having turned from the Gobi through little utterly barren and earthless hills of shattered rock, we heard all of a sudden the startling uproar of water running fast over stones.    It was so unfamiliar that I did not recognize it until my camel was snorting and shying at the edge of the stream.    I stumbled about that night as puzzled and haunted by the feeling of the not unknown but totally impossible as one sometimes is in dreams; for not only did we ford a deep, strong brook, but we camped on the stubble of harvested fields.

If at camping I had descended from something real, practical, and belonging to everyday life, such as a camel, into a dream of fantastic fields, tilled and harvested, I woke in the Earthly Paradise.    It was all hedged about with black and red stone hills and looked upstream into the larch and spruce forests and high snows of the Heavenly Mountains, as was only proper; but because the brook was set with long rows of slender poplars the caravan men called it White Poplar River. The valley is occupied by the People Who Bind Their Heads, the Turbaned People or *Ch'an-t'ou*, whose Chinese name has been conveniently corrupted into Chanto by many travelers' tales. They are the Turki, friendly and bearded and dressed in many colors (but in summer in white), and hereabouts they are all the subjects, almost the serfs, of the Khan of Hami or Qomul, on the southern side of the Qarliq Tagh, the easternmost oasis of Chinese Turkestan and the Camul of Marco Polo. The oasis has a true Turkestan character, but being the place where in all modern centuries the traffic coming from China proper by the Imperial Highway has entered the west, it shows the Chinese influence in many ways. The mountain subjects of the Khan, who rules the last of the once independent Turkestan principalities as a Native State under Chinese authority, are called Taghliq or "mountainy folk"; and it may be that they inherit some of the blood of earlier races. In these valleys they cultivate little patches of rice, on fields laboriously cleared of stones and flooded by channels from the rivers; they also herd a great number of sheep and ponies, mostly belonging to the Khan, in the higher valleys, where some of them lead a half-nomadic life in Mongol *yurts*.

The next day we moved downstream a little, with the camels breaking file and rioting through the rice stubble and the men dodging off to do a little trading at homesteads in buttons and braid and scented soap. Then, turning a spur, we started up another valley, until we reached a large village called Tuhulu. This is the Chinese T'u-hu-lu,[1] corrupted from Tur-khara. The name is found more than once in Zungaria and Chinese Turkestan, and according to Huntington[2] (who is not, however, concerned with this same Tuhulu) is from the name of an ancient

---

[1] A *t'u-hu-lu* in Chinese is "a bald gourd," the slang name for a man "as bald as an egg." Months later Moses was chatting with the Most Important Servant of the Most Important Foreigner in Urumchi, who asked what he had seen in his travels that was remarkable. "Tuhulu," said Moses with enthusiasm, thus causing an unfortunate situation in high servants' quarters, for the Most Important Servant was as bald as an egg, and the most assuaging diplomacy was needed to comfort him and quell the joy of his subordinates.

[2] *The Pulse of Asia.*

tribe. The village is evidently the Uturuk of Carruthers's map.[1]

This valley is well peopled, and in the hills about it are many hundred ponies belonging to the Prince of Hami. They are almost undistinguishable from the famous ponies of the contiguous Bar Köl range, and, though smaller than the average Mongol pony, are held in high repute for their gallant temper and endurance in travel, as well as because many of them are natural amblers.

In the Tuhulu valley I saw for the first time the true Mohammedan domes of mud-built mosques, as different as can be from the mosques of the Chinese Mohammedans, which have been accommodated almost exactly to Chinese temple architecture. On the gates or walls of the mosques were heads of wild sheep which the Turki peoples, from the Pamirs to Turfan and Hami, set up on their "high places" in lingering memory of some pre-Mohammedan Shamanistic practice.

The stubble everywhere swarmed with brown partridge and chukor partridge, enormously fat and incredibly tame. For several days I did not taste mutton. My shotgun was a thing of astonishment to the people of the valley, but their way of riding down chukor was quite as astonishing to me. Chukor are always more lively on the leg than on the wing, and at this season they were so fat that the onset of a bold Taghliq on a spirited pony made them look almost as helpless as so many dowagers. The riders begin in two parties. One puts up the birds, which fly toward the others, who ride them back at once, and then, each for himself, the riders keep hard after the broken coveys. After two or three flights like this the chukor get so tired that they can no longer fly; a few more minutes and they falter in their running; the men come up with them and, leaning from the saddles, strike at them with whips or throw stones which they carry in the breasts of their gowns. The riding was of the finest that I have ever seen, and the courage, dash, and endurance of the ponies was magnificent. They went up slopes of scree at a canter and down at a gallop, swerving round boulders, scrambling along narrow ridges, and turning just short of forty-foot

[1] *Unknown Mongolia.*

drops without an error. They were given a loose rein and a free head, and I never saw a mistake or a fall. The hardest riding comes in heading the birds away from the steepest rocks, where they can hide in gullies. I saw birds ridden to a complete stand-still, so that a man could dismount and pick them up in his hand, where they cowered in crannies with their heads hidden.

In following up the watered valley of Tuhulu we were going south, but at a few miles we bore off to the west again, up a huge sweeping valley, which offered an entry, as it were, between the Qarliq Tagh and the Metshin Ola, leading up to a pass that would take us sidling over the depression between the two con-verging ranges. The change from the warm, boxed-in, sun-filled lower valley was appalling. On the second day we could not break camp, for the wind came down the valley like the grand-father of all corridor drafts. Here we had camping close to us, for fear of Qazaqs in the mountains, two odd wanderers who had been following us at half-mile distances all the way from the Great Stones. Though they could only speak about a word and a half of either Chinese or Mongol I made them out to be Tanguts from somewhere away beyond Hsi-ning. They must have been from a remote district, or they would have been able to make shift with either Chinese or Mongol. One was an old lama who would have made a fine figure of a Benedictine abbot — a hale old man with those unmistakable ecclesiastical features, well boned but still more well fleshed, which belong more to the pontifical calling than to any one church, and are the same the world over. The other was his acolyte, a lad of twenty-odd, with the whitest teeth and the brightest black eyes that any hedge priest could want for a stock in trade. They had two fine camels, which had traveled hard and far but were still as fit as their masters; but though they were showily mounted they had a tent only just big enough for the two of them to squat in. It was of a single flimsy thickness of white cotton, walled about inside with the paraphernalia of their rites and exercises. The floor was spread with beautiful old carpet mats of several Central Asian makes, where they crouched over a handful of assorted dung, coaxing a little kettle to boil.

They had been on a praying tour through Outer Mongolia —
a venture in which Tangut lamas do very nicely for themselves,
not handicapped at all by difficulties of language, as they have
a wondrous reputation for magical powers, the reputation that
has hovered since time began about the fastnesses of Tibet.  They
should have returned to their own country by Ming Shui, entering Kan-su at Hsü Chou and going on through to Hsi-ning, but
had been scared out of their way by rumors of the defeated army
of Feng Yü-hsiang.  Therefore they were trying to make Hami
by the roundabout way of Barköl, hoping thus either to be set on
the eighteen Gobi stages of the cart road to Ngan-hsi or to be
directed by the main southern Turkestan road to Qara Shahr.
So far as I could understand their chatter and the way they drew
with bits of dung on the floor of their tent, they were sure of
finding Mongols who would send them across the Taklamakan
desert from Qara Shahr to Lop Nor, whence they would find a
way into Tibet through the K'un Lun.  If they really had that
idea, and I am fairly sure that I did not altogether misconstrue
them, it proves the surviving tradition of a road anciently well
known; for there is a road still known at the Lop Nor end of
Turkestan as the Kalmuk Road.[1]

During the night the wind eased down, and by morning the
weather was cold but calm, with clouds along the edges of the
snowy Qarliq Tagh, which marched dead straight on our left
hand.  Below the line of perennial snow we could see heavy
black forests.  We left in the early afternoon, and in two and a
half hours, passing the mud domes and cubes of a Taghliq burial
ground, were in sight of a large lake.  It appeared to be barred
across the middle by a spit of marsh.  The caravan men called
the two ends of it simply the East and the West Salt Pool; but it
is the Tur Köl or Tur Kul of Mr. Carruthers.[2]  The name shows

---

[1] *The Pulse of Asia*, by Ellsworth Huntington.

[2] In describing it he says: "An analysis of this water from the lagoons at the
eastern end of Tur Kul showed that it contained 34 per cent of salt, and in comparison I may mention that the water of the Dead Sea — the 'most saline of all
the world's important lakes' — contains only 25 per cent.  A thermometer boiled
in this water made the altitude of the lake at sea level! and it was not until we
found fresh water some miles to the east — where it first appeared above ground —
that we obtained a correct boiling-point reading for altitude."  He marks the
altitude at 6301 feet. — *Unknown Mongolia.*

an interesting affinity with Tur-khara or Tuhulu. For five and a half hours after sighting the water we went painfully on over snow; it was only two or three inches deep, but frozen so hard that the camels toppled and sprawled all over it. The evening was smoky with cloud and frosty mist, and the night, when we camped after a march of more than nine hours, brilliant and windless, but cold with the thin cold of high places. I experienced for the first time the celebrated phenomenon of having my breath frozen on my beard.

We were now placed at the foot of a pass leading over to Bar Köl. The caravan men call it Ssu Ta-tzu Liang, Dead Mongol Pass; because, by one account, of some particular Mongol who was frozen there, but, as others say, "because it is even cold enough to freeze Mongols," which is a camel puller's notion of superlative cold. The pass is considered closed to heavy caravan traffic from about the middle of October, though local Chantos, Qazaqs, and Mongols use it all winter, being able to wait for opportunity, since travelers in small parties can often worry through when it would be impossible to handle a large number of animals. This year, though the snow had begun early and fallen heavily, the pass was not yet closed, for we had questioned every caravan we met and they all had a good passage to report. Several other caravans were camped near the lake when we got there, some of them having waited three days for good weather. Even when the rest of the sky is clear there are usually clouds banked near Dead Mongol Pass; but unless it is wholly clear of cloud the caravans at this time of year will not attempt it. So far as I could see, the way in which the open upland valleys converge on the pass makes funnels at both ends of it, so that it is a trap for the deadly winds of the Central Asian highlands, though in actual height it is insignificant, being only about seven thousand feet.

On the day after our arrival we got off to what looked like a lucky start. The night before we had met fifteen unladen camels belonging to a trader, who had just come over, reporting that there was two and a half feet of snow in the pass, but well trodden and firm going. We had no wind at all and not the threat of a

36. DEAD MONGOL PASS
"It is even cold enough to freeze Mongols." (p. 271)

cloud. The wide valley leading up to the narrow gap was swept almost clean of snow by the wind, but when, just at sunset, we entered the mouth of the pass we found it a long, level floor of snow, dropping at the far end, a couple of miles away, to further vistas of snow. On our left hand — that is, on the slopes with a north aspect — were well-forested slopes of larch or spruce, high above us; but it is a peculiarity of the mountains here, confirmed by Carruthers, that none of the slopes with a south aspect are forested. On our right were black bare hillsides, impossible for laden camels to negotiate.

I began to feel uneasy. After all the talk I had heard among the caravans of the terrors of this pass it looked to me as though we might run a risk of being trapped in that long trench of snow, with no clear ground for camping and no fuel in reach — for there was heavy snow between us and the forest. It seemed amazing that even the caravan masters who had waited weather-bound for several days had not ridden up to make sure of the road before venturing their camels in it, and still more amazing that instead of rushing the pass in the first hours after dawn, which are always the most windless, they should attempt it at night, in the leisurely manner of open Gobi marches, in the treacherous falsely clear light of stars shining on unbroken snow.

I was well to the fore when we reached the snow. There was a little difficulty getting on to it. The crust was not everywhere firm, one could see that the wind had flawed over the regular track, and there were many places where a man on foot sank deep. I thought it would be better to camp on the clear ground just our side of the snow and wait for morning; but counsel of prudence was the last thing to utter in the face of established caravan masters, and after a short debate they decided to have a thrust at it. Had not three men with fifteen camels "folded over it," as they said, the day before? They went ahead, with the blind fortitude of men who are used to rely on luck and their power of endurance of suffering.

With all the caravans together there was a count of more than a thousand camels. The House of Chou was in the lead, with my eight camels at their tail. The file stretched behind us for at least two miles. Everyone had relied on the report that the pass was clear. Evidently there had been snow in it for a long time, but, being crossed almost day by day, a clear track had been packed hard. Then the wind that had held us to camp two days before had blown down snow from the hillsides, smothering Dead Mongol Pass from end to end. After a short progress there was no sign of the caravan that had crossed the day before. How they got over I am not sure, but I think that being light-loaded, and with a man to every five camels instead of one to eighteen, they had been able to keep high, skirting the rocks. Moreover, they had used the daylight and their eyes.

For about two hours we edged gingerly into the snow, until nearly all the hundreds of camels behind us were engaged. Then we came to a halt, and word of deep snowdrifts was passed back from the head of the line. Mounted men could not get more than a few feet ahead, and hardy adventurers on foot went in over the waist. At first there was an attempt at order. More mounted men came up and they rode across and across our front seeking for the trail, while men on foot wallowed in every direction, but without finding anything. Then the masters of the rearmost caravans tried to press forward, cursing us in the lead for having gone wrong; their ponies floundered in the soft snow at the side of what was left of the packed trail, and some of the camels, put out by the flurry, began sidling and fell into the soft snow, and in a few minutes there was bad confusion. We were hopelessly trapped, with deep snow on either hand, no place to camp and no room for turning. A wind came up ghoulishly out of the night, driving snow before it that rasped us like sand, and we had to give up.

The men, for a while, were on the edge of panic. Had the wind risen to a real gale, they would have dropped all and run. As it was, they openly cursed their caravan masters, and several times they nearly broke. It was only the work of controlling the camels that kept them warm enough and busy enough to stand by. Turning a thousand camels by files of eighteen in a strait gulf where those which get off the trail fall belly deep in soft snow is not a light matter. While we waited for those behind us to get clear we stood and suffered. The camels got a horrid doing. They stamped and fretted all night, shivering violently and shaking their loads. Mine would shake now and then so that he nearly threw me. They would try to dodge behind one another and start milling in circles, as all animals will in bad weather, the strongest pushing to the centre for warmth; and in the scramble they foundered one after another in the snow. The worst thing in the whole eerie night was the noise of the camels grinding their teeth; for camels, when they are cruelly cold, do not chatter their teeth but grind them, with a shrieking that goes through one's ears like a nail.

I was lucky, for I was never very cold. I had entered the pass walking as usual with bare feet in a pair of old brown shoes, which I changed for felt boots when I was ready to get on my camel. Some of the men felt it badly. The Wa-wa had to be sent back, his eyebrows frozen, to take shelter with the first caravan that should camp. Several others had a touch of frostbite in fingers or toes. Part of the time I kept warm by ploughing up and down the line to see what progress was being made; at other times I sat on my camel, where I could get the best view in the dim light; squatting in the snow being of no use, in spite of the comparative shelter from wind, because of the plunging camels, which kept routing one out.

My camels, with those of the House of Chou, suffered longest and most. Foot by foot we struggled back. The caravan just in front of us, which had been just behind, cast three loads in the snow in order to get the camels clear. Then two of their men, worn out in temper by the long strain, began a fight with teeth and nails that scattered blood and hair all over the snow. Others rushed at them to whack their heads because the struggle was frightening the weary camels, and we nearly had a free-for-all because a worn-out fellow had demanded help instead of asking for it. At one time camels were coming down right and left, but with digging and pushing and hauling and furious beating they were nearly all got out, though a number of loads had to be left in the snow overnight. One of my camels fell into a deep wallow, but by great good luck it was near a firm patch, and after slipping the load we hoisted out the camel and reloaded it. In the weary end, ten unimaginable hours after we entered the mouth of the pass, we drew clear and camped, or rather flopped, as the men said, on the first patch of bare ground. The final score to Dead Mongol Pass was a lot of scattered loads and two camels of the House of Chou.

It was then about half-past three. By six we were onloading again, to move down the valley to safer quarters. The camels were a battered lot. One of mine had to be lifted to its feet. Although tired to the bone, I turned back into the pass with the *hsien-sheng* of the House of Chou, who went to look at the two camels left the night before. At the low crest leading into the flat part of the pass I realized better than by the weaker light of evening the incredible folly of the caravan masters in venturing without reconnaissance, and not even by daylight, into a pass of evil reputation. They may well say that there are no men now who compare with the caravan masters of the last generation. From the mouth of the pass onward there was nothing but snow, reaching away down the almost level valley to what seemed a drop to a plain, and away below to the horizon.

One of the camels we could see at once was a total loss, but over the other we worked for more than an hour. The *hsien-sheng* was as pleased as a small boy at my idea of spreading under its knees and hindquarters the felts (with which it had been tented over in the night to keep out the worst of the cold) to give it a less slippery purchase when rising. When we had managed this with some sweating and shoving, I tugged at its nose cord with one hand, to rouse its interest, while lifting all I could at its shoulder, and the *hsien-sheng* lifted and twisted valiantly at its tail. The camel made a game struggle and got to its feet. We led it carefully for a quarter of a mile, but then it sprawled out on the frozen snow. After that it flatly gave up hope and refused to make another effort (camels are like that), in spite of all torture and the passionate addresses of the old *hsien-sheng*. "—— him with a ——," he said at last. " Will you not nourish an old age, you? Defile his ancestors, the grandson! Then let him feed the wolves, the ——!" and so took fare-

well of him with that word defined by the unerring Johnson
as "a term of endearment among sailors." To call a man a
grandson, it may be said, can be done by way of insult; for
ancestors are reverenced with the k'o-t'ou; therefore if you are
my grandson, I am your ancestor and you must abase yourself
with your head to the ground. By a pleasant analogy this oath
may be extended to camels.

On the way down we stopped at the first tent we reached, to
eat and drink. In the tent was a superb old Qazaq, who had come
in with a fox skin that he wanted to barter. He carried the
golden eagle that had caught the fox — a noble creature standing
about two and a half feet high, grave and docile in a plumed
hood. There was a Qazaq encampment in a branch of the valley
— thrusters, trying to establish themselves out of their own
country. The Qazaqs are not allowed on the south side of the
Bar Köl range, nor can they encroach on such of the territory
of the Khan of Qomul as is well defined; but the Metshin Ola,
bulging out at the side of the Bar Köl and Qarliq Tagh ranges
and easily approached from the outer desert, is a meeting ground
of Chinese herd owners from the Bar Köl side, Turki mountain
shepherds, and Qazaq nomads. While the Qazaqs must keep in
good standing with the Chinese and Turkis who have recognized
pasturing interests in these mountains, they are always ready for
pickings from the caravans who have not the support of any
locally vested authority, and steal at every chance.

That afternoon the wind began again, much worse than it
had been in the night, and held on for two more days and nights,
in which we kept close to our tents, unable to move and utterly
miserable with the cold. There was no fuel but the roots of a few
poor shrubs, reeds from the edge of the lake, camel dung from
old encampments, and cow dung left over from the summer
pasturing; but they all burned badly because of the dampness
frozen into the soil. Dung fuel is all very well until you cannot
shelter from a winter wind. After that only tamarisk will keep
the cold at bay.

In spite of the weather the Qazaqs came down to sell sheep
— the huge, fat-tailed Qazaq sheep which I saw for the first

time — and we had one good feed on blood sausages. This is a winter dish made from fresh casings from which the interior lining of fat has not been removed. They are stuffed with a pudding made from roasted flour and the blood of the sheep. We also made *yu-ch'a* or "fat tea," for which the men had been clamoring for days. According to rule there are two things which give the men a right to call for *yu-ch'a*. The first is when the tent is basted with a felt lining at the approach of cold weather; but as the House of Chou had done this during the easy marches in the warmth of Kuai-tze Hu when there was time to spare, the men had been fobbed off, while, as for me, I did not have enough felts to line my tent at all. The second and undeniable occasion is when the weather turns so cold that the camels must be left saddled all night, to give them some slight protection. We had done this at odd times during short cold spells, and regularly since leaving Tuhulu, and it was high time for *yu-ch'a*, which is one of the most admirable things that ever came out of Mongolia. It is made from mutton fat and flour dry-roasted on an iron plate or a shovel, and after being mixed can be kept in chunks ready for immediate use. As a cold-weather ration it is served out first thing in the morning and again as soon as the march is finished, the only further preparation needed being to put it in a bowl and pour boiling tea over it. This makes a genuine life-saving drink, which restores warmth and vigor. The Chinese administer it at once in cases of frost-bite because, they say, though a frozen foot cannot be put near the fire, yet there is no objection to warming it from the inside, and *yu-ch'a* gets there quicker than anything else.

The days of defeat in camp at the foot of Dead Mongol Pass were occupied in futile councils. No one in all the caravans had any idea of what to do, except the Chou caravan master, who said that he would not attempt the pass again at any price; in which his mind was made up for him by his men, who said loudly before him in the tent that if they were ever caught like that again they would not risk freezing for the sake of other people's camels. A small party of caravan masters, brought up with a round turn to face the value of wisdom, rode up into the pass to look for a way through.  They reported that there was indeed a way through the drift, practicable by daylight, and they had even pushed on for a couple of miles, when an onset of wind and cloud drove them back.  These were men whose camels had been in the rear on the night of failure; they were fit for an effort and still thought the thing could be done.  I myself, though full of sorrow at missing Barköl, made up my mind to turn back with my friend Chou.  I had no faith in the half-hearted reconnaissance.  The men had not pushed on to the end of the snow; there might have been other drifts that they had not seen, the continued wind might have swept down more snow, and I had to admit that my camels were knocked out of time.  They could not stand such another night; those long hours between sunset and sunrise had more visibly damaged them than all the hard marches of the Khara Gobi.  Nor was Tur Köl a place where they could make anything like a recovery in two or three days — not in winter.  There was nothing for them to eat but tall tufts of dead *chih-chi* grass, and that had little virtue in it, while everything that resembled true pasture had been cropped short by sheep.  They spent most of their time shambling about, drifting in front of the wind, and if anything they were a little weaker every day.

My plain course was to get out of this high country on to the Gobi again, and to follow round the mountains to Ku Ch'eng-tze by the longer way, which is the recognized way in winter.  There was a pass, quite obvious and probably easy, at the eastern end of Tur Köl, giving a direct escape northward, but everyone was afraid of ice, or of unknown snow.  I could hardly press the matter, seeing that the pass was quite unknown, after we had failed so ignobly in Dead Mongol Pass, which, after all, was well known.  The heart was taken out of my swaggering camel man; he knew none of the ways and there was not a guide to be had.  Several of the caravans together tried to hire a Qazaq guide, but the Qazaqs refused to understand anything but the selling of sheep.  A caravan in straits was the kind of caravan they liked to see.  It meant salvage for them.  They had already nipped in and taken the better of the two camels abandoned in the snow, which they must have done by bringing camels of their own to drag it out. I had urged the House of Chou to have a try at this, but their caravan master, never much of a fellow, did not dare challenge the surliness of his men, who were almost out of hand. Getting away, then, meant going back to Tuhulu, so in the end we made two heavy, dispirited marches down the high, noble, but savage valley of the Dead Mongol Pass approach, down to the kindlier valley of Tuhulu. The others waited by Tur Köl, all of them watching for fit weather and each of them hanging back for someone else to take the lead. I am not even sure of my dates and the count of days just at this time. I had been too crestfallen to enter up my journal for several days. Just before Tuhulu we gathered in two small caravans, which turned back with us. We reached the friendly village in some disorder. Moses had sprained an ankle, two of my camels were far gone, and three of the Chou camels were in such a bad way that they had to be exchanged against local camels. I put in a couple of days shooting chukor and watching the huge clouds of pigeons that wheeled rustling through the sky. I did not shoot any of them, because the Turkis regarded them as privileged if not sacred. It seemed astonishing that the fields of a few score people could support so many thousand pigeons. There were also a few duck, lingering through the winter along the stream, but they were far too shy for shooting.

During the stay we laid in a few provisions, mostly in the way of delicacies. What I appreciated most were onions — a mild kind of Spanish onion with a sweet sub-flavor. The Chinese here in the west call them *p'i-ya*, probably in adaptation of the Turki name. They are not, I understand, an onion native to China, and may even in Turkestan be of Russian origin. They were the only fresh vegetable I had, because the sack of garlic with which I had started from Kuei-hua had been spoiled by frost. Garlic, once frozen, turns yellow after thawing and loses all its savor; but onions do not have this disability. Here I got also dried melon rind, a famous delicacy brought over the mountains from Hami. In the oases of Turkestan proper there is such an intense dry heat that melons can be cut in strips and dried in the sun, becoming perfectly preserved before they start to decay. The strips are then woven into braid and the braid fixed spirally on two crossed twigs, making a flat round cake.

From Tuhulu there were two courses and a hazard for our consideration. In the first place we could go back on our way of entry, by White Poplar River; but this would have meant an easterly setback that it would have taken two extra marches to make up. In the second place we could follow down the stream from Tuhulu, which reaches the desert through a gorge; but the gorge, as we were told, was hard going at all times and was now likely to be still harder because of ice at the edge of the water. We therefore took the hazard, a new, third course, hiring a guide to get us out of the valley and through the Metshin Ola by a westerly route; and at last, on the sixteenth of November by my reckoning, we made a fresh start.

# XVIII

## BACK TO THE DESERT

THE guide who gave us our new lead from Tuhulu was a man marked unmistakably by the fabulous west, the adventurer's land where fortune and failure shoulder each other. He had been born on a farm in the outlying settlement of San-t'ang Hu, where he learned to speak Mongol and Turki from his childhood. The free life on the edge of the desert had weaned him from the ancestral Chinese passion for mere farm grubbing, and from a half-Mongol upbringing he graduated to the life of a mounted peddler, riding at large between the Mongols and the outer Chinese and Turki holdings, on the lookout for odds and ends of trade. In this he had prospered so rapidly — aided, they say, by luck in pony dealing and pony stealing — that he became the chief landowner in his own settlement, a trader in a large way, and the owner of a caravan of two hundred camels, going between Kuei-hua and Ku Ch'eng-tze. He reached the top of his fortunes about the time when the troubles in Outer Mongolia forced the establishment of the Winding Road, of which he was a conspicuous pioneer. The knowledge of his old peddling days made him the man called on to " tread open," in the phrase of the caravan men, the stages of the Winding Road which lead by the Spring of the Wild Rose to No Man's Land and the House of the False Lama — a service for which he received fees that have already been exaggerated to a legendary sum.

This very road, however, brought his ruin on him. Instead of handling his own caravan he made it over to a caravan master, himself retiring to his home to smoke opium, confident in his fame and wealth in hand. Now the losses in camels during the first years of the Winding Road were beyond anything before known to the trade, until the caravan masters were seasoned to a knowledge of its conditions. His caravan was crippled in its first journeys, and the camels he went on buying to recruit it were cast away one after the other. When the end came he was already sodden in opium. He left his family in destitution and his sons to become laborers on the land he had once owned, and bolted to Tuhulu, where, being under the local jurisdiction of the Khan of Hami, it was difficult to press him for his debts. He was picking up a living as camel and horse doctor to the chief Turki of the place, the overseer of the Khan's pony herd, and he talked of recovery and a new fortune, but the opium had too much hold on him and he could not last. Still, poor as he was, he had a smart ambling pony to ride. "Look at that for a Westerner!" said the caravan men. "Poor clothes on his back and precious little food in his belly — but he must ride a fine pony, dogs defile him!" This was the man, once rewarded with bulk silver for marking out a great caravan road, who had come down to setting us on our way for the fee of one silver dollar, two bricks of tea, and three packets of tobacco.

He took us by a short steep side valley up from Tuhulu into the foothills of the Metshin Ola, from which he began to work us out into the foothills of the foothills. We camped after a long stage in rolling country, on a sort of under-plateau. The next morning the guide pointed out a broad valley running across our front, coming down from the very same pass that we had seen at the eastern end of Tur Köl. We were not, however, to follow it to its opening on the Gobi, but to cross it, pass over the high ridge bounding it on the far side, and come down to the desert by the next big valley, a lateral traverse which would save us a couple of marches. Then he rode back, and we, in spite of the bearings he had given us, went scrambling off into the hills to lose ourselves. The ridge was simple in outline, and from camp we could plainly see the nick in it by which we were to cross, but as we sweated up the slow slopes on the far side of the valley the lower hills hid the gap from us, and as we entered the approach valley we took the wrong fork. Sometime in the middle of the night, when we came to the crest, we found that we were on the edge of a slope of at least seventy degrees, which looked in the starlight like a sheer precipice. There was nothing for it but to camp all jerrycummumble up and down a valley so narrow that the loads were scattered over a distance of at least a mile.

In the morning the position was clear enough. We were astride a magnificent ridge running straight out from the central mass of the Metshin Ola. To the southeast, at the edge of the desert but out of sight, we knew was the point where the water of the Tuhulu valley clears the hills, forming a small oasis called Wei-tze Hsia — that is, the Reeds Below, or the Lower (Place) of Reeds. The water then sinks in the sloping desert, but far away at the foot of the slope it reappears, making a second oasis, called Lao-mao Hu,[1] which we could see faintly. These two places are marked on Carruthers's map by their Turki names of Adak and Nom.

Right across our front was the big valley for which we had been told to look, running like an avenue to the open Gobi. Even so the men were unwilling to go on. This getting lost in waterless hills, on top of the bad business at Dead Mongol Pass, had brought back all their panic and disaffection. They demanded that we return to the other main valley and follow it to Wei-tze Hsia, where the camels could be watered and we could all sit down and think, and lament. This would have meant a loss of at least three days, so before they could get much further with their counsels I sought out the master of one of the small caravans which had joined us, the only man who seemed to be keeping his head, and sent him back to look for the place where we had gone wrong in the night. Then I started to follow up the ridge, to see if I could prove the pass. After about half a mile I came to a sudden drop, and, sliding and scrambling down into it, found that it opened easily into the big

---

[1] *Lao-mao* must stand for *Nao-mao*, which would be a reasonable Chinese equivalent for Nom (the *hu* being merely descriptive). In the Kan-su dialects (which carry over into those parts of Hsin-chiang, where the settlers are of Kan-su stock) initials *l* and *n* are confusingly interchangeable in many words. Thus *nei-pien* (there) becomes *lai-pang-ko*; *nan* (south) becomes *lai*, and *liang-ko* (two) becomes *niang-ko*. Another weird pronunciation is *fei* for *shui* (water). My Chen-fan Wa-wa, when he wanted to say either *che-ko* or *chei-ko* (this) or *na-ko* or *nei-ko* (that), would merely grunt *ah!* at the same time thrusting his chin out toward whatever he was talking about.

37. LOST CAMP, METSHIN OLA (APE MOUNTAINS)

valley.   Hurrying back down our side of the pass I met the caravan master, who for his part had found where the two valleys branched.   When we got back to camp the men agreed to have another try.   All this time the Chou caravan master, who had been in the lead when we went wrong, and who had quite lost his " face " and his nerve, had been lying in the tent with his face covered, while the men talked loudly against him.   After that day he rarely spoke a word if he could help it.

While scrambling in the hills I noticed a little group of stone sheepfolds, from which I infer that the Qazaqs, as the snow comes down farther and farther during the winter, move their camps to these outer flanks of the Metshin Ola.   There is a good deal of "white grass" growing in small tufts, but the country is no good for pasturing sheep until there is enough snow for the animals to eat.   It looks as though it were excellent game country, but the only proof I saw was a large ibex horn, which had lain rotting for a long time.   At Tuhulu I was told that all the lower ranges were fine wild-sheep ground when the snow was heaviest in the high hills.

It was an unhandy business marshaling all the camels in our narrow defile and getting the loads on, but at last we got them headed back to the fork, then up the true approach and over into the big valley, down which we marched away for the desert and hour after hour in the night through the desert, swinging left-handed to the northwest, making up enough ground to be able to strike water the next day.   We camped at a place where low earthy mounds, breaking the smooth sweep of the desert, and a few haggard shrubs showed that water came almost to the surface.   Twenty-five miles on the next march brought us to both water and good grazing, which the camels needed more than water.   The heavy work in the hills and the two full-length marches afterwards had set them back almost to the pitiful condition in which they had left Dead Mongol Pass.   A number of them were footsore, all were thin, and some were so done up that if they had stumbled and gone down while on the march they could not have been got on their feet again.   In the big Chou caravan there were no more spare camels; the loads had long ago been split up so that every camel fit for work was carrying as much as he could stand up under, while at the end of almost every file two or three camels followed unladen, their stiff walk and loose humps showing how tired and thin they were. On the march one could see the sure sign of worn-down camels; instead of striding well out they hung back until the cord from the peg in each camel's nose by which he is tied to the pack before was pulled straight; only the constant painful tugging at their nostrils kept them going, and scarcely one of them was not bleeding from the way that the peg stretched the tender cartilage. I was getting my first lessons in the way that camels can be forced on and on and on when they have reached the edge of the limit of their strength. At the end of every march it looked as though several camels would never start again, but after a few hours' rest, a little chewing of sapless grass or fibrous tamarisk and a handful of dried peas for real food, they would lurch to their feet again and keep on their feet, hour after hour.

They were given some respite now, for we had struck into a series of curious oases which run like a fringe along the outer edge of the Metshin Ola. There is a wide gap between Weitze Hsia and the first of these, Sha-tsao'rh Ch'üan or the Spring of the Wild Jujube, but then they lie closely strung together for seventy miles. They follow the level where water from the mountains, after sinking under the piedmont gravel of the outer slopes, reaches the surface again, so that most of them are long and narrow, running parallel with the distant range, as the water does not flow far into the desert before sinking again or evaporating. Here the gravel sprinkling of the desert vanishes, churned up in the water-softened underlying clay. Wherever the water tends to form pools grow high reeds, while the drier ground is thick with *chih-chi* grass,[1] phœnix trees, and wild brier roses. Oases of this kind, depending entirely on an underground water supply (for away from the mountains rain almost never falls, and the winter snow is usually light), are known to the Chinese locally as *hu* — a peculiar extension in meaning of the

[1] *Chih-chi* grass appears to be a sign of subsoil drainage. It is very tough, growing in bunches to a height of about three feet. When green, I believe it makes excellent forage, but when sere it has no "body."

word for a lake,[1] corresponding very exactly to our use of the word "oasis."

At the Oasis of the Wild Jujube [2] are the mud ruins of at least one deserted farm, said to have been tenanted years ago by Turkis, who spread out the available supply of water by irrigation channels, but abandoned the place because the water brought with it saline deposits which gradually made the fields untillable. Farming is carried on like this once in a long span of years in many of the smaller oases, but when the fields become barren through excess of salt they must be allowed to go back to fallow until a land-hungry family in the next generation has another try. Abandoned by men, the sheltered oasis swarmed with antelope (*Gazella subgutturosa*), come in from the desert to take up winter quarters. Although they are so shy on the open plains, these antelope seem to suffer a complete change of nature when they come in to shelter, being more doltish and easy to kill than so many rabbits. On the plains they rely almost entirely on their eyesight and seem to have an acute sense of the range of firearms; but among thickets they have poor senses of hearing and smell, and unaccountably drop their guard. A few miles farther west we began to see numbers of sheep, cows, and ponies, also driven in to the oasis for the winter and left untended unless a herdsman rides out once in a while to see that wolves have not been too busy. The antelope seem to take these herdsmen for granted, paying no attention to them; nor would they run far or fast from the caravans, were it not for the dogs.

It was warm among the thickets, and we went easily and gently along, until at the end of the march we crossed a strip of desert and entered the next watered land, called Niu-chuan-tze Hu or the Oasis of the Cowyard. Here we found a family of poor squatters and a rich family well known as the owners of a large caravan. They lived in a patriarchal state. The poor family were almost serfs of the rich, farming their land for them. The ancient father of the family lorded it over the rich household;

---

[1] Cf. *supra*, page 175, note 2.
[2] I have translated *sha-tsao'rh* as "wild" jujube, but literally *sha* is sand; compare "sand onion" for wild onion. Perhaps "desert onion," "desert jujube," would be truer renderings.

his eldest son was his bailiff, the second son was apprenticed to a business house at Ku Ch'eng-tze, the third son (the pick of the lot, because, owing to his hard life, he smoked little opium) was master of the family caravan, while two younger sons were little more than superior servants. A few Chinese retainers completed the establishment, and for supernumeraries there were several Mongol families, strays from Outer Mongolia, who worked off and on as herders, camped in the poorer parts of the oasis. The family, with the wives and children of all the sons, were quartered together in a compact group of mud buildings about a mean court, where they lived with little visible luxury except for the jewels and festal clothes of the women, a few carpets, and a superb old bronze pan for tamarisk coals.

At some time in the past a line of *karez* had been dug to extend the area of cultivation; it must have been a success, but had become useless through increasing salinity, so a fresh line was being dug by Turki laborers hired from a distance—the Chinese never having mastered the art of digging *karez*. This method of irrigation is of Persian origin; it was introduced in the Turfan depression (where, according to Huntington[1] about 40 per cent of the population is now dependent on it) in the eighteenth century, but I do not know of its ever having been extended to the northern or Zungarian side of the T'ien Shan system except of recent years, in this one series of oases. To irrigate by *karez* it is necessary first to determine an underground flow of water, then to make sure from the slope of the land that the water can be conveyed to cultivate fields. A well is first dug to tap the water; another well is then sunk a few yards away, and a tunnel bored through from it to the first, to conduct the water in the desired direction; then another and another well, each going to a slightly lesser depth, and so on until the water can be made to flow out over the surface. A large capital, judging by local standards, is necessary for an enterprise of this sort; the work must be done by skilled men, who are highly paid, and there is always the hazard that the water may contain a strong impregnation of salts which in a few years will make the fields barren.

[1] *The Pulse of Asia.*

So far from digging *karez*, hoarding silver in the ground, and putting on airs, the prosperous family at Niu-chuan-tze Hu would have been the most miserable kind of squatters had it not been for the Winding Road. Otherwise they would have had no market for their surplus grain and meat except a long way off at Barköl and Ku Ch'eng-tze, cities which are glutted with cheap food. Being on the caravan road, however, they could sell provisions and camel fodder at fancy prices to caravans coming from the east. We stopped there for several days, while the Chou caravan, which had run short, laid in a quantity of bread, and all of us rested our camels.

Owing to the halt I fell in with a most remarkable brigand, Li Erh, the Raider of the Qazaqs. Li Erh, or Li the Second, was the second son of a respectable family who owned a few camels and an inn on the K'o Chen side of the Wu-kung Pa, the pass from Kuei-hua to Mongolia, where I had stopped for lunch and where I first met the Eldest Son of the House of Chou. He had begun as a camel puller, but the dissipations of Ku Ch'eng-tze suited him so well that he deserted the caravans and took to a roving life among the Qazaqs and Mongols, learning to speak both languages. In more than twenty years he had only once been back to Kuei-hua, on a kind of furlough, having made the west too hot to hold him for a while. On that visit he had sheltered with my camel man, who had been mixed up in some pony-stealing villainies of his at Barköl, but who attempted to sell him to the Kuei-hua police, so that there was now a bitter quarrel between the two men. He had several times been in a fair way to fortune, but "his hand was big," as the Chinese put it, so that whatever he took in the desert he always squandered in Ku Ch'eng-tze. In latter years, getting bolder than ever, he had made a spectacular reputation as a strong man going out against the strong, a raider of the Qazaqs who raid the Mongols and the caravans. There are fighting bandits in plenty among the Chinese, and they are hardy fellows if well led, but courage of the single-handed kind is rare among them; the only other lone-hand robber that I heard of in the west being an adventurer who some years ago terrorized the Russian border near Chuguchak.

The corner stone of the fame of Li Erh was his way of fighting at any odds. They said that he shot well from horseback, and that, hanging himself all over with automatic pistols, he would ride into a Qazaq encampment, scatter all the ponies, and drive off the pick of the camels, which he would hide for a while before selling them on the Ku Ch'eng-tze market or passing them to the caravans. His last big exploit had been a running fight the year before when he staved off a number of Qazaqs and got clear away with more than twenty camels he had lifted from them. The Chinese authorities pay little attention to robbery among the nomads; if they did, they would have to keep a policeman in every camp. At some time after that, however, Li Erh had mixed himself up in an arms deal between a Chinese official and the Qazaqs — for, like the Mongols, when he was not at feud with the Qazaqs he went freely enough among them. The official was hiring "government" arms to the Qazaqs, who went raiding with them into Outer Mongolia, bringing back great herds of live stock, and it was a profitable business for everybody until the governor of the province had the official shot. Li Erh had then taken cover, and was living here in perfect security, a few miles from a border patrol, on the charity of the Kuei-hua caravans. A caravan man by origin, he had never robbed the caravans, so that he was always sure of food and shelter with them. Not only did he sell them camels on the quiet, but when they had camels taken by the Qazaqs, if he were anywhere to be found they would set him after the thieves, whom he frequently succeeded in overtaking and routing.

It was lucky for him that he could count on friends, because he was nearly blind from an inflammation of the eyes, made worse by some filthy nostrum that he had procured from Ku Ch'eng-tze. As soon as he came to camp the men brought him to me, and I worked a miraculous cure with argyrol, for which he thanked me extravagantly, promising me the loyal aid of all his automatics any time that I might have dirty work to be done. He was one of the most beautifully built men I have ever seen, more than six feet tall, I should think, in his heelless Mongol boots, but narrow-waisted and with a lithe grace of carriage that disguised the breadth of his shoulders.  He wore his half-Mongol dress with, I am sure, a sense of its dash and color, what with the squirrel-skin crest on his round, gold-braided felt cap, his wide half-boots, his gallant sash, and his embroidered silk tobacco pouch with the jade mouthpiece of his pipe showing from it. He had an arrogant way of talking and a kind of swashbuckling fine manners, but his strong features and handsome bearing were indescribably marred by the sinister droop of his bestial under-lip, which sagged like a dewlap and brimmed forever with saliva.

We moved on by easy stages through the oases of Tung Chuang (East Village, where there were one and a half families of Chinese and a small Mongol encampment), Ulan Bulak (Red Spring, a Mongol name), Shih-pan Tun (Stone Slab Tower; a poor spot, more a halting point than an oasis), Ssu T'ang (Fourth Stage), and San T'ang (Third Stage).  Tung Chuang was the only inhabited place, but everywhere could be seen abandoned fields and an occasional ruined hut.  At Shih-pan Tun, Ssu T'ang, and San T'ang there were beacon towers of an age that I could not possibly determine.  I looked for the fascine construction found by Sir Aurel Stein in the old line of Chinese fortifications based on the Jade Gate, at the Kan-su approach to Chinese Turkestan, but there were no signs of it, as the towers had easily been constructed without such aids out of flat slabs of black rock, of the same origin as the black gravel of the Khara Gobi, which lay plentifully on the low hills. Neither local people nor caravan men had any tradition about the founding or age of these towers, but in all likelihood they date back to one of the early Chinese occupations of the Bar Köl region; perhaps to the second century A.D., when the Chinese for a while had the upper hand of the Huns, who from their stronghold in the Bar Köl range for centuries threatened the Chinese in Kan-su and disputed with them the northern access to Turkestan, which belongs strategically to whoever holds the Bar Köl mountains.

All along the oasis line we had sunny, pleasant days, though the nights were cold; but at Ulan Bulak, which is higher and more exposed, we were raked all night by the worst wind we had yet known in Mongolia, which blew my tent flat and held us abjectly in camp all the next day. At San T'ang we were visited by a caravan master who is accepted from end to end of Mongolia as the chief inheritor in his generation of the great school of desert craft. He made his reputation in the year of the Chinese Revolution (the winter of 1911–12), being then in charge of a caravan going down from Ku Ch'eng-tze, with fifty or sixty "passengers," besides goods. The travelers were all men returning to their homes, most of them carrying all their savings in lump silver and gold dust. As they came near to Kuei-hua they picked up the news that the last stages were more dangerous than they had ever been; not only were the bandits out in force, unchecked, but the boldest youngsters in Outer Mongolia had ridden down for their share of the plunder. The terrified travelers offered to put up two thousand silver taels if the caravan master would find a guide to take them across country to safety; but he answered them honestly, telling them to keep their money, because no guide to be found near the main caravan route could be trusted to keep his mouth shut. Then, on his own responsibility, he turned off into unknown mountains. Now if there is anything that upsets the ordinary caravan master it is to get off the known road, where he has to look up pasture and water for himself, and if there is anything that terrifies the ordinary Chinese it is to venture into mountains of which no respectable predecessors have left any record. This man took his caravan for twenty-odd days through unpeopled ranges, and at every halt he found concealment, grazing for more than two hundred camels, and water for several score men. Once only he paid twenty taels to a wandering Mongol to accompany them for two marches, partly as guide and partly to make sure that he would not give the word to any marauders. When at last he dodged safely through the Ta Ch'ing Shan into Kuei-hua by a smugglers' valley, he had not lost a single camel, nor had there been one alarm, though almost every caravan that year was either plundered outright or made to pay heavy toll. Since then travelers have paid premiums to go with his caravan.

He was a bluff, strong, brutal man with a cheery manner, and he sat for a while in the tent of the House of Chou, passing the news of the road before mounting to ride after his caravan, which had gone by us at a little distance. He told us that the caravans from which we had parted at Dead Mongol Pass had got through with mixed luck; this time the leaders had had the best of it, but those behind had been caught by a storm, the snow blowing down on them so heavily that a number of camels were buried and suffocated. All of the caravans had been forced to turn out of the mountains again, and were now on our own road, only a few days ahead of us; but for our halt at Tuhulu and our losing ourselves in the Metshin Ola, we should have been in the lead ourselves. As for him, he had been coming from the west by the road "inside the mountains," with the snow getting heavier all the time. When he heard of the state of Dead Mongol Pass he determined to get on the Gobi road, but unless he had gone back for several stages the only known pass was full of snow. Nevertheless he struck out boldly, found snow-free valleys that no one else had ever attempted, and got safely to the Gobi without losses.

We marched that afternoon about ten miles, camping on the edge of the most important of the oases, San-t'ang Hu, or the Oasis of the Third Stage, which borrows its name from the Third Stage which we had just left, which in turn probably owes its name less to being a formal stage than to the old watch-tower, which makes a convenient landmark. San-t'ang Hu, like Ming Shui, pops up as a sudden name in the blank wastes of the map, where it is spelled Santohu. The spelling is probably due to the early Russian surveys on which most Mongolian mapping is based; but God, for the greater mystification of travelers, invented the Russians with a complete inability to hear or pronounce the Chinese language correctly. They cannot, in spite of their reputation for facility in foreign speech, even lay their tongues accurately to the bare necessities of life. For instance, *chiu,* the word for wine or spirits, which Russians in these parts have to use forty-eleven times a day, and the sound of which only varies from the word "Jew" in that it is pronounced with a sort of lingering affection, they call *dzun;* and they will go on calling it *dzun* until it is all finished. But let me confess, on top of this bit of snobbery, that it really is difficult to get the right hang of San-t'ang Hu, as the slovenly local speech makes it more like San-t'ao Hu; though the analogies of Ssu T'ang and San T'ang[1] ought to make it clear enough.

At San-t'ang Hu we had completed the Winding Road proper, for here the Great Road comes in from the northeast, after crossing the Black Gobi in two stages and passing the Lao-yeh Miao, that once-famous temple of which I have spoken. The oasis has a striking advantage of position in lying north of the Bar Köl mountains, Barköl town being about eighty miles away. Caravans coming from Mongolia can go on either by Barköl town and the road called the Road Inside the Mountains, through the foothills of the Bar Köl and Bogdo Ola ranges, or if the snow is too heavy they can keep on along the fringes of the Gobi, by the Road Outside the Mountains to Ku Ch'eng-tze. Whichever way they go, San-t'ang Hu is the pivotal point, and as many caravans are short of provisions when they get there, the people do a handsome business in supplying them. Moreover, another road, also going north, but diverging from the Great Road, comes in five or six stages to Tengku Nor,[2] at which place there is a Mongol temple, the trading centre of the Mingan *hoshun*. All the Chinese of San-t'ang Hu speak Mongol as readily as Chinese and have even little Mongol touches in their costume. Before the disorders in Outer Mongolia they claimed a large share in the Mongol trade of Barköl.

We halted for several days at San-t'ang Hu to lay in oats for camel feed, as the camels were going on their last reserve of strength, and the grazing for the rest of the way to Ku Ch'eng-tze was of the poorest. This halt led to my being arrested by a Chinese border patrol. We had already met a few troopers in the oases to the east, but on being shown my passport, which they could not read, they passed me along. At San-t'ang Hu were

[1] *T'ang* is not the regular word for "a stage." Its most common use is as the numerative of journeys: "He has gone the third time," or "on the third journey," is *t'a tsou-lo ti san t'ang*.

[2] I have no idea of the correct Mongol spelling or pronunciation of Tengku; *teng*, as I have written it, is pronounced like "tongue."

two officers, however, both of subaltern rank. The senior was a good enough fellow, and would have let me pass; but unfortunately he was quite illiterate. His junior was the "adjutant" of the command; he could read in a stumbling way, and he thought he saw a way to discredit his superior and gain promotion for himself on the score of zeal. He therefore declared that my passport, which was endorsed with a Chinese translation and the seal of the Bureau of Foreign Affairs at Peking, was a Japanese or Russian forgery; that I was a highly suspicious character on account of my arms, and that I must be detained until word could be sent to Barköl and a telegraphic inquiry be made from Barköl to the provincial capital at Urumchi.

Having thoroughly frightened his senior, the two of them began to search and list my belongings; but when I found that even if my arms and ammunition corresponded to the list on my passport they would not let me proceed, I refused to allow it. After a whole day of wrangling I was moved down to the village for detention, in quarters next to the officer commanding; and a couple of days later I parted in sorrow from the House of Chou, who went clanking and shuffling away into the desert, my friend the Eldest Son very much cast down and with a quivering lip, for he was sure that he would never see me again. I had even to send my dog Suji on with them, for I had no way of feeding him. I had a small store of silver dollars with me, but I saw at once that I must hide them, otherwise I might not be allowed to go until they had all been squeezed out of me. Suji had to be dragged away, fighting. They told me later that they made a rope collar for him and attached him by a swinglebar to a similar collar on a big bitch they had, which was in heat; but even so he tried for days to run away. I went, under armed guard, to see them off; and when they had gone I went back to the village, to await an unconjecturable fate.

# XIX

## THE OASIS OF THE THIRD STAGE

ALTHOUGH at first it looked as though my detention — it was more a detention than an imprisonment — were due to no more than the ignorance and stubbornness, complicated by the petty jealousies, of a couple of unimportant patrol officers, I soon found that there were heavier matters in the background which lent them their incongruous authorities. I had come within the play of curious border policies, having in fact thrust myself across the danger line of Central Asian affairs of the day.

The Governor of Hsin-chiang — that is, of Chinese Turkestan and Zungaria — had shouldered his way to power by bold action at the fall of the Manchus in the Chinese Revolution of 1911. From that time he had been holding the Chinese power, sometimes by sleight and sometimes by force, over the ambitions and interests of all the subject races in the vast province. The first danger to the ruling Chinese minority was from the Mongols, for in the year of the revolution a wind of independence blew through Mongolia, especially in the west, where the Manchu-Chinese hold was least evident and formidable. There was a danger that the numerous Mongol tribes in Hsin-chiang might join the clans of Western Outer Mongolia in a bid for autonomy. The danger was weathered, largely by the help of a powerful Mongol prince who favored the Chinese, but the danger of its recurrence had to be held in mind. After this the province was kept in good order by playing off the Qazaq and Mongol nomads against each other, and the Chinese against the Turki and T'ung-kan in the settled communities. Then came the War, the break-up of Imperial Russia, and the irruption of defeated Imperialist bands into Northern Hsin-chiang and

Mongolia, often pursued by Red detachments.    The danger from the armed Imperialists seemed worse than it was, since in the end they defeated themselves by their own violence and stupidity; but when they had finally been disarmed and dispersed Outer Mongolia remained under the domination of Soviet Russia. This meant, in the first place, that Mongol hostility to the Chinese rule was fortified, and led inevitably, when the Soviet power had been confirmed in Russia and the new Russia was able to face outwards, to a complete repudiation of Chinese authority, except in Inner Mongolia and Alashan, which lie open to China strategically and have always been under a stronger Chinese influence.

In the meantime the Governor of Hsin-chiang, while working energetically to keep his subject races both well affected and impotent, had to deal with new problems on the side of China. The period of Chinese civil wars had set in, and he had to walk with increasing wariness to avoid being involved in one or another of them.    It was his good fortune to be protected by deserts on that side which made it difficult to invade his province; but the interests of his people suffered from the disorganization of trade and the insecurity of traffic over long, awkward routes obstructed by armies and brigands.    The question of trade was of the first importance, because the Governor relied heavily on the material prosperity of all his peoples to keep them politically contented, his maxim being that a subject race is far less likely to think of revolt when it has wealth at stake.

With the old Imperial Highway, the cart road to China, no longer open to safe traffic, Chinese trade with Chinese Turkestan was thrown entirely on to the Mongolian caravan routes; but here again the handicap was added to year by year.    The policy of Soviet Russia in Outer Mongolia was directed toward the total exclusion of the Chinese and their trade, in order that Russia, still too weak for open competition, might benefit by an unhindered access to all the resources in raw materials of the country.    From about the year 1923 Chinese caravans going between Turkestan and China were denied the Great and Small Roads through Outer Mongolia; but by the establishment of the

Winding Road through Inner Mongolia, Alashan, and No Man's Land communication was still maintained. The run of the cards, however, was with the Russians. While choking Chinese trade, both direct and in transit through Outer Mangolia, they were creating for themselves an effective monopoly of the trade of the Chinese province of Hsin-chiang, with which, from the Siberian frontier, they maintained cordial relations. The Governor, though losing ground, worked hard to keep his markets open and competitive; but trade he must have, for the sake of prosperity and political security, so that, as the buying power of the Chinese markets diminished, he was forced to encourage the Russian trade. He and his able subordinates must have been galled by the irony of having to lay more and more stress on the cordiality of relations with Russia, all the time that market values were being forced down by the lack of competition against the Russian buyers. At last, after the shuffling of policy and expedience, the paradox stood clear: the province of Hsin-chiang, ruled by Chinese but virtually disengaged from any Chinese central government or home authority, was in friendly relations with Russia and relied on Russia for the major part of its foreign trade — but on the other side of another long open frontier stood Outer Mongolia, which under Soviet advice and encouragement had made good a quasi-belligerent break with the Chinese and all their works.

The situation became more acute and the paradox more distressing just at the time of my journey. The penning of the Christian Army of Feng Yü-hsiang in the Northwestern Province by the anti-Communist alliance headed by Chang Tso-lin, the prospect of its defeat, and the different possibilities of its retreat or dispersal had borne a full crop of lusty rumors throughout the hinterland. It was known that the Christian General was heavily committed to his Russian supporters. What actually happened was that, with all the troops he could extricate, he made his way toward Ho-nan Province, there to carry on the turbulent new-thought, New-China, sometimes pro-Christian, often pro-Russian, and usually antiforeign cause; but that did not matter at the time. The weight of Chinese opinion was that he would withdraw more to the northwest, into Kan-su Province, which he controlled, there to recuperate, and that very likely he would still further retire into Hsin-chiang, — his army and transport, though impaired by defeat, being quite sufficient to overrun the province, — where he could create an independent power in close touch with his Russian sympathizers. Why he should not have done so is no part of my story here; what bore on my affairs at the time was the obvious danger of his taking this move.

While an unprovoked invasion of the neutral province of Hsin-chiang was thus generally feared, from the Kan-su side, it was also charted among the possibilities that the retreating army, in whole or part, might attempt to gain Hsin-chiang by the Mongolian routes — the Outer Mongolian routes especially, as they presented less difficulty of transport and commissariat. The Governor of Hsin-chiang had dealt with these possibilities to the best of his power. A concentration of such troops as he could offer had been made at Hami, to protect the Imperial Highway coming in from Kan-su; but the closing of his Mongolian frontier was not so simple. The danger there was in the mobility of the Mongol tribesmen, the probability that all Outer Mongolia would be thrown into turmoil if the Christian Army marched through the country to the occupation of Hsin-chiang, and the possibility that the Mongols under his own rule would move to join the Mongols on the other side of the dividing Altai range. To prevent a coalescence of the subject Mongols and the free tribesmen, a policy of segregation had already been roughed out. To retaliate against the embargo on the Chinese caravan trade, an embargo had been laid from the Hsin-chiang side on the export of grain and flour to Outer Mongolia. This was the only trade with Hsin-chiang which the Mongols wanted, for they had come during the long peaceful years of the Manchu Empire to depend largely on grain for winter stores. At the same time the Governor began to sharpen a sword ready to his hand, the Mohammedan Qazaq tribesmen, who were encouraged to carry themselves more proudly against the Mongols. To stiffen the Mohammedan nomads against the Mongols was a total reversal of what had been the Manchu-Chinese policy through all the nearer past.   In Central Asia the Mohammedans had been looked on as the most inflammable material for revolt, and the Mongols had accordingly been favored against them, to keep them chastened.   The Qazaqs had since ancient times been in touch with the Mongols along the Altai — on the westerly side for the most part, but up towards Kobdo on the easterly slopes also.   Under the Manchu dynasty those who guided the Chinese Empire had ruled that all the nomad lands belonged of original right to the Mongols, and that the Qazaqs must therefore pay grazing fees in rental to the Mongol tribes.

Under the pressure of new events, the Mongols having become the more dangerous, favor was withdrawn from them.   The Qazaqs were encouraged to strike for their own betterment; arms began to be found in plenty among them, and arms were withheld from the Mongols.   The perennial hostility between the two races of different faith and tradition, kept alive by cattle raidings, stirred into a more open enmity, and within a few months the Qazaqs had cut a wide swathe between Outer Mongolia and Hsin-chiang; what had been before a mountain boundary was made over into a belt of desolation, raided across and across by Qazaq bravoes.   Mongols who belonged under the rule of the Governor of Hsin-chiang Province withdrew for safety farther into the province; while the emboldened Qazaqs pushed their raids well to the northeast of the Altai, plundering almost unchecked among the Mingan Mongols, who, as one of them said to me, were "harried into nothingness."   The Mongols under the authority of the Governor of Hsin-chiang were thus surgically divided from the independent tribes of Outer Mongolia, and all communication between them was at an end.

To complete the segregation, the embargo on trade between Outer Mongolia and places like Ku Ch'eng-tze, Barköl, and the outer oases from San-t'ang Hu to Bai was rigidly enforced. At first, after the announcement of the measure, it had been regarded as a weapon ready but not urgently needed; the people of San-t'ang Hu, for instance, had made fortunes by running grain, flour, and trade goods across the Gobi to Tengku Nor, and more than one official had profited by keeping his head turned. That time was now over; several men had recently been shot for smuggling, and the border patrols, like that at San-t'ang Hu, were under such emphatic orders that the petty officers no longer dared to countenance illegal trade. To recoup themselves, they were keeping a strict watch on all the regular caravans, frightening those caravan masters whose documents might be regarded as in the least bit irregular into paying them well for permission to pass, enforcing a check on the amount of provisions which each caravan might carry, and exacting a commission on the sale and purchase of supplies at San-t'ang Hu.

This was the net of suspicion, intrigue, and obstruction into which I had thrust myself. Of the two officers, the man in nominal command was too much afraid to be anything but impotent; the " adjutant," the semi-literate one, was more concerned to intrigue against his superior than to give me a just consideration. Knowing that the responsibility was not his, he let his fancy loose in wild theories. He announced his opinion that my American passport, with its Peking endorsement in Chinese, was definitely spurious, but he would not commit himself to a decision that it was a Japanese forgery, — an idea that occurred to him, I suppose, from ancient reports of anti-Japanese feeling near the coast, — for he had an alternative suspicion that I was engaged in selling arms, or again might be a Communist emissary come to spread disaffection, or yet again a Russian officer in the pay of the Christian General sent in advance to determine a line of invasion. The day after my detention a rider was dispatched to Barköl to carry the word to higher authorities, " for instruction and necessary action." I was not allowed to send out any word myself, for fear I might, as I had claimed, have friends in the province who would stir themselves to bring discredit on good, active, honest soldier-men. In spite of that I sneaked off a letter to be posted at Ku Ch'eng-tze by my friends of the House of Chou, and a few days later, having hired a pony from a Mongol, I got my camel man away to Barköl — where he was himself anxious to go, in search of a reckoning with the family of the long-unheard-of caravan man who had first hired camels to me and then sublet the contract to him.  One of my letters was to the two Protestant missionaries whom I knew to be stationed at Urumchi, the capital, the other to my friend Pan,[1] addressed to the capital with instructions to forward.

Thereafter I could do no more, but set myself to wait.  My only real discomfort was in being vilely lodged, for I was not allowed to pitch my tent, but had to stay in a derelict room next to the quarters of the officer commanding.  Parts of the sleeping platform had caved in, so that it could not be heated in the regular way by lighting a fire in the stove at the front, from which the smoke ought to be drawn off by flues, warming the whole platform.  More than half the room was taken up by the platform, the k'ang, which measured about seven feet by ten; the rest made as it were a well, about five feet by ten, in which was piled the whole of my gear.  The only way of getting warm was to light a fire on the mud floor in what was left of the sunken part of the room, squatting beside it close to the ground in order to keep below the smoke — or else to go visiting.  I spent most of the time visiting, when I was not in the open, but at night Moses and I and the camel man, when he returned from Barköl, had to share the k'ang, after putting out the fire.

San-t'ang Hu is the kind of place that most travelers leave as soon as they can, writing it down in their accounts as "a miserable hole" or "a collection of wretched hovels."  The Chinese themselves, in those regions, have a pat phrase for such outposts of the back of beyond, calling them Gobi-t'an'rh-shang, which is as much as to say "on the flat of the Gobi," meaning that they have no amenities whatever.  It was the only settlement of the kind at which I ever made a long stay, and I was glad afterward that I had been kept there long enough to feel the pulse of that kind of frontier life.

Knots and ridges of low black Gobi hills, thinly sprinkled with snow, broke the slow swell of the black Gobi plains outside the western Metshin Ola which divided the hu from Bar Köl.  In the deepest depression among the desert hills rose the springs which brought the oasis to life.  The main trend of the watered

[1] See Chapter I.

land, instead of lying parallel to the mountains as usual, went away to the north, following a small stream that ran briskly for several miles until it encountered the irredeemable water-swallowing desert. The umbilical village of San-t'ang Hu was at the sources of this brook, but farms and small clusters of huts were scattered to the west and north, some of them depending on other springs, so that in the whole area included under the name of the Oasis of the Third Stage there must have been over thirty families. These people are all of one stock, being sons and grandsons of immigrants from Chen-fan, — Little Mice they are called, being at one or more removes from the Chen-fan born who are the only true Sand Hollow Mice, — and they are all prosperous and incredibly stingy, laying interest to interest when business is in their favor, but repudiating contracts when it goes against them. The townsfolk of Barköl have a bad enough name, not only from the few travelers who have visited the place, but among the Chinese as well. I am not the one to mitigate this repute, seeing how badly I was used by the Barköl man who in the first place was under bond to take me through Mongolia; but I put it on record that in the mouths of the Kuei-hua caravan men the people of Barköl are open-handed and noble beside the mean nigglers and hagglers of San-t'ang Hu.

During my stay of about a fortnight among these people I saw well enough how set they were on maintaining a technical ignorance between the doings of their left and right hands, and came to a poor opinion of them. I talked and listened endlessly in their company, sitting on the sleeping platforms of all the foremost villagers in turn, while they smoked opium, chaffered with the masters of one caravan after another about the price of grain, and sometimes in whispers laid open before me the politics of the frontier. Also all the folk, when they heard that I made no charge, began to court me for my medicines; but as there was nothing in the world wrong with most of them except opium (that, the usual boils and bowel troubles, and a tendency to tuberculosis and secondary venereal disease) I did little good. It is poor practice putting drugs into a man the whole tone of whose system is set by opium. Both men and women were notable smokers; but then, as Moses put it, "What amusements do they have all winter in a place like this, except opium and women? And look at the women!" — for they were a skinny lot of shrews, the young with the old.

The strange thing was that while the women were old at twenty-five, largely through their smoking, the men on an average were strong, well built, and active, keeping their health so long as they stayed out of doors, farming and riding and herding and traveling; especially if they smoked fresh opium, leaving alone the dottle or pipe scrapings with which real "fiends" bemuse themselves. The onset of danger in such a community is among the children. The village headman, though past sixty, was a thick-chested, heavy-boned fellow who did not look more than forty, and had only a year or two ceased from the handling of his own caravan. This man had a late-born child of less than two, by a youngish wife. Every evening before the baby was rolled up in its quilts they brought it to the k'ang where the father lay with his pipe, and the father puffed opium smoke into its face that it might not cry all night. I was told that this is commonly done with fretful, weakly children born when both the parents have long been opium smokers. There can be nothing but a poor chance for a second generation which, yet unweaned, cannot sleep until the craving has been allayed. The heads of several families I knew were pioneers of the early settlement, men between sixty and eighty who were still in fine vigor, taking whole bellyfuls of smoke with unshaken calm. These were the men who had made their own land and set up their own fortunes, earning their vices as they went along; but among the grandsons of such men, born to an easy initiation, there showed few who were not weak and purposeless.

Next door but one to me were an old couple, in their fifties, untimely senile, who were playing out the end of their tragedy. It was less than a year since their only son had died — of tuberculosis, as far as I could determine. Denied posterity, which was about all the hope or idea that he had of immortality, the man had allowed what little he owned to go to ruin; for there are fewer women than men in San-t'ang Hu, so that he could not afford another wife. The woman, who was past bearing, understood that the chief burden of sin was on her soul, and from the day of calamity had done nothing but weep and invite death. I went into her dark kennel to see what I could do, but there was nothing left of her but a few old bones wrapped in rags and a fleshless head under a shock of dusty hair. She had even lost her voice, except for a deathly wordless whisper, and lay twitching under her rags with big tears dripping down her face, while another unsightly hag was getting the opium pipe ready. It was quite plain that she was past help, but as they told me that her throat pained her I gave her some cough drops and aspirin. The next day she died. Luckily I had made the visit only when urged by an officer who, by virtue of his command, was lord of the village, so that no accusation was made that I had hastened her death.

The stretching, waking, and burial of the corpse made an agreeable diversion for several days, during which I sat in at a series of feasts given by the neighbors. Not only Moses but one or two Kuei-hua caravan visitors were hugely taken with the priestly part of the ceremonies, which they declared to be quite different from the ritual in their own parts of the country. Taoist priests, the inheritors of the different schools of primitive magic all over China, are usually put before Buddhists and all comers at funeral pomps. Unfortunately I did not know enough to appreciate the peculiarities of the local rite, and still more unfortunately I was unable to keep up my journal all the time that I was at San-t'ang Hu, for fear of suspicion, so that I came away without notes. What interested me most was that none of the officiants were priests by calling, the community being too small and too stingy to support stipendiary clergy, though they had a number of shrines and a temple down the stream which was visited by touring priests from Barköl at periodic festivals. For funerals they relied on a guild of amateurs, who were equipped not only with robes, musical instruments, and other furniture, but with false hair made up in the priestly style. The robes, though old, were not of a high quality of embroidery or brocade; they had been brought from Chen-fan by the original settlers, and I suspect that they and the rest of the paraphernalia had been inherited from an original body of Taoists who had disappeared, abandoning celibacy and being absorbed into more profitable lay occupations after transplantation.

In another major case on which I was consulted at San-t'ang Hu I failed to bring off a miracle. My camels were at pasture at the edge of the oasis, under the charge of the Chen-fan Wa-wa, who was quartered in the *yurt* of a Mongol, and one day while I was there drinking tea with milk and salt in it, and talking about all matters that interest men within the four edges of Mongolia, the Mongol put out an elbow toward the side of the *yurt*, where a figure lay inert under a covering of antelope skins. It was his daughter, he said, who lay sick; were I to bring a few medicines with me the next time I came, he would appreciate it. He had none of the fawning ways of the Little Mice of San-t'ang Hu; he did not hint that my Chen-fan Wa-wa was living in his *yurt* at his charges; he merely hoped that I might take an interest.

I found that the girl was tall and would have been comely but for the dry fever that was wasting her. The mother said that the sickness began on her return from a search for lost cattle. After finding the cattle she had come in the way of a snowstorm; she had not been able to herd them against it, and, fearing that they might stray farther before the wind, she had stayed with them, a night, a day, and another night, without shelter, fire, or food. When the storm passed she brought the cattle back, in the way that a Mongol girl must do. It was a usual chance of Mongol life; but the girl had been taken with a sickness.

I thought that the girl must have pneumonia; but after I had been coming several days to do what I could, giving instructions about keeping her well warmed and sheltered (which were not followed, for she rose in her sickness to do her own share of work, gathering fuel and tending the fire), the mother brought out further words. She thought that the girl was turning to recovery. It was well; the girl, in truth, was a girl, but the

eldest of the children now, and the most able to work; it would
have been bad to lose her, too.   They had all had the sickness —
father, mother, the big son, this daughter, the two little children,
an impish boy and girl.   "The big son?" I asked.   "Out there,"
she answered with her chin.   I went out before long to look for
the Chen-fan Wa-wa.   "The big son, yes," he said; "he was the
one who died.   His body is there, a hundred paces from the *yurt*,
in a hollow.   They did not throw him far enough from the *yurt*;
therefore the wolves have been afraid to come.   You know the
Mongols.   They think there are devils in it.   They are giving
money, food, and already a pony to that wandering lama who
camps away down there.   He is not a good man.   He comes
from a long way — a place in Alashan, which I know.   He was
going to Koko Nor, but he turned aside, because of much talk;
they say there is trouble, and the roads are closed.   He will take
everything he can from this Mongol, who is a good man, for
prayers to lift the curse from the body of his son; then he will
order that the body be thrown farther off, and the wolves will
eat it, and they will say that it is well."

But I was thinking of something else.   I knew now what the
"pneumonia" was.   Typhus had been through that *yurt*.   It
made me a little queasy to think of the lice that must be crawling
over the felts in it, and on the people with whom I had huddled
about the fire.   I looked up typhus in my little book, which en-
joined nursing more than any remedy for that sickness.   I knew
that what little books call nursing was the last attention a Mongol
girl could expect; but with urging I got rest for her, at least,
and in another week she began to pull around.

Her father was a grave, solid man, getting on for fifty, with
a handful of names, both Mongol and Chinese.   He belonged to
a fine class that is not being recruited in large numbers in these
days, being one of those Mongols who used to enter the Chinese
caravans.   Beginning as a camel puller, he had risen to be master
of Chinese caravans, but had left the profession after the closing
of the old roads he favored, and had settled at this place just
over the border from his own tribal country.   As he spoke the
Chinese of Kuei-hua to admiration and had moved among well-

considered men, but remained a sterling Mongol in carriage and instinct, there was much to be learned from his talk.

He stood friend, as openly as he dared, to a couple of Mongols on whom justice was done while I was at San-t'ang Hu. They had stolen half a load of cloth from a caravan, whose mounted men, scouring the country the next day, had overtaken them. They were such inexpert thieves that they confessed their guilt at once and showed where they had hidden the cloth; but the unforgiving Chinese had nevertheless brought them before the officer commanding the post at San-t'ang Hu. As the cloth had a value of more than a hundred Hsin-chiang paper taels, they had laid themselves open to the penalty of death. (A hundred Hsin-chiang taels are roughly equivalent to thirty silver taels, and this sum would equally have merited the sentence of death under the rule of the Christian General at Kuei-hua.)

My friend the officer commanding convened a summary court-martial. After a short address, in which he pointed out to the offenders that, having the good fortune to be within the Chinese boundary and safe from the unleashed disorders of Outer Mongolia, they ought to be more grateful than to start thieving, and recommended them to take notice of his clemency in not sending them to the civil court at Barköl, which would have ordered them to be shot, he gave judgment that they be beaten with three hundred strokes each, on the heel of the left hand. This is a traditional Chinese military punishment, administered with a short stick, flattened at the striking end. The blows do not seem to be more than a sharp tapping, but they can reduce a man's hand to a shapeless pulp. In the civil courts of Ku Ch'eng-tze a similar beating is frequently ordered for inveterate thieves, but on the ankle bone; the bone can be smashed in this way, crippling a man for life.

The Mongols were then held under guard for the night, to be sent back the next day to the *yurt* of the man who had been appointed head of all the Mongols of this fringing territory, and made answerable under a heavy bond for the future good conduct of the two thieves. Before they were dispatched, however, a Chinese came to lay his own case before the commander

of the post. Two ponies of his had been stolen some weeks
before, and two Mongol thieves had now been caught.  If they
had not taken his ponies, they might very well know who was
concerned.  The officer therefore reappointed himself as a court
of inquiry and judge the following day.  The terrified Mongols
could only plead that they were newcomers; that they could
establish that they had only come down from Outer Mongolia
since the theft, and that they had at no time been within a day's
ride of the holding of the Chinese accuser.  The officer retorted
firmly that they were proven caravan robbers and therefore pre-
sumptive horse thieves, and that, being Mongols, they were
beyond doubt incorrigible liars.  He ordered that they be put to
the question under the lash.

This beating was given with the braided lash of a horsewhip,
about seven inches long, between the naked shoulders.  By paying three dollars each to an underofficer and making presents
worth two or three dollars more, the Mongols obtained a false
count of six in ten.  The men who laid on the lashes sang out
the count so skillfully that it would have been hard to detect the
dropped numbers had one not known the procedure.  It must
have been plain enough to the presiding officer; but it was the
custom, and he paid no heed.  In this beating also each lash, as
it was given, did not seem to be heavy; but even so the backs
of the writhing Mongols, held on their knees by men standing on
their legs and holding their outstretched arms, swelled as I
watched into pulpy weals running with blood.  Once the second
in command, the same officer who had set himself against me,
cried out that the lashing was not hard enough, and, snatching
the whip, struck as hard as he could; but though they yelled
pitifully from the moment that the presiding officer gave the
awful word "Strike!" and though an interpreter standing by
gave a cursory rendering of their howls, and in the pause between
each hundred strokes they were commanded to confess their
knowledge and complicity, the two Mongols, seeming to wither in
stature as they blubbered on the ground, could do no more than
promise that they would aid in looking for the stolen ponies.

I saw the two the next day, in the *yurt* of my own Mongol

38. LI ERH, THE LONE-HAND ROBBER ON HIS BARKÖL PONY
"A raider of the Qazaqs who raid the Mongols and the caravans." (p. 288)

39. AUTHOR AND CAPTOR
"San-t'ang Hu is the kind of place that most travelers leave as soon as
they can." (p. 301)

40. "TAOIST PRIESTS," SAN-T'ANG HU
"For funerals they relied on a guild of amateurs." (p. 304)

41. JUSTICE AT SAN-T'ANG HU
"Being Mongols, they were beyond doubt incorrigible liars. He ordered that
they be put to the question under the lash." (p. 308)

friend. Their left hands were very lame and their backs were not comfortable; but they were eating heartily. Both of them were wearing ragged trousers which had once been wadded with cotton — trousers such as soldiers wear. They had both been wearing, when they were brought in, not only good sheepskin trousers but good sheepskin overtrousers on top of all. The escort who was to see them off was now wearing a set of trousers like that.

Both men looked simple and docile. I am quite sure that neither of them harbored any newfangled thoughts about justice and a fair trial. They were primitive Asiatics, and the only thought that would occur to them was that they had offended, not Justice, but Power. If ever they were to drift back to the Mongol side of the border and, by chance, help in half beating the life out of some Chinese who had offended against Power, they might indeed take a vague pleasure in the thought that they were getting a bit of their own back; but the most definite thought likely to be in their heads would be that it was nice to be on the lucky side, and dealing out Justice — I mean Power.

In the meantime I had got on the best of terms with the senior officer, with whom I messed and who allowed me to go where I pleased during the day, so long as I was under escort. He was a good enough fellow, who, after committing himself thoroughly by sending a dispatch to Barköl, began to be afraid that he had gone too far in stopping me at all. Almost every day I went out after antelope, which crowded in every evening to the edge of the oasis to shelter from the worst wind and cold. Each morning a herd of them could be found starting to graze away from exactly the same place, within ten minutes' walk of the village, no matter how often they were thinned out by shooting. They knew a man with a rifle well enough by sight, and would withdraw when they saw me; but until then they would feed calmly within two hundred yards of shouting Mongol and Chinese herd boys. I spent some time in drawing all the wild-poplar thickets around the oasis until I found that up to about ten in the morning, when they went out to the open Gobi to lie in the sun during the warmer hours, becoming automatically true unapproachable desert creatures once more, all that was needed was to stroll up to the nearest camel-herding urchin and ask him where the antelope were.

The first sign that I had not been forgotten by the authorities was the return of my camel man from Barköl. He reported that he had not been able to settle his affairs with the family of the Barköl caravan owner. The man's caravan had reached Barköl many weeks before, but had just gone on to Ku Ch'eng-tze, under the charge of a younger brother; but the old father would not pay up the money owing either to the camel man or to me, saying that the agreement was to be met at Ku Ch'eng-tze, and that the presence of his camels there was good enough security for both of us.

While in Barköl he had been summoned before the Civil Governor, who told him that my passport was in order, but that he could not effect my release from the military arm until confirmation was obtained from the capital. It came out in the end that the Civil Governor was at odds with the Military Governor, who disputed his authority, saying that, as martial law was being enforced along the border, I was a military prisoner, and used my capture to discredit the Civil Governor. He had enough pretext for his action in that the news of my intended arrival, forwarded by the Bureau of Foreign Affairs in Peking to the Governor of Hsin-chiang, had only been circulated to the civil authorities; whereas he claimed that my capture by a military patrol, and my possession of arms, made it necessary for him to refer again to the capital for direct sanction before admitting me to the province. The Civil Governor, however, sent two runners of his *ya-men* out to San-t'ang Hu, with a courteous letter to me and another to the village headman, ordering that I be furnished free with all necessary supplies and given any aid I might require. The headman had been friendly enough with me all during my stay, but, being of the true San-t'ang Hu breed, he stopped short of any expense to his pocket. Seeing that his village was in possession of the military arm, he deferred rather to the soldiers than to the Civil Governor to whom he was nominally responsible.

A day or two later still word came through from the Military Governor, stating that I was to be allowed to proceed, but giving no other orders, so that I was still in a tight place over supplies.[1] I was in urgent need of food for the men, and as for the camels, though I did not own them and by the strict rules of travel they were no affair of mine, it was imperative to take on a ration of feed to carry them through the snowy stages ahead. As the military order had done no more than release me, without restoring me to an honorable position, the prestige I had from the Civil Governor was very shaky. I had said boldly at the beginning that I had no ready cash, so that to bring out money and offer to buy would have spoiled all the prestige that did remain to me; the rapacious villagers would have taken every cent, giving inadequate supplies in return. My only course was to force the requisition of what I needed.

Here Moses and the blessed Tientsin speech bore me to triumph. The only man in San-t'ang Hu not of the scurvy Chenfan blood was the caretaker of the priestless village temple. By his turn of speech he was undoubtedly a Tientsin man, probably from one of the villages near the sea, whose men are called *Hai lang-t'ou*, Sea Hammers, because their bold talk is so forceful that it carries them everywhere. He wept openly when he met Moses; between them the mere community of speech was a sure bond, and when he found that I had the same speech he swore himself unreservedly to my service. He would never tell us his true name, but in his emotion at finding "kinsmen" in his exile among barbarians he spoke out so freely that we soon knew that he had been wanted for desperate murder in Tientsin, had fled to the west, had been proscribed in this province for other crimes, and had at last withdrawn to this oasis at the world's end, where he kept in order the empty temple buildings and raised enough melons against the sunny walls to defray his living in a forgotten old age. Moses found that he had a rich memory of the tales in which men delight who have grown up at village fairs in the talk-loving province of Chih-li, and with

[1] My release was hastened by the representations made on my behalf by the missionaries at Urumchi, the Postal Commissioner, and Mr. Pan — without whose intervention I might never have been allowed to enter the province at all.

that we warmed up a small pot of spirits and invited him to an assemblage, where he enthralled us and the slow-tongued western men with wars and embassies and the doings of prodigious heroes away at the eastern end of the Great Wall, where it abuts on the sea and in time past all things were ordered correctly, the barbarian being held in check on the one side, while in hither China civilization rested.    When the gathering broke up, the exile had so wrought on himself that he confided to Moses an obscure message, which delivered in a certain shop in a certain street in Tientsin would be carried to the right ears, that the remaining relatives might know he was secure in his last years.

To this man Moses, being suddenly inspired, confided that I was the nephew of Dr. Tenney, whose name was wonder-working in Chih-li Province because of things done by him for Chinese friends in the Boxer year, and who had later been American Chargé d'Affaires in Peking.    Nephew I was not; but no matter.    What would have been thought a lie had Moses given it out of his own mouth unsupported was accepted as momentous when it was found that another Chih-li man really knew of a great man whose name was Ting Chia-li, who had done thus and so was linked with this one and that other among the mighty.    I became first the Nephew of the American Ambassador, and then the Nephew of the American Prince, who was of the blood of the American Emperor.

When the retired desperado heard that the villagers of San-t'ang Hu were being sticky about sending me off with due honor, he saddled a donkey and came to my door trembling with anger.    For a whole morning there was talk worthy of a Sea Hammer; the villagers were browbeaten, the *ya-men* runners of the Civil Governor were scourged out of their opium apathy, my enemy the Adjutant was reduced to nerveless terror, and my friend the officer commanding was emboldened to give orders, and everything was set before me.    The nameless old man, still trembling, was put on his donkey.    Bowing, he made his farewells.    He was not yet wholly assured, he said, that the honor of Chih-li Province was beyond reproach; but at least, if the necks of the evil generation of San-t'ang Hu were stiffened against me before my departure, I must let him have word, and he would come up from the patch of sun between the walls of his priestless temple to do a further cleansing.

Not for nothing is it said: " Ten Oily Men from Peking are not the equal of one Boastful Mouth from Tientsin, and ten Boastful Mouths are not the equal of one Dog's Leg of Pao-ting Fu." [1]   " And over and above these three kinds of talking men," said Moses, " you have to reckon with the Sea Hammers."

[1] *Kou-t'uei-tze*, Dog's Leg, is a slang name for the *ya-men* runners of Pao-ting Fu, formerly the capital of Chih-li Province. As this was the high court of appeal for all civil and criminal procedure in the province, these hangers-on had a sinister power on the undersides of the law. (Peking, in the same province, was not the provincial but the Court and Imperial capital.)

# XX

## ORDEAL BY SNOW

It was on the sixteenth day after my arrival at San-t'ang Hu, and the fourth after the order had been given for my release, that we got away; we should have started a day earlier but for a storm that broke the long spell of fine weather, which had lasted over my detention. At San-t'ang Hu we had joined the old Great Road, so that my camel man was at last in country known to him; but still, the last marches between us and Ku Ch'eng-tze were not to be lightly undertaken. The end of the Great Road is, in reality, a choice of three routes: one going straight to Bar Köl and thence by the Road Inside the Mountains, through hilly country, emerging by Mu-li Ho and Ta Shih-t'ou almost at the gates of Ku Ch'eng-tze; one following the outer edge of the mountains for a number of stages, before entering them and joining the first; and a third skirting the mountains all the way. The first two are better than the open desert until the winter has fully set in, but once they are encumbered with snow the only safe way is by the open desert, where in an ordinary winter snow lies neither long nor deep. This route is reckoned at eleven or twelve stages, but owing to unusual snow we had in the end to keep still farther out from the mountains, the distance, at my estimate, running to 230 miles.

What made the prospect most serious for us was that we could count on no company. During my stay at San-t'ang Hu every Kuei-hua caravan had gone by, the last one leaving five days before us. As they were all made up of camels which had been gathered behind the hills north of Kuei-hua during the summer, and had got away, like us, just before the Christian Army surged out of the northwest in retreat, it would be months before another caravan could be assembled at Kuei-hua, as the retreating soldiery must have swept even the outlying hills bare of every kind of transport. Moreover, the season was late, and it was reported that more snow had fallen than had been known for years, though this seemed hard to believe while I was yet in the sunny little *hu* sunk in a hollow in the Gobi, where during the day I did not even have to wear sheepskins when I went out to shoot. The news, however, could not be denied; just before we started a caravan came in from Ku Ch'eng-tze, the last which had attempted the passage Inside the Mountains, where it had been overwhelmed with snow. Out of sixty camels, carrying only travelers and their provisions, and contracted to make a quick journey to Kuei-hua, more than twenty had been "thrown away" in the snow before they could get clear of the hills, and during the struggle the travelers had gone fireless day after day in deep drifted snow. They had been a month on the way.

My own camels were my chief cause for worry. When I had been halted, they were badly worn down by more than three months of travel through lean pastures; but what was left of them was hard and stubborn. Two of them, if they had stumbled on the march, would have gone down and nothing would have got them on their feet again; but it used to amaze me how they would slog along to the end of a forced march, if put to it, and after a rest of twelve or fifteen hours be able to go on again. Indeed, *lo-t'o tung-hsi hao tung-hsi,* "camel things are good things," as the men said; "sweet water, salt water, bitter water, no water; good pasture, bad pasture, no pasture — each day you pull a day, and just the same the camels walk it out." This is the way with camels, however; when they are going on their last strength you may nurse them here a day and lay them off there a day, but on the whole you must keep them moving. If you do not keep them up to the effort they slack away, and then nothing will restore them but the next summer grazing. In fifteen days on a warm pasture ground my camels had gone limp and weak, their tired, stringy muscles relaxing into soft tissue. When they got out of shelter they flinched from the unabated

Gobi wind, hanging back until the tugging nose pegs made them bleed, and one could see that they would be a poor gamble in the stages we had to cover.

Our last send-off was from the good Mongol who had watched over the Chen-fan Wa-wa and the camels while my camel man was away at Barköl. After reciting carefully all the stages and all the chief marks of the road, he presented us with a snow rake, a thing with a solid blade of iron set on a long haft, used to scrape a place for the tent in the snow, and we got away on an afternoon of pale sunshine to make a short initial march. We camped on the open Gobi of black gravel and tamarisk, and the next day were wind-bound in camp, cowering from a vicious gale that plucked at the tent until dark. Just at sunset we had a good omen; I was on my heels by the fire when Moses, who had stuck his nose out to take a look at the signs of the weather, popped back grinning and said, in his best guest-announcing manner, " Old Man God with a present of meat." Moving over to his side of the fire, I could see two half-grown antelope feeding on tamarisk tops within a hundred yards of the tent; whereupon, uncasing the rifle, I squatted comfortably by the fire and dropped one of them. I think this must be a record. The other ran for about twenty yards, then turned to stare. As I could no longer see him from the fireside, I went out of the tent, but the bitter wind rocked me as I knelt, and before I could aim had numbed my bare hands, so that several shots went wild as the second antelope trotted slowly away. When I went to bring in the one I had killed, I found that the tent was wiped out of view by the glare of sunset, and I can only suppose that the antelope, feeding directly toward the sunset, had also failed to see it. I paced the distance at ninety yards.

In the next two marches we passed along at the foot of the lowest of the hills which hedge Bar Köl away from the Gobi; we were never in sight of the lake, but at intervals we could look over to the splendid alignment of the Bar Köl range, noble in height and covered with the aching white of snow, which rose to the south of it. At a point where the outer hills, falling away, allow an easy exit from the lake basin, a road practicable for carts

issues from Barköl town. Here we found an old watchtower
and a solitary decaying inn, which was occupied by another
patrol in the chain marking all the openings between Turkestan
and Mongolia.

Ever since leaving San-t'ang Hu we had been checked by
strong head winds, against which the camels labored without
heart, and the camel man, the only one of us who knew what
trials must lie ahead, brooded over the black bitterness within
him until he was more nearly insane than he had yet been. He
harbored a hate against me because my luck had led us to the
detention at San-t'ang Hu; a hate against Moses because he was
devoted only to my interest, a hate against the Chen-fan Wa-wa
because, he said, the Wa-wa had not looked properly to the grazing of the camels during the last fortnight, so that they had lost
their strength, and a hate against the family of the long-missing
caravan owner who had first united our fortunes, because their
camels had already left Barköl, so that he had neither been able
to hand me over to their care nor yet claim the money they owed
himself. All of these interwoven hates he vented on the Wa-wa,
threatening day and night that he would cast him off, that he
would throw him on the Gobi, that he would turn him away to
starve or freeze. On the morning that we left this desolate place
he spoke to the Wa-wa with worse cruelty than ever, and when
the Wa-wa was stung to an answer he seized the snow rake and
tried to brain him. Moses and I smothered him, and after a
while calmed him enough to get the loads up and start off; but,
knowing that in his wild talk he had shown how he hated the lot
of us, he became more darkly savage than ever. That night,
as we made camp, he hammered in the tent pegs with a horrible
frenzy; the act of striking seemed to waken all his passion again
and he muttered that there was more than one way of dealing
with enemies, that he well knew what could be done with an
iron hammer in the dark of the night when men slept, and so on.
Moses lifted an eyebrow at me, but we took no open notice, not
even whispering together. Fortunately, we both slept light at
that time; there was more toil in every march as we went forward, and what with the nervous tension and the overweariness

that comes from slow plodding against an unrelenting wind, under a fettering weight of clothes, our sleep was always broken. We no longer rode at all; the wind searched one out so on the top of a camel that it could not be borne for long, and as all the camels were so weak it was urgently necessary to divide the loads and ease them as far as possible.

The Qarliq Tagh, the Bar Köl range, and the Bogdo Ola make in general a straight line, but between the ends of the Bar Köl range and the Bogdo Ola there is a gap filled in with rough-and-tumble hills which are not aligned with the same unity of direction. It is through these hills that the roads called Inside the Mountains pass; but as we could not take any of these roads, and as the hills bulge out more to the north than do the massive key ranges, we had to cast to the north in a long slow curve. The first march on from the opening of the Bar Köl depression took us by a group of coal workings, from which coal is hauled in bullock carts to Barköl town. Most of the workings are simply open pits, the coal being exposed at a depth of about two or three feet and having a great thickness; others go farther down, making it necessary to haul up the coal in baskets at the end of a rope which is passed over a wooden wheel and drawn by a bullock which walks from the edge of the pit straight into the desert until the basket reaches the surface, and then returns, to allow the basket to go down again. Much of the coal is burned into coke on the spot.

On the next march I shot a fine antelope buck, which ran across our front at a small distance. We saw many antelope which allowed us to pass amazingly near, because we had no dog; camels and men on the line of march did not worry them in the least. But if I left the line to get nearer them they would be off in a flash.

This march brought us in view of the Baitik Bogdo, a range on our north running up to a central mass of bold peaks, a southern offshoot of the Great Altai. March by march the snow grew deeper, until it was the *ching mien'rh pai*, the "clean face of white" dreaded by the caravans. Several times we met caravans from the west whose masters told us that the farther we went the deeper we should find the snow, and that we should have to expect blizzards every few days. The prevailing wind was from the north or northwest during the day, but after nightfall there came regularly what the Chinese call the "down-the-mountain wind" from the ranges to the south, which struck through tent, sheepskin sleeping bag, and the fur clothes I wore when I slept, even when there was a hot fire of tamarisk burning all night. Then for some days we drew away from the zone of tamarisk growth and could afford ourselves only a small fire of the branches of spindly stray tamarisk we picked up during the day. At times we crossed exposed plains where the snow, worked on unceasingly by the wind, lay only in sharp-edged, frozen riffles; but in general it varied from a few inches to a yard in depth, blanketing any grazing the camels might have had. On account of the extreme cold and the difficulty of grazing, we abandoned the usual routine of night marches. We would break camp in the morning, and make a temporary camp about the warmest time of day, turning the beasts loose to console their tucked-up bellies with what firewood they could see above the snow, while we ourselves gathered bundles of fuel. Then in the late afternoon and evening we would make another short march.

On the eighth day out from San-t'ang Hu, passing over a low, snow-filled divide between indeterminate hilly groups, we came down to a Chinese frontier post established in a rotting fort of mud and stone and brick called Tse-fang. The fort, which was intended to effect a control over the narrowest part of the desert gap between the Baitik Bogdo (a summer range of the Qazaqs) and the Bogdo Ola–Bar Köl mountains, was held by a few "mild-eyed melancholy lotus-eaters" of the least Tennysonian, under the command of an old Manchu. He had been, under the Empire, a high official in Barköl, but under the Republic was glad enough to house the wreck of his fortune in these decrepit walls. He had a moustache of five spiritless hairs on the one side and an icicle on the other; he cultivated a few scratch fields near the fort, kept a few sorry cattle, a scrawny wife, and an emaciated daughter, smoked opium, and allowed me to pitch my tent in the shelter of the fort walls. The only fuel he could furnish was frozen cattle dung, which, when placed on the fire, thawed out damply, giving off a damnable smoke and precious little heat.

Tse-fang has an evil name for winds, of which there was proof in the sharp ridges of frozen snow. As we blundered ahead the snow lay deeper, and we began to come on bare patches scraped in it where one caravan after another had "flopped," as the men say it, unable to face the winds and make the regular stages, making forced camps at intervals of three or five miles without shelter or fuel. On the eve of the twenty-third of December the wind stopped and snow began to fall. "This," said my camel man, "is the famous hoarfrost of Ku Ch'eng-tze, which rimes the whole world from evening until morning"; but I thought that it looked uncommonly like snow. In the morning I was proved right; and, what was more, the snow was still falling. We made an effort to go on, but within a quarter of a mile foundered hopelessly, having veered off the snow-buried trail. The minor undulations of the plain became terrible ditches filled with soft new snow in which the camels lurched to a standstill, waving woebegone heads on long haggard necks. Even their full manes and heavy winter pelage did not disguise their wretched condition. We camped at a loss, while the camel man and I plunged off in the blandly, steadily falling snow, casting for the trail. As a man could not see for more than a few yards, and the snow hushed all shouting, we dared not go far. When we had both returned without any luck the camel man broke down like a craven. He wanted to abandon the loads and turn back for Barköl, saying that neither would he be able to find his way to Ku Ch'eng-tze nor could his camels live to get there. He moaned and whimpered all night, though it did not seem to me that there was any pressing danger. We must be almost within hail of the track, and even if all the camels died we had enough food to last until a caravan came by. The trouble was that, with all the Kuei-hua caravans ahead of us, if we were forced to wait for rescue it would mean being taken in the other direction, back to San-t'ang Hu or Barköl.

The next morning, Christmas Eve, broke dazzlingly clear.

Even the camel man pulled himself together, when we found
the trail half a mile off, a broad avenue running dead straight
through a thin tamarisk growth, the tamarisks having been
cleared off for a width of twenty yards by the ceaseless passing
of caravans. Before long we passed a dead camel and two still
alive — the first abandoned camels we had seen that had not yet
succumbed to the terrible weather — and at the end of the stage
we came into a sheltered hollow in the plain, among low, rounded,
sandy hummocks. The place is called Wu-t'ung Wo-tze, the
Nest or Shelter of Phœnix Trees (Wild Poplars). It swarms
in winter with antelope, and was formerly a well-known wild-ass
ground; but the wild ass in this region has been almost killed off
by the Qazaqs. Both Mongols and Qazaqs will put themselves
to more trouble to bag wild ass than almost any other game;
they consider the meat to be the most delicate eating, while antelope they judge rather inferior to mutton. Wu-t'ung Wo-tze is
one of the winter camping grounds of the Qazaqs, but we saw
none there. They also use it as a halting point when migrating
between their winter grounds and the Baitik Bogdo. When they
are not in camp at the spot, it is one of their favorite ambushes
when they are out raiding caravans, owing to its isolation and
shelter. We kept a watch all night, but there was little danger,
as the severe weather would have kept the boldest raider to his
home camp. We had fuel enough here to burn logs of wild
poplar all night, but they did not make so hot a fire as the blessed
tamarisk, which glows until there is nothing left but an ash of
soft gray powder.

Wu-t'ung Wo-tze is an outcrop of sand a little beyond the
extreme point of an arc of low dunes which runs out from Ku
Ch'eng-tze. Between the dunes and the Bogdo Ola a number
of trails run in to the caravan city, of which we were bound to
take the most northerly, near to the dunes, to keep as far as
possible from the foot of the mountains and the deep snow.
Leaving this camp on Christmas Day, we traveled over a plain
where the wind had scoured the snow to a minimum depth. It
is called Ssu-shih li P'ing-tan, or the Forty Li Level Flat. The
whole plain is grown with nothing but one of the two kinds of

Bar Köl poison grass (really a low shrub, looking very much like tamarisk shoots) and on it somewhere is Yasu Obo,[1] the Obo of Bones. Years ago a Kalgan caravan traveling for the first time by this route, not knowing the poison grass, turned their camels out to feed here and lost almost the whole herd; and their bones have been heaped into an *obo* for a landmark and a warning.

At Wu-t'ung Wo-tze we had camped on bare soil cleared by another caravan, pitching our tent over the still-glowing coals of their fire. This caravan could be only a day ahead of us, and must, we knew, be the one which had started from San-t'ang Hu five days before us. Plenty of signs gave the reason of their slow progress; we were now rarely out of sight of camels cast either by them or the caravans just in advance of them. Many of these camels were still living, and by the way they were plated with frozen snow on one side it was plain to see that the earlier caravans had been impeded more by blizzards than by snowfall. Even when a camel is too numbed and weak to stand, his incredible vitality may keep him living for five or six days, and that under the torture of successive blizzards. They do not get even the cruel mercy of death from the wolves, for, though a wolf will pull down a standing camel, he is daunted by the unnatural sight of a living camel that lies still and waits. Hungry wolves will wait for days until the camel rolls over on his side in the spasm of death. Some of the castaways we saw, however, had not so much as stretched out on their sides, but had died huddled with their legs under them and their necks turned back in a posture of agony, showing how they had tried to shield their heads from the wind, frozen as they lay. Those that still lived would turn their heads, their bodies being powerless, to watch our approach; then turn to the front to follow us with their gaze. I could not shoot them; there was too much at stake, for if I had shot and the weather, say, had turned against us, it would have been attributed to the uneasy ghosts of camels dead by unfitting violence, and blamed on me, and there would have been panic.

[1] It is typical of the half-Mongol character of the Chinese caravan men that they should give this *obo* a Mongol name.

But I remembered the sentry chain of death across the Black Gobi, and thought this worse.

Just before entering Wu-t'ung Wo-tze we had seen, to one side of the clear sunset, a small blue triangle seeming to be lifted above the levels of snow — the veritable Man-t'ou Shan, the Mo-mo Shan, Bread Mountain, the Snow Mountain of Ku Ch'eng-tze, the Great Bogdo, the central peak of the Bogdo Ola. It is a hundred and fifty miles beyond Ku Ch'eng-tze, and we were another hundred miles out. We saw it once more at another sunset, this time with all the range in view, but for most of the day sight would be obscured by a strange dry mist of frosty particles glittering in the sun. I was told that the dunes were not far to our right; at times we could see the loom of them through the mist, and one day we passed two small herds of ponies strayed from Qazaq winter quarters among the sands. On the twenty-sixth of December we caught up with the caravan next before us — a double caravan, an unusual formation, of three hundred camels, the men being divided into two tents under two caravan masters because of their numbers. This was one of the two double caravans belonging to T'ien I Tsan, the richest of all the firms now engaged in the caravan trade. Long ridges of heaped snow showed where they had been digging out their loads. The men said they had been two days in this camp, having been pinned to it by two blizzards, and that they had been through one storm after another — storms that we had missed by a day or two — all along the road since leaving San-t'ang Hu. Three other caravans had been camped with them; these others had got away in the morning, but they had remained, partly because of the number of loads they had to dig out, partly for the sake of some of their camels, which lay by the tents, badly numbed, but perhaps recoverable. It was an unchancy place for a camp, badly exposed and too far from fuel for either comfort or safety, but I weakened as much as the others to the temptation of company, and we took up the cleared space and living coals left by one of the other caravans.

The next morning broke still and fine — clear, that is, overhead, but misty around the horizons. Fair pasture was to be

42. THE AUTHOR'S CARAVAN PASSES AN
ABANDONED CAMEL
"To kill it might make its troubled soul follow the other camels . . .
bringing them ill luck." (p. 115)

found about two miles to the north, on the verge of the dunes, so the camels were sent out to get a bite. About noon a breeze moved over the plains from the mountains to the south; in a quarter of an hour it had swollen to a *buran*, a kind of gale with more terror in it than any wind I know. Overhead the sky remained a thin, pale, cloudless blue, but across the plain there blew steadily, without gust or lull, a barrier of dry driven snow ten or fifteen feet in height. The Chen-fan Wa-wa was out with my camels, along with the T'ien I Tsan herd. The T'ien I Tsan people, knowing they could not work three hundred camels back against such a wind, told him it was sure death to try to get back to the tents. They could only huddle in the lee of their camels, digging down into the snow, and wait for the end of the storm; but he said stubbornly that he must go back. He had just loaded one of the camels with tamarisk, and stringing the eight together he worked his way back, half the time on his hands and knees. He said that he nearly missed the tent, as he could neither see nor hear, but that just as he was passing he " smelt camp." The camel man had started out to retrieve his camels at the beginning, but came back whimpering that it was all up; it was *yao-ming, yao-ming* — sure death, sure death. I had also made an attempt, but I could not stand upright even going before the wind; and realizing that I did not know exactly where the camels were, and could not get back if I found them, I came into the tent again. When the boy reached us his face, throat, and chest were sheathed in ice.

We turned out, scrabbled a hole in a drift where the camels might kneel, and stacked the loads for a windbreak. In a few moments they were covered with snow, which kept them warm. The wind roared with the same appalling steadiness for hours, driving harsh grains of snow through the double cotton-canvas thickness of the tent that stung and numbed us with a creeping cold. The tent, though we banked it high with snow, sagged far over, and only in the lee of the fire was there any warmth. Some time after dark — I think it was only about half-past seven — the wind shut off as though a gate had been closed. There was an awful, ringing silence for a few moments, then a backwash of wind from the north in a few gusts, then peace. "It came like a train and it stopped like a train," said the Chinese. "'Toot!' she comes and 'Bang!' she stops." We hovered by the fire, dozing, for we dared not lie down. The fuel was running out, and the cold when the wind blew was nothing to the cold that settled down on us when the wind had passed.

At about four in the morning we heard bleating, and a young Qazaq crawled in at the door of the tent, speechless and dizzy with exhaustion. Like the Wa-wa, his throat and chest were in a cast of ice — which really, by allowing a thin film of body warmth to form between it and the skin, is a protection against frostbite. This was the first time I had heard a man's breath rattling in his throat, and at first it scared me. After ten minutes in the warmth of the fire, but not too near it, he began to recover a little. He had been rounding up strayed sheep and goats when the wind caught him; he had kept on his feet and kept his flock together as only a nomad could have done, and after lasting out the storm had struggled on until he saw our light. Had he not seen it, he would have died, for he was far gone and the temperature was dropping steadily. My fiendish camel man was picking up his courage again, in the way he had; he wanted to throw the man out " for a thief of a Ha-sa (Qazaq)," and would give him neither food nor tea, which so angered me that I gave him half the bread that remained to us — we had not enough left for a full meal, as, owing to the long time we had been over these few stages, our food had given out, and there were no more antelope to shoot. The Qazaq ate dejectedly, dipping the bread in tea.

At dawn the hardy young devil, still weary but a little stronger, went off with his flock toward the dunes, while we packed up to run from the place of ill omen. The tent was rigid with ice so that it could not be rolled, but had to be draped on a camel; and the camels so badly done that they could not rise until dug free of the snow. One of them, carrying only a light half-load, had to be lifted to its feet by three men. The wind rose again that morning to a great fury; but, though we could see the barrage of snow rushing across the plain behind us, we were already on the edge of the deadly place, and, descending slowly, got clear away. We had been able to run for it because we had four men to handle only eight camels; but the big double caravan, slow in assembling, failed to get away and for the third day in succession " found weather."

We came down to the dunes, which here curved across our way, the place being called Sha Men-tze, the Gates of Sand, and fetched up with the three caravans of which we had already heard. Two of them were small, traveling very light. They belonged to traders who had failed in a clever enterprise. Their plan had been to smuggle grain and flour into Mongolia, exchange them for ponies, and, to avoid the risk of entering Hsinchiang again, go on to sell the ponies at Kuei-hua; but, owing to the disagreement between the Civil and Military *ya-men* at Barköl, their bribery of underlings had gone amiss, and they had been so heavily fined in both courts that the owners were faced with ruin. With one of them was a young Chih-li trader who had taken the opportunity of trying to collect some debts owing to his firm in Mongolia; and, being ill at ease alone among western men, he clave at once to Moses and me for comfort. In the same caravan was a pock-marked Sand Hollow Mouse, the only one of his kind I ever found to have bowels of kindness, who knew the Wa-wa's family by name and offered to help him in Ku Ch'eng-tze for old sake's sake.

My camel man, instead of improving in temper as he got his camels nearer to Ku Ch'eng-tze, grew more morose at every stage, and again began to turn his senseless and evil spite on the Wa-wa. As for me, I had been lying back for months, waiting for my revenge, and now at last his insane passion delivered him into my hand. After a night spent shivering in a hole in the snow, without enough fuel, the Wa-wa went off to the tent of his new-found friend. He spent the whole morning there, while the camel man grew black in the face with wordless anger. When it came time to load and start, and the work had been done and the camels kicked and lifted to their feet, he spoke to the Wa-wa a few low words, with the narrowed eyes and the snarl that meant he was looking for trouble. The Wa-wa was not up to the challenge, but fell back — ordered off into the snow to shift for himself, hopeless and ready to sit down and die, in the way that his kind have when their spirit is broken. Seeing what was on, I spoke to him, telling him to follow us and appear at camp, when I would make things right. Then I told Moses to speak with the Chih-li man in the other caravan, telling him to stand by for a row. He did this very quietly; then the two of us fell in behind our few camels and we were off, well in advance of the other caravans.

I could see what was in the camel man's mind. What he had done was in part to ease his blind hate of all the world and his own destiny; but in part it was to free himself of an obligation and to discredit me when we arrived in Ku Ch'eng-tze. The Wa-wa, though nominally in his employ on the promise of wages, was really under my protection and had been living on my food. This was known throughout the caravans, and if I abandoned the Wa-wa it would be a public sign that the camel man had mastered me. There was also the matter of the camels, which had undoubtedly been saved by the Wa-wa when he brought them out of the blizzard into a measure of shelter; if he arrived in Ku Ch'eng-tze without having been sacked, he would have a strong claim against the camel man.

Moses and I took further counsel as the camel man, striding ahead, put more swagger into the swing of his shoulders at every step. The Chen-fan Wa-wa, unless I came to his aid, would be in a bad way. His only friend was a camel puller, and that friend would not be able to bring him into his tent. The law of the caravans was very plain. It was not the business of any caravan master to look into the right and wrong of a quarrel between a camel owner and his servant; if the servant was cast off, no other caravan master could take sides by admitting him to more hospitality than a casual meal between marches. The Wa-wa might perhaps reach a village; but village folk are hard, and the west is full of rogues. A vagrant coming in from the desert must obviously have been driven out from a caravan, and they would think him evidently guilty of some bad crime, and refuse to aid him. So far as my camel man was concerned, he had knowingly uttered sentence of death.

Moses at first was inclined to counsel submission and advise me to let the Wa-wa abide by his destiny, which was obviously full of evil, while we settled our own affairs in Ku Ch'eng-tze. He himself had had most of the heart taken out of him by cold and privation; but when I insisted that the issue must be forced, he pulled himself together and we soon had our business before the meeting under its different heads. In the first place there was the old reason for not walloping the camel man in a forthright manner as he deserved: namely, that the affair would immediately be regarded as one between foreigner and Chinese, and I should be put hopelessly in the wrong. In the second place, we must keep on the right side of caravan custom, in so far as it could possibly apply to a quarrel out of the ordinary run of caravan troubles. This brought us to grips; the camel man's offense against me must be strained into an offense against caravan custom. Before long our plan grew out before us with the devastating logic of true inspiration.

"When we have made camp," said Moses, "you will talk softly with the camel man. You will ask him as a favor to take back the Wa-wa. But, because you did not challenge him at the moment he turned off the Wa-wa, he will think you are afraid of him; therefore he will heap humiliation on you, that he may have things to boast of in the future. He will refuse to take back the Wa-wa. Then you will say, 'But let the Wa-wa eat my food and follow our camp, and have nothing to do with you, but let me at least have a little merit.' Thereupon the man, being carried away, will threaten you and refuse to carry you and your loads if you have anything more to do with the Wa-wa; and then we will strike." That was it. We both well knew that the core of the whole caravan code and tradition is that the carrier must deliver loads and travelers. He may exceed the time limit, infringe one clause or another of the agreement, cumber his case with sins of commission and omission; but at the latter end he must deliver his loads intact and in good order or be deprived of all standing in the craft.

The plan worked like doom. We reached that night a deserted inn at a place called Hsi Ch'üan, the West Spring, overtaking yet three more caravans. All the caravans planned to halt at this place and send a few men and picked camels through the snow to a village to the south, to get provisions, of which we were all desperately short. Our camp was in shelter of the old inn yard, and for fuel we had the rafters of the buildings. We could stand a siege, for the others would share their provisions with us even if they gave no other support. When all was in order I approached the camel man diffidently. He was sitting next the door of the tent, making tea for himself, looking at us sardonically but not speaking. He heard me out; then said brutally that he had taken his decision; I might like it or lump it, and the Wa-wa might freeze or starve—he wished to hear no more pleadings. Then I suggested, still mildly, that the Wa-wa's wages be forgotten; he ought to be grateful only for being taken to Ku Ch'eng-tze. Let him live quietly in the tent, which, after all, was mine, and eat my food, and let the camel man ignore him. The fellow sat back and filled a pipe. Then he said, tasting his triumph in every word, "If he comes along and uses your tent, let him carry your tent. My camels will not carry it. If he uses your food and cooking pot, let him carry them—not my camels." "Do you mean to say," I asked, still deprecatingly, "that you will not carry these things, which are mine?" "Of course I won't," he answered.

Then I changed front. "If you won't carry my things," I said, "get out of my tent, and get out quickly. I have finished with you." He began to mitigate his words, at that; but "Too late!" I said, and "Go!" I said, and "Go!" said Moses; and, taking him by the neck and the trousers, we heaved him into a deep bank of snow. As he fell I locked his neck in chancery and twisted it, but took care not to mark him, for at all costs we must remain in the right. When he got up, Moses first getting off him as he lay sprawled, I warned him away from my tent under threat of treating him as a thief, while Moses made haste to get in the first word at as many tents as possible. The formal ejection was nicely touched off by the arrival of the Wa-wa, who came straggling in just in time to see the satisfaction which we consummated after so many tens of days.

It was a beautiful feeling. I had my revenge, I had it complete, and I had it in such a Chinese dressing that no one could round on me with the countercharge of having behaved like a Frightful Foreigner. It was common knowledge among all the caravans that I had stood more than any Chinese traveler has to suffer. Also my fine fellow had committed the ultimate crime of his craft: he had refused to carry me or my goods, according to contract. The repudiation was his. When the news spread through camp, the bitter laughter of Asia went up. Everyone was glad to see the swagger taken out of the man. Then, as the more sober among them began to think how this business would look in Ku Ch'eng-tze, they took other counsel. After all, to say in the middle of a desert of snow that you will not carry your passengers is no light threat. The man would be irretrievably ruined. Peacemakers came before me. Would I not be a little easy?

I stuck to my point. Everyone could see that I was not pressing this quarrel except in the name of fair dealing, so that all men might judge between me and this other for righteousness. I must clear my name and dignity. I would not hush up the quarrel, nor would I talk again with the man. If he had a case, let him not put it here through peacemakers, but come to Ku Ch'eng-tze and go with me before a magistrate. Then a committee of caravan masters came to present other arguments. They had the Chinese distaste for pushing a thing to extremes, and a Chinese preference for settling disputes in a guild court, as it were, and above all they were anxious not to take too strong a part against a man of the same craft; but I was unshaken still. I said I would leave Moses and the Wa-wa in charge of my camp and make my own way to Ku Ch'eng-tze, to get other camels. At this point the Chih-li trader came in strongly to my support, as I had known he would, not being embarrassed like the others by being of the caravan trade. In the end I secured all I wanted, and the master of the unladen caravan made me a ceremonial offer of free transport into Ku Ch'eng-tze " for the good name of all the caravans."

Of course the long-faced, black-hearted camel man was

brought low forever, and at the same time all my affairs in Ku Ch'eng-tze were simply resolved. The original caravan owner whose contract I held still owed me one hundred dollars and one hundred and twenty taels to the camel man. When I demanded my hundred dollars, his brother must pay at once or come before a magistrate who would hear that the family representative had passed on the contract to a notorious rogue, who by his own boast had been a runner to bandits. On the other hand, this man would certainly not be paid his hundred and twenty taels, nor could he get it without going before a magistrate. But if a magistrate knew that he had openly repudiated his contract, and that he was known to be an associate of bandits, he would condemn him to imprisonment if not to death, and at the least would have all his camels confiscated. Had he not boasted that at least two had been presented to him by bandits?

And so it fell out. My affairs went nicely enough; I never knew how he arranged his, but he was refused payment and was stranded in Ku Ch'eng-tze without a cent and with eight worn-out camels that could not sell for anything like their real value. He came once to beg my intercession; but he did not get it. I was going out that day to a feast, with my very good friend the Eldest Son of the House of Chou; and Moses went too.

We halted another full day by the deserted inn; then, provisioned again, we took up the march for Ku Ch'eng-tze. Only three or four stages remained, but they were long, and men and camels were pushed to the last possible effort. I became so tired and cold that I let my journal go, and afterwards, running day and night together in my memory, could not even be sure of my count. I had now only one desire: to make Ku Ch'eng-tze, conclude the settlement of my caravan affairs, and hurry on a hundred and fifty miles more to Urumchi, where I should get the first news of my wife, without which I could neither concert our plans for meeting far and far away on the Siberian border nor sketch out our further journeys in Chinese Central Asia.

Also it was necessary to get Moses in to shelter and a little

rest at least.   He plodded along — the cold made riding unthink-
able — with slow, solid determination, never complaining except
with a joke, like the good fellow he was; but the long exposure
was telling on him.   His eyes were hollow, his sometime plump
cheeks were colorless and pasty, and he moaned and muttered
in his sleep.   What was discomfort to me was privation to him,
and he had done gallantly for a fattish man of forty, who for
near twenty years had confined his exercise to walking a mile
or so to market and coming back in a rickshaw.

As for me, I was, by the end of it, leg-weary and dizzy with
strained fatigue; but yet I cannot remember without exaltation
the magnificent sense of brutal, long-drawn effort and slow at-
tainment in those last stages of the last twenty-odd days between
San-t'ang Hu and Ku Ch'eng-tze.   The snow got deeper every
mile, until it was impossible to travel except on a narrow trail,
less than a foot wide, packed and frozen so hard that the camels,
not being designed for slippery going, could hardly stagger on
it and would continually plunge off to welter in soft drifts.   We
sweated as we lurched ahead, and froze the moment we stood
still.   I remember that we entered a series of depressions along
the foot of the Bogdo Ola, the winter grounds of the Erh-hun-tze,
the Bastards, a mixed race descended from Chinese fathers and
Mongol mothers who are found in these mountains and of whom
I had also seen a few in the Metshin Ola.   Here the snow was
broken by spikes of *Chih-chi* grass.   We were out of the winds,
but a still, ringing, iron cold closed in on us.   The end of it was
that we reached an inn, joining the summer cart road that goes
Inside the Mountains; and on the last day I rode ahead with
the Chih-li trader, he dressed as a Mongol, as is the custom of
the Chinese who trade among the Mongols.   Our riding camels
came down time and again on the slippery footing, pitching us
off, until at last we were forced to lead them, scrambling and
falling ourselves.   Then the mist lifted — it was not long after
sunrise — and I, one hundred and thirty days and more out from
Kuei-hua, it being now about the second of January, 1927, saw
Ku Ch'eng-tze lying before me in a hollow, a walled city muffled
in snow: the far city of the caravans, the gate of Inner Asia.

Mongolia was cast behind. An hour later we led our camels under the city gate, and almost the first voice I heard was a hail from the camel puller with the nickname too wonderful for print, he of the House of Chou whom I had treated for the bellyache when everyone else thought he was possessed of a ghost.

"And this really means," I thought a little mournfully in my triumph, "that I am hardly any more a traveler. I have been a traveler."

43. THE AUTHOR WITH THE VILLAINOUS CAMEL PULLER AND
ANTELOPE (GAZELLE) NEAR SAN-T'ANG HU
"The long-faced, black-hearted camel man was brought low forever." (p. 330)

44. ROOFS OF KU CH'ENG-TZE
"A walled city muffled in snow." (p. 332)

45. CARAVAN MERCHANTS' GUILD, KU CH'ENG-TZE
"The gate of Inner Asia." (p. 332)

46. SHENSI MERCHANTS' GUILD, KU CH'ENG-TZE
"The Tower of Springs and Autumns."

# APPENDIX

## SUMMARY OF ROUTE, STAGE BY STAGE, KUEI–HUA—KU CH'ENG–TZE

*(Directions and distances by rough estimate)*

| Date | Days out from Kuei-hua | No. of stage | | Total in miles from Kuei-hua | General direction |
|---|---|---|---|---|---|
| 20 Aug. '26 | 1 | 1 | Leave Kuei-hua, travel over open farming country to inn at opening of valley into Ta Ch'ing Shan. Name of halt, Pa K'ou (Mouth of Pass). Distance of stage 7 miles. | 7 | N |
| 21 Aug. '26 | 2 | 2 | Ascent by valley bed over Wukung Pa (Pass), then a long slow pull up again to the open rolling country of the Mongolian plateau. Halt at village within sight of K'o Chen. Distance of stage 23 miles. | 30 | N |
| 22 Aug. '26 | 3 | 3 | Pass, without entering, K'o Chen (Mongol name Kukuirghen, Blue Cloth; Chinese *K'o* stands for *kuku, Chen* means, according to context, a military post or a township; official Chinese name, Wuch'üan Hsien, District City of the Five Springs. Headquarters of Chinese settlement on the plateau in this region. Telephone communication with Kuei-hua). From here follow any one of a number of cart roads connecting villages to NW; occasional villages and farmed land; much good grazing. Halt at | | |

| Date | Days out from Kuei-hua | No. of stage | | Total in miles from Kuei-hua | General direction |
|---|---|---|---|---|---|
| | | | Chao Ho (Temple River), Mongol name Shara-muren (Yellow River). Small stream flowing inland; catchment area of Yellow River and Pacific drainage now over-passed. Mongol temple, with Living Buddha; mud fort of Pao Shang T'uan. Here formerly point of divergence of roads going to Urga, Uliassutai, and Ku Ch'eng-tze. Distance of stage 25 miles. | 55 | NW |
| 23 Aug. '26 | 4 | 4 | Continue over rolling country, passing Ulan Nor (Red Lake), a small tarn of salt water. Halt at Ts'a-ts'a (Chinese name adapted from Mongol). Up to this village, cheap grain supplies can be had, but little else. Distance of stage 25 miles. | 80 | NW |
| 24 Aug. '26 | 5 | 5 | Rolling plateau country, fine pasture. Cross grass-grown dike of indeterminate length, evidently relic of earthwork fortification. Halt at Pai-ling Miao (Temple of the Larks). Small stream flowing NE. Small hills all about. Caravan pastures now reached. This is now true starting point of all caravan routes from Kuei-hua. Distance of stage 40 miles. | 120 | NW |
| 25 Aug. '26 | 6 | — | Halt. | | |
| 26 Aug. '26 | 7 | — | Halt. | | |
| 27 Aug. '26 | 8 | 6 | Rolling country, first-class pasture. Halt at Suji (Mongol name for one of the bones of a sheep), a well and | | |

| Date | Days out from Kuei-hua | No. of stage | | Total in miles from Kuei-hua | General direction |
|---|---|---|---|---|---|
| | | | camping ground. Distance of stage 25 miles. | 145 | W |
| 28 Aug. '26 | 9 | — | Halt. | | |
| 29 Aug. '26 | 10 | 7 | March through fine rolling pasture. Range on North, Mongol name Boyeh Bogdo; Chinese name Hei Shan (Black Mountains). Halt at Erlidsengegen; a small pool, a tiny stream, some marshy bottom land. Chinese cultivation advancing from South due to occupy this land next year. Distance of stage 12 miles. | 157 | W |
| 30 Aug. '26 | 11 | 8 | Fine pasture. Pass to North of two small lakes, Bagan Nor and Ikki Nor. Halt on verge of hilly country. Distance of stage 13 miles. | 170 | W |
| 31 Aug. '26 | 12 | 9 | Advance into hilly country. (There is another way round, to N.) Halt at Chinese camel-tax inspectorate. All this country called Yang-Ch'ang-tze Kou, the Valley or Valleys of Sheep Stations. Distance of stage 7 miles. | 177 | S of W |
| 1 Sept. '26 | 13 | 10 | Through low rounded hills. Halt in watered valley. Yang-ch'ang-tze Kou, general name of district, belongs to this valley in particular. Due to be occupied by Chinese settlers next year. Distance of stage 14 miles. | 191 | SW |
| 2 Sept. '26 | 14 | 11 | Out of watered valley (which corresponds probably to Khundu-ling | | |

| Date | Days out from Kuei-hua | No. of stage | | Total in miles from Kuei-hua | General direction |
|------|------|------|------|------|------|
| | | | Gol of Prjevalsky and Muli Ho of Younghusband) through hills for 5 or 6 miles; then long plain. Road from Pao-t'ou converges on Small Road. Hills of decayed rock on N, Wu-la Shan on S. (Mountains of the Oirat Mongols, a division of Ulancahp League.) Distance of stage 26 miles. | 217 | W |
| 3 Sept. '26 | 15 | 12 | Follow base of N hills, then enter them to pass round Mongol temple. Halt in low barren hills. Camp called by several names, of which one is Gaidsegai-khutu (*khutu* probably for *khuduk*, Mongol for well). Distance of stage 22 miles. | 239 | W |
| 4 Sept. '26 | 16 | — | Halt. | | |
| 5 Sept. '26 | 17 | 13 | Morning march through arid country to brackish pool in sight of lamasery called by Chinese Hoshatu Miao (10 miles). Evening march still through arid country. Halt by brackish pool called Hasakhutu (16 miles). A few Oirat Mongols. Distance of stage 26 miles. | 265 | W |
| 6 Sept. '26 | 18 | — | Halt. | | |
| 7 Sept. '26 | 19 | — | Halt. | | |
| 8 Sept. '26 | 20 | — | Halt. | | |
| 9 Sept. '26 | 21 | 14 | Hilly country, slightly better pasture. Ten miles NW to an *obo*; 7½ miles W to lower country; 2½ miles S, turning away from the | | |

| Date | Days out from Kuei-hua | No. of stage | | Total in miles from Kuei-hua | General direction |
|---|---|---|---|---|---|
| | | | Small Road to Morhgujing (approximate version of Mongol name). This is beginning of the Winding Road. Camping place a depression with poor pasture among low, barren hills. Distance of stage 20 miles. | 285 | W |
| 10 Sept. '26 | 22 | 15 | Through small gap in hills into uneven country of loose, sandy soil. So far as this, easy going for carts; henceforward it would be difficult for anything on wheels. Pass *obo* called Ulan-gangan Obo; marks end of Ulangangan hills, which are outliers or an extension of Wu-la Shan. Descending slowly, halt in front of Lao-hu Shan (Tiger Mountains) which presumably connect to NW or WNW with Hurku hills of Prjevalsky and Younghusband, and to S or SE with Lang Shan. Distance of stage (5 miles NW, 5 miles SW) 10 miles. | 295 | W |
| 11 Sept. '26 | 23 | 16 | Through Lao-hu Shan; 6 miles NW to top of pass; 2½ miles W over small plateau; ½ hour descent, then 11½ miles SW over sandy, hummocky plain to Chaganerlegen (said to mean White Springs). Water by digging in dry stream bed. Distance of stage 20 miles. | 315 | WSW |
| 12 Sept. '26 | 24 | 17 | Through same sort of country. Cultivated land about 35 miles to S. Few Mongol *yurts* and camps of Chinese selling grain. Halt at Modajing (Chinese corruption of Mon- | | |

| Date | Days out from Kuei-hua | No. of stage | | Total in miles from Kuei-hua | General direction |
|------|------------------------|--------------|--|------------------------------|-------------------|
| | | | gol name). Hills in front, called Khara-terugen, said to mean Black Hilltops; to SW a glimpse of blue mountains, the main range of the Lang Shan. Temple in sight to S. Distance of stage 16 miles. | 331 | SSW |
| 13 Sept. '26 | 25 | 18 | Ascend into Black Hilltops, which must be foothills of Khara-narin of Prjevalsky, which in turn are evidently the Lang Shan. Better pasture in small isolated areas. Cross small streams. Camp among hills. Mongols very few. Distance of stage 19 miles. | 350 | SW |
| 14 Sept. '26 | 26 | 19 | On through Khara-terugen. Road cut up by gullies, small but difficult for loaded camels. Camp with no name. Distance of stage 13 miles. | 363 | SW |
| 15 Sept. '26 | 27 | 20 | Out of Khara-terugen to camp at group of traders' posts in shallow dry valley with gravelly clay banks, close to Large Mongol temple called Shandan Miao (Mongol *shandan*, said to mean a small brook, Chinese *miao*, a temple). A traverse from here North to Small Road and across it to Urga. Poor country, but important junction of trade routes. Western limit of Ulanchap League and true Inner Mongolia; beyond is Alashan. "Shandan" marked on Prjevalsky's map. Country between Morhgujing (where my route left that of Younghusband, who fol- | | |

| Date | Days out from Kuei-hua | No. of stage | | Total in miles from Kuei-hua | General direction |
|---|---|---|---|---|---|
| | | | lowed the Small Road) and Shandan Miao previously unexplored. Distance of stage 12 miles. | 375 | SW |
| 16 Sept. '26 | 28 | 21 | Pass near temple. Enter heavy dunes. Camp at Ulan Nor (Red Lake), a salt pool on a clay floor among dunes. Distance of stage 13 miles. | 388 | W of S |
| 17 Sept. '26 | 29 | 22 | Out through the dunes, which extend in a huge sweep N and NW. Then loose, sandy country, spear grass, and thorns. Few Mongols. Camp by very low clay hills at well called Hoshatu (Mongol name, said to mean The Hollow Place, or The Gap). Distance of stage 16 miles. | 404 | W of S |
| 18 Sept. '26 | 30 | 23 | Heavier sand; in places ankle-deep. Halt by knot of clay hills, called Hasabuchi. Group of *yurts*, some belonging to Chinese traders. Cultivated land now left behind, the nearest being to SE. From high point near camp sand hills can be seen to N; more sand hills to S and SW, backed by blue hills. Southerly course followed for last few marches is to get through sandy area at its most practicable. Distance of stage 12 miles. | 416 | W of S |
| 19 Sept. '26 | 31 | 24 | Slowly down to big depression. Halt by a salt mere, partly smothered by dunes. Huge dunes on S. A few elms, all old. Distance of stage 13 miles. | 429 | NW |

| Date | Days out from Kuei-hua | No. of stage | | Total in miles from Kuei-hua | General direction |
|---|---|---|---|---|---|
| 20 Sept. '26 | 32 | 25 | Up from depression to plain of sandy clay, arid and poor pasture, passing temple called Tukomen Miao — by presumption, the Baintukhum of Prjevalsky. Halt by big dunes on S, at small pool. To N, wide clay plain, clay buttes. Mongol camps in distance. Saline water. Camp, or pool, called Jagasatai (approximate pronunciation), probably compounded from Mongol word pronounced by Chinese *jagang*, a tamarisk. Distance of stage 16 miles. | 445 | WNW |
| 21 Sept. '26 | 33 | 26 | Skirting dunes, then leaving them behind, pass through strip of tamarisk jungle, the first seen. Then arid, hard plain. In spite of poverty and emptiness of country, Chinese traders encamped at two places. Halt at well called Shihni-usu. Distance of stage 15 miles. | 460 | N of W |
| 22 Sept. '26 | 34 | 27 | Over plains; into and out of depression representing ancient lake bed. Poor grazing everywhere. Halt by two wells, called Dir Usu (Bad Water?) also Khayir-khutu (i.e. Khayir-khuduk, Pair of Wells). Camp of Chinese trader. Distance of stage 20 miles. | 480 | W |
| 23 Sept. '26 | 35 | 28 | Arid country, but several traders. Low barren hills close on N, distant blue mountains to S said to be the border of Kan-su; possibly beginning of Yabarai range indicated by Kozloff. Distance of stage 17 miles. | 497 | W |

| Date | Days out from Kuei-hua | No. of stage | | Total in miles from Kuei-hua | General direction |
|------|------|------|------|------|------|
| 24 Sept. '26 | 36 | 29 | In morning 4 miles W to camp near trader. In evening NW through low, barren, red hills, passing some elms in dry watercourse; out of hills to camp in flat, circular plain. Distance of stage 20 miles. | 517 | NW |
| 25 Sept. '26 | 37 | 30 | Through sandy, hummocky country to well. Distance of stage 17 miles. | 534 | WNW |
| 26 Sept. '26 | 38 | 31 | Through desolate country, stratified clay showing above thin, loose sand; bear N to round hills on S; then up to higher level with hills on S and N, to camp with thin, black, slaty or volcanic gravel overlying sandy soil. Distance of stage 17 miles. | 551 | W |
| 27 Sept. '26 | 39 | 32 | Through region called Kharajagang, the Black Tamarisks. Skeleton growth of dead tamarisks. Black and yellow sand, outcrops of black rock, all shivered in a flat stratification, like slate. Barren hills on front, larger hills at distance S, probably the Yabarai; road through these to Chen-fan. Traders in two places in apparently uninhabited country. Water from wells, bitter. Hills on front rise to triple peak called Soyakheilikun (? Sayir-khayir-khan) said to mean Overlapping Teeth. Pass by these through dry hills by narrow dry gullies; camp at Sharahulasu (? Shara-khur-usu, Yellow Reed Water). A small marsh | | |

| Date | Days out from Kuei-hua | No. of stage | | Total in miles from Kuei-hua | General direction |
|---|---|---|---|---|---|
| | | | smothered in sand; water yellow and viscous, bitter from tamarisk roots. An outer scarp of hills bars camp from open desert; barren hills S and W, probably backbone of Sands of Badain-jarenghi of Kozloff; skirts of hills buried in sand. Distance of stage 24 miles. | 575 | WNW |
| 28 Sept. '26 | 40 | 33 | Scramble out through sand on to desert; low clay bluffs showing through sandy soil; small dunes blown up against hills. Track bears away from hills. Camp in unrelieved desert; said to be well at some distance, but of bad water. Distance of stage 18 miles. | 593 | W |
| 29 Sept. '26 | 41 | 34 | Ten miles over hard, flat, sandy gravel. Then 2 hours through heavy dunes, with tamarisk growth. Then sandy hummocks, and past an *obo* marking two wells close together; then another well, where camp. This is beginning of region known to caravan men as Kuai-tze Hu, the Depression of Goitso of Kozloff. Country from Bain-tukhum (Tukomen Miao) to this point previously unexplored. Distance of stage 16 miles. | 609 | WNW |
| 30 Sept. '26 | 42 | 35 | Sandy for 5 or 6 miles, then pass *obo*. At 11 miles through small dunes for ½ hour. Country so far very much smothered by sand. At 14 miles a well called the Well of the Wu-t'ung (*toghraq* or wild poplar). Then wells every mile or so. Camp at Obo Ch'üan (Spring | | |

| Date | Days out from Kuei-hua | No. of stage | | Total in miles from Kuei-hua | General direction |
|---|---|---|---|---|---|
| | | | of the Obo). Big pool near by and wide reedy swamps, perhaps masking other pools. Distance of stage 23 miles. | 632 | W |
| 1 Oct. '26 | 43 | 36 | Through half-marshy country to camp near large reed beds trending N. The heavy dunes are here well to S. Distance of stage 14 miles. | 646 | W |
| 2 Oct. '26 | 44 | 37 | Same half-marshy country. Keep nearer to dunes on S. Small pools and runlets of water, many reeds. Water gradually becomes less evident. Distance of stage 15 miles. | 661 | W |
| 3 Oct. '26 | 45 | 38 | Country becomes drier. Camp in small plain of soft earth and cropped-off reeds. Dunes now close in on left and left front, going away to NW in big sweep. Good well, unlimited water, but tastes of soda. This is last camp in Kuaitze Hu. Distance of stage 8 miles. | 669 | W |
| 4 Oct. '26 | 46 | 39 | Enter dunes at once, about 60 feet high; vigorous growth of tamarisk. At 2 miles, a well; at 2½ hours the dunes are bare of tamarisk. In another hour, tamarisks again. Halt by big *obo* of tamarisk boughs; shrine inside *obo*. Distance of stage 17 miles. | 686 | W |
| 5 Oct. '26 | 47 | 40 | Bare dunes again; reaching, say, 100 feet in height. Still higher dunes in view both N and S. Even between highest dunes are sometimes bare patches of clay. Dunes gradually get lower, and tamarisk | | |

| Date | Days out from Kuei-hua | No. of stage | | Total in miles from Kuei-hua | General direction |
|------|------|------|------|------|------|
| | | | growth increases. Camp when dunes begin to decline to mere hummocks. No well. Distance of stage 18 miles. | 704 | W |
| 6 Oct. '26 | 48 | 41 | Shallow sand most of the way; tamarisks and other desert plants. Then a few small dunes, from which emerge into plains. Camp near line of wild poplars marking dead stream. Several wells, called Bo-er Ch'üan — a bastard name. Distance of stage 14 miles. | 718 | WNW |
| 7 Oct. '26 | 49 | 42 | Wide plains, rather soft soil, ancient reed beds, much cropped off. Steep clay buttes on every side. Pass one well. Camp in a knot of clay hills; a few wild poplars and scrub willows; no well. This camp cannot be far to S of Khara-khoto, ancient city of Etsina. Between this camp and the previous one a route diverges SW to Kan-su border and Kan Chou; indicated by Kaznakoff, of Kozloff's expedition. The same route followed in the reverse direction must lead to Outer Mongolia; it is little used, but known. Distance of stage 15 miles. | 733 | WNW |
| 8 Oct. '26 | 50 | 43 | Across a table-land rifted with wide, steep-sided gullies, which are probably all ancient flood beds of Edsin Gol. In gullies a few wild poplars, with tamarisk, willow scrub, and desert plants. Table-land dead flat, clay sprinkled with flat black fragments of stone. From this descend to Eastern arm of | | |

| Date | Days out from Kuei-hua | No. of stage | | Total in miles from Kuei-hua | General direction |
|---|---|---|---|---|---|
| | | | Edsin Gol, cross it and camp. Distance of stage 16 miles. | 749 | WNW |
| 9 Oct. '26 | 51 | — | Halt. | | |
| 10 Oct. '26 | 52 | 44 | Ascend to table-land; not broken by any rifts; sometimes a little sand, a few reeds, tamarisks, and wild jujube thorns. Camp at Western branch of Edsin Gol. Distance of stage 20 miles. | 769 | W |
| 11 Oct. '26 | 53 | 45 | Cross Western branch of Edsin Gol and several dry flood channels. Ascend slowly to desert plain — clay covered with flat pieces of black stone. Tiny tamarisks and a very few desert plants of the smallest size. Camp in open plain; flat circular horizon; no well. Distance of stage 20 miles. | 789 | W |
| 12 Oct. '26 | 54 | 46 | Continue over plain. Tops of hills come in view on NW front. Halt at small, half-dead oasis; a few sandy mounds, scattered wild poplars; a few stumps of reeds, of which new growth must depend on exceptional rains. Name of camp, White Earth Mounds or White Earth Well (Pai-t'u Ka-ta'rh, Pai-t'u Ching). Distance of stage 20 miles. | 809 | N of W |
| 13 Oct. '26 | 55 | 47 | Same plain. Camp in shallow bed of vanished stream. Small tamarisk shrubs; dead reeds (cropped off); good well. Shrine of tamarisk boughs. Name of camp, Lu-ts'ao Ching, Reed Grass Well. Distance of stage 5 miles. | 814 | N of W |

| Date | Days out from Kuei-hua | No. of stage | | Total in miles from Kuei-hua | General direction |
|---|---|---|---|---|---|
| 14 Oct. '26 | 56 | 48 | Ascend gradually on to Khara or Black Gobi. At 2 miles leave softer soil for hard sandy clay overlaid with black gravel. At 4 hours drop into ravine, climb out and enter hills, direction erratic. At about 10 hours begin to clear hills. At about 11–12 hours (exceptionally fast going) camp, marked by tamarisk *obo*, in an elliptical plain, with hills curving on N and S. Here the Two Dry Stages way diverges. No well. No grazing but very small dry shrubs. Distance of stage 32 miles. | 846 | N of W |
| 15 Oct. '26 | 57 | 49 | At 7–8 miles reach hills running NE to SW; turn along them, climbing slowly, dipping in and out of shallow gullies. At 22–23 miles cross over divide and descend slowly, bearing more to NW, into broken country, where camp. Same lack of vegetation and water. Distance of stage 30 miles. | 876 | S of W |
| 16 Oct. '26 | 58 | 50 | Skirt low hills which lie on N for 12–13 miles. Then other hills close in on S. Pass over low divide, descend slowly, and at last enter small confined depression among steeper hills, to camp at Shih-pan Ching (Stone Slab Wells). Plentiful water, slightly saline. Grazing still poor. Distance of stage 31 miles. | 907 | W |
| 17 Oct. '26 | 59 | 51 | Turn S out of hollow; then W; at 5 miles cross dry stream bed; well and scanty "red-willow" scrub. | | |

| Date | Days out from Kuei-hua | No. of stage | | Total in miles from Kuei-hua | General direction |
|---|---|---|---|---|---|
| | | | Then SW past a spur of black hills, then W and camp on flanks of hills. A little more scrub; no water. Distance of stage 16 miles. | 923 | W |
| 18 Oct. '26 | 60 | 52 | Skirt hills for 2 hours, then incline NW into valley ascending to narrow pass; bad going for camels for 10 minutes. On coming out of defile there is a well or built-up spring lying away from track, called Yeh-ma Ching (Wild Horse Well). Then descend smooth slope of piedmont gravel to camp in huge wide valley. This marks descent from central mass of Khara Gobi. No water at camp; slight increase of desert scrub. Distance of stage 12 miles. | 935 | W |
| 19 Oct. '26 | 61 | 53 | Cross valley for 5 miles, slight ascent. Then enter black hills, with reddish tinge, by valley in which there is some scrub, and ascend in 2 hours to a plateau, on which camp by boggy, wide hollow; water in muddy pools from exceptional summer rains; otherwise not usual to halt here, as this is first of so-called Three Dry Stages. Distance of stage 13 miles. | 948 | NW |
| 20 Oct. '26 | 62 | 54 | Desert less severe than Central Khara Gobi. Gradual ascent for about 8 miles, then some clay mounds, then slowly downward to camp. Range of mountains comes in sight on SW front. Said to be beginning of Ma-tsung Shan (Horseshoe Hills) — compare | | |

| Date | Days out from Kuei-hua | No. of stage | | Total in miles from Kuei-hua | General direction |
|------|------------------------|--------------|---|------------------------------|-------------------|
| | | | Madzi-shan of Ladighin, of Kozloff's expedition. Pasture slightly improved; a few wild onions, indicating summer rainfall. Distance of stage 16 miles. | 964 | WNW |
| 21 Oct. '26 | 63 | 55 | Ascend very slowly for 7–8 miles, then gradual descent. Direction NW to about 15 miles, then incline slowly more to W. At about 21 miles, Ho-shao Ching (Well of the *hoshun*, indicating a route toward Outer Mongolia). Small, dried-out marsh, a little "red-willow" scrub, white efflorescence on soil. Take on drinking water and continue 3–4 miles to better camel pasture. This marks end of Three Dry Stages. Distance of stage 25 miles. | 989 | WNW |
| 22 Oct. '26 | 64 | 56 | Ten or 11 miles through scrub, in which there is a little coarse grass. Then strike a knot of detached low hills, at the end of a mass of barren hills to the N and NW. Here is a marshy depression running SW to NE, in which are plentiful springs. It is called Kung-p'o Ch'üan, the Spring of the Hillside of the Duke. Here is the fortress of the False Lama. By the fortress the depression curves round to W and NW, linking with a series of oasis pastures, treeless but inhabitable. Trail from Yunbeize comes in here; also Two Dry Stages route rejoins main route. Passing ruins, camp in soft soil, much soda efflorescence, springs, called T'iao Hu. A trail | | |

| Date | Days out from Kuei-hua | No. of stage | | Total in miles from Kuei-hua | General direction |
|---|---|---|---|---|---|
| | | | somewhere to S goes through Ma-tsung Shan to Hsü Chou in Kan-su. Somewhere in this region the line followed from N to S by Ladighin, of Kozloff's expedition, is crossed; from the Edsin Gol to this point, previously unexplored. Distance of stage 16 miles. | 1005 | WNW |
| 23 Oct. '26 | 65 | — | Halt. | | |
| 24 Oct. '26 | 66 | 57 | Through poor oasis country. At 4 miles a well, but no good pasture. At 8 miles camp among hillocks. Distance of stage 8 miles. | 1013 | NW |
| 25 Oct. '26 | 67 | 58 | Enter series of semicircular foot-hill ranges, the lower hills of the Ma-tsung Shan, of which main range, to S, is masked. A few Mongols. At about 7 miles, good water from a pair of wells. Halt in open hill country; no water close at hand. Distance of stage 12 miles. | 1025 | NW |
| 26 Oct. '26 | 68 | — | Halt. | | |
| 27 Oct. '26 | 69 | 59 | Ascend shallow valley, filled with scrub; cross easy divide, descend slowly to more barren country. Mongols camped at distance. Halt by Hsien-ch'ih Ching (Salt Pool Well). Water vile. Distance of stage 11 miles. | 1036 | NW |
| 28 Oct. '26 | 70 | 60 | In and out over horseshoe hills; no wells until at 7 hours reach Ming Shui (Clear Water). Ascend easy valley beyond, camp among hills, | | |

| Date | Days out from Kuei-hua | No. of stage | | Total in miles from Kuei-hua | General direction |
|------|------------------------|--------------|---|------------------------------|-------------------|
| | | | with view of much larger hills to W. Near this camp, group of small *obo* to mark crossing of routes. One comes from Outer Mongolia, one from Hsü Chou and Kan Chou; one goes to S side of end of Qarliq Tagh, to reach Ch'ing Ch'eng and Hami; finally there is the main caravan road. From stage 56 (House of the False Lama) to Ming Shui previously unexplored. Distance of stage 20 miles. | 1056 | W |
| 29 Oct. '26 | 71 | 61 | Bear away to N from hills on W. Flat going for 6 hours, then approach isolated double peak with saddle between, called Tuei'rh Shan (Twin Mountains). A slightly saline spring here. Continue 2 hours to camp. The Ma-tsung Shan are now all overpassed. Distance of stage 20 miles. | 1076 | NW |
| 30 Oct. '26 | 72 | 62 | Long downward slope, at foot of which a marsh, called Chiao Ch'üan (Saltpetre Springs). On W a wide trough; barren hills rising on far side; beyond them, magnificent view of central mass of Qarliq Tagh. Distance of stage 22 miles. | 1098 | NW |
| 31 Oct. '26 | 73 | 63 | Through broken country in gap between Chiao Ch'üan and foothills of Qarliq Tagh. A good deal of poison grass on this march. Poor pasture. No water. Distance of stage 13 miles. | 1111 | NW |
| 1 Nov. '26 | 74 | 64 | Continue toward Qarliq Tagh, engaging in low outer hills. At | | |

| Date | Days out from Kuei-hua | No. of stage | | Total in miles from Kuei-hua | General direction |
|------|------------------------|--------------|---|------------------------------|-------------------|
| | | | entrance to small valley pass a few wild poplars, from which camp at well higher up same valley is called Erh-chia Wu-t'ung (Two *toghraq*). Qarliq Tagh now masked by foothills. Distance of stage 11 miles. | 1122 | NNW |
| 2 Nov. '26 | 75 | 65 | Through foothills; pass through narrow valley; at 3 hours camping place called Hsiao Shih-t'ou (Small Stones, Small Rocks); direction becomes erratic. Valley opens out; at 5 hours, closes again. At 6 hours, halt at Ta Shih-t'ou (Big Rocks). Distance of stage 15 miles. | 1137 | NNW |
| 3 Nov. '26 | 76 | 66 | Reach crest of foothills; small plateau, sight of Qarliq Tagh. Descend sandstone gorge, direction erratic; at mouth, springs on hillside, Ts'u-mei Ch'üan (Spring of the Wild Rose). Turn out of hills and camp on open plain. From Ming Shui to this point previously unexplored. Distance of stage 21 miles. | 1158 | N |
| 4 Nov. '26 | 77 | 67 | Short stage over plain of clay, gravel, and tamarisks, seamed with small dry channels. Distance of stage 8 miles. | 1166 | W |
| 5 Nov. '26 | 78 | 68 | Over sloping plain; minor hills on right front; nearing these, there is a diversion of routes, the more northerly skirting the outside of the mountains all the way to Ku Ch'eng-tze. Taking S route, bear towards Qarliq Tagh; at 10 hours a well among low barren hills. | | |

| Date | Days out from Kuei-hua | No. of stage | | Total in miles from Kuei-hua | General direction |
|---|---|---|---|---|---|
| | | | Then strike a strong mountain stream flowing N, called by Chinese Po-yang Ho (White Poplar River) and camp. Distance of stage 28 miles. | 1194 | S of W |
| 6 Nov. '26 | 79 | 69 | Turn downstream (N) as far as general junction of streams coming from mountains; then upstream, past small clusters of dwellings, to main village of Tuhulu (supposedly Chinese corruption from Tur-khara or Turqara: cf. Tur Köl). This village is marked Uturuk on Carruthers's map. At about 3 hours, passing upper village marked by Carruthers Urge (?), turn W away from watered valley, ascending easily into huge valley between Qarliq Tagh and Metshin Ola, and camp. No well near camp; sparse pasture all through this valley. Distance of stage 14 miles. | 1208 | S of W |
| 7 Nov. '26 | 80 | — | Halt. | | |
| 8 Nov. '26 | 81 | — | Continue ascent of great valley. Group of shepherds' huts seen on left; this is Tomdun (Carruthers). Pass Turki cemetery. Valley dips at head into big depression between Qarliq Tagh and Metshin Ola, in which is salt lake of Tur Köl. Past upper (W) end of lake valley forks; N branch leads up into Metshin Ola, S branch goes over into Bar Köl depression. At E end of lake a pass leads N to desert, by which outer route may | | |

| Date | Days out from Kuei-hua | No. of stage | | Total in miles from Kuei-hua | General direction |
|---|---|---|---|---|---|
| | | | be joined. Camp beyond head of lake. Distance of stage 21 miles. | | |
| 9 Nov. '26 | 82 | — | Start ascent of pass; it is indicated on Carruthers's map. Height about 7000 feet. Easy ascent as far as pass proper, which then becomes a narrow trough. Turned back by snow. Camped at mouth of pass. Distance, camp near Tur Köl to mouth of pass, about 10 miles. | | |
| 10 Nov. '26 | 83 | — | Return to Tur Köl. | | |
| 11 Nov. '26 | 84 | — | Halt. | | |
| 12 Nov. '26 | 85 | — | Start back to Tuhulu. | | |
| 13 Nov. '26 | 86 | — | Reach Tuhulu. | | |
| 14 Nov. '26 | 87 | — | Halt. | | |
| 15 Nov. '26 | 88 | — | Halt. | | |
| 16 Nov. '26 | 89 | 70 | Turn W out of Tuhulu valley by steep ascent into foothills of Metshin Ola; then N or NW. Camp with a little rough grazing; no water. Distance of stage 21 miles. | 1229 | NW |
| 17 Nov. '26 | 90 | 71 | Ascend to a main spur of Metshin Ola, which run out to E. Camp on ridge, having lost way (correct way quite easy). Distance of stage 12 miles. | 1241 | NW |
| 18 Nov. '26 | 91 | 72 | Descend on N side of spur; turn out by big, easy valley to skirting plains; camp in full desert. Distance of stage 21 miles. | 1262 | NW |

| Date | Days out from Kuei-hua | No. of stage | | Total in miles from Kuei-hua | General direction |
|---|---|---|---|---|---|
| 19 Nov. '26 | 92 | 73 | Continue over desert, following round outer hills of Metshin Ola; halt at Sha-tsao'rh Ch'üan (Spring of Wild Jujubes). Distance of stage 25 miles. | 1287 | WNW |
| 20 Nov. '26 | 93 | 74 | Through oasis country to Niu-chüan-tze Hu (Oasis of the Cow Yard). Distance of stage 13 miles. | 1300 | W |
| 21 Nov. '26 | 94 | — | Halt. | | |
| 22 Nov. '26 | 95 | — | Halt. | | |
| 23 Nov. '26 | 96 | 75 | Pass Tung Chuang (East Village; 1½ families) to Ulan Bulak (Red Spring). Distance of stage 12 miles. | 1312 | NW |
| 24 Nov. '26 | 97 | — | Halt. | | |
| 25 Nov. '26 | 98 | 76 | Pass small empty oasis of Chagan Ch'üan Ching (Mongol-Chinese: White Spring Well) to halt at spring. Distance of stage 10 miles. | 1322 | NW |
| 26 Nov. '26 | 99 | 77 | To half-desert camp called Shih-pan Tun (Stone Slab Tower); ancient watchtower. Distance of stage 12 miles. | 1334 | W |
| 27 Nov. '26 | 100 | 78 | Pass Ssu T'ang (Fourth Stage; ancient tower) to San T'ang (Third Stage; ancient tower). Distance of stage 15 miles. | 1349 | W |
| 28 Nov. '26 | 101 | 79 | Small stretch of desert to San-t'ang Hu (Oasis of the Third Stage). Distance of stage 8 miles. | 1357 | W |
| 29 Nov. '26 | 102 | — | Halt. | | |
| 30 Nov. '26 | 103 | — | Halt. | | |

| Date | Days out from Kuei-hua | No. of stage | | Total in miles from Kuei-hua | General Direction |
|---|---|---|---|---|---|
| 1 Dec. '26 | 104 | — | Official detention. | | |
| 2 Dec. '26 | 105 | — | "          " | | |
| 3 Dec. '26 | 106 | — | "          " | | |
| 4 Dec. '26 | 107 | — | "          " | | |
| 5 Dec. '26 | 108 | — | "          " | | |
| 6 Dec. '26 | 109 | — | "          " | | |
| 7 Dec. '26 | 110 | — | "          " | | |
| 8 Dec. '26 | 111 | — | "          " | | |
| 9 Dec. '26 | 112 | — | "          " | | |
| 10 Dec. '26 | 113 | — | Order given for release. | | |
| 11 Dec. '26 | 114 | — | Provisioning and overhauling. | | |
| 12 Dec. '26 | 115 | — | "          "          " | | |
| 13 Dec. '26 | 116 | — | "          "          " | | |
| 14 Dec. '26 | 117 | 80 | Desert plain; slight ascent, camp in desert. Distance of stage 13 miles. | 1370 | S of W |
| 15 Dec. '26 | 118 | — | Halt. | | |
| 16 Dec. '26 | 119 | 81 | Pass camping ground called T'ien-sheng Chüan (Heaven-born Enclosure) closely skirting Nrim of Bar Köl depression. Tamarisks; no water; a little snow. Distance of stage 18 miles. | 1388 | S of W |
| 17 Dec. '26 | 120 | 82 | Through low, black hills; poor pasture; a few sheep. View of Bar Köl range to S. Pass gap giving NW egress from Bar Köl depression. Halt near solitary inn, Tung | | |

| Date | Days out from Kuei-hua | No. of stage | | Total in miles from Kuei-hua | General Direction |
|---|---|---|---|---|---|
| | | | Ch'üan (East Spring). Watchtower called Pai Tun (White Tower). Distance of stage 11 miles | 1399 | W |
| 18 Dec. '26 | 121 | 83 | Bear more to N, passing minor range on S. Pass coal mines (surface workings). Halt in shelter of small knolls. Distance of stage 13 miles. | 1412 | W |
| 19 Dec. '26 | 122 | 84 | Uneven Gobi, growth of low tamarisks. Baitik Bogdo to N, running W. At 3 hours, a way S into hills, joining route "Inside the Mountains." Camping ground called Tuan-chia Ti (probably Land of the Tuan Family). Distance of stage 13 miles. | 1425 | N of W |
| 20 Dec. '26 | 123 | 85 | Descend to slightly marshy hollow; then hills on S bulge toward N; route bears N to avoid snow. Camp in snow at foot of rise. Distance of stage 15 miles. | 1440 | NW |
| 21 Dec. '26 | 124 | 86 | Ascend small rise, descend slowly to frontier post called Tse-fang. Camp within fort. Distance of stage 15 miles. | 1455 | W |
| 22 Dec. '26 | 125 | 87 | Continue through heavier snow. Hills on S appear to round away to SW. Camp in snow. Distance of stage 14 miles. | 1469 | W |
| 23 Dec. '26 | 126 | 88 | Snowfall; no wind. March one mile, then forced camp. Distance of stage 1 mile. | 1470 | W |
| 24 Dec. '26 | 127 | 89 | Continue descending slightly. S hills at increasing distance. A | | |

| Date | Days out from Kuei-hua | No. of stage | | Total in miles from Kuei-hua | General Direction |
|---|---|---|---|---|---|
| | | | range on N represents spurs of Baitik Bogdo. Halt among low, round mounds, called Wu-t'ung Wo-tze (Nest or Shelter of Wild Poplars). Distance of stage 14 miles. | 1484 | W |
| 25 Dec. '26 | 128 | 90 | Route begins to bear SW toward Ku Ch'eng-tze. Peak of Bogdo Ola can be seen in clear weather. To N a route to Uliassutai, through Baitik Bogdo. A number of possible routes to Ku Ch'eng-tze, but when snow deep necessary to keep well out. Cross plain of Ssu-shih Li P'ing-t'an, Forty Li Level Flat, known for poison grass. Camp in open. Distance of stage 12 miles. | 1496 | SW |
| 26 Dec. '26 | 129 | 91 | Rolling country; dunes to right. Increased growth of tamarisk. Camp in open. Distance of stage 12 miles. | 1508 | SW |
| 27 Dec. '26 | 130 | — | Blizzard. | | |
| 28 Dec. '26 | 131 | 92 | Descend gradually to hillocks of sandy earth at place called Sha Men-tze (Gates of Sand). Distance of stage 10 miles. | 1518 | SW |
| 29 Dec. '26 | 132 | 93 | From Sha Men-tze continue over flat; all landmarks obscured by hoary mist. At 4 hours round more sandhills; camp in snow. Distance of stage 16 miles. | 1534 | SW |
| 30 Dec. '26 | 133 | 94 | Over snowy plain to well and solitary inn called Hsi Ch'üan (West | | |

| Date | Days out from Kuei-hua | No. of stage | | Total in miles from Kuei-hua | General Direction |
|---|---|---|---|---|---|
| | | | Spring). Village somewhere to S. Distance of stage 8 miles. | 1542 | SW |
| 31 Dec. '26 | 134 | — | Halt. After this, journal not kept. Approximate details: — | | |
| 1 Jan. '27 | 135 | 95 | Approach Bogdo Ola range and strike line of hollows; winter quarters of Chinese-Mongol half-breeds. Distance of stage 20 miles. | 1562 | between W and S |
| 2 Jan. '27 | 136 | 96 | Similar march, to small village, where cart road is joined. Distance of stage 20 miles. | 1582 | between W and S |
| 3 Jan. '27 | 137 | 97 | Enter Ku Ch'eng-tze. Distance of stage 5 miles. | 1587 | between W and S |

In the above summary, in order to make the estimate of the distance from Kuei-hua to Ku Ch'eng-tze as nearly as possible correct, the marches from Tuhulu to Dead Mongol Pass and back have not been counted as "stages." The average length of march for the 97 days counted as "stages" is therefore just under 17 miles.

# MAPS

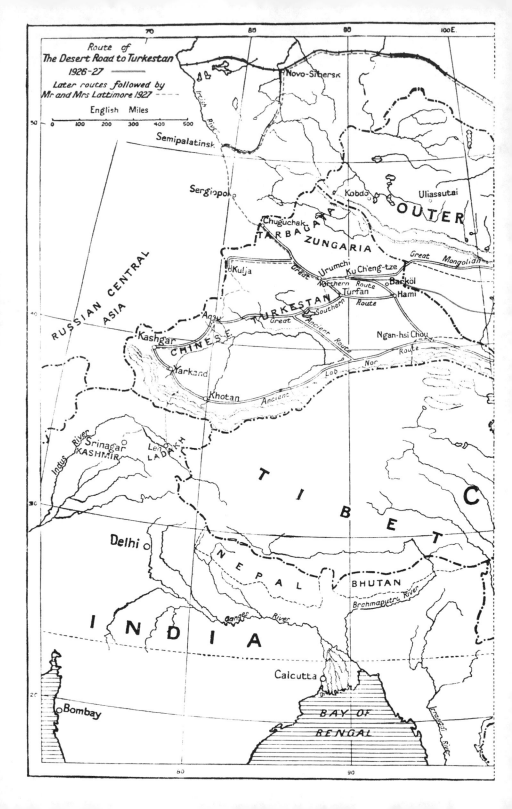

Route of
*The Desert Road to Turkestan*
1926-27 ————

*Later routes followed by
Mr and Mrs Lattimore 1927* - - - -

English Miles

0    100   200   300   400   500

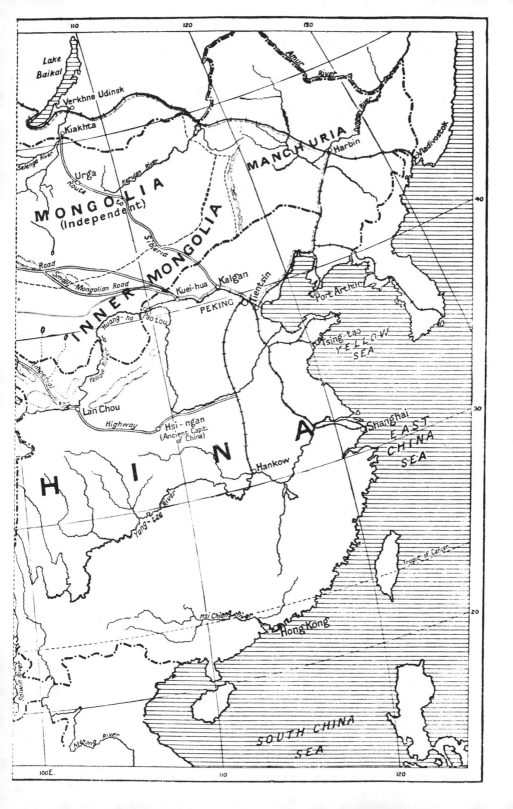

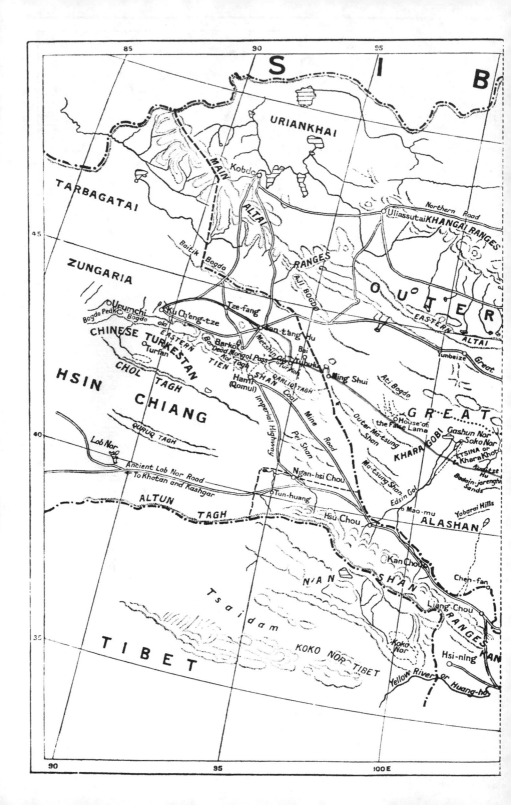

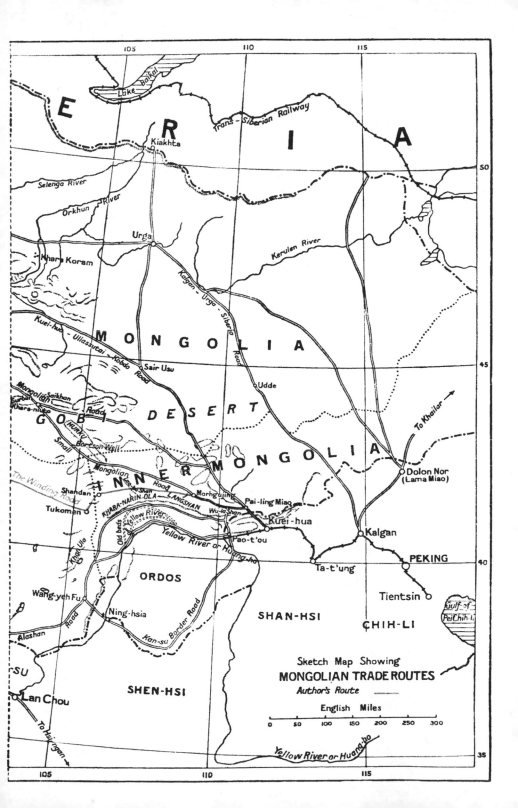

Sketch Map Showing
**MONGOLIAN TRADE ROUTES**
*Author's Route*

English Miles

0    50    100    150    200    250    300

# TABLE OF NAMES

| Usage in The Desert Road to Turkestan | Pinyin Usage | Other Common Usages |
|---|---|---|
| Adak | Weizi Xia | |
| Aji Bogdo | | Aj Bogd Uul |
| Alashan | Helan Shan | |
| Altai | Aletai | Altay, A-la-t'ai |
| Badain-Jarenghi-Ilisu | | Badain Jaran Shamo, Pa-tan-chi-Lin Sha-mo |
| Bai | Baicheng | Pai-Ch'eng, Bay |
| Baitik Bogdo | | Baytik Shan |
| Barköl, Bar Köl | Balikun | Barkul, Barkol, Pai-li-k'un |
| Bogdo Ola | Bogeda Shan | Bogda Shan |
| Chao Ho | Erfenzi | Erf-fen-tzu |
| Chen-fan | Zhenfan, Minqin | Min-ch'in |
| Ch'ien Lung | Qianlong | |
| Chih-li | Zhili | Hebei, Hopeh |
| Ch'ing-chen | Qing-zhen | |
| Ch'ing Ch'eng | Qincheng | Ch'in-ch'eng |
| Chin-t'a oasis | Jinta | |
| Chuguchak | Tacheng | Ta-Ch'eng, Qopek, Tarbagatai |
| Edsin Gol | Ruo Shui, Ejin Qi | Jo Shui, Etsina |

| Usage in The Desert Road to Turkestan | Pinyin Usage | Other Common Usages |
|---|---|---|
| Erh-hun-tze | Er Hunzi | |
| Erh-Lang | Er Lang | |
| Fan-tze | Fanzi | |
| Feng-chen | Fengzhen | |
| Gaidsegai-Hutu | | |
| Gashun Nor | Gaxun Nur | Ka-Shun No-erh, Chü-yen Hai, Gaxun Nur |
| Hai Lang-t'ou | Hailangtou | |
| Hami | Hami | Qomul, Kumul, Camul |
| Ho-nan | Henan | |
| Hsi Fan-tze | Xi Fanzi | |
| Hsin-chiang | Xinjiang | Sinkiang, Chinese Turkestan |
| Hsi-ngan | Xian | Sian |
| Hsü Chou | Xuzhou, Jiuquan | Chiu-ch'üan |
| Hurku | | Hörh Uul |
| Jao Lu | Rao Lu | |
| Kan Chou | Zhangye, Ganzhou | Kan-chou |
| K'ang Hsi | Kangxi | |
| Kan-su | Gansu | |
| Karakoram | | K'a-la-k'un-l'un |
| Khara-narin | | Hara Nariin Uula |
| Kharashar (See Qara Shahr) | | |
| Khotan | Hotan | Ho-t'ien |
| Khutukhtu | | Khutagt |

| Usage in The Desert Road to Turkestan | Pinyin Usage | Other Common Usages |
|---|---|---|
| Kiakhta | | Kyakhta |
| Kirghiz | | Kyrgyz |
| Kobdo | | Khobdo, Hovd, Jargalant |
| K'o Chen | Wuchuan | Wu-ch'uan, Kuku-irghen |
| Koko Nor | Qinghai | Ch'ing-hai |
| Ko-lao Huei | Gelao Hui | |
| Kuai-tze Hu | Guaizi Hu | |
| Ku Ch'eng-tze | Qitai | Ch'i-t'ai |
| Kuei-hua | Guihua, Huhehaode | Huhhot, Huhehot, Hohhot, Old City |
| Kung-P'o Ch'üan | Gongpoquan | |
| K'un Lun | Kunlun Shan | |
| Ku-yang Hsien | Guyang | |
| Lan Chou | Lanzhou | |
| Lao-Mao Hu | Naomaohu | Nom |
| Liang Chou | Liangzhou | |
| Liaotung | Liaodong Bandao | |
| Lien San Han | Lian San Han | |
| Lien Ssu Han | Lian Si Han | |
| Lop Nor | Loulan Yiji | Lop Nur, Lo-pu Po |
| Lu-ts'ao Ching | Lu Jing | |
| Man-t'ou Shan | | Bogda Feng |
| Mao-mei · | Dingxin | Ting-hsin |
| Ma-tsung Shan | Mazong Shan | |
| Ming Shui | Mingshui | |
| Mu-li Ho | | Mori, Mu-lei |

370

| Usage in The Desert Road to Turkestan | Pinyin Usage | Other Common Usages |
| --- | --- | --- |
| Ngan-hsi | Anxi | An-hsi |
| Nge-lu-te | | Ölöt |
| Ning-hsia | Ningxia | Ninghsia |
| Olöt | | Eleuth |
| Pai-ling Miao | Bailing Miao | Darhan Muminggan, Lianheqi, Temple of the Larks |
| Pai-ling Ti | Bailing Di | |
| P'an Ta-jen | Pan Daren | |
| Pan Tsilu | Pan Jilou | |
| Pao Shang T'uan | Bao Shang Tuan | |
| Pao-ting Fu | Baoding | |
| Pao-t'ou | Baotou | |
| Pei-le | Beile | |
| Pei Shan | Bei Shan | |
| Pei-tai Ho | Beidaihe | |
| Qara Qash (River of Black Jade) | Moyu | Karaksh, Karakax |
| Qara Shahr | Yanqi | Yen-ch'i |
| Qarliq Tagh | | Kar Lik Shan, K'a-erh-Li-K'o Shan, Karlik Tagh |
| Qazaq | | Kazakh, Kazak |
| Samarqand | | Samarkand |
| San Pu-kuan | Sanbuguan | |
| San T'ang Hu | Santanghu | |
| Shan-hsi | Shanxi | Shan-hsi |

| Usage in The Desert Road to Turkestan | Pinyin Usage | Other Common Usages |
|---|---|---|
| Shan-tung | Shandong | |
| Sha-tsao'rh Ch'üan | Sha zao'er Quan | |
| Shen-hsi | Shaanxi | Shan-hsi |
| Shihni-usu | | Xin Us, Hsi-ni Wu-su |
| Shih-pan Ching | Shiban Jing | Stone Slab Wells |
| Soko Nor | Suoguo Nuoer | So-Kuo No-erh, Sogo Nur |
| Ssu-shih li P'ing-tan | Sishi Li Pingdan | |
| Ssu T'ang | Sitang | |
| Ssu Ta-tzu Liang | Si Dazi Liang | |
| Suji | | Suj, Su-chi |
| Ta Ch'ing Shan | Daqing Shan | |
| Ta Chüeh Ssu | Da Jue Si | |
| Taklamakan Desert | | Taklimakan Shamo, T'a-k'o-la Makan Sha-mo |
| Tarim Desert | | T'a-li'mu P'en-ti, Tarim Pendi |
| Ta Sheng K'uei | Da Sheng Kui | |
| Ta Shih-t'ou | Da shitou | |
| Ta-t'ung | Datong | |
| Ta-tze | Dazi | |
| Teng-k'ou | Dengkou | Bayan Gol |
| T'ien I Tsan | Tien Yi Zan | |
| T'ien Shan | Tianshan | |
| Tientsin | Tianjin | T'ien-chin |
| Ts'ang Chou | Cangzhou | |

| Usage in The Desert Road to Turkestan | Pinyin Usage | Other Common Usages |
|---|---|---|
| Ts'u-mei Ch'üan | Cumei quan | |
| Ts'ung I Ho | Cong Yi He | |
| Tsun-kung | Xi gong | |
| Tuei'rh Shan | Dui'er Shan | |
| Tuhulu | Yiwu | I-wu, Aratürük |
| Tukomen Miao | | Tohom, T'u-k'u-mu |
| Tung Chuang | Dongzhuang | |
| T'ung-kan | | Dungan |
| Tung-kung | Donggong | |
| Turki | | Uygur, Chanto |
| Uighur | | Uygur |
| Uliassutai | | Uliastay, Javhlant |
| Urumchi | Wulumqi | Urumqi, Tihwa |
| Wei-tze Hsia | Weizi Xia | Adak |
| Wu-la Shan | | Urad, Urat |
| Wu-t'ai Shan | Wutai Shan | |
| Wu-t'ung Wo-tze | Wutongwazi Quan | |
| Yabarai | | Yabrai Shan, Ya-pu-lai Shan |
| Yeh-ma Ching | Yema Jing | |
| Yüan Dynasty | Yuan | Mongol Dynasty |
| Zungaria | | Dzungaria, Chun-ka-erh P'enti, Junggar Pendi |

# NOTES TO PP. ix–xxiv

1. After that David taught Chinese history for twenty years at Dartmouth College. He was the first, as I (his namesake) am the third Lattimore in direct succession to work as a full professor without a Ph.D.

2. Several have the family as subject, and although the names are altered, the drawings are apt as likenesses; in one, *Jerry and the Pusa* (New York, 1932), the hero is actually Owen as a boy in Baoding. To distinguish her from my mother, Eleanor Frances was called "*Xiao* Eleanor," Little Eleanor. Her illustrations for my mother's *Turkestan Reunion* appear in the Kodansha Globe edition (New York: Kodansha America, 1994).

3. Eleanor Frances Lattimore Andrews, "Some Recollections of My Childhood in China; European Interlude; China Again" (typescript), p. 2.

4. Marcel Wolfers, "Alexander Lattimore, Tientsin, China, 1918–1927" (typescript, 1953), p. 1.

5. Owen Lattimore, *High Tartary* (New York: Kodansha America, 1994), p. xxxv.

6. Owen Lattimore, *Studies in Frontier History: Collected Papers, 1928–1958* (London: Oxford University Press; Paris and The Hague: Mouton and Co., 1962), preface, p. 12.

7. Ibid., p. 14.

8. Ibid., p. 15.

9. Under the Kodansha Globe imprint, Kodansha International has now reissued both of these books by my father, as well as my mother's lively narrative of the trip from her distinctive viewpoint, *Turkestan Reunion*.

10. In Paris, the worst of it was that Eleanor lay immobilized for two weeks in the American Hospital at Neuilly not from illness, but so as to come out of her operation without a scar. She had fallen into the hands of a surgeon who specialized in scarless appendectomies for chorus girls, and his professional standards did not permit him to release a patient while any scarring could still develop from body movement.

11. Owen Lattimore, *Mongol Journeys* (New York: Doubleday, Doran, 1941; New York: AMS Press, 1975).

12. I have written briefly about my mother's life in a biographical note added to the Kodansha Globe edition of *Turkestan Reunion*, and Orville Schell, in his introduction to the Kodansha reissue of my father's *High Tartary*, gives an excellent summary of my father's life, especially his involvement with Senator Joseph McCarthy.

13. Owen Lattimore, *The Desert Road to Turkestan* (Boston: Little, Brown, 1929; New York: Kodansha America, 1995), p. xvii.

14. Owen and Eleanor's faithful and indispensable companion Li Baoshu (Moses) served

them for another eleven years, although mostly in China, where he returned in 1927. The immigration laws did not allow his permanent entry to the United States. He received help from my parents from 1945 to 1949.

15. See Owen Lattimore et al., *Pivot of Asia: Sinkiang and the Inner Asian Frontiers of China and Russia* (Boston: Little, Brown, 1950), pp. 52–65.

16. This information came from a Nationalist official who had combed through the provincial archives before transporting them to Taiwan in 1949.

17. It is noteworthy that he traveled more than 1,350 miles without seeing an inhabited village or town.

18. Owen Lattimore (compiled by Fujiko Isono), *China Memoirs: Chiang Kai-shek and the War Against Japan* (Tokyo: University of Tokyo Press, 1990), p. 85.

19. See Robert P. Newman, *Owen Lattimore and the "Loss" of China* (Berkeley: University of California Press, 1992), pp. 526–27.

20. See Owen Lattimore's introduction, in Owen Lattimore and Fujiko Isono, eds. and trans., *The Diluv Khutagt: Memoirs and Autobiography of a Mongol Buddhist Reincarnation in Religion and Revolution*, Asiatische Forschungen 74 (1982).

21. See James Cotton, *Asian Frontier Nationalism: Owen Lattimore and the American Policy Debate* (Atlantic Highlands, 1989), p. 51.

22. Ruth W. Dunnell, review of *The Perilous Frontier: Nomadic Empires and China*, by Thomas J. Barfield, in *Journal of Asian Studies*, 50, no. 1 (February 1991): 127.

# INDEX

# INDEX

# KODANSHA GLOBE

International in scope, this series offers distinguished books that explore the lives, customs, and mindsets of peoples and cultures around the world.

**A NATION IN TORMENT**
*The Great American Depression, 1929–1939*
Edward Robb Ellis
New Preface by the Author
1-56836-113-0

**SEX AND SUITS**
*The Evolution of Modern Dress*
Anne Hollander
1-56836-101-7

**JERUSALEM**
*Battlegrounds of Memory*
Amos Elon
Updated by the Author
1-56836-099-1

**THE LIFE AND MANY DEATHS OF HARRY HOUDINI**
Ruth Brandon
1-56836-100-9

**SETTING THE EAST ABLAZE**
*Lenin's Dream of an Empire in Asia*
Peter Hopkirk
1-56836-102-5

**CATS AND PEOPLE**
Frances and Richard Lockridge
Drawings by Helen Stone
1-56836-115-7

**CHARTING THE SEA OF DARKNESS**
*The Four Voyages of Henry Hudson*
Donald S. Johnson
1-56836-105-X

**VOICES OF DEATH**
*Letters and Diaries of People Facing Death— Comfort and Guidance for All of Us*
Edwin Shneidman
New Preface by the Author
1-56836-112-2

**PROPHETS WITHOUT HONOUR**
*Freud, Kafka, Einstein, and Their World*
Frederic V. Grunfeld
New Introduction by Michael Brenner
1-56836-107-6

**THE HUMAN ZOO**
*A Zoologist's Classic Study of the Urban Animal*
Desmond Morris
1-56836-104-1

**ALL ABOARD WITH E. M. FRIMBO**
*World's Greatest Railroad Buff (Expanded Edition)*
Rogers E. M. Whitaker and Anthony Hiss
New Preface by Anthony Hiss
Illustrated by Mark Livingston
1-56836-114-9

**THE PRIVATE WAR OF MRS. PACKARD**
*The Dramatic Story of a Nineteenth-Century Feminist*
Barbara Sapinsley
New Introduction by Phyllis Chesler
Foreword by Eric T. Carlson, M.D.
1-56836-106-8

To order, contact your local bookseller or call 1-800-788-6262 (mention code G1). For a complete listing of titles, please contact the Kodansha Editorial Department at Kodansha America, Inc., 114 Fifth Avenue, New York, NY 10011.